Frank McDonald **The Construction of Dublin**

Frank McDonald

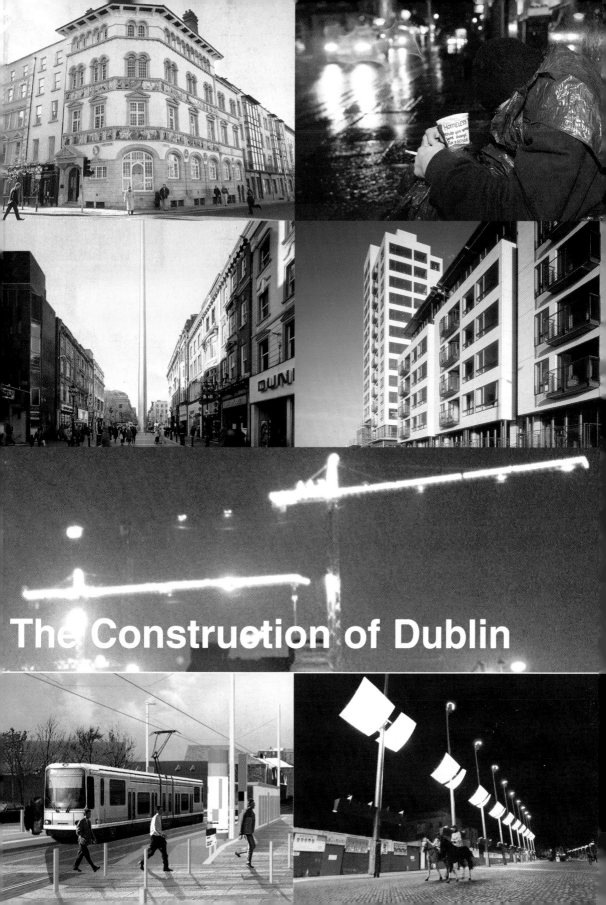

The Construction of Dublin

THE CONSTRUCTION OF DUBLIN
by Frank McDonald

© Frank McDonald and Gandon Editions, 2000
All rights reserved

ISBN 0946846 499 hardback / 502 paperback

Designed by John O'Regan (© Gandon, 2000)
Produced by Nicola Dearey, Gandon

Repro by Lens to Image, Dublin
Digital illustrations processed by Gunther Berkus, Cork
Printed in Ireland by Betaprint, Dublin

GANDON EDITIONS
Oysterhaven, Kinsale, Co Cork, Ireland – tel: +353 (0)21-4770830 / fax: 4770755
e-mail: gandon@eircom.net / visit our web-site: www.gandon-editions.com

Gandon Editions is grant-aided by The Arts Council / An Chomhairle Ealaíon

Albert Leary & Son, 1995

Dedicated to the memory of
Deirdre Kelly (1938-2000)

This is a book about the future of Dublin at a very critical turning point in its history. It had been playing on my mind for some time, but what galvanised me to start writing it in late-October 1999 was a deep sense of foreboding after I had read, and absorbed, the most recent population projections, and talked quite animatedly, as I recall, to an Irish student who was doing an MA thesis in Liverpool on transport in Dublin. But I could not have written it at all without the generosity of the *Irish Times* in giving me three months paid sabbatical leave and, after that period of grace expired, being quite indulgent as I sought to meet the alarmingly short publication schedule set by the extraordinary pair of publishers, John O'Regan and Nicola Dearey of Gandon Editions.

In a sense, this work is a sequel to *The Destruction of Dublin* and *Saving the City*.* The title was chosen as much for its ironic quality as its nutshell description of the awesome task that lies before us. Yet it could not have been written under more different circumstances. The two earlier books date from the bleak period of the mid- to late-1980s. The first of them was written in longhand from files stored in an orange box, and then typed up on a rented electric typewriter. It was easy then to take nine months off because there was so little happening in the city. Dublin was in the doldrums, and we all had the luxury of time to undertake original research or engage in polemics. Now we are so run off our feet by the Celtic treadmill that we barely have time to think.

The Construction of Dublin was written in the midst of a maelstrom of activity generated by Ireland's booming economy. Against that frenetic background, it represents something of a snapshot of the city at a particular moment in time. Some of the cases it deals with, such as the massive scheme proposed for Spencer Dock, were not fully resolved at the time of writing, and, to that extent, it is incomplete. But there is so much going on that it would have been quite impossible to deal with everything and tie up all of the loose ends as long as the boom continues. That, too, looks more uncertain, with inflation at double the EU average already providing evidence of serious overheating. Nonetheless, in recounting the principal sagas, the book should give readers some idea of the forces that are shaping 21st-century Dublin, for good or ill.

For ease of assimilation, it is divided into themes. The first chapter, 'Changing Fast', sets out where we stand and sketches the main tasks facing us in this decade. The second, 'Going Up', deals with the high-rise debate, focussing in particular on George's Quay, Spencer Dock and the millennium 'Spike' for O'Connell Street. The third, 'Getting Around', treats the main traffic and transport issues, including the Luas and Port Tunnel controversies. The fourth, 'Spreading Out', deals with the emerging Edge City and alternative models of urban development, such as Temple Bar and Docklands. Finally, 'Muddling Through' covers a broad sweep of territory, concentrating on the decision-making process. Inevitably, some of the content – particularly on traffic and transport – has been drawn from my own work for the *Irish Times*; I am grateful to the

Editor, Conor Brady, for permission to rework it, and also to the Picture Editor, Dermot O'Shea, and the Irish Times Studio Manager, Tony Cerasi, for making so many illustrations available free of charge. That being said, most of it is new material, particularly on the personalities involved and their respective roles in the construction of Dublin.

I am indebted to a large number of people for giving me the benefit of their insights and opinions. So many needed to be interviewed that I resorted to the stratagem of hosting a series of informal colloquies with many of the principal players. Much of what they had to say has found its way into this book in one form or another; but then, the future of Dublin is, or should be, a collective effort. Any errors or omissions – and I'm sure there must be some, human fallibility being what it is – are mine, made during a three-month period when my study became a cave from which I emerged every so often to take screen breaks from a trusty Apple computer.

I am particularly grateful to Jim Barrett, Richard Barrett, Eamonn Brady, Brian Brennan, Tim Brick, Gerry Cahill, Willy Clingan, Paul Clinton, Eddie Conroy, Ciarán Cuffe, Paul Cullen, Nicola Dearey, Jack Fagan, John Fitzgerald, Dick Gleeson, John Graby, John Henry, Owen Hickey, Jim Horan, Brian Hughes, Phillip Jones, Owen Keegan, Garrett Kelleher, Paul Keogh, Fergal MacCabe, Colm McCarthy, Pat McDonnell, Bernard McHugh, Laura Magahy, Donal Mangan, John Mulcahy, David O'Connor, Joan O'Connor, Seán O'Laoire, John O'Regan, John O'Sullivan, Shane O'Toole, James Pike, Tony Reddy, Johnny Ronan, Bride Rosney, Eamonn Ryan, Michael Smith, Terry Thorp, Fergal Tobin, Ciarán Treacy and Derek Tynan.

I would also like to express my thanks to Paul Allen, Dorothy Barry, Gordon Benson, Seán Benton, Charlie Bird, Ciarán Blair, George Boyle, Alan Bradley, Francis Bradley, Mark Brennock, Gen Bunyan, Christoph Burgener, Joan Burton, Una Carmody, Fintan Cassidy, John Cassidy, Denis Coghlan, Diarmuid Collins, Frank Connolly, Peter Coyne, Hugh Cregan, Richard Cremins, Mick Crowley, Rory Deegan, Ronnie Devlin, Martin Donnelly, Miriam Dunn, Eamonn Elliott, Conor Falvey, Noirin Finnegan, Mick Foster, Joanne Geary, John Gibson, Pete Hanan, Seán Harrington, Paul Hayden, Mary Hetherington, Sharon Hutchinson, Mandy Johnston, Martin Jones, Matt Kavanagh, Seán Kearns, Eamonn Kelly, Margaret Lee, Simon Lincoln, Ian Lumley, Frank McCabe, Oliver McCann, Niall McCullough, Tom McEnaney, Des McMahon, Ciarán McNamara, Eamonn Maguire, John Maher, Alan Mee, Hugh Mohan SC, Colm Moore, Tom Moriarty, Ann Mulcrone, Pat Mulcrone, Valerie Mulvin, Esther Murnane, Mary Murphy, Paul Murray, Deirdre Ní Raghallaigh, Ciarán O'Brien, Paul O'Brien, Robert O'Byrne, Donal O'Connor, John O'Connor, Kevin O'Hare, John O'Mahony, Susan O'Regan, Lindis Page, Simon Perry, Paddy Prendiville, Deirdre Reddy, Fionnuala Rogerson, David Rooney, John Smyth, Noel Smyth, Irene Stephenson, Vanessa Sweeney, John Vincent and Mark Ward. By publicly acknowledging all of them for their assistance, however, I do not mean to imply that a particular piece of information or unattributed quotation can be sourced to any of those named. There were others who helped on the basis that they would remain anonymous, and I am happy to respect their wishes while expressing my gratitude to them, too.

The book is dedicated to the memory of Deirdre Kelly, one of Dublin's greatest champions until she was finally defeated by cancer less than two months into the new millennium. Deirdre was a bundle of energy, passion and commitment, who threw herself into epic struggles from Hume Street to Wood Quay, as well as fighting numerous battles against destructive office development and road-widening schemes. She was a radical, in the truest sense, in that her ideas and the stances she took were way ahead of their time. In the early 1970s, when the inner city was being remorselessly evacuated, she founded the Living City Group, holding out a candle in the dark for the centre of Dublin. In a way, every new apartment block built in the inner city since the early 1990s is a tribute to her. She was also the guiding light of the Dublin Crisis Conference in 1986, on which we worked closely together, as well as the author of *Hands Off Dublin*, which documented and denounced the Corporation's wretched road plans, *They're All Outta Step But Our Corpo*, which showed what other European cities were doing, and *Four Roads to Dublin*,[†] a meticulously researched and illuminating history of her beloved Ranelagh, Rathmines and Leeson Street. To me, Deirdre was both a friend and an inspiration over many years, and, while we all miss her terribly, I am delighted to be able to make this small gesture to acknowledge my own long-standing personal debt to her.

Finally, no words could express my heartfelt thanks to Eamonn Slater, who has stood by me through thick and thin. Along with Brian Yore, he kept me going through a very intensive period, not least by providing buckets of moral support. I also want to thank my dear parents, William and Maura McDonald, for everything they have done for me over the years, and to wish my marvellous and spirited mother a full recovery from the setback she suffered last December.

FRANK McDONALD
Temple Lane, Dublin
1st May 2000

[*] Frank McDonald, *The Destruction of Dublin* (Gill & Macmillan, Dublin, 1985); *Saving the City* (Tomar, Dublin, 1989)

[†] Deirdre Kelly, *Hands Off Dublin* (O'Brien Press, Dublin, 1976); *They're All Outta Step But Our Corpo* (Dublin, 1980); *Four Roads to Dublin* (O'Brien Press, Dublin, 1995)

1. Changing Fast

t is important to start by acknowledging how far we have travelled. In the 1980s, Dublin was so down in the dumps that one former Lord Mayor – Jim Mitchell TD – said it had 'about as much character as a second-rate knacker's yard'. This damning line, quoted in the introductory chapter of *The Destruction of Dublin*, was uttered in a time of bleak depression, even despair, when the inner city was littered with derelict sites and dilapidated buildings and public policy was haphazardly pointed in the wrong direction. High Street, once the main thoroughfare of medieval Dublin, was so stripped of its architectural fabric that the street sign had to be put up on a pole. Parliament Street, right in front of the City Hall, was so dead that all it lacked was a gravestone to mark the spot. And most of the Liffey Quays were threatened by destructive road-widening schemes. Anyone with a sense of shame meeting friends from abroad at Dublin Airport used to devise circuitous routes to avoid the worst eyesores, but the urban blight was so endemic that blindfolds might have been a better option. The state of the place was so shocking that, when Dublin was designated European City of Culture for 1991, Peter Pearson, artist, author and conservationist, together with An Taisce's Ian Lumley, who has done more than anyone to protect the city's architectural fabric, came up with the idea of convening an Urban War Crimes Tribunal. Loosely based on the model of Bertrand Russell's Vietnam War Tribunal in Stockholm, it was to be a theatrical affair staged just for one day, with Senator David Norris in powdered wig as the judge, Lumley acting as chief prosecutor, Pearson doing his devastating mimicry of the principal suspects – Charlie Haughey, Padraig Flynn, George Redmond, etc – all of them represented by cardboard cut-outs in the dock, and the audience serving as an informal jury. But nobody got their act together, and in the end Lumley devised a simpler format, the Nicolae Ceausescu Memorial

A bird's-eye view of Kevin Roche's master plan for Spencer Dock, at the confluence of the River Liffey and the Royal Canal, with the proposed National Conference Centre in the foreground.

Awards for the Destruction of Dublin, presented *in absentia* to a rogue's gallery at his home in Henrietta Street.

Dublin today is a different place; it has been reinvented. The whole atmosphere of the city has changed utterly over the past decade or so, since Frank Feely's historically dubious but immensely successful 'Millennium' in 1988. That year-long circus helped to focus attention on the inner city, encouraging everyone in Dublin – notably the vast majority living in the suburbs – to consider it in a new, more positive light. So did initiatives like the visionary Dublin City Quays project, co-ordinated by Gerry Cahill at the UCD School of Architecture, and the seminal Dublin Crisis Conference in the old Synod Hall at Christchurch. Aided by urban renewal tax incentives, developers began moving into areas which they had ignored for years, such as the medieval city and the Liffey quays. At first, this new activity was confined to own-door office blocks and even the odd petrol filling station, but it eventually encompassed the construction of apartment buildings right in the heart of the city to meet a huge suppressed demand, from younger people, in particular, for living space close to where they worked. Incredibly, there was not one private flat available for purchase anywhere in the city centre until 1990, because it simply did not rate as a residential location. Since then, at least 13,000 apartments have been provided in new or refurbished buildings dotted around the inner city, injecting new life into previously run-down areas and reversing decades of relentless population decline. And while the quality of these new living spaces was highly variable, ranging from tiny shoe-boxes to generous penthouses, the spin-off benefits of having so many new residents has contributed enormously to Dublin's rediscovery of itself as a self-confident European dot.com capital.

The city has a palpable 'buzz' about it, and this liveliness makes a huge impression on first-time visitors. In August 1999, the *Observer* ran a piece describing Dublin as 'the richest, happiest city in Europe', though its author admitted that this was a superficial judgment based on one fun-filled weekend. Four years earlier, in a special supplement on cities in the *Irish Times*, architect Seán O'Laoire wrote that any visitor to Dublin 'would be struck immediately by the intensity of activity right through the urban core, with all the late-night liggers, nightclub goers, strollers, revellers, down-and-outs, policemen, ambulances in one vast urban drawing room'. Not surprisingly, tourist numbers have soared, putting Dublin among the first rank of European cities for short breaks, and allowing the city to proclaim itself as 'the party capital of Europe'. Walk down any main street these days and you are almost as likely to hear a foreign language being spoken as English. Dublin has become consciously cosmopolitan, so much so that even Northern Ireland unionists are quite gobsmacked by this bustling capital of an increasingly secular state. 'Open-air movies on balmy summer nights, café-bars serving the best cappuccino, any number of nightclubs and restaurants catering for almost every taste, 24-hour city-centre convenience stores swarming with late-night "ravers", and an annual festival featuring Mardi Gras-style street theatre and spectacular fireworks displays', gushed the latest *Insight* guide. 'Put all of this together with a booming economy, the emergence of a confident contemporary architecture and the extraordinary asset of having the youngest population in Europe and what you get is Dublin, one of the most transformed cities anywhere in the world. All that's missing is a Mediterranean climate that would match its mood.'

Dozens of new hotels have materialised, some in the most unlikely places, and others are being built or planned. Yet all of these are merely part of the biggest building boom ever to hit the city, with more tower cranes decorating the skyline than at any time in its history. We have lost count of the number. There are so many cranes and they move around so much that it's hard to tell. Is it twenty-five, thirty, thirty-five or forty? Probably more, anyway, than any other European capital apart from Berlin. What is certain, however, is that the Dublin of the 21st century is taking shape right before our eyes, and that 1999 offered us 'the last glimpse of ourselves as we scurried raggedy-arsed out of the old century', in the words of Tom Humphries, one of the finest journalists of his generation. 'Religious orders packing their bags. Boom, boom, boom down at the registry office. Charlie Haughey, his reputation gobbled by social ebola, raging through the Four Courts like Lear on the heath. Stretch limos. Fox-hunting. Eco-warriors. On our knees to Puff Daddy and the boys from MTV. Romantic Ireland dead and gone and with Jack Lynch in the grave. Minor British royals giving face to good Irish cameramen. Lordee. We could never have imagined these images. Even ten years ago, we couldn't have conjured them. If we'd known in 1974 what we'd look like in 1999, would we have even kept turning the pages?' And now, suddenly, 'we have little freckle-faced Donald Trumps running about the place.'

Part of the reason for its current success is that Dublin has developed a critical mass in European terms, which is why it has attracted such big players as Intel, Hewlett Packard and IBM as well as most of the world's leading financial institutions, at least for back-office activities. In 1997, *Fortune* magazine noted that banks such as Barclays, Chase Manhattan, Citicorp and Sumitomo run everything from treasury operations to fund management from Dublin, and ranked it ahead of Amsterdam, Barcelona, London and Milan as the best city in Europe for doing business. The International Financial Services Centre became the gleaming, power-dressed symbol of the 'Celtic Tiger' economy – so successful, indeed, that it generates £430 million-plus per annum for the Exchequer, even at a 10% corporation tax rate. Much to the amazement of everyone who lived through some of its darkest days, Dublin now stands at the forefront of European cities in terms of its prosperity, its urban environment and social ambience. After years of neglect, the inner city suddenly has a real value. It may be measured, however crudely, by the staggering prices being paid for parcels of property with development potential. A quarter-acre site at the corner of Harcourt Street, for example, was sold for £8.8 million in December 1999 – equivalent to an all-time record of £32.5 million per acre – without the benefit of outline planning per-

John Searle / Gandon Archive

The Bookend building on Essex Quay, designed by the late Deirdre O'Connor of Arthur Gibney & Partners. Since 1990, at least 13,000 apartments have been provided in the inner city, injecting new life into previously run-down areas.

Members of the Mardi Gras-style street theatre group, Aquatic World, weaving their way down Dame Street during the first St Patrick's Day parade of the new millennium.

Alan Betson / *Irish Times*

Alan Betson / *Irish Times*

Tower cranes working on Citibank and several other office blocks in the extended IFSC area beside Jury's Inn. Counting the number of cranes on the skyline was a preoccupation in the earlier period of the property boom.

The International Financial Services Centre at the Custom House Docks, power-dressed symbol of the 'Celtic Tiger' economy, seen from Matt Talbot Bridge.

Richard Kelly

Matt Kavanagh / *Irish Times*

Frank McDonald

Mountjoy Square, for long a ruinous spectacle on the way in from Dublin Airport, has been miraculously put back together again.

A 1987 photograph of part of the west side of Mountjoy Square, showing a derelict site and the remains of a house demolished as being 'dangerous' by Dublin Corporation.

John Searle / Gandon Archive

The Curvilinear Range in the National Botanic Gardens, Glasnevin, designed by Richard Turner, and restored by an Office of Public Works design team headed by Ciarán O'Connor.

mission for the scale of office development required to turn a profit on the deal. Meanwhile, Georgian town houses in and around Merrion and Fitzwilliam squares were being converted back into fine residences, after years of dead-after-dark office use, by the likes of Edward Haughey, Louise Kennedy and Tony O'Reilly. Even Mountjoy Square, for long a ruinous spectacle on the way in from Dublin Airport, has been miraculously put back together again, even if Dorset Street still presents a depressing introduction to the city. So, too, has Turner's great Curvilinear Range in the National Botanic Gardens, one of numerous major projects by the Office of Public Works to restore or recycle a wealth of historic structures – including Government Buildings in Merrion Street, Charlie Haughey's magnum opus. Our former great leader took such a close personal interest in this £18 million project that he rejected the original design for a muted grey carpet on the corridors, with a jagged red line running through it that vanished under the door of the Taoiseach's office; he thought it might be misinterpreted as a trail of blood. And that wouldn't do at all for the man who was referred to by his press secretary, PJ Mara, as 'Il Duce' or, more frequently, as 'El Diablo'. Mara's most memorable line, delivered after Haughey came under fire from Des O'Malley, was: 'Uno Duce, una voce – in other words, no more nibbling at my leader's bum.' But fair dues to CJH. Only he would have embraced the challenge of remaking and refurbishing Government Buildings; his predecessor, Garret FitzGerald, would not even have noticed that the old Taoiseach's office

Irish Times

Government Buildings on Merrion Street – Charlie Haughey's magnum opus. The former UCD School of Engineering (completed in 1922) now houses the Department of the Taoiseach.

Our former great leader, 'now raging through the Four Courts like Lear on the heath', on the steps of Government Buildings in December 1991, attended by one of his leading acolytes, Bertie Ahern, then Minister for Finance.

Eric Luke / *Irish Times*

Archer's Garage on Fenian Street, a Grade 1 listed building, demolished in June 1999 by Noel O'Callaghan, hotelier, property developer and director of Bord Fáilte.

A perspective view of the planned L-shaped office building on the site of Archer's Garage, showing the demolished garage reinstated in the foreground.

Hotelier Noel O'Callaghan pictured with the Taoiseach Bertie Ahern celebrating the 'topping out' of the Stephen's Green Hotel in April 1999, two months before Archer's Garage was demolished.

was like a parish priest's parlour.

The picture is not uniformly rosy. Conservationists complain that the city continues to lose irreplaceable elements of its historic fabric, including some worthy interiors, because of the development stampede; they call it 'death by a thousand cuts'. Most shocking, by a long shot, was the illegal demolition by leading hotelier and property developer Noel O'Callaghan of Archer's Garage on Fenian Street over the June bank holiday weekend in 1999, when there was nobody around to stop it. There had been some confusion about the status of this landmark building, dating from the romantic era of motoring in the 1940s, but there was no doubt in the end that it had been included on List 1 in the final version of the City Plan, adopted three months earlier though still not published at the time. Because it was not a Georgian house in Merrion Square, O'Callaghan may have thought that he could get rid of it with impunity, clearing the way for an office development on the site. Instead, all hell broke loose, with calls from right across the spectrum that he should be prosecuted, facing a fine of up to £1 million and/or two years in jail on indictment. With the Mont Clare, Davenport, Alexander and St Stephen's Green hotels under his belt, as well as a directorship of Bord Fáilte, O'Callaghan was compelled to sign a legally enforceable agreement with Dublin Corporation that the demolished garage would be faithfully reconstructed, a daunting task made somewhat easier by the availability of many original drawings and plans. Meanwhile, in Sandymount, people are still in mourning for the loss of another landmark – the 150-year-old Presbyterian Church on Tritonville Road. Despite an outpouring of public protest, it was razed to the ground in September 1999, on foot of dubious claims that it was 'dangerous', to make way for a misconceived development by the Presbyterian Residential Trust, consisting of fourteen sheltered housing units and eight private apartments. The fact that the building was unlisted and that local residents had missed out on two opportunities to make their views known on the trust's planning applications did no credit to the conservation cause. But then, as this sorry saga showed, the planners didn't cover themselves in glory either.

Anyone who has been away from Dublin for ten years would hardly recognise the place, and they are bound to feel disorientated by other changes, too. The preposterous 'refurbishment' of the interior of Bewley's in Grafton Street, the 'legendary, lofty, clattery café', must be one of the most telling metaphors for the 'new for old' psychosis. Brown Thomas has turned into Marks & Spencer, while Switzer's has been replaced by a Dallas-style version of BT's. But then, the consequences of globalisation have been particularly evident in the retail trade, as indigenous Dublin outlets are replaced by foreign-owned retail multiples. The Jervis Centre, that groundscraper built by Paddy McKillen on the site of one of Dublin's best-known hospitals, has Argos, Boots, Debenhams, Dixons, M&S and Tesco. You could just as easily be in Manchester. Here Today is gone from South Anne Street, Our Boys from Wicklow Street, and chandlers McCann Verdon from Burgh Quay. The oldest shop in Dublin, Read's Cutlers on Parliament Street, is

Anyone who has been away for ten years or more would hardly recognise Grafton Street. Brown Thomas has turned into Marks and Spencer, while Switzer's has been replaced by a Dallas-style version of BT's.

The Morrison Hotel on Ormond Quay Lower, designed by Douglas Wallace Architects. Along with the Life bar in the Irish Life Centre, Pravda, GUBU and Zanzibar, it qualifies as 'one of those southside embassies on the northside'.

Irish Times

Frank McDonald

The Adelphi cinema in its heyday *(above)*, and as it is now *(right)*, with the cinema's once-bustling foyer occupied by the breeze-block jaws of Arnott's multi-storey car park and service dock shuttered, its name purloined for a trendy pub next door. On Ormond Quay, Lawlor Briscoe's antique furniture emporium has given way to Zanzibar, a cavernous souk conjured up by publican Liam O'Dwyer. Together with the Life bar in the Irish Life Centre, Pravda, GUBU and the Morrison Hotel, it probably qualifies as 'one of those southside embassies on the northside', a generic title coined by the *UCD Rag Mag*. Cinemas have also disappeared, with the Savoy the only survivor in O'Connell Street, while in Middle Abbey Street the Adelphi's once-bustling foyer is now occupied by the breeze-block jaws of Arnott's multi-storey car park and service dock. Churches, too, have been transfigured, with St Andrew's taken over by Dublin Tourism, St George's serving as the Temple Theatre music venue, St Mary's on its way to being converted from a paint shop to a pub, and SS Michael and John's, the earliest purpose-built Catholic church in Dublin, carved up for a Viking Adventure. Some major alterations to the urban landscape go unnoticed or, at least, unremarked upon. There was no comment in the media about the fact that the all-singing, all-dancing red brick wall of the new women's prison at Mountjoy has obliterated the grim, forbidding gateway of the old jail, which had long been a landmark on the North Circular Road.

The pace of change is so spectacular that nobody has a handle on it – not Dublin Corporation, not the banks or property developers, not even the Government. Since the mid-1990s, planners have been run ragged trying to deal with a torrent of planning applications and appeals, while the construction industry is so stretched that electricians, plumbers and carpenters are commuting from Holyhead every Monday on the Stena HSS service in their transit vans. They have become known collectively as 'the Welsh choir'. Some architects also find it difficult to get office boys anymore because 'they're all into IT now', in the words of Betty Ash, of the St Andrew's Resource Centre in Pearse Street. Meanwhile, almost everyone in an office environment is working harder than ever, inundated by a flood-tide of post, 'landline' and mobile phone calls, voice-mail messages, and reams and reams of e-mail. 'To an English visitor, Dublin is repeating, on a larger scale relative to its smaller size, the experience of London during the Thatcher years, when the promised deregulation of the financial services sector triggered a massive building boom', according to architecture critic Martin Pawley, writing in July 1999. 'To anyone who remembers London in the mid-1980s, the similarity is uncanny. There is the same sense of a city possessed by tremendous economic forces. The rules and regulations drawn up for the measured control of development in quieter times can no longer be made to fit. The forces of movement have seized the initiative and, on every side, there are indications that it is not time to pause, but rather to spring onto the back of the Celtic Tiger and ride, ride, ride.'

Whatever about Pawley's rip-roaring advice, there can be no doubt that the momentum generated by the current economic boom is confronting the city with huge pressures for development and expansion. As the City Manager, John Fitzgerald, said in April 1999, Dublin is 'awash with potential developers who

Paddy Whelan / *Irish Times*

The Boyne Hall housing estate outside Drogheda. Many of the new estates on the outskirts of towns throughout Leinster are, in effect, little bits of Dublin way beyond the metropolitan area.

have buckets of money to spend' – some of them, indeed, at war with each other over the spoils in areas they would have ignored just five years earlier. One of Fitzgerald's tasks is to manage the boom, insofar as he can, and seek to ensure that beneficial development is directed into the right areas before the economy runs out of steam. 'It's a great time for me to be doing what I'm doing. There'll never be a better time', he declared confidently. Never has the demand for office space been so strong, both in the city centre and out on the urban periphery. Never have we been faced with so many plans for high-rise buildings, shopping malls, office parks and leisure facilities. And never has Dublin had to deal with the immense challenge of providing at least 200,000 new homes – that's nearly half as much again as all the houses and apartments already built – to accommodate a steep increase in population over the next ten years. Where these homes are built, and in what form, is clearly an issue of overwhelming importance, because we are not going to get another chance. After 2011, when the present economic boom has fizzled out and the population of the Greater Dublin Area begins to level off, we will have all the houses and apartments we need. By then, as the ESRI has said, Dublin will be 'cast in concrete', and it will be too late to undo mistakes made over the next decade or to mitigate the many errors already made during the past thirty years.

In the meantime, we congratulate ourselves on our new-found prosperity, even though few among us have any real idea what exactly is fuelling the 'Celtic Tiger'. All we know is that 'for the first time in our history, we are able to decide what we want and go out tomorrow and pay for it', as the Taoiseach, Bertie Ahern, put it in August 1999. But the boom has yielded some strange results. There is a sense that Dublin has fallen into the hands of a changeling species, a new 'me generation', with no experience of thrift, still less of poverty, and no folk memory of the Famine. 'One of the things that acquisition and the pursuit of wealth induces is amnesia', according poet Eavan Boland. 'And those who seek them will not only forget, but *want* to forget, the levels of strength and survival and near-to-the-edge dispossession that we once had as a people.' A culture of conspicuous consumption has taken a firm hold of Irish society, as we babble away on slimline mobile phones, leaf through brochures marketing exotic foreign holidays, purchase gourmet convenience food at outlandish prices, and sign up for low-interest bank loans to buy the latest top-of-the-range car or that dream home on the Costa del Sol. Idealism, too, seems to have been forgotten. Successful people, in the materialistic sense, care less and less about those being left

One of Dublin's homeless begging on a wet winter's night. The Simon Community has been having trouble finding local volunteers for its soup runs in the city's ever-growing netherworld.

Bryan O'Brien / *Irish Times*

behind. Even the Simon Community has been having trouble finding local volunteers for its soup runs in Dublin's ever-growing homeless netherworld, and the same problem is reported by the Society of St Vincent de Paul. Surely it couldn't be true, as Louise East has written in her *Irish Times* 'Winging It' column, that the younger generation has no opinions or convictions about anything other than 'nightclub openings, shopping must-haves and holiday options'. Another *Irish Times* writer, Orna Mulcahy, vividly captured the atmosphere of an upmarket Thai restaurant, improbably called Diep Le Shaker, on Pembroke Lane, where 'ranks of tables were filled with well-dressed, well-heeled, hair-slicked-back rich people out for the night enjoying their money ... Champagne is the tipple of choice here and snipes of Veuve Cliquot were flying.' In the middle of her meal, 'a flustered-looking waitress went around all the tables asking if anyone had parked a 92 D Mercedes outside. At every table, she seemed to be getting the same wisecrack – "What? Only a 92?. You must be joking, har har har!".' Mulcahy concluded, tongue-in-cheek, that the unknown 'vehicularly challenged person' might have been one of the other waitresses, or perhaps even the kitchen porter. Her piece was headed, aptly enough, 'A place to move and shake'.

Is it all a flash in the pan? Or is there something more fundamental going on? Perhaps what we are witnessing is the reclamation of Dublin by a new generation of Irish people who have travelled widely and even worked in other European cities, shed their cultural baggage, and now returned home to demand the same sort of lifestyle they experienced elsewhere. They see no reason why the Hibernian metropolis should be less civilised or interesting to live in than, say, Amsterdam, Paris, Munich or Barcelona. But there are two seemingly inescapable downsides to Dublin's prosperity – horrendous traffic congestion and spiralling house prices. The city's diversity is threatened by the astronomical value we now place on residential property, because people on lower incomes – actors, artists, nurses and waiters, even teachers and gardaí – may no longer be able to buy or rent homes conveniently located to their workplaces. With single-storey cottages selling for £150,000 or more, and two-bedroom flats renting for up to £800 per month, they are being forced to look further afield. God be with the days when Dubliners used to complain that the city was being overrun by 'culchies'; now some Dubliners who can't afford to buy homes in their own city are becoming reluctant migrants to provincial towns such as Gorey, Mullingar and Tullamore, where houses are considerably cheaper. New housing estates on the outskirts of these towns and many others are, in effect, little bits of Dublin way beyond the metropolitan area. Do the children reared in such places grow up as Wexford, Westmeath and Offaly people, even while their Dublin-born parents continue to commute to work in the capital? But unlike those who travel by rail from as far north as Lurgan and Newry, most of the migrants to the outer Leinster towns tend to drive their cars on the much-improved national roads radiating outwards from Dublin. The provision of these virtual motorways has facilitated suburban sprawl, judging by the number of new housing estates springing up along their routes, and given long-distance commuters an edge over those living closer to the city centre in, say, Templeogue.

In the thirty years to 1992, an estimated 100,000 one-off houses – bungalows or two-storey dwellings on individual sites – were shovelled into the countryside throughout the Greater Dublin Area, including Meath, Kildare and Wicklow, and there is no reason to believe that this trend is not continuing, even at an accelerated pace. A drive along the backroads from, say, Baltinglass to Oldcastle reveals the extent of this suburban colonisation of the capital's rural hinterland, and the consequential traffic congestion it creates in every village and country town. For the truth is that most of these houses are urban-generated, owned and occupied by people who work in Dublin or one of the towns in the region. Farmers are only too willing to sell off acre or half-acre sites to bungalow-builders, often to provide collateral for bank loans. Those with land on the periphery of Dublin or of the larger Leinster towns are even more entranced by the prospect of making huge windfall gains from the sale of their holdings for more concentrated suburban development. Over the years, they have found that many county councillors are well attuned to the needs of the marketplace, demonstrating their willingness to rezone land at the drop of a hat – or, in some cases, a brown envelope – whether or not it makes any sense in planning terms. In successive county development plans since the early 1970s, thousands of acres of good agricultural land have been rezoned for suburban housing, against professional planning advice, at six or eight houses per acre with little or no reference to the availability of public transport. But whether the planners won or lost, the result was the same – formless low-density housing that spreads across the landscape, engulfing whole villages along the way. Ballymore Eustace, in Co Kildare, is just one example. On foot of a rezoning vote by county councillors, planning permission was granted for a suburban estate of 450 houses on the outskirts of the village. Though overturned on appeal by An Bord Pleanála in September 1999, the threat remains that it will be inflicted with a dormitory more than half its size, whose bread-earning residents, as Kevin Myers (who lives nearby) wrote in the *Irish Times*, 'are gone by 6.30 in the morning, are not back until 8 o'clock in the evening, and who know as much about the community they have landed in as they do about Pluto's outer moons'.

Traffic is one of the inevitable consequences of earlier plans to create a motorised city. Now that we've got it, we're beginning to realise that it doesn't work. And with at least a thousand cars now being added to Dublin's roads *every week*, the gridlock we face is directly related to fact that it occupies a land area twice the size of European cities of comparable population, notably Copenhagen. Day after day, horror stories multiply about the side-effects of this process of self-strangulation. Traffic chaos has become part and parcel of Dublin life, and it's getting perceptibly worse year by year. And though every city suffers from traffic to some degree, the problem here is aggravated by suburbs extending, in reality, from Dundalk to Baltinglass. Nearly everybody can now see that the city is facing heart seizure, with all of its arteries clogged by cars, and the Liffey quays, in particular, choked by a growing fleet of trucks heading to and from the port. Just ask the bleary-eyed commuters who must leave their homes fifteen or twenty minutes earlier in the morning than they did last year to be sure of getting to work on time. Or consider the shocking estimate that Dublin's economy is losing at least £1 billion every year because of the time being wasted sitting in traffic jams. Ten years ago, the morning peak period extended from 8 o'clock to 10.00. Now it runs from 7.00 to 10.00, and the volume of traffic is also much greater. Congestion is no longer confined to the city centre and the main roads leading into it. The suburbs, too, are becoming saturated with cars, as more and more motorists join the fray. According to the Dublin Transportation Office, there are 137,000 cars hitting the road every morning throughout the city and its hinterland. That's 45,700 more trips than what was anticipated by transport planners in 1994. They had not bargained for a booming economy and, with it, an unprecedented surge in car sales. Each of the last four years produced a record for new D-registered cars, climbing from 44,487 in 1996 to 50,916 in 1997, to 56,064 in 1998 and 64,361 in 1999, and these figures do not include new registrations in the adjoining commuter belt counties of Meath, Kildare and Wicklow. Car dealers have never had it so good, with the latest models flying out of their showrooms. By 6th January 2000, the Swiss ambassador's wife was surprised to see that the new '00 D' registrations had already topped 3,600. Such was the double-zero's mesmeric attraction that 42,000 new cars were sold throughout the State before the end of the month, representing a 55% increase on the figure for the previous January. Many of the purchasers were young and buying a car for the first time, lured by the promise of freedom held out so tantalisingly by every TV advert. An EU-funded study by the sociology department at Trinity College concluded that the right to own a car has become almost synonymous with citizenship, quite apart from its value as a status symbol and, for many, a social necessity. 'Passing a driving test is a far more important social ritual than exercising the vote for the first time', it said. As a result, people are pulling up plants and getting rid of lawns to make room for two, three and even four off-street car-parking spaces, as sons and daughters acquire their own private chariots. Cars lined up outside the ostentatious homes of the nouveaux riches are seen as sleek symbols of social success.

For years, car ownership levels in Ireland were artificially depressed by heavy excise duty and VAT on cars, parts and petrol, as well as road taxation running ahead of inflation and a high-cost insurance regime skewed against the under-thirties. These factors created the pent-up demand which has now been released by the booming economy. The extraordinary, almost exponential increase in car ownership and use was not anticipated by anyone involved in drafting the DTI (Dublin Transportation Initiative) strategy in the early 1990s. Its forecasts are officially acknowledged as being 'very much off target', with the current batch of transport planners now scrambling to catch up. This failure in

Newly arrived Toyota cars lined up in Dublin Port. Car dealers have never had it so good, with the latest models flying out of their showrooms – 42,000 in the first month of this year.

A DART train at Lansdowne Road station. Only prejudice against public transport can explain why not one extra carriage was added to the electrified rail system despite a doubling of passenger numbers since it came into service in 1984.

forecasting has been compounded by delays in delivering long-planned infra-structural projects – notably Luas, the Port Tunnel and the southern leg of the M50. All of these are behind schedule, in some cases by several years. Meanwhile, public transport remains pathetically inadequate due to serious under-funding. For years, it was perceived as a residual service for those too poor to have their own cars. The rule of thumb applied by successive governments, reinforced by the Department of Finance, was that public transport loses money, therefore we shouldn't invest in public transport. How else is it possible to explain why extra carriages are only now being added to the DART fleet despite a doubling of pas-senger numbers since the electrified service was introduced in 1984? What other explanation can be offered for the appalling conditions on the Maynooth line, for example, with its decrepit stations and trains so overcrowded that commuters must squeeze into the guard's van? Or for the fact that Dublin Bus is forced to operate with the lowest level of public subsidy of any urban transport service in Europe?

Many car-commuters simply don't have an alternative. Due to the negli-gence and prejudices of successive governments, the city does not have anything approaching a public transport *system*. Thus, the DART is largely confined to the 'Gold Coast' around Dublin Bay. Elsewhere, there are only buses or often-decrepit suburban trains, and it's not even possible to transfer from one to anoth-er without paying a second fare. Links between bus and rail services are tenuous, adding to the unreliability of public transport and making car use more likely. The Luas light rail lines planned to link Tallaght, Sandyford and Ballymun with the city centre should help, of course. And while the new trams will provide an attractive alternative to travelling by car on the routes they serve, Luas will not on its own give Dublin the transport system it so desperately needs. What Luas has going for it is an upmarket image that should appeal to those motorists who firmly believe that 'buses are for losers', even where quality bus corridors (QBCs) have been provided to speed their passage into town. 'Even if Dublin Bus was to collect these people from their houses every morning, drop the kids off to school and then serve them a champagne breakfast in club class conditions on the way into town, they still wouldn't get the bus', according to Owen Keegan, Dublin Corporation's Director of Traffic. Measures such as the Stillorgan Road QBC, introduced in late August 1999 despite howls of protest from the car lobby, are aimed at those who are prepared to make the switch to public transport. But it is clear that many motorists are infuriated about the priority being given to Dublin Bus in the allocation of road space, about all the ramps designed to deter rat-run-ning through residential areas, and even about the whole idea of 'traffic calming'. Having once felt superior as they drove past rain-soaked bus queues, they sud-denly found that the tables had been turned on them. Now they were constrained for space as the buses whizzed by on the inside lane. It isn't just on the routes where bus corridors have been implemented that traffic congestion is evident. The disease has spread along all the main arteries throughout the Greater Dublin

Area, provoking daily outbreaks of road rage directed at cyclists, pedestrians and other drivers. 'It's all upon us now, the fact that money wasn't invested in public transport', sighed one senior planner.

And the indications are that car ownership levels will continue to soar. Throughout the State, there were 1.5 million vehicles registered at the end of 1998, up from just over one million in 1990, with a similarly large increase in vehicle miles per capita. Yet we are still well below the European Union average of 423 cars per thousand in population. In a 1998 paper for Earthwatch, Sadhbh O'Neill indicted increasing car use for degrading the city and severing its communities. 'As roads become more dangerous for cyclists and pedestrians, more journeys are carried out by car. In response to people's increased mobility, planning decisions are made which assume most people have access to cars', she wrote. And this represented a 'terrible tyranny' for those who don't – mainly women, older people, the poor and disabled. The environmental consequences are also alarming. According to O'Neill, 'every piece of evidence and every study carried out in recent years points to the disturbing fact that the rise in car ownership and usage will certainly bring about a much lower quality of life, less mobility for some groups in society, and poorer health. The car-culture advocated by car advertising tries to tell us that "my journey is more important than yours", yet the cost of everyone's journey is borne by society and the environment as a whole: the air we breathe, the streets we live on, and the fragile health of many members of society, including the one in seven children who suffer from asthma.' The most recent air-quality report by the Environmental Protection Agency warned that increasing volumes of traffic will make it difficult for Dublin and Cork to stay within new EU limits on nitrogen dioxide and particulate matter (microscopic dust known as PM_{10}). Indeed, the PM_{10} limits are already being exceeded on about 40% of days in the year at College Street, in the centre of Dublin, mainly because of the dirty diesel engines in buses and heavy-goods vehicles. Traffic is also the fastest growing contributor to the greenhouse gas emissions blamed by scientists for global warming – no longer a distant threat we can afford to ignore, but a phenomenon that is already happening.

How did we walk – or, rather, drive – ourselves into this quagmire? After a century-long love affair with the car, traffic is moving at about the same speed as it was in the era of the horse and cart. The very proliferation of automobiles, as Americans call them, has set aside the promise that they would give us freedom of movement. According to John Henry, director of the Dublin Transportation Office (DTO), we failed to appreciate the crucial link between land use and transportation. 'Land use is where it all started to go wrong,' he said. 'We put industrial estates here and residential estates there in separate single uses. Tallaght is a good example. We moved the people out and they had to travel back to the jobs. But then, we all wanted our own semi-d with front garden, back garden, a sense of home and place.' And it is precisely because Dublin is far from compact that we now have a transport crisis, while Copenhagen doesn't. The city was not designed to facilitate public transport. Had it been so designed, its expansion would have been planned along rail lines or high-capacity bus routes. And despite the Government's endorsement of higher housing densities, particularly close to public transport nodes, land is still being rezoned in the Dublin area for car-dependent, low-density development. Some pro-motoring pressure groups still believe that we can build out way out of the problem, with such expensive schemes as the Eastern Bypass motorway, but other European cities have found sensible ways to tame the traffic, and this book explores some of the novel ideas they have adopted in recent years.

As for those who wonder whether we should spend billions to provide the city with a functioning public transport system that only a minority might use, what we should be doing is designing communities around new high-grade public transport routes – Luas, DART, suburban rail and a partly underground Circle Line in the city centre with a spur to Dublin Airport and a new line to Navan. Establishing such a symbiotic relationship between land use and transportation is now the most critical task we face. If we pull it off, Dublin has as much chance as any other European capital of becoming a 'sustainable city' for the 21st century. If we don't, or don't even try, it will be a disaster of our own making. For the future shape of the metropolitan area and much of Leinster will be set for decades to come by what happens in the next ten years. That much is clear, whether or not Brian Hughes, lecturer in urban economics at the Dublin Institute of Technology, is correct in forecasting that the Greater Dublin Area could have a population of 1.9 million by 2011, based on a 'business-as-usual' planning scenario and the continuation of strong economic growth. According to Hughes, the GDA is now emerging as 'Ireland's city-state of the 21st century', and any attempt to constrain its growth by interfering with the market-led demand would mean that 'all of Ireland will be the loser'. This is hardly a view that the Council for the West, for example, would endorse. Like many others over the years, it has been campaigning for balanced regional growth, to bring jobs and hope to depressed areas along the Atlantic seaboard, instead of allowing Dublin, willy-nilly, to become a bottomless pit for inward investment.

Hughes's forecast is substantially in excess of the 2011 target figure of 1.65 million in the Strategic Planning Guidelines for the Greater Dublin Area, drawn up in 1999 for its seven local authorities by a consortium of consultants headed by Brady Shipman Martin. However, his figure is curiously similar to the 1.85 million projected by ERDO, the Eastern Regional Development Organisation, in its very controversial settlement strategy published in 1985, two years before it was wound up. In the depressed late 1980s, with the rate of population growth falling rapidly, ERDO's forecast was regarded as wildly over the top. The fact that its strategy also wrote off the entire inner city, saying that it did not have the capacity to house even an extra 10,000 people without major changes in public policy, and focused instead on blanket suburban development, did not help either. At the memorable Dublin Crisis Conference in 1986, team leader Len O'Reilly defended the ERDO study. 'The 1.85 million figure is not an objective, but who is to say it could not happen?' he said. 'When you think of what happened in the 1950s when the region was growing at a rate of only 1,800 per annum and yet we had this huge resurgence in the 1960s and 1970s with the migrants coming back. Who can say now that this won't happen again? We are in the middle of a very bad recession and yet the population is still growing at 12,000 to 13,000 per annum. These people have to be accommodated. They are not Martians. They are our children and your children. We must accommodate them.' But no more than any economist at the time, O'Reilly and his largely in-house study team did not hear the distant roar of the 'Celtic Tiger' and, with it, the advent of unprecedented levels of in-migration, not only by returning Irish emigrants, but also by foreign nationals. That influx, which reached a record 45,000 in 1999, is largely responsible for boosting the Republic's population by 1,000 *per week*. Two-thirds of this growth is happening in the GDA, adding to the pressures brought about by our new-found prosperity. The results are evident in high house prices, maddening traffic congestion, and an 'infrastructural deficit' that has deprived Dublin of an adequate supply of housing and a functioning transport system. Much-needed infrastructure to make good this deficit has frequently been delayed by endless rounds of public consultations and/or legal actions. In some cases, indeed, the long-established NIMBY (Not In My Back Yard) syndrome has been replaced by what has been termed the BANANA (Build Absolutely Nothing Anywhere Near Anything) factor, of which a subsidiary is NOTE (Not Over There Either).

If Hughes is right, we would need to provide some 25,000 housing units per annum, significantly more than the figure envisaged under the Greater Dublin Area Strategic Planning Guidelines. Failure to do so and to deal with other deficits would imply 'a continuing nightmare scenario of under-providing for housing, transportation and infrastructure', he warned. But plans for higher-density housing, large elements of infrastructure, and the various other facilities required by an exploding city-region will not be achieved painlessly. We will also have to adjust to living in an increasingly multicultural metropolis, quite unlike Dublin in the Rare Oul Times, as refugees and economic migrants continue to be attracted to Ireland in search of a better life. The crunch issue is where all the new housing is to be built. If policies favouring higher residential densities are not properly implemented, the relentless sprawl of Dublin will continue – not only at the periphery of the existing built-up area, but also popping up around provincial towns within a fifty-mile radius of the city, such as Carlow, Drogheda, Navan and Portlaoise. This phenomenon of 'leap-frogging' beyond traditional dormitory towns like Bray or Maynooth has created a housing boom in the more distant towns, as they are drawn into an extended commuter belt, according to two other DIT academics, Brendan Williams and Patrick Shiels. Drogheda's annual output, for example, went up by nearly 300% in three years, while Portlaoise's population is expected to double from 9,000 in 1996 to 18,000 in 2001. 'Cluster effects' can also be observed in Maynooth/Leixlip/Celbridge as the three towns gradually coalesce. In their paper, *21st Century Dublin – the Edge City and Commuterland*, Williams and Shiels also drew attention to the continuing trend of major multinationals such as Amdahl, Dell, Intel, IBM and Hewlett Packard locating in a ring around the outskirts of Dublin, in an incipient American-style 'edge city' that also includes hotels, shopping malls and business parks.

Thus far, at least, we have avoided the terrible 'doughnut effect' so characteristic of most urban areas in the US. The influx of population into the core of the city has seen to that. But while its population is rising for the first time in more than seventy years, the reverse is happening throughout the older suburbs. The conversion of large houses from bed-sits to single-family use, the increasing prevalence of the 'empty nest' syndrome as older couples are left rattling round in houses far too large for their needs and the flight of their grown-up children to homes of their own elsewhere have all contributed to plummeting residential densities throughout the inner suburbs, in particular. Even in newer suburban areas, such as parts of Tallaght, the population is now falling quite dramatically as the sons and daughters of young couples who moved out there in the 1970s leave the family home to repeat the cycle in Leixlip, Carlow or wherever. As these areas are thinned out, leaving a lot of elderly residents without the vibrancy and purchasing power to sustain the corner shop or neighbourhood centre, new suburbs will be built on greenfield sites further out, requiring a whole new range of social facilities. By 2011, according to the Strategic Planning Guidelines, the population will increase by 14% in north-east Kildare, 31% in the rest of Kildare, 24% in north-east Wicklow, 28% in the rest of Wicklow, 40% in Meath, 46% in south Fingal and 48% in north Fingal. By comparison, Dublin city and Dun Laoghaire-Rathdown are anticipated to rise by just 4% and 5% respectively. In the case of the city, population increases in growth areas such as Docklands would be all but offset by falling numbers in more established built-up areas.

Brian Hughes believes the SPG estimates are grossly understated. His own figures suggest much higher growth rates, ranging from a low of 8.7% in the city area to a staggering 101.5% in north Fingal. In the real world, as he put it, Greater Dublin's population is growing more than twice as fast as the rest of the country, largely because of strong in-migration induced by its disproportionate level of economic growth and much higher rates of household formation, particularly by young single people. If this trend continues, the GDA would account for more than half of the Republic's total by 2047 at the latest. Such a prospect raises serious implications for housing, infrastructure and other elements of the built environment, according to Hughes's latest paper on the subject, published in October 1999. 'The failure to plan or to build anywhere near sufficient residential units in the GDA is the prime cause of the housing affordability crisis that now so seriously threatens the momentum of the Celtic Tiger', he wrote. 'For every 100 housing units the GDA should be producing, it is only building 61 units ... Such a dismal level of production is not compatible with sustainable planning.

Specifically, the housing units are not being built where the jobs are being created, thus inevitably adding to longer home-to-work journeys.' Though 60% or 65% of population growth is in the GDA, it accounts for only 30% to 35% of the housing output. This mismatch between supply and demand turned housing into a hot political issue and, in late 1997, the Government responded by commissioning economic consultants Peter Bacon & Associates to prepare a major report on the measures needed to curb steeply rising property prices. It recommended that optimum use should be made of land already zoned for development by increasing residential densities and accelerating investment in water and sewerage infrastructure – proposals that were accepted with remarkable alacrity by ministers. The Department of the Environment was already committed to promoting higher housing densities under the previous government's Sustainable Development Strategy. Now it was pledging vastly increased resources to deal with the infrastructural deficit. A second Bacon report, in March 1999, claimed credit for taking some of the heat out of the market, though house prices continued to increase, if not quite so sharply, and there were still problems on the supply side, with new houses being snapped up as soon as the plaster was dry, and even sooner in many cases.

Clearly, there is a danger inherent in making population projections based on a three-year upward trend and the assumption that a high-growth economy will be sustained. But even if the rate of growth is slowed down by some external shock, Dublin's population will continue to rise over the next decade, providing an engine to drive development. At least 200,000 new homes, and possibly as many as a quarter of a million, *will* be built throughout the Greater Dublin Area, so where that engine is directed has become absolutely critical to achieving a sustainable future. There is every reason to believe that the gains made over the past decade in reversing inner-city decline will be consolidated, with Docklands offering the best prospect for area-wide regeneration. However, this is likely to be counterpointed by endless peripheral expansion and a simultaneous decline in the population of older suburban areas. The truth is that nobody has a map of where we are all going, and there are few enough signposts either. Given that most of the housing built in Dublin over the past thirty years was developer-led, it is a reasonable bet that market forces will play a dominant role in determining the future of the region. What seems to be happening is roughly along ERDO lines, though with somewhat higher housing densities and more development in the inner city than Len O'Reilly and his team envisaged in 1985. Ostensibly, the Strategic Planning Guidelines propose to 'consolidate the metropolitan area in line with the principles of sustainable development', to concentrate development throughout its hinterland in major centres such as Navan, Naas-Newbridge-Kilcullen, Drogheda, Balbriggan and Wicklow, and to 'provide a better balance between public and private transport'. In effect, John Fitzgerald and the six county managers had a cake to cut, and each of them ensured that he (all of them are men, of course) got a fair slice of it. According to Fitzgerald, the indicative pop-

Frank Miller / *Irish Times*

Noel Dempsey, Minister for the Environment, pictured at the Fianna Fáil ardfheis in March 2000. By introducing a requirement that up to 20% of new housing schemes must be 'social or afford-able' housing, he seemed to be taking on the party's old pals in the building industry.

ulation target of 1.65 million in the current guidelines is 'the prudent one to aim for', but he maintains that the monitoring system is flexible enough to respond to changes. [The figure was revised upwards to 1.76 million in the April 2000 review.] 'There's no reason why we couldn't plan for a higher figure, if required', he told the *Irish Times* in September 1999. The Dublin Transportation Office was also working to the 1.65 million forecast, and said that if it was higher, 'we would have to do things quicker'. The only thing certain about different population projections, according to John Henry, is that they will probably all be wrong.

Rigid social stratification – or 'spatial apartheid', as Jim Walsh of Combat Poverty calls it – is another unfortunate feature of housing in Dublin and everywhere else in Ireland. Witness the half-stifled outcry from the building industry after the Minister for the Environment, Noel Dempsey, introduced legislation in July 1999 giving powers to the local authorities to acquire up to 20% of any residential development site, at little more than its agricultural value, for 'social or affordable' housing. In doing so, he seemed to be taking on Fianna Fáil's old pals in the construction and development sector at a time when they had 'never had it so good', in Harold Macmillan's immortal phrase. Knowing full well that failure to deal with the housing issue will do no favours for his party in the next general election, Dempsey extolled this courageous initiative as 'the most radical ever brought forward' by an Irish government to deal with spiralling house prices. The development lobby was furious, and there were mutterings about challenging the constitutionality of the Minister's measure. One of its main concerns was that Dempsey's move would depress the value of residential development land, especially in the more sought-after areas, because house-purchasers would not pay good money for homes on new estates when they might end up living cheek by jowl with an enclave of social housing. In future, according to Alan Cooke, chief executive of the Irish Auctioneers and Valuers Institute, people would speak of pre- and post-1999 housing, depending on 'whether they live in mixed developments or are among the lucky few residing in segregated private schemes'. In his view, the resale value of private homes on mixed estates would take a hammering because of the close proximity of social housing. He reiterated this point in a letter to the Minister, perhaps not realising that he had grown up in a house built by Meath County Council. Yet even Cooke could not deny that there was a pressing need for more social housing in the city. Despite Dublin's loss of EU Objective 1 status, it still contains nine of the eleven classified areas of social deprivation nationally, and seven of these are in the Corporation area. Since John Fitzgerald made housing one of his top priorities, well over £100 million has been found to 'fix the bricks and mortar' and regenerate marginalised communities, with the aim of bringing them back into the city's mainstream. Leaving them to fester in ghettos is simply not an option, especially when the funds are available to achieve a quantum leap in social conditions.

But the real issue in the debate on Noel Dempsey's proposal had nothing to do with lifting people out of poverty. It was all about what his opponents saw as a blunt instrument of social engineering to enforce a level of housing integration which was unacceptable to the wider public. It didn't matter that the '20% requirement' would include houses available for purchase by people on moderate incomes as well as those built by housing associations and local authorities. In November 1999, Dempsey offered an olive branch in the form of an amendment to his own bill, permitting the local authorities to purchase houses at cost price plus an element of construction profit, as an alternative to acquiring a portion of the overall site. But since they would first have to prepare housing plans before the relevant provisions of the Bill came into operation, there was a window of opportunity for landowners to offload residential sites to beat the deadline, and no doubt that many of them availed of it. Certainly, the very 'threat' that future schemes would have to include a sizeable element of social housing loosened up land banks, releasing a substantial amount of residential land for development. But with demand for housing almost insatiable, prices remained high and would be passed on to purchasers – whether private or public – in the exorbitant unit cost of house sites. In theory, higher densities should mean lower costs. In practice, any gains in this area were offset by rising prices as housing demand continued to outstrip supply. Moreover, if the current economic momentum is sustained, even at the more moderate 5% growth rates predicted by the Economic and Social Research Institute, house prices are set to rise even more as we move steadily closer to the per capita income of some of the richest countries in Europe.

Whatever way one looks at it, the first decade of the new millennium is make or break time for Dublin. Not since its golden era in the late 18th century has it been at such a critical crossroads. The future shape of the city and its hinterland – indeed, of the country as a whole – will be determined by the decisions we make during these years of unprecedented prosperity. Just as we are still living with the legacy created by the Duke of Ormonde and the Wide Streets Commissioners, future generations of Dubliners will long be living with the physical shape of the city we leave to them. Thus, the course we choose to follow in catering for the current surge in population really is of overwhelming importance. We could, of course, continue travelling down the same road by allowing the capital to sprawl out over the countryside, gobbling up some of the best agricultural land in Ireland. Or we could attempt to consolidate the existing built-up area by developing housing at higher densities, especially in areas close to public transport routes. After all, it was the inauguration of the Kingstown railway line in 1834 that allowed Dublin's upper middle classes to colonise Merrion, Blackrock and Dun Laoghaire, just as the Harcourt Street line opened up Dundrum, Foxrock and Carrickmines, and the old tram lines did the same for Rathmines, Rathgar, Churchtown and Clontarf. Yet despite an allocation of £1.58 billion in the National Development Plan for public transport in the Dublin area, there is no real indication that the Government fully appreciates the crucial connection between transport and land use in determining how a city develops. Almost everyone involved in the planning arena is nervous about what may happen. Indeed, many anticipate chaos for the next few years as we feel way towards a more environmentally sustainable path of development.

The choice facing us now is stark: either the capital continues to expand endlessly on its periphery and pops up in the form of suburban housing estates tacked on to Carlow, Portlaoise, Tullamore, Mullingar, Navan, Drogheda, Dundalk and other provincial towns within an ever-growing commuter belt, or we learn from the lessons of other European cities which have confronted the problems associated with population growth and made a very good stab at solving them by consolidating the built-up area and developing new towns at higher densities linked to high-grade public transport systems. Every man, woman and child in the Greater Dublin Area is directly affected in one way or another by the direction the city will take. If we travel down the first road, we would end up with our own version of the car-dependent American 'edge city', sprawling out formlessly across the landscape. But if we choose to travel down the second road – and we can still make that conscious choice – there is a chance that we might end up with something approaching a more compact, European-style sustainable city. 'A strategy that promotes increased usage of the private car is unsustainable, and existing problems in the Greater Dublin Area indicate the consequences of following such a path', the Strategic Planning Guidelines state bluntly. 'The conclusion is that there is no alternative to a sustainable, public transport-based solution and that failure to implement the appropriate measures could seriously prejudice the economic and social growth of Dublin.'

And so, for the second time in its history, Dublin has reached the point where things become fixed for two or three hundred years. This may not be widely understood, even by most of our political leaders, but it is nonetheless a fact. Perhaps we have been so distracted by raking over old coals to focus on the future. Acres of newsprint and countless hours of broadcasting air time have been given over to coverage of the various tribunals – and there can be no doubt that we've learned a lot about the interaction between business and politics, as well as Charlie Haughey's penchant for Charvet shirts and much else besides. But despite the Government's commitment to invest £40 billion under its National Development Plan between now and 2006, there has not been nearly enough public debate about where this is likely to lead us and what kind of Dublin we will be left with after its share of the money is spent. Based on what has been going on over the past ten years, as documented in the themes of this book, only the most blinkered optimist could have any real confidence that we will get it right.

2. Going Up

Anyone over forty will remember the thrill of seeing Liberty Hall for the first time. It shone like a beacon of modernity, a symbol of the transformation of Dublin from the black-and-white era of drab tenements in the Georgian slums to an almost blinding Technicolour future, laden with all sorts of possibilities. The city, we thought innocently, was dusting off its old cobwebs and embracing the 20th century. Gazing in awe at what was then the Republic's tallest building, it seemed to us that Dublin had arrived at last. Despite SIPTU's recent efforts to brighten it up, Liberty Hall stands as a shabby monument to misplaced optimism as well as being an unfortunate addition to the visual clutter around the Custom House. Equally, few can be found today to say a good word about O'Connell Bridge House or about the lumpen cluster of taller-than-average office blocks in and around Poolbeg Street, of which Hawkins House – headquarters of the Department of Health – is unquestionably the most odious, quite apart from the fact that it stands on the site of the Theatre Royal. Indeed, it was the appearance of this unfortunate group in the 1960s that persuaded Dublin Corporation to adopt stricter policies aimed at protecting the city's generally low-rise skyline.

Successive city plans, from 1971 onwards, had laid down a fourteen-point set of criteria for dealing with planning applications for high buildings. Issues to be taken into account included overshadowing and overlooking, disruption of the scale of an existing streetscape, detraction from important landmarks or structures and spaces of architectural or historical importance, detrimental effects on spires, domes and the skyline in general, scale in relation to surrounding open space, visual relationship to the River Liffey, the canals, St Stephen's Green and other important areas, and whether the civic importance of a proposed high

Zoe Developments' sixteen-storey apartment tower at Charlotte Quay in the Grand Canal Docks. Designed by O'Mahony Pike Architects, it was cited by the *Irish Times* as 'an example of how high buildings can contribute positively to the urban environment'.

Terry Thorp / Irish Times

Despite SIPTU's recent efforts to brighten it up, Liberty Hall stands as a shabby monument to misplaced optimism.

Estate agent Ken MacDonald was one of the first spokesmen of the development sector to advocate 'well-designed multi-storey buildings' on landmark sites.

building would justify its prominence. These criteria were quite restrictive, and helped to fend off most, though not all, proposals for high buildings, commonly defined as 'those which significantly exceed the general building heights of their surroundings'. Thus, Dublin managed to retain its characteristic low profile and human scale, even if this necessarily produced 'a sprawling city with little skyline interest', as a 1998 draft of the Corporation's new high-building policy guidelines put it. That document was itself the product of a renewed debate about the appropriateness or otherwise of high buildings in the city, led by a development lobby brimming with the confidence engendered by a burgeoning economy. Its view was well represented by Ken MacDonald, managing director of estate agents Hooke & MacDonald, which specialised in selling city-centre apartments of highly variable quality. Writing in the *Irish Times* on 31st December 1997, he argued that higher densities were needed in Docklands, with 'well-designed multi-storey buildings' on landmark sites to pave the way for a population of 100,000 – four times what was envisaged in the area master plan adopted earlier that month. 'What's wrong with twenty or thirty storeys if it is going to enhance the city and be functional as well?' he asked. There was also a strong view among developers that the increasingly buoyant office market in Dublin could absorb more than a few skyscrapers. Indeed, the Construction Industry Federation argued that there should be no limit at all on the size of office blocks in the city. It was this type of pressure, as well as a marked preference among some senior Corporation officials for a few 'architectural spikes', that prompted a review of policy on the future of Dublin's skyline in the first draft of the new City Development Plan, published in March 1998. Though it accepted that, generally speaking, Dublin is not a high-rise city, it put forward the proposition that there 'may be requirements for high buildings in certain locations in the future', and said each case would be judged on its merits 'in terms of sustainability, development control policies, transportation and employment policies, local plans and the definite need to regenerate certain areas of the city'. This was in line with the Corporation's recognition of Dublin's emergence as 'a significant world financial/ commercial centre' and its concern to 'ensure that a high buildings policy does not unreasonably deter or deflect inward investment'. One of the key consider-

courtesy of Dublin Corporation

City Manager John Fitzgerald at his desk in Wood Quay. Described as 'the Jack Charlton of Irish local government', his style of leadership is firmly focused on substance rather than style.

ations would be whether any proposed high building was 'elegant, contemporary, stylish, and, in terms of form and profile, makes a positive contribution to the existing skyline'.

The progressive, hands-on City Manager, John Fitzgerald, who had taken over from Frank Feely in June 1996, denied that such a move would give Dublin a Pittsburgh-style skyline. He said it was generally accepted that the low-rise character of the city centre should be protected, but there was 'scope for creativity' in the Docklands and elsewhere. Though he conceded that this was a 'radical departure', he felt it was appropriate in 'a changing city, one that's changing faster than any other city in Europe'. Fitzgerald had inherited a deeply demoralised bureaucracy, and he was determined to turn it into a 'proactive' organisation. Initially, he insisted on being photographed seated at his desk rather than on the roof terrace of the Civic Offices, with its panoramic views of the Liffey quays and the domes, spires and tower cranes on the skyline. That would have been too much like the 'master of all he surveys' mode favoured by his predecessor. The enigmatic Limerickman wanted to mark the transition from the *ancien régime* to a

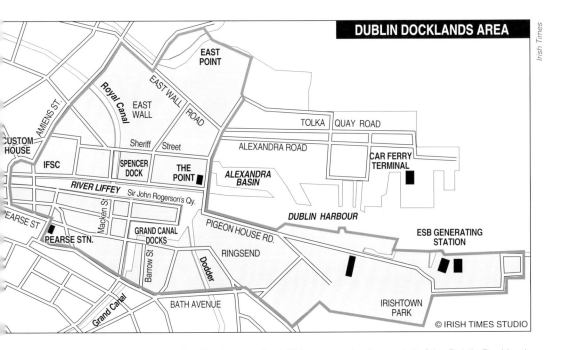

Irish Times

Map of the Dublin Docklands area, the 1,300 acres under the control of the Dublin Docklands Development Authority

Elevation of one of the central elements of the Barrow Street scheme by O'Mahony Pike Architects for Zoe Developments – a circular block of apartments, rising to nine storeys, installed inside the skeleton of a Victorian gasholder, with car-parking beneath.

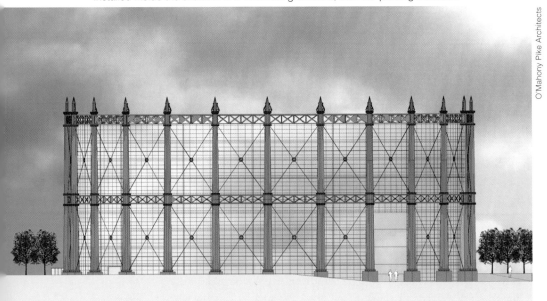

O'Mahony Pike Architects

different type of corporate leadership, firmly focused on substance rather than style. As South Dublin's first county manager over the previous two years, he had been so successful in moulding a team spirit that he was dubbed 'the Jack Charlton of Irish local government'. One of his first acts on taking over at Wood Quay was to establish a management team consisting of himself, three assistant managers, the finance and personnel officers, the city architect, the city planning officer and the city engineer. They meet once a week, on Tuesdays, for an hour-and-a-half to 'hammer out a corporate consensus', as he terms it. He also set about 're-educating' some two hundred people in management posts, sending groups of up to twenty at a time to Tulfarris House, in Co Wicklow, for two-day sessions to begin forging a new ethos, based on thinking more strategically and making a better job of managing the Corporation's 6,500 staff. A 'can do' philosophy began to permeate the Civic Offices, after the fashion of Yosser in *Boys from the Black Stuff*, and senior officials seemed to have a new spring in their step, with bold initiatives in every area of activity giving weight to the Corporation's new slogan, 'Leading Change in the City'.

Of course, there were opposing views on the high-rise issue. On one side, conservationists argued that Dublin is a low-rise city and should always remain so. On the other, development interests made the case that the time had come to go up rather than out. 'We've always said that it's not a question of either/or, because we've achieved good densities in the city centre without going too high', Fitzgerald told the *Irish Times* in January 1999. However, he added that the whole issue of high buildings in the city was 'new territory, we haven't been there before'. Asked why the Corporation had not conducted a series of visual analysis studies to determine more precisely where high buildings might be located, Fitzgerald said the draft plan had avoided being 'over-prescriptive' to help develop a consensus on the issue. 'There's a very strong consensus that the core of the city, especially the Georgian core, is sacrosanct, but also that there are points outside it where high buildings could be a feature. So what we propose to do is to carry out a skyline study to identify these locations.' But long before the looser policy on high buildings was eventually adopted by the City Council in March 1999, or the skyline study had been commissioned, gung-ho developers stole a march on the planners with audacious schemes such as the 'towers of light' proposed for George's Quay, directly opposite the Custom House, and the immensely more ambitious £1 billion development earmarked for a 51-acre site at Spencer Dock and North Wall Quay, including the long-delayed National Conference Centre. The flurry of high-rise applications also included tall blocks for the former gasworks in Barrow Street, one encased in the steel formwork of a listed Victorian gasholder, and for Thorncastle Street, on a site adjoining the River Dodder. Zoe Developments Ltd, Dublin's most prolific builder of apartment blocks, had even managed to persuade An Bord Pleanála to reinstate four floors omitted by the Corporation from its sixteen-storey apartment block at Charlotte Quay, in the Grand Canal Docks. What Zoe produced there was quite elegant –

a slender tower designed by O'Mahony Pike, rising from the corner of the dock basin and mimicking the profile of a nearby grain silo on the inner dock, with no negative impact on the city centre skyline. According to the *Irish Times*, it was 'surely an example of how high buildings can contribute positively to the urban environment'.

But the Corporation's loosening of its guidelines seemed to mark the declaration of an open season for erecting 'skyscrapers', and to suggest that Dublin was navigating into dangerous waters without the aid of an Admiralty chart. There was also a perception that the Corporation itself was promoting the use of big-name architects from abroad, on the basis that Dublin was now 'a world-class city that needs world-class buildings by world-class architects, particularly if the scheme involves high-rise buildings', as one resentful local architect complained. In this context, George's Quay and Spencer Dock are worth examining in some detail because they illustrate how difficult it was to adjudicate on mega-development schemes in the absence of a detailed visual analysis of the city. In the case of George's Quay, the Cosgrave Property Group had astonished other developers by engaging the high-flying international architects, Skidmore Owings & Merrill (SOM), to design a high-rise scheme for the balance of the site assembled so painstakingly in the 1970s by Irish Life. The group, run by brothers Joe, Michael and Peter Cosgrave, had previously availed of the services of Ambrose Kelly, an architect who would not be eligible for membership of the Royal Institute of the Architects of Ireland because of its insistence on recognised academic qualifications. His firm, organised on profit-centre lines, charged cut-price fees and excelled at producing humdrum exercises in Georgian pastiche such as Custom Hall on Gardiner Street – admittedly a very brave development for its time – or Ha'penny Bridge House on Lower Ormond Quay, with its kitsch references to the famous iron bridge. Kelly is an incredibly successful businessman, who once booked the entire Abbey Theatre, with Taoiseach Albert Reynolds as guest of honour, to say thanks to all of his clients and associates. His practice grew from the Ambrose Kelly Partnership into the Ambrose Kelly Group (chairman: Ambrose Kelly), before this amiable and wily impresario felt he should change the name to Project Architects Ltd after becoming embroiled with his friend, crane-hire king Dermot O'Leary, in the fallout from boardroom carnage at CIÉ in 1995. It was Kelly who suggested commissioning SOM, when he realised the awesome scale of the Cosgrave brothers' ambitions for George's Quay. They had followed their father Jack, a one-time milk delivery contractor for Hughes Dairies, into the property business, and were so proud of their own achievements that they always put a 'Cosgrave Bros' date plaque on their completed buildings, in the Kilroy-Was-Here style.

Now, the Cosgraves were going stratospheric. In 1997, they had paid £11 million for a two-acre derelict site behind the quite undistinguished office buildings on George's Quay, designed for Irish Life by Keane Murphy Duff and occupied by Ulster Bank and Coopers & Lybrand. Instead of simply proceeding with the construction of a moderately high-rise cluster of seven blocks to the rear, for which An Bord Pleanála had granted a ten-year planning permission in June 1991, the Cosgraves were tempted to test what appeared to be the new enthusiasm for tall buildings among senior officials of Dublin Corporation – notably City Architect Jim Barrett, Deputy City Planning Officer Dick Gleeson, and even the City Manager. And so, they hired the biggest guns they could find, bearing the initials SOM, which knew practically everything there was to know about high-rise buildings. Founded in 1936 in Chicago, the home of the skyscraper, Skidmore Owings & Merrill had become a global practice, with free-standing offices in New York, Boston, San Francisco, Hong Kong and London. Its catalogue – in fact, a lavishly illustrated, large-format, hardback book – detailed major projects, often 'superscale office towers', ranging round the world 'from Manhattan to Moscow, Chicago to Shanghai, London and Berlin to Kuala Lumpur, Jakarta and Ho Chi Minh City (Saigon)'. Two of its supertowers are among the world's top three tall buildings – the 442-metre Sears Tower in Chicago (1975), and the 420-metre Jin Mao building in Shanghai (1998). But these megastructures will be surpassed by even taller towers, including one which SOM has designed for its home-base in Chicago, which will rise to a building height of almost 470 metres. For the purposes of comparison, the Canary Wharf tower in London, by Cesar Pelli, is a mere 237-metres high. Everywhere SOM oper-

Irish Times

Ambrose Kelly, the incredibly successful architect-businessman whose firm excelled at exercises in Georgian pastiche.

The Sears Tower in Chicago, which rises to a height of 442 metres, was one of the many super-scale office buildings designed by international architects SOM.

Frank McDonald

ates, according to its glossy catalogue, 'it redefines modern architecture's tradition of "problem-solving".' And what distinguished the firm's work, it said, was 'its masterly ability to translate contemporary traditions of practice into an exacting and sophisticated art of building'.

SOM's only previous involvement in Dublin was the ill-fated bus station and transportation centre, planned by CIÉ for the Temple Bar area in the mid-1970s. Now, more than twenty years later, Roger Kallman, the urbane American who heads its London office, was back in town to sell a spectacular high-rise scheme for George's Quay. This was going to be something special. Three curvaceous office buildings, joined at ground level by a three-storey glazed atrium on the axis of the Custom House dome, and two inter-linked apartment buildings would read as 'transparent sculptural forms' rising up behind the bland blocks on the quay frontage. Their irregular shape and crystalline quality would be stunning on the landscape, Kallman enthused. But both he and the New York-based project architect, Roger Duffy, were initially quite coy about the dimensional heights of the taller buildings. They talked in terms of twenty-four storeys for the central tower – on the face of it, just seven floors higher than Liberty Hall – but it was clear even from the watercolour bird's-eye view issued by the developers and from a rather crude block model that the building would be much higher, given the floor-to-floor clearances required for 'third generation' office space.

It was not until the planning application had been lodged in April 1998

SOM's plans for the ill-fated CIÉ bus station and transportation centre in the mid-1970s would have consumed the core of Temple Bar and much of Ormond Quay.

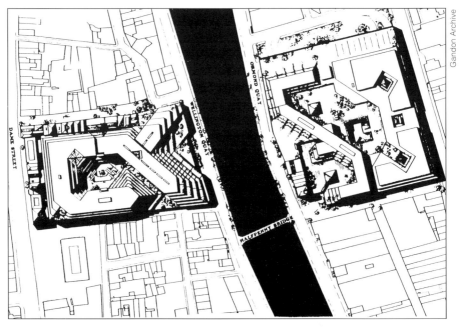

that the full truth emerged – the central office tower was to rise to 100 metres, or nearly twice the height of Liberty Hall. Perspective drawings showing the scheme in relation to its surroundings, particularly the Custom House to the north, were not made available to the media, presumably in an effort to avoid controversy. By that stage, Cosgraves had engaged Bernard McHugh, one of the busiest and most astute planning consultants in Dublin, to progress the project. 'For the whole of the 20th century', he wrote, 'the making of tall buildings has been an important part of architectural endeavour. They have often been adopted as symbols of civic pride. In the 1960s, Cork and Dublin competed for the tallest building in Ireland, with Liberty Hall losing out by a few feet to Cork County Hall. It is not a coincidence that with Ireland enjoying its first sustained period of economic growth since the 1960s, there should again be proposals for tall buildings. It would not be surprising if tall buildings were again seen as symbols of progress and of the nation's success, though, as current debate would indicate, this is unlikely to be a universally accepted view.'

McHugh conceded that the 'areas of concern' for local residents included traffic and parking, building heights, light and shadowing effects, water supply and drainage, noise, construction impacts, wind, air quality, and the overall impact of the scheme on the community. 'It should be noted at the outset', he wrote, 'that buildings at latitudes outside the tropics will never be free of shading in daylight hours, for simple reasons of solar geometry.' However, the George's Quay site had one overwhelming advantage. By virtue of its location beside the DART station at Tara Street, it was 'one of the most accessible parts of Dublin city and indeed of the State'. And because it was so accessible to public transport, its development would be in line with the Strategic Planning Guidelines for the Greater Dublin Area, even if the new buildings proposed were bound to be 'the subject of aesthetic debate'.

In September 1998, having spent six months considering the case, Dublin Corporation decided – against the advice of City Planning Officer Pat McDonnell – to grant planning permission for the George's Quay project, subject to the tallest block being reduced in height from 100 to 80 metres. If built, even at the lower height, this shimmering glass tower would have been the highest building in the Republic, outstripping Liberty Hall by 21 metres (70 ft) and Cork County Hall by almost as much. The decision, signed by the Assistant City Manager Seán Carey, said the height reduction of the tallest block was required to 'reduce its negative visual impact on surrounding areas and the extent of its protrusion above the existing skyline'. The other four buildings were to be correspondingly reduced in height to retain what was described as the 'dynamic tension' between the various elements of the complex. Carey, a politically astute GAA enthusiast who had come in from rezoning-mad Fingal County Council in 1997, was seen by some as the hatchet-man for John Fitzgerald's bold visions. Jovial but single-minded, he enjoyed meeting property developers with big plans for the city, and did what he could to 'get things moving'. Before doing so, however, he would

Assistant City Manager Seán Carey, seen by some as the hatchet man for City Manager John Fitzgerald's bold visions.

City Planning Officer Pat McDonnell, a sensitive and laconic architect-planner, who is regarded by many conservationists as something of a hero.

instruct other Corporation officials in hurling parlance to 'mark' this guy or that, and 'never lose sight of the ball'. Pat McDonnell, who is regarded by many conservationists as quite a hero, had become increasingly isolated from the various project teams set up by Carey to deal with major schemes. Though he had only been appointed as City Planning Officer in 1995, he was treated as a relic of the *ancien régime*, even as many of his own ideas were coming to fruition – notably the move towards integrated area plans. Now 'out of the loop', this sensitive, laconic architect-planner who has been with the Corporation for thirty years found himself living on information so that he could continue to play a meaningful role. And one of the crucial areas where he was determined to make an impact was the Corporation's high buildings policy, where he had little sympathy for the vaulting ambitions of Dublin's new breed of developers, not to mention some of his own colleagues.

In a 36-page report on the George's Quay scheme, Pat McDonnell strongly recommended that planning permission be refused because of the 'unacceptable impact' it would have on the environment of Trinity College, the setting of the Custom House, and on views from Kildare Street, O'Connell Bridge, the Ha'penny Bridge and Grattan Bridge. And although he recognised that SOM's design had 'many fine qualities', he felt that this 'forthright architectural statement' was a 'deliberate attempt to impose ... a very prominent and assertive building' on the city's skyline. But the urge to facilitate a major development triumphed over any lingering doubts, as well as the implacable opposition of the Dublin Docklands Development Authority, which said the complex failed all the criteria for high buildings laid down in the 1991 City Plan and the City Planning Officer's view that it would have a 'detrimental' impact on the skyline. As a result, Seán Carey had to rely on a brief, three-page report from the City Architect to justify granting permission subject to twelve conditions, including an overall reduction in height. Jim Barrett argued that SOM's scheme had 'a positive architectural and sculptural tension'. It also had 'distinct advantages' over the 1991 cluster of seven office blocks with 'no public realm' and a building form and content 'which has been accepted by urbanists everywhere as undermining the historic nature and potential of cities'. As well as providing a 'focal landmark feature' in the city centre, SOM's scheme would bring 176 apartments into the area, and it also presented an opportunity to create a substantial pedestrian precinct next to Tara Street railway station, long the busiest in Ireland. Barrett's view prevailed, not least because of his close relationship with John Fitzgerald, for whom he provided a continuous stream of architectural and urban-design ideas. The exuberant Corkman had been head-hunted by the Department of the Environment to become Dublin City Architect after establishing a well-deserved reputation for his visionary role in transforming the fortunes of Limerick by turning the city around to face the Shannon. His only failing is that he has little sympathy for historic buildings.

Conservationists were appalled by the Corporation's decision, which Carey had justified 'in the anticipation that this development at George's Quay will become an important landmark in the city centre'. Ciarán Cuffe, an architect and Green Party councillor, was the first to lodge an appeal with An Bord Pleanála, claiming that the tallest block would resemble 'a giant stump' that would 'dominate the city's skyline from every angle'. The Corporation's decision was also denounced by the Irish Georgian Society, the Dublin Civic Group and

City Architect Jim Barrett, an exuberant Corkman who was headhunted by the Dept of the Environment after his visionary role in transforming the fortunes of Limerick.

Ciarán Cuffe, the Green Party city councillor, who was the first to appeal against Dublin Corporation's decision to approve SOM's high-rise plans for George's Quay.

Paddy Whelan / *Irish Times*

An Taisce. In a joint statement, they warned that an unrestricted proliferation of high-rise buildings would pose 'unprecedented risks to the fabric of the city', and called on the Corporation to reinstate the fourteen criteria contained in the 1991 City Plan for assessing their visual impact. What SOM had proposed for George's Quay would be, in the civic group's words, an 'architectural colossus ... totally alien to Dublin'. They were particularly surprised that the Corporation planners did not exercise their discretion to request an environmental impact statement from the developers, even though the site was below the two-hectare (4.8-acre) threshold specified for an EIS. As far as they were concerned, Dublin should be following the examples of Paris, Rome and Helsinki by imposing 'strict limita-tions' on building heights to preserve the characteristic low-rise nature of the city's historic core. Kevin B Nowlan, the veteran conservationist and chairman of the Civic Group, said this was one of Dublin's main selling points. 'Tourists won't come here to see Frankfurt or Manhattan', he declared. 'To have a series of enormous buildings overwhelming Trinity College, the Custom House and the Georgian squares would present a totally different reality to the history of Dublin.' Mary Bryan, conservation officer of the Irish Georgian Society, said there was a 'huge money factor' involved. 'People making decisions about our buildings are paying too much attention to the "Celtic Tiger", which has very greedy paws, and not enough to the goose that laid the golden egg.'

Lined up alongside them was the DDDA, which was given a mandate in 1996 to develop a 1,300-acre area stretching from Butt Bridge to the Poolbeg peninsula. Arguing that the scheme did not comply with the Docklands master plan, the DDDA said that its predecessor – the Custom House Docks Develop-ment Authority – had taken 'considerable trouble' to create buildings in the International Financial Services Centre 'which, whilst unashamedly modern, sought a scale appropriate to the existing scale of the city' and were designed in particular to defer to the importance of the Custom House. In the 1987 compe-tition to develop the IFSC's original 27-acre site, it recalled, proposals based on 'imported images of large-scale and substantial heights' had been rejected as 'inappropriate and harmful to the visual image of the city'. There was also strong opposition from residents of the immediate area and Docklands in general. 'No High Rise' billboards and 'Docklands Not Shadowlands' posters appeared in prominent locations, appeals were made to An Bord Pleanála and statements issued to the media. They were heartened by the board's early decision to request an EIS from the developers, interpreting this as a sign that it, too, was uneasy about the scheme. Meanwhile, SOM availed of the board's request to look again at the original design, as amended by the Corporation, and this exercise resulted in the scheme being substantially recast, with the central office tower reduced fur-ther in height to 73.7 metres. With a corresponding reduction in the height of the

SOM's revised plans for George's Quay, which the architects said would read as 'a cluster of building forms that create a sculptural massing', with the Custom House in the background.

Eric Luke / *Irish Times*

A 'No High Rise' billboard in Townsend Street, one of many indicating the strength of local opposition to developer-led proposals, such as the 'towers of light' scheme on George's Quay.

adjoining apartment blocks, the architects said that 'the resulting building expression is no longer that of a tower with lower buildings flanking it, but rather a cluster of building forms that create a sculptural massing.'

A Bord Pleanála oral hearing on the scheme dragged on for four days, with a stunning model by David Murphy's ModelWorks of SOM's revised proposal prominently displayed for all to see. Roger Duffy, the project architect, had flown in from New York to present his case, floridly arguing that his 'towers of light' would be infinitely preferable to the 'portals of darkness' of the 1991 scheme by Keane Murphy Duff. But he was clearly unprepared for the level and ferocity of the opposition, saying it 'would never have happened in the US', and flew home somewhat shell-shocked. What amazed the community groups at the hearing was Duffy's regular first-name references to senior Corporation officials, such as Jim Barrett, Pat McDonnell and Seán Carey. 'It seemed to them that there had been a whole lot of meetings and discussions behind the scenes, from which they were excluded, and this made them feel like second-class citizens', Cllr Cuffe said afterwards. Nonetheless, the community groups were well represented, and managed to get across their point of view because they had the status of appellants rather than mere observers. Their concerns were powerfully reinforced by another appellant, Brian Hogan, whose long professional experience as the architect of several major schemes in Dublin from the 1960s onwards carried considerable weight with the planning inspector, Karl Kent. In a ninety-page report that pulled few punches, he endorsed Hogan's contention that SOM's bulky towers lacked 'the more elegant proportions of Liberty Hall', and said he also agreed entirely with all of the objectors on 'the need for a coherent height strategy for the city'.

In North America, as this perceptive planner noted, 'there are wonderful cityscapes, the most admirable being probably that of Chicago. The soaring buildings of this city form an incomparable environment. Unfortunately, where attempts have been made to transplant this, particularly to the United Kingdom, the results have been lamentable. The historic skyline of London has been irreparably affected. This is the city to which Dublin has most often been compared, but the differences in scale of the historic centres are quite enormous. Adverse impacts from high buildings, noticeable in London, would become overwhelming in Dublin', he wrote. Neither did the inspector accept that the proposed towers would have such an 'ethereal quality' as portrayed in the architects' presentation. Because of their height and massing, they would dwarf existing high buildings in the vicinity, including Liberty Hall and Hawkins House, with 'a wholly detrimental effect on Trinity College' and a 'fairly severe' impact on the Custom House. Though he agreed that SOM's towers – described by Jim Barrett as 'timeless architecture' – had 'very great subtlety', he felt this quality 'would be lost to a great extent, particularly under the grey skies of Dublin'. Kent also referred to the Corporation's declared policy that high buildings 'will not be allowed within the city centre', and said it was not clear to him how this had been addressed in deciding to grant permission for the George's Quay project.

The board's verdict, when it came in September 1999, was a devastating refusal, in line with Kent's recommendation, and signed, incidentally, by Michael Wall, then its only architect-member. Given the site's location at the edge of Dublin's historic core, close to buildings and areas of architectural heritage value, it said the height and bulk of the scheme 'would detrimentally affect the historic precincts of the Custom House, Trinity College and the Liffey Quays'. It would also 'seriously injure the amenities of residential property in the vicinity' due to overshadowing, and 'materially contravene' the City Plan. This latter judgment was a stinging rebuke for the Corporation because it suggested that the whole scheme should have been voted on by the City Council, instead of being decided by executive fiat. That the project would have given employment to five hundred construction workers and supported up to 3,000 jobs on completion was neither here nor there. The booming economy had given the appeals board the luxury of being able to say no. Job creation was no longer to be cited as a reason for approving schemes that raised serious environmental doubts. It seemed that the board – and even its then chairman, Paddy O'Duffy, a stickler for procedures and propriety – was disowning the thesis, once expounded by O'Duffy himself, that the interest of 'Ireland Inc' was a relevant planning consideration which had to be taken into account. With the onset of prosperity, the board could now 'afford to be more discriminating about development', as he put it. What sunk George's Quay was a photomontage of the scheme, seen from the mid-point on Gardiner Street, showing the 'towers of light' looming up behind the dome of the Custom House. And though the decision was taken by a clear majority, according to sources, it was immediately seized on by the development lobby as evidence that An Bord Pleanála was now 'anti-development'. Just a few years earlier, curiously, it had been perceived by conservationists as being very much 'pro-development'.

But there was some irony in the board's comprehensive rejection of SOM's bold venture. Fifteen years earlier, in 1984, it actually granted full planning per-

mission to Irish Life for an office tower up to forty storeys high on the George's Quay site. It was the last thing Irish Life expected, because it had applied for a much more modest high-rise scheme designed by Keane Murphy Duff. But the late Robin Walker, then a member of the appeals board, had written the conditions in such a way as to contrive a skyscraper. Walker had put forward a 22-storey tower in the competition for the Civic Offices at Wood Quay back in 1967, and was deeply disappointed when it didn't win. Now, in 1985, he had a chance to impose a high-rise building on the Liffey quays, albeit by another firm of architects, and he was not going to shirk this fortuitous opportunity. But Irish Life balked at anything so bold, and after doing its sums and having a look at a few skyscrapers in the US, dropped the idea of building anything so tall at George's Quay. It had discovered that high buildings carried a high price tag. Once an office block goes above seven storeys, it needs reinforced foundations and double the number of lifts, toilets and fire-escape stairs. And since all of this expands the service core, the critical ratio of a building's gross area to its net lettable floorspace is undermined, threatening the profitability of the whole project.

An Bord Pleanála's decision to reject SOM's scheme was immediately seen by opponents as a vindication of the stance taken by the Corporation's embattled City Planning Officer and, simultaneously, as a teacher's slap for the City Architect. Michael Smith, who had just been elected as national chairman of An Taisce, said the board's refusal 'could not be more subversive of incongruous high-rise schemes for the city centre which overshadow historic buildings and established communities'. It was also a blow to the 'aspirations of the City Architect and city management who in practice have been pushing an allegedly "exciting" brave new world of high-rise'. This charge was emphatically rejected by City Manager John Fitzgerald, who expressed surprise that An Taisce would issue 'such a wildly inaccurate statement'. And though he was 'obviously disappointed' by the board's ruling, he insisted that the Corporation had dealt with George's Quay in a professional manner. An *Irish Times* leader said the real import of the board's decision was that the Corporation needed to devise, sooner rather than later, a credible strategy for the city's skyline. 'Had the appeals board decided to sanction the high-rise scheme designed by international architects Skidmore Owings & Merrill, it would almost certainly have been interpreted by developers as the signal for a free-for-all. That the board has firmly rejected SOM's "towers of light", using words that leave no room for equivocation, sends out quite the opposite message. It also lays down a clear marker on the acceptability, in urban-design terms, of high-rise schemes in close proximity to the city's historic core ... Dublin has much to learn from other cities with experience of

A model of the Keane Murphy Duff scheme for George's Quay, approved by An Bord Pleanála in 1991. The unbuilt central cluster was characterised by SOM's project architect, Roger Duffy, as the 'portals of darkness'. And below (seen from a different angle), the revised KMD scheme, commissioned by the Cosgrave Property Group after SOM's plans were rejected.

high-rise development. Few visitors to Paris are not impressed by the manner in which it has retained its 19th-century skyline. After making one disastrous mistake with the Tour Montparnasse, office towers were consigned to La Défense, on its perimeter. By contrast, London adopted an ad hoc approach, allowing skyscrapers to spring up in the West End, the City and Canary Wharf, not to mention East Croydon. A more judicious planning strategy is clearly required to avoid a repetition in Dublin of monstrous errors that cannot easily be undone, while not closing our minds to the idea that well-designed high-rise buildings have their place in an increasingly complex urban hierarchy.'

The Cosgrave brothers were shell-shocked by the decision. It was a crushing blow. For the first time in their careers, they invested heavily in high architecture and had been counting on SOM's dramatic design to carry the day. Now they had nothing to show for it. Throughout, they had made it clear that if SOM's 'towers of light' were rejected, their only option would be to revert to the 'portals of darkness' of the earlier scheme by Keane Murphy Duff. After all, it had received a ten-year permission from An Bord Pleanála in 1991, so there would still be time to build it before that decision ran into the sands of time in June 2001. There was also an almost insatiable demand for new office space because of the booming economy, and not enough space coming on stream to meet it, especially in the Dublin 2 and Dublin 4 postal districts. But given the changing needs of the office market, as well as the passage of time, it seemed improbable that they would simply start building the 1991 scheme, which would provide a cluster of seven office blocks in the middle of the site and two more on its Moss Street perimeter. If it was a case of 'back to the drawing boards', it should have been possible to devise a low-rise, high-density scheme for the site to provide a more appropriate urban design 'fit' than the inferior, dated cluster of office blocks – one higher than Liberty Hall – for which permission was granted by the appeals board in 1991. But with office vacancy rates as low as 1% in the city centre, the Cosgraves parted company with SOM and commissioned Keane Murphy Duff to dust down their old plans, lightening the architectural treatment by trying to capture some of the quality of the failed scheme. Meanwhile, they could console themselves with the success of their SAS Radisson Hotel at St Helen's in Booterstown, designed by Burke-Kennedy Doyle, and a stylish commercial development by Scott Tallon Walker on the former Ibex site overlooking Dun Laoghaire Harbour. But just as major excavation work got under way at George's Quay, a local resident who had objected to the SOM scheme for the site, sought a judicial review of Dublin Corporation's decision to approve KMD's revisions to its 1991 plan without reverting to the public.

There can be no doubt that An Bord Pleanála's ruling in the George's Quay case represented a significant setback to Dublin's skyscraper lobby. The fact that it followed refusals by the appeals board of high-rise schemes for Barrow Street and Thorncastle Street on grounds of height and bulk, among other considerations, sent a powerful message to developers with soaring aspirations that 'skyscraper' projects were premature, pending the outcome of a Corporation-commissioned skyline study to establish what locations in the city could 'take' high-rise buildings. This study had been promised by the City Manager following complaints that the Corporation had failed to spell out precisely where such 'focal points' could be built when it reformulated its policy by removing or rewriting many of the restrictions contained in successive city plans. Its new approach, amplified by a policy document published in November 1998, conceded that high buildings 'represent a major change in the city's basic form and character', and said that any such change 'must be set within a well-directed and controlled framework'.

The purpose of the skyline study is to lay out a level playing field on which the whole issue of height in urban-design terms can be judged. This is of particular importance in relation to the impact on historic buildings and precincts, as well as residential areas. In the case of George's Quay, the objectors made it clear that they were not opposed to high buildings per se, nor indeed to the high standard of SOM's architectural treatment. It was the location, sandwiched between the Custom House and Trinity College, that presented a real problem. An Bord Pleanála's decision to reject it was also an endorsement of the more conservative approach of the Dublin Docklands Development Authority, whose 1997 master plan was cited by the appeals board as one of the planks for its refusal. The principal reaction of opponents of the scheme was one of 'profound relief', in the words of Mary Bryan of the Irish Georgian Society, because of the precedent that would have been created 'if such a radical change in building height was permitted so close to the city centre'. The local communities were delighted because they had 'put a lot of work and effort into it and fought a good fight', as Bryan noted approvingly. The South East Network, which co-ordinated this campaign, was 'absolutely thrilled' that the board had listened to their concerns. Alan Curtis, the network's co-ordinator, said the board's decision 'just goes to prove that you don't need thousands of pounds to put a good case forward'. This theme was taken up by Michael Smith of An Taisce, who said there was a need for a genuine dialogue with communities in areas that may be deemed to have a 'carrying capacity' for high-rise buildings. 'The aim should be to ensure that there would be so much planning gain in terms of excellence in architecture and a broad range of social facilities – green spaces, community centres, social housing and local employment – that local people would actually become enthusiastic about the prospects.' But first, the Corporation would have to complete its strategic skyline study before any further planning permissions were granted. In the meantime, community groups throughout the Docklands formed an alliance, with the active support of An Taisce, to oppose 'the developer-led high-rise schemes which are plaguing our areas', and girded themselves for the mother of all battles over Spencer Dock and the National Conference Centre.

No major scheme in the Republic, apart from the Burren visitor centre in Co Clare, has been so bedevilled by delay, uncertainty and bad blood as the proposed National Conference Centre. More than ten years after it was first mooted, the failure to deliver this 'flagship project' became acutely embarrassing, especially following the successful completion in 1997 of Belfast's magnificent Waterfront Hall. It seemed to underline, yet again, our almost unbelievable inability to handle major infrastructural developments. The root cause of this fiasco was that successive governments expected to procure the NCC at no cost to the public purse, either in terms of capital investment or running costs. They wanted something for nothing, and appeared to believe that it could be produced by waving some sort of magic wand. Indeed, the initial thesis was the inherently loss-making conference centre would need a casino to provide a 'financial engine' to support it. That's what encouraged the US Ogden leisure group to pursue its hugely controversial Sonas Centre plan for the Phoenix Park racecourse site, even in the teeth of ferocious local opposition. But after it had secured planning permission from An Bord Pleanála in 1996, the Rainbow Coalition government effectively scuppered the £250 million project by saying that it would not amend the Gaming and Lotteries Act to license casino gambling. Under pressure from voters in the marginal constituency of Dublin West, even Fianna Fáil rowed in, and Bertie Ahern parted company with his old school friend, Ogden's Robert White, to promise that they would not be granting a casino licence either.

The Ogden group had been one of the main contenders for the National Conference Centre in a competition for developers held in 1995 by the then Minister for Tourism, Enda Kenny. However, just before the final fence was reached, the competition was aborted and Kenny announced that his Department and Bord Fáilte would be entering into exclusive negotiations with the Royal Dublin Society to develop the centre on its Ballsbridge site. One of the prime factors in this dramatic U-turn was that the RDS, as a quasi-public institution, might qualify for a higher level of EU aid under the Operational Programme for Tourism – an assumption that turned out to be false. The designation of the RDS as the 'preferred location' also suited powerful hotel interests in the area, even though it should have been clear to Kenny that traffic-choked Ballsbridge needed a conference centre like a hole in the head. And since there was no provision in the City Plan for such a major public facility in this location, it was bound to run into serious planning problems. Kenny's unilateral decision – taken, he maintains, with the acquiescence of EU Commissioner Monika Wulf-Mathies – ignored the fact that Dublin Corporation had already granted full permission for a rival conference centre scheme on the site of the Carlton Cinema and adjoining properties in O'Connell Street. Its promoters, led by businessman Richard Quirke, were aghast at being ruled out of contention in favour of the RDS. Backed by Dublin City Centre Business Association, the Carlton Group subsequently complained to the European Commission, claiming that they had been

Bryan O'Brien / *Irish Times*

Belfast's magnificent Waterfront Hall, designed by architects Robinson McIlwaine and built at a cost of £32 million, with the British Telecom tower and the Hilton Hotel in the background.

The Ogden Group's Sonas Centre scheme for the Phoenix Park racecourse site, designed by Burke-Kennedy Doyle & Partners, was scuppered by the Government's refusal to grant a casino licence.

Barry Mason / *courtesy of Burke-Kennedy Doyle*

unfairly treated, probably because of a deep-seated prejudice against O'Connell Street and a failure by everyone involved, including Bord Fáilte, to recognise the NCC's value as an anchor for urban renewal. The complaint was treated very seriously in Brussels, and was still being investigated when Jim McDaid took over as Minister for Tourism after the June 1997 general election. With Dublin Chamber of Commerce loudly complaining that persistent delays in progressing the project were costing the economy £30 million per year in lost tourism revenue, he was left with no option but to hold yet another competition in a last-ditch effort to procure the conference centre. This he regarded as 'the key achievement' of his first fifty days in office.

At the time, it was estimated that the conference centre would cost between £35 and £45 million, with the EU chipping in 50% of the cost, up to a maximum of £26 million. Bord Fáilte's overly prescriptive brief required a 'state-of-the-art' public building with a gross floor area of 18,000 square metres (194,000 sq ft), including a raked auditorium with seating for 2,000, a full stage and orchestra pit for up to ninety musicians, and a separate banqueting hall, twice the size of the Burlington's with tables for up to 2,000 diners. It was all to be provided in a landmark building of high architectural merit that would 'last for 100 years'. The aim, as ever, was to capture for Dublin a share of the estimated 350 major conferences held in Europe annually, and bring in an extra 30,000 high-spending visitors, such as salesmen on incentive holidays whose principal goal is to 'get laid', as one of those involved in an earlier bid for the project put it. Five potential developers entered the competition for the contract, including, much to everyone's surprise, the Office of Public Works. It proposed to build the NCC on a rather obscure site at Infirmary Road beside the Phoenix Park, which was later reserved as a headquarters for the Department of Arts and Heritage. Not unreasonably, senior OPW officials let it be known that had they been asked by the Government to build the NCC, it would have been 'up and running' years earlier. In the mid-1960s, Raymond McGrath, the OPW's chief architect, had designed a huge concert hall for the site of Beggar's Bush barracks, but it was never built because the Government balked at the £4 million estimate. Other entrants were the Sonas Centre group, having one last spin on the merry-go-round; Mountbrook Holdings, run by Seán Dunne, the Gandon-lookalike developer who had carved up St Helen's in Booterstown for housing and now had his eyes on the 24-acre gasworks site around the Grand Canal Docks; the RDS, somewhat reluctantly this time; and the Spencer Dock consortium of Treasury Holdings, controlled by Richard Barrett and Johnny Ronan, in partnership with CIÉ and Harry Crosbie, the Docklands entrepreneur. The Carlton Group, which had brought about the latest competition, decided not to enter because it had lost faith in the whole process. There was also a Canadian company called Moytura Developments, which made a lot of noise about its interest in the gasworks site, but did not submit a tender in the end. It was feared that this company, whose headquarters was tracked down by Treasury Holdings to a lakeside bungalow near Toronto, might take a legal action challenging *any* decision to award the contract, though these fears turned out to be unfounded.

Barrett and Ronan were used to playing for high stakes and winning. Treasury Holdings, which they decided to set up in 1992 at the Olympic Games in Barcelona, had built or acquired property assets in Ireland and elsewhere with a capital value exceeding £400 million. Treasury takes its name from Ronan's earliest flagship project, the conversion of the sizeable Bolands bakery on Lower Grand Canal Street into a post-modern office block, which ultimately netted the National Treasury Management Agency as principal tenant. Completed in 1990 at a time when there was nothing happening in the office market, it was a remarkably courageous project, towering over the virtual tented village of Robert Neill's two- and three-storey, depression-led Clanwilliam Square office scheme next door. Ronan, who enjoys a commanding view of Dublin from his cluttered Hollywood producer-style office on the penthouse floor, is the accountant son of a wealthy Tipperary farmer who had diversified into office development in Dublin. He took over the business after his father's death in 1983, and immediately set about expanding it, showing great nerve in the process. Five years later, he teamed up with his one-time Castleknock College classmate, Richard Barrett, a shrewd Ballina-born barrister, whose separate suite of offices are located on nearby Grand Canal Quay. They would be just as

Johnny Ronan, Barrett's partner in Treasury Holdings, who looks like a buccaneer, and sometimes even behaves like one. And below, cover story in the February 2000 issue of *Business & Finance* magazine.

likely to take momentous decisions over buffalo chicken wings and double espressos in the Elephant & Castle or fine food and wine in Cooke's Café or Patrick Guilbaud's as in a more conventional boardroom setting. But then, Ronan hardly corresponds with the image of a conventional property developer. With his black beard and long, sleeked back hair, usually glistening with gel, he looks like a buccaneer, and sometimes even behaves like one, slashing through Dublin's property world with a cutlass, and barking at anyone who gets in the way. Though he drives an American Hummer jeep and always seems to taking snappy calls on his mobile phone, he can be great fun off duty, and regularly tears himself away to go cycling at a fast pace in the Dublin Mountains with his old friend, champion Seán Kelly. Barrett, on the other hand, is the consummate legal eagle, with little of Ronan's explosive personality, though one senses a certain seething under the surface when things are not going Treasury's way. Tall, charming and quite relaxed in the company of friends, he rarely loses his cool and can always be counted on to spot things in the small-print of a folio or Finance Act that are to its advantage; he keeps on top of things by reading such heavy tomes as *Irish Land Law*, even on holidays in Spain, Florida or Latin America.

What this unlikely pair have in common is an insatiable devotion to every property developer's real 'high' – the art of the deal. They see themselves as the natural successors to a previous generation of Dublin proper-

The Treasury Building on Grand Canal Street, Johnny Ronan's earliest flagship project. A remarkably courageous scheme for its time, it towers over the virtual tented village of Robert Neill's two- and three-storey, depression-led office scheme next door.

opposite

Richard Barrett, consummate legal eagle and director of Treasury Holdings, pictured in 1995 in the atrium of the Treasury Building.

The almost-blank gable of the Treasury Building is enlivened by this engaging sculpture by Rowan Gillespie, of a figure – called *Human Endeavour* – climbing up to (or is it down from ?) Johnny Ronan's office is on the penthouse floor.

ty developers, such as John Byrne, Charlie Kenny and John Corcoran, but more attuned to what's going on abroad. 'With that goes the same buccaneering spirit as you'd see in New York with Donald Trump. The names may be different, but it's the same scenario', according to one of the many consultants who have worked for Treasury. Harry Crosbie, Barrett and Ronan's ebullient partner in SDDC, owns a large trucking fleet and also developed the Point Depot and the Vicar Street venue in the Liberties. Co-owner of the Clarence Hotel with members of U2, Crosbie acquired his part-share in the Spencer Dock venture by virtue of owning the Woolstore, a decaying listed building off North Wall Quay, and a substantial stretch of its campshire – that narrow strip of land between the roadway and the river. In 1993, he unsuccessfully sought planning permission to replace the disused sheds on the campshire with a six-storey Ambrose Kelly-designed block of three hundred flats standing on *piloti* over a surface-level car park on the quayside. This ill-conceived scheme was rejected both by Dublin Corporation and An Bord Pleanála because it would have run counter to the long-term objective of developing the campshire as an amenity area.

Treasury Holdings prefers to operate in Dublin 2 and Dublin 4, but its track record is somewhat less impressive than all the bluster would indicate. By the time it entered the lists for the NCC, the company had completed several office developments in the vicinity of Mount Street Crescent, including Peppercannister House, which was shovelled into the rear gardens of two houses on Herbert Place; a thin neo-Georgian office block that replaced an inoffensive petrol filling station on the crescent itself; and a preposterous mock-1930s block on the former Plantation site in Herbert Street, designed by Jimmy O'Connor of Arthur Gibney & Partners, and occupied by solicitors Matheson Ormsby Prentice. Other projects included a late-1980s office and residential scheme on the Grand Canal at Percy Place by Henry J Lyons & Partners, Treasury's most frequently used architects; the conversion of the former UDT bank on Fleet Street into the Temple Bar Hotel; an apartment block and new swimming pool on the site of the Markievicz Baths in Townsend Street, designed by Anthony Reddy & Associates; a dastardly plan to demolish Pelican House on Mespil Road, one of Dublin's finest office buildings from the 1960s, and replace it with a huge ground-scraper extending back along Burlington Road; and a hotel at the apex of D'Olier Street and Westmoreland Street, with a Manchester United shop to anchor it. But none of these schemes caused such a furore as the 164-bedroom Westin Hotel on nearby College Street. Formerly flagged for a Hilton, this was Treasury's most controversial development by a long shot. It involved the demolition of four historic buildings (one of which was listed) on the triangular site, which also fronts on Westmoreland Street and Fleet Street, the retention of other more important façades, notably the former Scottish Widows and Pearl Insurance buildings, and the erection of a huge mansard roof structure above the lot. Inevitably, this brought Barrett and Ronan – as well as AIB, which owned the site – into bitter conflict with the Dublin City Association of An Taisce and, ultimately, with the

Frank McDonald

Henry J Lyons & Partners

Treasury Holdings' controversial project at the edge of College Green involved demolishing all but the façades of notable historic buildings, including the former Dublin headquarters of the Scottish Widows (foreground) and the Provincial Bank of Ireland

Elevation to Westmoreland Street of the new Westin Hotel, which also has frontages on College Street and Fleet Street.

Michael Smith, national chairman of An Taisce since September 1999 and moving force behind Lancefort Ltd, with Dr Sara Dillon, Lancefort's legal adviser and co-founder of Friends of the Irish Environment.

Alan Betson / Irish Times

dreaded Lancefort Ltd.

Lancefort was established by Michael Smith, the association's chairman and, more recently, national chairman of An Taisce, in the immediate aftermath of An Bord Pleanála's decision in December 1996 to sanction the Hilton development. Tall and well built with poster-boy good looks, Smith is a non-practising barrister of independent means whose mission in life was, and is, to save Dublin from the dark forces that threaten its fabric. Day after day, almost on a full-time basis, this angry young man waged a guerrilla war on several fronts from his duplex flat in a late-17th-century listed building on Ormond Quay, poring over the planning lists and firing off detailed objections against any scheme which he believed would damage the environment. Like others without as much bravado in the past, he came to the conclusion that a legal entity was needed to fight significant planning cases through the courts, if necessary, and Lancefort was his chosen vehicle. Disparagingly dubbed the Lone Ranger, with fellow-barrister Colm MacEochaidh playing Tonto and Ian Lumley taking an off-stage role as technical adviser, he rode out to confront some of the cowboys cashing in on the Celtic Tiger economy. Developers became almost apoplectic about Lancefort's activities, as they never quite knew when, or where, they might be

Model of Mountbrook Holdings' remarkably modest scheme for the National Conference Centre and ancillary development at the Grand Canal Docks, with the Liffey in the foreground.

courtesy of Murray O'Laoire Architects

ambushed. This fear and loathing was compounded when Smith and MacEochaidh were unmasked by the *Sunday Times* in 1998 as the sponsors of a £10,000 reward, offered through a Newry firm of solicitors, for information on land rezoning corruption – a clever tactic that flushed out James Gogarty and ultimately led to the establishment of the Flood Tribunal.

Lancefort's first action was to set up a 'Think Again Hilton' web-site on the Internet, describing Treasury's £35 million scheme for College Street as 'the most destructive in Dublin for years', ignoring the fact that the company already had planning permission in the bag for an equally destructive office development on the site. Exaggerated claims were also made that eleven 'important historic buildings' would be demolished or gutted for the hotel scheme, a figure derived by double-counting the corner buildings and the former Provincial Bank of Ireland headquarters, a fine neo-classical edifice with frontages on both College Street and Fleet Street, whose elaborate Victorian banking hall is being retained. Nonetheless, Lancefort filed a High Court action seeking a judicial review of An Bord Pleanála's decision to approve the plans, claiming that there should have been an environmental impact assessment under EU law. This dragged on through 1997, running up an estimated £1 million in legal costs, and ultimately resulted in Lancefort losing the case. An earlier attempt by Smith's legal advisers to settle it in return for a substantial contribution to Lancefort's fighting fund had been rejected by Treasury because of the conditions attached, which included the retention of threatened buildings and an overall reduction in height. After Judge Catherine McGuinness delivered her judgment in March 1998, Richard Barrett made it clear that Treasury would be pursuing Smith personally for its costs, saying: 'His house is gone.' Throughout, the developers maintained that they could fall back on the alternative plan for an office development, involving an equivalent level of demolition and façade retention, for which planning permission had been granted by An Bord Pleanála in 1993. What their bankers did not realise was that this permission was effectively unworkable, and after that fatal defect had been exposed by the *Irish Times*, a £17 million loan facility for the office scheme was promptly withdrawn. By then, Hilton International had pulled out of the College Street project because it had been delayed so long, though the official reason given was that the US-based group, having seen alarming reports of heroin being sold openly on O'Connell Street, had become concerned about crime in the area. Some months later, after losing another deal with Sheraton, Treasury managed to sign up the Westin hotel group as its anchor tenant, and demolition work finally got under way, creating an enormous hole at the edge of College Green. But this hole was filled with remarkable speed, and it was clear at the time of writing that the new hotel, designed by Henry J Lyons & Partners, with its first floor given over to offices for AIB, was being finished to a very high standard. The curious set-backs on either side of the Provincial Bank façade on College Street was a rather silly planning requirement. In June 1998, as if to celebrate its famous victory over Lancefort, Johnny Ronan invited some fifty friends and associates to what the *Irish Times* property supplement described as a 'glittering gig in Modena', where Luciano Pavarotti sang for them in the garden of his villa. Smith hit back by suggesting that the invitation list should be published, and later wrote a libellous 'rant' for *Magill* alleging cozy relationships between Treasury Holdings and elements of the media, including myself, and complaining that Lancefort had been 'the victim of a lazy, well-dined and often malicious press'. It resulted in the magazine's January 1999 issue being pulped on legal advice.

Meanwhile, Bord Fáilte's requirement that all five of the contenders for the National Conference Centre would have to confirm ownership of their chosen sites was presenting an acute problem for Seán Dunne and Mountbrook Holdings. Though Dunne was convinced that his Murray O'Laoire-designed scheme for the Grand Canal Docks area – which seems remarkably modest, in retrospect – had a real chance of success, the fact was that Bord Gáis Éireann had refused to entertain any proposal for the property, and was in the process of transferring it to the Dublin Docklands Development Authority at a discounted price to reflect the cost of decontaminating it after decades of town gas manufacturing. No amount of effort by Mountbrook's chairman, banker Jim Lacey, could remove this irritating obstacle to Dunne's ambitious scheme, even though he had an inside track as a Fianna Fáil appointee to the DDDA's executive board. At one point, he was requested to leave a meeting of the board while it discussed a letter from Mountbrook seeking an exclusive right to develop the BGE site. Lacey had relinquished his chairmanship of Dunne's principal vehicle on joining the authority's board in November 1997, but five months later his position became untenable in the wake of the National Irish Bank scandal, prompting him to resign as a director and also as chairman of the Irish Aviation Authority. With no movement on releasing the Bord Gáis site, a fifteen-strong evaluation team acting for Bord Fáilte's grandiloquently titled Management Board for Product Development ruled it out of contention before recommending in favour of the Spencer Dock proposal. Dunne had argued that the Treasury Holdings-led consortium was in the same boat, since it did not have full title to CIÉ's rail freight marshalling yards and that, in any case, both of the Docklands contenders had received 'letters of comfort' from the DDDA saying it would facilitate whichever scheme emerged victorious. CIÉ also needed to watch its step. It had also found itself in hot water a few years earlier when it sold a site at Horgan's Quay in Cork to developer Owen O'Callaghan without bothering to advertise a public tender. As a result, all semi-state companies with redundant property in the Docklands area had been instructed by the Government in November 1997 to deal exclusively with the DDDA in relation to any land disposals. Either of the NCC schemes in Docklands would have provided an 'anchor' for the renewal of the area, in line with the DDDA's master plan – though, somewhat surprisingly, given that it would be the biggest 'anchor' around, the plan made no explicit provision for the conference centre.

The Spencer Dock consortium probably had the better site, pivotally located on North Wall Quay half-way between the International Financial Services Centre and the Point Depot, and just over one kilometre downstream of O'Connell Bridge. It also held what it saw as a trump card – its conference centre had been designed by Kevin Roche, the renowned Irish émigré architect, and it would be his first ever building in the country of his birth. He was also probably the only person that Barrett and Ronan listened to without interruption. Johnny Ronan had long admired Roche's architecture, and commissioned him to design Treasury Holdings' entry in the abortive 1995 competition for the conference centre, in somewhat unhappy collaboration with Scott Tallon Walker. Though disillusioned by the outcome of that competition, remarking to his clients that modern Ireland didn't seem to be much better than a banana republic, he was persuaded by Ronan to undertake the project for a second time after Jim McDaid had announced the new contest two years later. Winner of nearly every architectural award worth having, Roche was born in Dublin in 1922 and grew up in Mitchelstown, Co Cork, where his father managed the famous creamery. He was educated at Rockwell College and went on to study architecture at UCD, almost by accident, drawing acanthus leaves and fluted classical columns in its Beaux Arts era. After working with Michael Scott & Partners on Donnybrook Garage and Busáras, he left for the US in 1948 to do a postgraduate course at the Illinois Institute of Technology, studying at the feet of that great apostle of Modernism, Mies van der Rohe. Instead of coming home to depressed 1950s Ireland, he stayed on in the US and got a good job in Detroit with the Finnish-American architect, Eero Saarinen. Following Saarinen's untimely death in 1961, Roche and a brilliant Dutch-born structural engineer, John Dinkeloo, took over his practice and completed such major works as the Gateway Arch in St Louis, Missouri, and the brilliantly aerodynamic TWA terminal at Kennedy Airport, designated a New York landmark in 1997. The same status was also con-

Location map of CIÉ's 51-acre Spencer Dock site, halfway between Connolly Station and the Point Depot, currently used as a rail-freight marshalling yard.

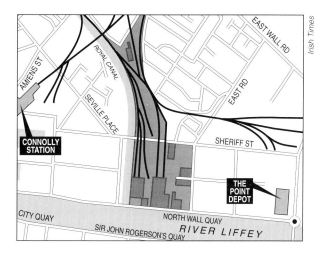

Ezra Stoller, ESTO

One of Roche Dinkleloo's best-known works, the Ford Foundation headquarters in New York, completed in 1968, has been described as 'probably one of the most romantic environments ever devised by corporate man'.

opposite

Kevin Roche, Ireland's leading expatriate architect, with a model of the proposed National Conference Centre at Spencer Dock, flanked by Dermod Dwyer, chairman of the development consortium (left), and Harry Crosbie.

ferred on Roche Dinkeloo's Ford Foundation headquarters on East 42nd Street, which was the first modern building to be laid out around a plant-filled atrium. Writing in the *New York Times*, Ada Louise Huxtable said it was 'probably one of the most romantic environments ever devised by corporate man'.

Now in his late 70s, Roche could look back on a lifetime of architectural achievements. Altogether, as his impressive practice brochure noted in 1998, Kevin Roche John Dinkeloo & Associates had designed five museums, three research laboratories, several centres for the performing arts, and no less than thirty-eight corporate headquarters, including many high-rise blocks, which had been 'woven into the skylines' of New York, Chicago, Atlanta, Tokyo, Singapore and Kuala Lumpur. Some of them, such as the General Foods headquarters at Rye in upstate New York, were almost self-contained universes with no relationship to their surroundings. It was one of his regrets that the only thing he hadn't done was to leave a major legacy in Ireland, so he was genuinely delighted when Johnny Ronan invited him to design the National Conference Centre. What he came up with was a large, stone-clad cube with a dramatic tilted cylindrical atrium on its Liffeyside frontage, and switchback escalators rising up through it. The building, which would rise to a parapet height of 43 metres (150 ft), was to be located in a four-acre zone at the southwestern corner of the Spencer Dock site,

Eric Luke / *Irish Times*

courtesy of SDDC

A night-time view of the proposed National Conference Centre, a large, stone-clad cube with a dramatic tilted cylindrical atrium on its Liffeyside frontage. This was the only image of Spencer Dock released at the outset.

leaving a narrow strip between the dock basin and its largely blank gable wall – a feature reminiscent of the face presented to the River Lee by Cork's Opera House. Harry Crosbie enthused that it would be 'the finest public building that could be given to the city in this generation', designed by Ireland's leading expatriate architect. What wasn't at all clear at the time was what the developers were planning for the remainder of their site. Ballpark figures on the quantum of ancillary development then envisaged – 1.3 million square feet of offices, one million square feet of apartments, a pair of 250-bedroom hotels and 140,000 square feet of retail and leisure facilities – were in the public domain, but the architectural implications had not been spelled out. And though it was one of Bord Fáilte's requirements that all five contenders had to indicate the scale of ancillary development accompanying their conference centre schemes as part of the assessment process, that was all happening behind closed doors in an atmosphere of heightening tension.

By May 1998, Government ministers were said to be 'running around like headless chickens' wondering whether the National Conference Centre would ever come home to roost, as the latest competition to procure it – the third in ten years – turned into yet another fiasco. Day after day, crisis meetings were taking place to see if there was any way of salvaging this landmark project, following a decision by Bord Fáilte's Management Board for Product Development to reject its own evaluation team's recommendation in favour of the £79 million Spencer Dock scheme. One of its complaints was that details of the ancillary development planned for the 51-acre site, which would obviously be crucial to subsidising the loss-making conference centre, had not been submitted for evaluation, as required by the competition brief. It had also become apparent that the DDDA was unhappy with the scale of this development proposal, and not just because it would encroach on an urban park envisaged by its own master plan. It would also put an end to the prospect that the CIÉ-owned site might be acquired by the authority at a knockdown price. According to sources, the DDDA offered CIÉ about £33 million for the Spencer Dock site, valuing it at less than £1 million per acre. Yet the authority itself had been *selling* land on the adjoining twelve-acre site, west of Spencer Dock, for up to £10 million an acre. No wonder the board of CIÉ stuck to its guns and held out for the proposed joint venture with Treasury Holdings and Harry Crosbie.

Peter Coyne, Scottish-born chief executive of the DDDA, with a scale model of the Docklands area. He later described his dealings with the Spencer Dock developers as 'the worst three months of my life'.

Joe St Leger / Irish Times

This deal, which had been recommended by three independent property advisers, was potentially of enormous benefit to the cash-starved State transport group because it would retain freehold title to the entire 51-acre site, currently used as a rail freight marshalling yard, while the land was developed for higher value activities. Estimates by CIÉ sources put the long-term benefit to the group as high as £360 million over twenty years, given the scale of the master plan being devised by Kevin Roche's office in Hamden, Connecticut. Not surprisingly, with adjoining land selling for fantastic sums of money, CIÉ came to regard Spencer Dock as a cash cow. It could, of course, have made a major killing by selling off all fifty-one acres in tidy parcels to private developers, netting millions of pounds for its nearly empty coffers. Had it done that, however, the proceeds would have been recouped not by the company itself to fund much-needed investment in the railways, but by the Exchequer. There was nothing in it for CIÉ. Its deal with Treasury Holdings, on the other hand, would bring in an annual rental income for as long as it retained the freehold, and meant that it could keep all the money for its own use. It was for this reason that CIÉ was dismayed when much of its Spencer Dock site was zoned for an urban square and linear park in the DDDA's master plan – a factor which had allowed the authority itself to value twenty-eight acres of the holding at just £23 million. Spurred on by its fast-talking chairman, Lar Bradshaw, it wanted to get its hands on all or part of CIÉ's land, either by purchasing it outright or acquiring a share in it through a joint venture. Bradshaw saw this as the only way to achieve the master plan's social objectives, including the provision of affordable housing.

But CIÉ was having none of it. The group's chief executive, Michael

Lar Bradshaw, fast-talking chairman of the Dublin Docklands Development Authority and managing partner of the Dublin office of McKinsey International, the US trouble-shooting management consultants.

Michael McDonnell, who breezed into Heuston Station in 1995 as CIÉ's chief executive and began implementing a programme to develop the group's surplus property, including Spencer Dock.

Dara MacDonaill / courtesy of the *Irish Times*

Frank Miller / *Irish Times*

McDonnell, together with its head of programme and projects, Ray Byrne, and its property manager, Jim Gahan, were determined to realise the value of CIÉ's landholdings, going for what they saw as the best deal in each case. What they were doing, in effect, was following some free advice given repeatedly over the years by Seán Dublin Bay Loftus that the company should be developing surplus land adjoining the mainline railway stations and selling off the air space above them, instead of persistently increasing bus and rail fares. In a 1979 interview with Frank Kilfeather of the *Irish Times*, the eccentric alderman said CIÉ should be negotiating with planning officials in Dublin and elsewhere to see how best it could develop its railway property for offices, flats and retail facilities. 'It doesn't have to be tower blocks', he added. But the railwaymen within the company insisted on holding onto their territory and their Neanderthal view prevailed, at least until Michael McDonnell breezed into Heuston Station in 1995. Almost immediately, this very untypical semi-state chief executive, with a tendency to shoot from the hip, was talking about 'all the property we're sitting on', ultimately setting in train a programme of disposals and/or joint ventures to realise its value.

One of the issues that worried Bord Fáilte's Management Board for Product Development, in its assessment of the five tenders for the National Conference Centre, was that Treasury Holdings were putting virtually no equity into the Spencer Dock project and that it could 'fall on its face' as a result. What had been devised with its prospective partners, GE Capital, was a complex lending deal, crucially dependent on the assumption that tax incentives would be available. 'This project is a business and financial risk and would be impossible to rescue if it failed,' one source said at the time. 'Unless CIÉ are in the deal, it doesn't stand up. Otherwise, who will subsidise the losses? The difficulties that arose were clear-cut. It seemed that Treasury Holdings were trying to have an each-way bet.' As a result of this and other concerns, the board – chaired by Malachy Stephens, a Mullingar accountant appointed by Enda Kenny – voted by five to one against adopting its evaluation team's recommendation in favour of Spencer Dock. The only dissenter was Jim McGuigan, marketing services manager of Bord Fáilte, who had lived with the conference centre project since its inception. True to form, Treasury Holdings immediately initiated High Court proceedings for a judicial review of Bord Fáilte's decision to invoke a 'negotiated procedure', in EU parlance. What this meant was that all five contenders would be invited to resubmit their schemes to a new team of assessors who were to report back to Bord Fáilte 'as a matter of extreme urgency'. Richard Barrett and Johnny Ronan saw this as an attempt to overturn the original evaluation team's recommendation and award the contract to one of their rivals. After they agreed to withdraw the legal action, a new team of assessors headed by banker Richard Hooper endorsed Spencer Dock as the best scheme, and the Government decided in June 1998 to award them the contract, subject to a cost-benefit analysis to secure EU approval, a test which it apparently passed.

Work was to start three months later, but it became clear that the project was in danger of going off the rails. Firstly, there was the likelihood that it might not qualify for the full range of urban renewal tax incentives because of opposition from Brussels. Given that it was being financed on the assumption that such tax incentives would be available, it seemed that the sums no longer added up. And secondly, there was now serious tension between the Spencer Dock consortium and the DDDA. These factors delayed the finalisation of a Section 25 planning scheme for the site, which would have taken it out of the normal planning process, thus shortening its delivery time and meeting the deadline to 'draw down' the £26 million in EU aid. The authority even used its Section 25 planning powers as a negotiating chip, at one stage describing these powers as 'intangible assets'. This led to charges from Treasury Holdings that the DDDA was in the business of 'selling indulgences' and was actually seeking a 'contribution' of £50 million towards the realisation of its social objectives – an allegation which, of course, it vehemently denied. The authority's chairman, Lar Bradshaw, and Johnny Ronan had an appalling row over the alleged 'bung' at a stormy lunch in Cooke's Café in November 1998, 'fighting like turkey-cocks at the table', in the words of one observer. Relations between the two sides hit rock bottom when the developers discovered that the DDDA had lodged an objection with Dublin Corporation against their planning application for enabling works on the site, including the excavation of the 'largest hole in Ireland'. At issue was the authority's insistence that the conference centre should be pulled back 20 metres (66 ft) from the edge of Spencer Dock to facilitate the creation of a linear park along the Royal Canal, as envisaged in its own master plan. It believed that the clearance of just 6.5 metres (21.5 ft) between the dock basin and the massive gable wall of the conference centre, as approved by Dublin Corporation, would be far too narrow. The developers argued, somewhat unconvincingly, that Bord Fáilte's acceptance of their tender for the NCC was so site-specific that it could not be shifted eastwards, even slightly, without running the risk of losing the £26 million EU grant. Moving it would also mean having to relocate CIÉ's rail freight gantry, and it had to stay where it was for the moment. A crisis meeting between the two sides turned into another 'table-thumping session', with Barrett and Ronan seeking an unequivocal assurance that the DDDA would not take the matter to An Bord Pleanála. Days passed before such an assurance was received.

The proposed National Conference Centre was now enveloped in a poisonous atmosphere that seriously threatened its delivery. Week after week throughout the autumn of 1998, there were accusations of blackmail, bad faith, skulduggery and hidden agendas, and the Government was furious about it all. The Minister for the Environment, Noel Dempsey, who had political responsibility for the DDDA, was particularly concerned about what he saw as the antics of Barrett and Ronan, and sought to avoid any contact with them. At one point, after being flooded with letters from the developers detailing the authority's alleged duplicity, he wrote to them saying that he did not 'see much point in continuing interminable correspondence between you and me'. He was kept in touch with unfolding events by John O'Connor, the assistant secretary in charge of his Department's planning division, a member of the Docklands executive board. By August 1998, when the Tall Ships came to Dublin, it was becoming evident that there had been a complete breakdown of trust between the DDDA and the developers, Spencer Dock Development Company. They claimed that it was trying to scupper their plans by throwing an inexplicable series of spanners in the works, whereas the DDDA feared that it was being set up as a scapegoat should the developers fail to deliver the conference centre, and that it was already being painted into the black corner. SDDC's relationship with the authority deteriorated further after Richard Barrett lodged an official complaint to the Dáil Committee of Public Accounts, claiming that it was wasting public money in commissioning a limited Section 25 planning scheme for the conference centre, without reference to the rest of the site. The authority saw this move as another example of posturing by SDDC in the propaganda war between them. In a letter to Barrett, its Scottish-born chief executive, Peter Coyne, said he was 'very concerned that you may not be serious in your endeavour to secure the conference centre as you effectively disregarded our advice to you as to how best to proceed with the process. Furthermore, you have stated on more than one occasion that you would be much better off if the conference centre project were to fail and you were to develop CIÉ's land without it. That may be a simple statement of fact, but the implication is worrying.' And he added, bluntly: 'I am not prepared to have the Authority manoeuvred into the position of being the pretext for your withdrawal from the conference centre project. This Authority is 100% behind the project, and if you are also, you will stop all this adversarial posturing and give us your full co-operation.' Coyne, who had been a director of British Waterways with responsibility for canalside development in London, later described this period as 'the worst three months of my life'.

The DDDA refused to give a prior commitment that it would sanction a Section 25 planning scheme for the extended site until it first received a firm indication from SDDC on the form and content of what they were planning to build. But the developers were in a quandary. They had anticipated that IFSC-style tax incentives would cushion the project, cross-subsidising the conference centre's losses, which they estimated at more than £100 million in its first decade, including repayments of capital and interest. To compensate for the non-availability of tax incentives, it calculated that a much larger quantum of development – at least four million square feet – would now be required to secure funding for the centre. The financiers, in particular, would want to see how the space would stack up around it. After all, Bord Fáilte had accepted the figure of four million square feet, and the Government, in approving the project actually sought – and received – an indemnity for the Exchequer against any losses for twenty years. If the developers could not get approval from the DDDA for this enormous quantum of development, they would have to go somewhere else. When it became clear that the authority would not give SDDC what it wanted, there was no option but to go through the normal planning process, which is what the developers decided to do. They were clearly taking a risk, not least because of the time element involved. Had the DDDA not been so vehemently opposed to the sheer scale of their ambitions, they could have had a Section 25 approval within weeks. Making a planning application to Dublin Corporation, accompanied by a detailed environmental impact statement, and then defending it all in a Bord Pleanála appeal, was going to take nine months or more, jeopardising the prospect of meeting the deadline of end-2000 for the EU's £26 million grant.

However, the developers were convinced that they would get a more sympathetic response from the City Manager, John Fitzgerald. After all, he had publicly stated his belief that the conference centre was a 'must have' project for Dublin. What's more, explicit support for the proposal to locate it at Spencer Dock and North Wall Quay had been incorporated in the new City Plan, and the 'vibes' from the Civic Offices seemed to be very positive. But even though Fitzgerald was obviously keen to 'deliver' the NCC, he was also determined that the Corporation was not going to be taken for granted. As Richard Barrett and Johnny Ronan beamed with confidence, putting it about that the Corporation would see them right, Fitzgerald became increasingly irritated. He made it clear, even before SDDC's planning application was lodged, that what would count in the end at Spencer Dock was 'the proper planning and development of the area', in the words of the 1963 Planning Act. By then, the cat was out of the bag. On 15th December 1998, at a media briefing in the Merrion Hotel, hastily arranged by Frank Dunlop, the public relations consultant, Kevin Roche revealed his plans for the largest urban development project in the history of the State. As each illustration unfolded, there could be no gainsaying its enormous scale, with a curtain-walled tower, in blue-tinted glass, rising to a height of 128 metres (422 ft) – significantly taller than the curved glass block originally proposed by SOM for George's Quay, which was 'only' 100 metres high, and even exceeding the height of the slender millennium monument planned for O'Connell Street. It was to be flanked by a virtual wall of tall, bulky office buildings up to 84 metres (277 ft) high and surrounded by multi-storey hotels, apartment blocks and landscaped open spaces, as if Canary Wharf had come to Dublin, with the retained historic buildings on North Wall Quay reduced to mere outhouses. Even the lower-scale office blocks would have been higher than the ceiling set by the Corporation for George's Quay. Yet that decision had encouraged the developers and set the stage for Spencer Dock to soar. For some, it recalled the opening credits of *Dallas* or 'the bits of New York that don't work, like Battery Park City'. Opinion among Dublin architects was scathing. One called it 'the March of the Triffids', while another said it was 'the architectural equivalent of genetically modified organisms – once released into the environment, it will pop up everywhere.' It was, as Cllr Ciarán Cuffe put it, 'scary stuff'.

Senior Corporation officials were also taken aback by the enormity of what now confronted them. Though some had seen a video preview, Johnny Ronan's dramatic unveiling of a scale model of the scheme at a presentation in the Civic Offices still caused a sharp intake of breath. 'It was like a girl jumping out of a cake or something', one of those present recalled – except that nobody cheered. The stunned silence that followed was eventually broken by SDDC's project manager, Dermod Dwyer of Tourism and Leisure Partners Ltd, who said: 'Would somebody please say something?' Everyone gathered around the model as Ireland's most decorated architect took them through the various elements. But even though most of it had been generated by AutoCAD (Computer Aided Design), it was clear that the great wall of tall buildings now being proposed for Spencer Dock was bound to loom up over the roofline of Holles Street Hospital, detracting from the 'Georgian Mile' on Fitzwilliam Street, and would also be seen in the distance from numerous other vantage points in the city. But then, as Ronan pointed out, the Grand Arche of La Defense on the edge of Paris is visible from the Champs Elyssees. Roche gamely defended the height as a trade-off for the creation of extensive areas of open space, including a raised urban park in the middle of the site that would be larger than Fitzwilliam Square. Of course, it would have been possible to build lower, but in order to retain the same density of development, this would mean covering much more of the site. And that was the nub of the issue: though the scheme as presented was the 32nd version of Roche Dinkeloo's master plan for Spencer Dock, all of these options had been prepared under the stricture of producing an aggregate six million square feet of buildings on the site. Their clients would not budge an inch on that central point. For the architects, therefore, it must have been almost like playing a game of draughts as they moved buildings of varying mass around a virtual checquerboard. 'Obviously, Roche came over to do the conference centre and then got bounced into doing all the other stuff', one of his Dublin colleagues commented.

Everyone was becoming rather nervous as they waited for SDDC to reveal its final hand in a formal planning application to Dublin Corporation, which had set up a high-level project team to assess the scheme. One of its members, Dick Gleeson, so annoyed Roche in talking about the quality of urban space in European cities at a series of long sessions with the world master architect that he complained about being bullied by an uppity planner. It didn't help that Gleeson was deeply unimpressed by Roche's design for the NCC, though Pat McDonnell thought it had a 'rough-hewn, elemental quality'. Before the project team had even finalised a set of 'development principles' for the 51-acre site, planning consultants Frank L Benson & Partners submitted the application along with the required environmental impact statement. As the boxes containing some 2,400 drawings were carted into the Civic Offices on 2nd March 1999, an immensely chuffed Johnny Ronan was on hand to smile for the cameras and proclaim it a historic day, for it was the biggest planning application ever lodged with an Irish local authority, with a capital value of £1.2 billion, for what was probably the largest 'brownfield site' in Ireland. The scale of it was staggering. Not

courtesy of Dublin Corporation

Dick Gleeson, Deputy City Planning Officer. He so annoyed Kevin Roche in talking about the quality of European cities that Roche complained about being bullied by an uppity planner.

only did it provide a National Conference Centre, now bloated to include an exhibition centre with an overall price tag of £125 million, but also a two-storey podium covering a large part of the site, with 7,311 car-parking spaces on several levels below it; 3,012 apartments in eleven buildings, ranging from nine storeys above ground to seventeen storeys above the podium level; nine bulky office buildings rising from six storeys above ground to twenty-two storeys above the podium; two large hotels; twenty-one retail units, including bars and restaurants; a 'Technopole' housing major research and development facilities for Trinity College; a new underground station possibly serving as a terminus for a rail link to Dublin Airport; and extensive areas of open space. Though the tallest block, centrally positioned on the southern portion of the site, had been reduced in height to 95 metres (313 ft), the sheer scale of what was being proposed – a 'mini-Manhattan, a city in itself', as Senator Joe Costello (Labour) described it – remained quite breathtaking. Seán Carey, the Assistant City Manager, made it clear that the Corporation was 'very concerned about the height' of many of the buildings, and he said there would have to be 'significant changes' in the plan if it was to win approval. The Corporation's set of principles evolved from a series of brainstorming sessions with Michael Lowe, a director of Arup Associates in London who had wide experience of urban design with huge schemes such as Broadgate. Having familiarised himself with Roche Dinkeloo's master plan, he put it up to the Corporation's high-level project team to spell out what it wanted to see happening at Spencer Dock. 'So you've got a conference centre, a canal, a river, and existing or planned transportation links', one of the participants recalls him saying at one of the sessions. 'Forget about all the drawings. Don't start picking at the bits and taking them down in scale. You have to have a clear picture in your own minds of what *you* think should go there. So what in your wildest dreams would you put there, on this pivotal site downriver from the city centre?' Lowe then gave them all pens and paper and asked them to put names on the elements they would like to see, so they wrote down things like 'mixed uses', 'not a compound', 'an extension of the city centre', 'must face out', 'extrovert', and 'must have families'. Members of the team flew to London for a day and toured Broadgate, at the edge of the City, and Canary Wharf, that huge office complex on the Isle of Dogs. What they concluded was that Canary Wharf, with the tallest tower in Europe, was what cities end up with when the sky's the limit, whereas the much more densely built Broadgate would be preferable for Dublin. It was through such a process that the set of development principles emerged. They specified that any scheme for Spencer Dock 'must recognise the sensitive character of the skyline of the city' and respect the amenities of existing communities in the area. Apart from establishing a 'major civic focal point', it would also have to 'generate a sense of place', with a lively mix of uses, both during the day and at night, as well as achieving 'the highest architectural and civic design standards'. The Corporation also wanted to tease out the provision of social housing, because there didn't seem to be any in the scheme, as well as the traffic implications, which, on the face of it, were potentially horrendous.

Six weeks after the planning application was submitted, Harry Crosbie appeared on the *Late Late Show* with SDDC's model of the entire scheme, extravagantly extolling its virtues to a seemingly mesmerised Gay Byrne, just decorated as a Freeman of Dublin, with nobody present to challenge him. It was seen as a clever tactic by the developers to be represented on television by this charming 'real Dub', who, in Byrne's view, deserved nothing but congratulations for what he was trying to do for the city. However, Crosbie did manage to score an own goal when he referred jocosely to the local community, saying there was a perception that 'they eat their young down there'. People living in East Wall parish went bananas, and the trucking magnate, who was really referring to Sheriff Street in its car-burning days, had to apologise to anyone who thought he had implied that the area was not populated by 'a settled, respectable and thriving community'. But even as Crosbie maintained that it was a 'fear of the future' that preoccupied the locals, other more powerful forces had already intervened. Among the first objectors to make their views known to the Corporation was Dermot Desmond, the multi-millionaire financier and tax exile who is credited with originating the IFSC. In a document submitted on his behalf, planning consultants Reid Associates claimed that the Spencer Dock project had been 'driven purely by economic considerations of maximising commercial floorspace' on a pivotal site in the Docklands area. It also said there was no justification for excessively high buildings that would 'significantly obtrude on the skyline [and] detract from the importance of the Liffey as a major linear landmark of the city'. In their EIS, even the developers conceded that the erection of twenty-six mainly high-rise buildings at Spencer Dock would have a 'profound and permanent impact' on the landscape and skyline of the Docklands area. Ultimately, the historic buildings being retained, such as the former Midland Hotel and nearby Woolstore, would be 'the smallest on the site'. Existing views of St Laurence

O'Toole's Church would be obstructed, adjacent low-rise housing would be over-looked and overshadowed and more traffic would be brought into the area. On the plus side, the scheme would provide housing for more than 7,000 people – doubling the population of the north side of Docklands – and 11,000 permanent jobs when it was all built. Incredibly, the EIS estimated that at least 70% of the 44,000 trips per day which all this activity generated would be on public transport, foot or bicycle because, by 2010, the infrastructure would be in place throughout the city to 'bring about a radical change in people's travel behaviour'.

The DDDA, now out of the frame in terms of adjudicating on the scheme, told the Corporation that it was 'seriously concerned' about it on the grounds of over-development, poor civic design quality and traffic impacts. By then, of course, its relations with SDDC had deteriorated to such a low level that Richard Barrett actually advised an Institute of Directors conference on property invest-ment to avoid the Docklands area because 'it's too much trouble'. The final straw had broken when the authority, to Barrett and Ronan's intense annoyance, decid-ed to go ahead with the preparation of a Section 25 planning scheme for Spencer Dock – an exercise which the developers regarded as 'useless', given that they had already made a planning application to Dublin Corporation. The draft plan, pre-pared by Scott Tallon Walker and Urban Projects under conditions shrouded by the utmost sensitivity, offered little comfort to SDDC. What it recommended was that the volume of space on the southern portion of the Spencer Dock site – in other words, south of Mayor Street – should not exceed 3.5 million square feet. And with only a low-rise cluster to the rear, this would have given the developers no more than four million square feet in total, including the now gargantuan NCC. It is known, however, that this crucial finding was conveyed to the Corporation. The DDDA also pointed out that its own studies had shown that any building above 42 metres (138 ft) would also have an impact on the wider city skyline. With buildings of 80 metres or more, the impact would be 'very signifi-cant', particularly from the Georgian Mile. 'The proposed height and density of development will produce a poor-quality environment for both neighbouring property and for the future occupants of the proposed buildings, especially future residents', the authority's chief executive, Peter Coyne, said in his letter to the Corporation. It also 'ignored' one of the critical factors in urban design – that the quality of space between buildings was as important as the quality of the build-ings themselves. Many of these spaces would be in shadow, all but one of them lacked a sense of enclosure, and wind turbulence would create 'unpleasant con-ditions' at ground level, according to Coyne. Overshadowing would extend to the Royal Canal, on the western perimeter, as well as nearby housing. Referring to traf-fic impacts, he said existing critical junctions in and around Docklands were 'incapable of taking any further increases' in car-parking, at least until major infrastructural works are completed, including the Port Tunnel.

The scheme was considered by the City Council Planning Committee in April, though the councillors' role was merely advisory, as it was deemed not to require a 'material contravention' of the City Plan. Their reaction ranged from gushing enthusiasm, with both Carmencita Hederman (Ind) and Ita Greene (FF) describing it as 'the most exciting development' ever proposed in Dublin, to outright opposition from councillors such as Ciarán Cuffe, who warned that the conference centre – ostensibly the main event at Spencer Dock – would be 'dwarfed' by the higher buildings massed behind it, and Tony Gregory TD, who said the Corporation was being 'blackmailed into accepting this New York-style development' in order to secure the NCC. And so, in May, two months after SDDC's application was lodged, the planners issued a detailed request for 'substantial further information' to help clarify all of the issues. In a 53-page report, Deputy City Planning Officer John Martin, who has a well-deserved reputation for being thorough, identified the height and bulk of the buildings and the traffic implications of providing 7,300 on-site parking spaces as 'the

John Martin, Deputy City Planning Officer, pointing to the Spencer Dock scheme on the 1:1,000 scale model of the Docklands area and its hinterland requested by An Bord Pleanála to enable it to assess the impact of the proposed development.

most significant adverse impacts' of the scheme. The Corporation sought full-colour photomontages to show the proposed buildings in the context of surrounding streets, as well as what Spencer Dock would look like seen from distant vantage points. It also wanted further shadow studies, as well as an assessment of microclimatic effects, especially the wind turbulence associated with high buildings, and a retail impact statement, given that the 18,000 square metres (193,750 sq ft) of shopping proposed for the site would be 'larger than some existing suburban shopping centres'. Taking up a point made by Dermot Desmond, the planners also sought further information on the implications of concentrating 204,380 square metres (2.2 million sq ft) of office space at Spencer Dock. That's what made it, in the words of Cllr Dermot Lacey (Labour), 'a very greedy application' requiring a thorough economic analysis. It seemed to some that Treasury Holdings was trying to corner the Dublin office market, because in addition to the enormous quantum of space proposed for Spencer Dock, the company was simultaneously pursuing plans for an extensive office park on the Legionaries of

A bird's-eye view of the Roche Dinkeloo master plan for Spencer Dock, with the proposed National Conference Centre in the foreground, at the confluence of the River Liffey and the Royal Canal.

Perspective view of Kevin Roche's National Conference Centre from the Macken Street suspension bridge designed by Santiago Calatrava.

ARC Digital / SDDC environmental impact statement

A perspective view of the Spencer Dock scheme from the north-east shows that it would be like 'living at the foot of the Grand Canyon or the Cliffs of Moher with windows', in the words of Fr John Wall of St Laurence O'Toole's Church, whose spire would be dwarfed by the scheme.

Colossal scale: a computer-generated perspective of the Spencer Dock scheme, looking west along Mayor Street Upper, with the existing terrace of two-storey houses shown right.

ARC Digital / SDDC environmental impact statement

Christ land in Leopardstown, close to the M50. Altogether, what it had on the stocks was equivalent to a four-year supply at current take-up rates.

As the architects and other consultants involved in the Spencer Dock project worked around the clock to provide the planners with the additional information they required, their clients went to the Civic Offices for a tense and decisive meeting with Seán Carey. He told them that the most they could expect to get was 4.5 million square feet, including the NCC, which by then had an overall floor area of 425,000 square feet (39,480 square metres). This leviathan, more than double the size Bord Fáilte had in mind, had been created on the advice of the operators of Britain's National Convention Centre in Birmingham, bumping up the price tag to £125 million. The developers continued to insist that 5.5 million square feet of space was needed to subsidise the centre, which they believed would lose £6 million a year, and with the Government determined to insulate itself against exposure to such losses, it could only be funded by the quantum of development proposed. Although only four of the twenty-six buildings proposed in Roche Dinkeloo's master plan had been designed in detail, SDDC was seeking full planning permission for the lot, with the balance subject to further applications for approval on foot of that 'parent' permission. The developers needed this, above all, to secure a financial package for the £1.2 billion scheme from GE Capital, which would obviously want to see what's stacked up along the road, as it were, before finally committing itself. Cocksure as ever, Johnny Ronan had already been pictured signing a contract with Sisk's to build the conference centre. A huge billboard was erected on the site proclaiming its imminent new role, and a quite lavish suite of temporary offices installed there to house Dermod Dwyer and members of the fifty-strong team of consultants.

Dublin Corporation was caught in a cleft stick, between wanting to facilitate the NCC project on the one side, and being unable to swallow the enormous scale of the underpinning ancillary development on the other. For a start, the 51-acre site was twice the area of Temple Bar, and the planners could hardly have failed to notice the urban diversity which can be experienced on its network of narrow streets compared to, say, the introverted and sterile enclosure of the IFSC. Yet what was being proposed for Spencer Dock was much more like the IFSC, but on an incomparably larger scale. At six million square feet, it was actually larger than the first phase of Canary Wharf, and had 'more in common with Detroit than Dublin', as Ciarán Cuffe put it. The configuration of the buildings was also problematic, with the tallest block perhaps inevitably positioned in the middle of the site when it could have been located at the edge of the dock basin. No compositional studies had been submitted to justify the configuration proposed, though such studies were a key element in planning the second phase of Canary Wharf. Close-up views illustrated the colossal scale of the scheme, though it had to be conceded that much of the low-rise 'brownfield' foreground would inevitably be redeveloped to a higher scale. More distant views, intended to gauge its citywide impact from such locations as Dunsink Observatory, Howth Head and the playing fields near Mount Argus, conjured up a false city centre. Anyone not familiar with Dublin's skyline would almost certainly have thought that Spencer Dock was the heart of the city, even though it was as far removed from it as Canary Wharf is from London's financial district. The developers made no concessions to the Corporation's well-flagged concerns about the nature and scale of the overall scheme. Apart from reducing the number of basement car-parking spaces by five hundred, not one iota had been changed. Instead, they maintained that its density was 'not excessive'. The plot ratio (derived by dividing the gross floor area of the a development by its site area) was put at 2.58:1, excluding the NCC, and this seemed moderate compared to, say, George's Quay. However, it transpired that this plot ratio had been calculated across the entire site, including parts which could never be developed, such as a 600-metre stretch of the Royal Canal, the roads that traverse the site, and the campshires along the Liffey and on both sides of Spencer Dock. Traffic was also a huge issue. The implications of providing more than 7,300 on-site parking spaces on-site in an area with a 'sparse and discontinuous' road network – to quote the developers' environmental impact statement – could barely be imagined. Without a new bridge at Macken Street and the Port Tunnel, it would mean gridlock.

CIÉ made a detailed submission, as part of the additional information response, outlining plans for the development of public transport to serve the

The suspension bridge designed by Catalan architect-engineer Santiago Calatrava to cross the Liffey at Macken Street. With a spear-like pylon as high as Liberty Hall, it is pivoted to swivel, thereby allowing the odd ship to dock near the Custom House.

Dave Meehan / courtesy of Dublin Corporation

scheme. But its scattergun approach failed to resolve one of the most crucial issues of all – the provision of a strategic rail link between Spencer Dock and Barrow Street to bypass congestion around Connolly Station. Apparently, what it envisaged was that the proposed Dublin Airport rail line would terminate underground at the eastern end of the Spencer Dock site, and that a quite separate rail link would bridge the Liffey from the western end. Unfortunately, this would run right alongside the sensational cable-stayed road bridge designed by Santiago Calatrava on the axis of Macken Street, with a pylon as high as Liberty Hall and a pivot to allow ships to dock near the Custom House. A second Loop Line very close by would detract from the sculptural drama of the Catalan architect-engineer's creation. For this reason, the Corporation made it clear that it favoured an underground link between Spencer Dock and Barrow Street. 'A high-level rail crossing of the river would not be acceptable because of detrimental effects on visual amenity and severance of property', the planners said firmly. It also emerged that CIÉ's own Light Rail Project Team had lodged an objection to the scheme, in which its parent group was directly involved, because it would 'severely compromise' the efficiency of Luas by providing a reservation on Mayor Street wide enough for single-track operation only. After the Corporation requested CIÉ to clarify its position on the matter, the light rail team was bluntly instructed to withdraw its objection. It was clear that property development considerations were taking precedence over the needs of public transport, even within CIÉ. Dúchas, the State heritage service, also insisted that a proposed bridge over Spencer Dock itself should leave sufficient headroom for navigation, in line with plans to restore the Royal Canal.

There was also the history of comprehensive redevelopment in Dublin to consider, and it was far from encouraging. Even sites of just four acres had often taken nearly two decades to redevelop. The most relevant and salutary case was the 27-acre Custom House Docks site, for which hugely overblown claims were made in 1987. It was to be developed 'with style, flair and imagination' to create an 'exciting people place' where there would be 'an unfolding pageant of events' offering 'a variety of sensory delights' to the people who would work or live there. Charlie Haughey, borrowing the mantle of Leopold Bloom, had even suggested that it was destined to become 'the new Bloomusalem in the Nova Hibernia of the future'. However, as Senator David Norris pointed out, this quotation from *Ulysses* was particularly ill-chosen because Bloom was 'hallucinating when he made the speech, his audience was a collection of whores and drunkards, the location was a brothel and none of the prophesies came true'. And though the Dermot Desmond-inspired International Financial Services Centre turned out to be a roaring success, netting the Exchequer hundreds of millions of pounds even at a 10% tax rate, it could hardly be defined as 'an exiting people place', still less a 'new Bloomusalem'. Indeed, the Custom House Docks site is still a controlled, almost moated, enclave, rather that a natural extension of the city centre.

But the Corporation had a hot planning application on its hands and had to make a decision. The City Manager set a clear direction that however much a conference centre was desirable, the decision must be based on proper planning and development considerations and 'doing the right thing for Dublin'. Senior officials worked long hours wrestling with the issues, knowing in the back of their minds that whatever decision they made it was bound to involve some compromise, while fearing that, if they granted SDDC permission for a large quantity of office space at Spencer Dock, it might be challenged in the High Court by envious rivals. 'We don't like it, we would rather it wasn't here, but it's here', Jim Barrett said at the time. 'We have to act responsibly and make a decision. It's not going to be popular. Whichever way it goes, it's going to hurt.' The Corporation was on its own. Bord Fáilte, as the commissioning agency for the conference centre, took a back seat while the proposed development weaved its way through the planning process. It did not even have anything to say publicly about the fact that the NCC had more than doubled in size. Politicians at national level also remained extraordinarily silent on the issue, despite the huge scale of the scheme, its likely impact on the Docklands area and the city in general, both in the sky and on the ground, and the fact that it was to be located in the Taoiseach's own constituency.

Quite shamelessly, the Government turned a blind eye to the NCC developers' plan to create an additional 5.5 million square feet of offices, apartments, hotels and retail facilities at Spencer Dock on the basis that all of this was required to pay for the conference centre. It left Dublin Corporation, as the city's planning authority, holding 'the shitty end of the stick' – in Ray Burke's memorable phrase – forced, in effect, to approve a too-large quantum of development on the 51-acre site in order to secure this 'must have' project. Ten years earlier, when the State was nearly bankrupt, it was perfectly understandable that the Government expected the private sector to step in and finance both the construction and operational costs of the proposed conference centre, with the only 'public money' coming from Brussels. But now, the Exchequer was almost groaning under the volume of revenue rushing in from tax receipts and the sale of Telecom Éireann, netting a surplus of nearly £6 billion for 1999 alone. As one economist put it, the Department of Finance 'doesn't have a basement big enough to hold all the money that's rolling in'. The Government could have broken the Gordian knot between the NCC project and the massive bulk of buildings stacked up behind it by dipping into this honeypot to pay for the conference centre, just as it managed to find £23 million to purchase Farmleigh, the Guinness estate on the edge of Phoenix Park. Operating losses, estimated by SDDC at £6 million per year, could have been funded by a marginal tax on hotel bedrooms above a certain standard. A levy of £1 per room per night for three-star hotels, £2 for four-star hotels and £3 for five-star hotels would raise £3 million per year, based on 65% occupancy, and the remainder could have been raised by increasing the yield from commercial rates.

But then, maybe Dublin didn't need a conference centre at all, if its purpose was simply to boost tourism. By 1999, the city was awash with tourists. The number of hotels had increased from eighty-one in 1993 to 122, while bed capacity doubled to 19,800, and a further twenty hotels were being built or planned. This reflected the fact that Dublin had suddenly become one of the fastest-growing tourist destinations in the western world, attracting 3.4 million overseas visitors in 1999, roughly three times its population. So why should the city still be chasing the marginal increase that a conference centre would bring when not having one hadn't made a blind bit of difference to its new pulling power? The factors which gave rise to the NCC plan had changed fundamentally, yet we were still stuck in the same old groove. But if the price to be paid was a massed Pittsburgh-style skyline at Spencer Dock, there was a growing conviction that it was too high a price. As for the EU grant of £26 million, even if the deadline for drawing it down was extended, one senior official with strong reservations about what was being proposed shook his head sadly and said: 'It could be the most expensive EU money we'll ever get.'

As the August planning deadline loomed, the developers engaged the critical eye of Martin Pawley, one-time architecture correspondent of the *Guardian* and author of provocative books such as *Terminal Architecture* and *Theory and Design in the Second Machine Age*. He was paid by SDDC to write an article for publication in the *Irish Times* in which he described the massive scheme for Spencer Dock as 'a model for tomorrow', saying it was 'following the course charted by Canary Wharf'. The conference centre itself was 'an epic structure ... [with an] urbane but assertive design', Pawley enthused. 'Critics who carp at the large amount of supporting accommodation called for by the developers fall silent at the thought of losing the NCC without it. In the same way, critics who complain that they do not yet know what all the supporting buildings will look like are given pause by Kevin Roche's standing in the architectural firmament.' Many were not given such pause. Pawley's piece was a commissioned response – and rightly described as such in the *Irish Times* – to a much earlier broadside in the newspaper by Dublin architect Paul Keogh, which had utterly incensed Johnny Ronan. In it, Keogh argued that Roche had no experience of working in a European city of Dublin's scale, and, 'after fifty years largely spent in the US corporate culture, he may well be culturally disconnected.' His master plan for Spencer Dock, Keogh wrote, would not only represent 'the squandering of a unique opportunity' to create a sustainable urban community, 'it would also be a reversal of the aspirations of Dublin as a European city and would set a precedent for further such schemes.' It was 'no coincidence that the predominant architectural influence behind the pressure for this type of high-rise development is American – Skidmore Owings & Merrill at George's Quay and Roche Dinkeloo at Spencer Dock'. The developers trawled through the world of architects and critics in an effort to find somebody of standing who would respond to this indictment. Their only other fan was Pat Liddy, author and illustrator of several books on Dublin, who had penned a piece for the *Irish Times* suggesting that the strength of Spencer Dock was its sheer scale, because it would 'galvanise the State' to invest in 'the urgent installation of the necessary infrastructure' to serve the Docklands area. By the time they found Martin Pawley and commissioned him to write his glowing notice in July, it was too late to have any real impact.

Given the complexity of the issues facing it, Dublin Corporation's August 6th planning decision on Spencer Dock seemed like Solomon's judgment. The tactics employed by SDDC, on the lines of 'don't hit me now with the child in my arms', did not produce the result they were seeking because the child in question – the National Conference Centre – was now virtually an orphan. Of the twenty-six buildings proposed in March, the developers received full planning permission for just two – the NCC and a single adjoining office block – and even this was conditional on the submission of an immense amount of further details. Only outline planning permission was granted for the rest, subject to a 'cap' of 4.6 million square feet on the overall development – 25% less than SDDC sought. The Corporation's 32-page planning decision also made it clear that 'the layout proposed, including all details of buildings, structures, open spaces, paved areas, circulation areas and access points, are specifically excluded from this grant of outline permission.' In other words, Kevin Roche's master plan had been emphatically rejected by Dublin's planners. This slap in the face was serious enough, but what really wounded Roche was that even the text of the decision referred to 'the lack of evident urban design character of sufficient quality in the layout and spaces, as well as the repetitive and undifferentiated language of architectural expression' – hardly a ringing endorsement of his work. City Planning Officer Pat McDonnell, in a voluminous 163-page report, was even more scathing in his assessment. 'Most of the problems result from the specific design and resultant dubious environmental quality of much of the layout', he wrote. 'Apart from the main conference building, which is plain but forceful in its design, the rest of the precinct has adopted a somewhat anonymous style of speculative commercial architecture which in total, it must be said, produces a rather low-key, bland appearance provoking images of North American city core development.' McDonnell recommended that no building on site should exceed 54 metres (178 ft), though City Architect Jim Barrett felt that there would be opportunities to increase building heights in the middle of the site – a disagreement, one of many between them, which was left to the skyline study to resolve.

Apart from fundamental objections to the design, including the 'divisive and intrusive' podium, one of the main reasons why only outline permission was granted for most of the scheme was that it could not be allowed to proceed 'pending a decision by the competent State authorities in relation to the vertical and horizontal alignment of the cross-river rail link', as recommended by the Greater Dublin Strategic Planning Guidelines. Endorsing the view taken by CIÉ's Light Rail Project Team, the Corporation specified that adequate provision would also have to be made for a future twin-track Luas line through the area, that on-site car-parking was to be drastically reduced from 6,805 spaces to a maximum of 2,000 'to avoid gridlock on the surrounding road network', and that the developers would have to contribute £2 million towards the cost of constructing the Calatrava-designed Macken Street bridge. The planners also wanted to see more 'family-orientated housing' on the 51-acre site, to create a sustainable community in the long term, with more open space and children's play areas. But even though the Corporation believed that the conference centre would be 'beneficial' to the city, the net effect of its decision was to put the project in jeopardy. In a statement issued by Frank Dunlop, the developers warned that the planning conditions 'will seriously inhibit further progress on the NCC [which] cannot be built and funded on an ongoing basis without significant supporting development on the remainder of the site'. The statement added that the centre would have to be operational by 31st December 2000 to avail of the EU grant. That time frame was 'rapidly diminishing', and the money could 'fall by the wayside. Sadly, in such circumstances, so will the National Conference Centre.' Their reaction was understandable. After all, they had invested enormous financial and intellectual resources to progress the Spencer Dock project, with twenty-two firms of consultants employed and £10 million racked up, mainly on professional fees. Richard Barrett told the *Irish Times* that they would seriously consider any initiative by the Government to provide public funding for the NCC to make up for losing 25% of their master plan. No such initiative was forthcoming, and it began to look as though the centre was doomed.

Eight appeals were lodged with An Bord Pleanála against the Corporation's decision, including an Exocet from Dermot Desmond. He had read Paul Keogh's critique in the *Irish Times* and hired him to make an elaborate case on architectural and urban-design grounds, stating that his client's 'over-riding concern is for the quality of the city's future urban environment'. He argued that the development of a fully detailed master plan for the 51-acre site – twice the area of Temple Bar – was a public responsibility and should not be 'governed by economic expediency'. As for Roche Dinkeloo's proposals, even the conference centre was 'gargantuan [and] grossly out of scale with every other building in Dublin', including Liberty Hall, O'Connell Bridge House, the Central Bank and the Civic Offices. 'Why is it that the size, bulk and profile of the scheme are more reminiscent of an aircraft hanger than a building of national prestige?' he asked. And notwithstanding Kevin Roche's pre-eminence among Irish architects, the photomontages of what he had proposed for the rest of the site showed 'images of an architecture of frightening brutality ... virtually identical to any number of projects by him for American cities'. To accept this style of architecture on such colossal scale, Keogh warned, would be a major travesty in terms of its visual impact on the city, the precedent it would set for future developments, and the negative effect it would have on Dublin's architectural culture. This was not something that would be tolerated in other European historic cities, such as Amsterdam, Edinburgh or Vienna.

It could all have been so different. Had the relevant authorities decided in the first instance where the National Conference Centre should be located – and Spencer Dock was as good a location as any – and then invited tenders for its construction, Dublin might have acquired a truly remarkable civic building comparable to the Sydney Opera House or the Guggenheim Museum in Bilbao, or having something of the interaction with its surroundings as the Centre Pompidou in Paris. It could have become the centrepiece of a vibrant urban neighbourhood that would also have related Docklands to the wider city, as Paul Keogh said. But this could only have happened if the conference centre was paid for by the Government, thereby detaching it from the gargantuan scale of the ancillary development said to be required to subvent its losses. As it was, not even CIÉ's parent department had been given sight of its contract with the Spencer Dock developers. Nobody other than the parties involved knew whether there were any sub-clauses which might result in the site becoming a somewhat less lucrative 'cash cow' than the bosses in Heuston Station hoped for and expected. Whatever the eventual outcome, Treasury Holdings had managed to lock the national transport group in a golden handcuff when it should arguably have followed the example of Bord Gáis Éireann and entered into an arrangement with the DDDA, based on the site's full market value. It was also obvious, even as the developers argued their case before An Bord Pleanála, that they were unlikely to get a more favourable decision from the appeals board than they received from Dublin Corporation. Even their coup in recruiting architect Donough Murphy as a consultant within three months of his retirement from the board after ten years as a member – a move that put him in conflict with its code of practice – was not going to tilt the balance in their favour. Indeed, long before the case was determined, Kevin Roche himself came to the depressing conclusion that the entire project would never happen, not even his much-prized NCC. And though he had designed major buildings on three continents, he never felt so dumped on as he did in Dublin.

Apart from the development of the IFSC extension on a twelve-acre site just west of Spencer Dock, where the greatest concentration of tower cranes in Dublin had gathered, nothing much seemed to be happening in Docklands. DDDA board meetings, under the chairmanship of Lar Bradshaw, were long and tedious, with a lot of time given over to conciliating local community interests, in line with the DDDA's mandate to achieve the social and economic as well as the physical regeneration of the area. Bradshaw, who runs the Dublin office of McKinsey International, the US trouble-shooting management consultants, had been a Rainbow Coalition appointee, though he managed to strike up a good relationship with Noel Dempsey. Said by some to have an ego in inverse proportion to his size, Bradshaw was fond of 'shooting the breeze' and left the careful, low-key Peter Coyne to get on with the day-to-day work of managing the authority's affairs. But neither of them became a high-profile spokesman for Docklands in the way Laura Magahy did for Temple Bar. Although the Tall Ships visit to

Dublin in August 1998 helped to put Docklands on the map and gave people a glimpse of its potential, the DDDA's master plan failed to capture the public imagination. All of its 'anchor projects', such as a Science Museum or Centre for the Performing Arts, were merely indicative, and even the target additional population of 25,000 over fifteen years appeared somewhat conservative. Projects that would have made a big difference, such as replacing the visual barrier of the Loop Line bridge with a more slimline structure, or building a barrage (or weir) to hold the Liffey at a constant level, were not regarded as priorities – although, in November 1999, the authority commissioned consultants to devise a 'river generation strategy' for the Liffey downstream of Butt Bridge, and to look at Dublin's potential as a cruise tourism venue.

The only really daring scheme for Docklands had been put forward by Dermot Desmond – a huge, glazed 'ecosphere', as high as Liberty Hall, filled with tropical flora and fauna and plonked in the middle of George's Dock, right in front of the IFSC. It became known to sceptics and detractors as the 'Gorillas in the Mist' project. Even if this extraordinary proposal was hubris on his part, nobody could deny that Desmond was the quintessential northside boy made good, with a net worth of several hundred million pounds and a nickname, The Kaiser, to go with his distinctive *fin de siècle* moustache. He founded National City Brokers in 1981, turning it into one of the most successful stockbroking firms in Ireland, and masterminded such megadeals as the 1988 takeover of Irish Distillers by Pernod Ricard. In the High Court, it was claimed that Desmond had boasted of his access to the corridors of power while Charlie Haughey was Taoiseach, and won a number of State commissions, including the flotation of Irish Sugar as Greencore plc. What wasn't known, until the Moriarty Tribunal started inquiring into it, was that he had joined Ben Dunne in supplying Haughey with money to support his lavish lifestyle, picking up an 'insignificant' bill of £75,000 in 1990 for the refurbishment of the then Taoiseach's yacht, *Celtic Mist*. In that same year, he was one of the key figures involved in the controversial sale of Johnston Mooney & O'Brien's bakery in Ballsbridge to Telecom Éireann for £9.4 million, after it had been purchased for £4.5 million from United Property Holdings, a company in which his friend, plutocrat Michael Smurfit, then chairman of Telecom, had an interest. 'Greed is a great motivator of people', Desmond once said. John Finnegan, the charming, roguish estate agent and alleged Ansbacher depositor, had even billed Telecom for a 'finder's fee' of £120,000 for pointing out the derelict bakery to his friend Smurfit. He was paid £39,000. When details of the Byzantine transactions over the site were first exposed in September 1991, Desmond memorably maintained that he had only provided 'mezzanine finance', but a Government-appointed inspector, John Glackin, concluded later that the Isle of Man company involved, Freezone Ltd, was owned by the financier – a finding hotly disputed by him at the time, though it has since emerged through the Moriarty Tribunal that it was through this offshore vehicle that the £75,000 had come to pay for Haughey's yacht repairs. The

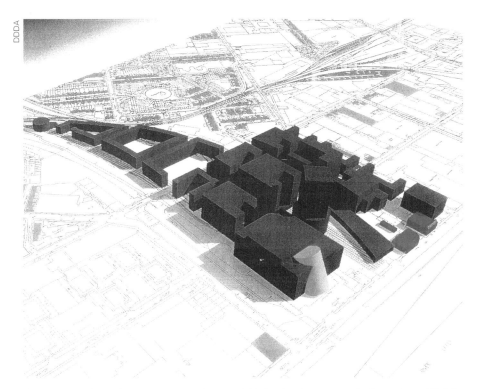

An axonometric projection, prepared by the DDDA, showing what a built version of Dublin Corporation's August 1999 planning permission for Spencer Dock would look like, interpreted from the ground rules laid down by the Corporation's architectural adviser, Michael Lowe.

Dermot Desmond as Superman, zooming over streets of terraced cottages in the North Wall area. His intervention in the struggle over Spencer Dock turned it from David v Goliath into Goliath v Goliath, with David cheering from the sidelines.

disclosures resulted in a 'bonfire of the vanities', with Desmond having to step down as chairman both of NCB and Aer Rianta, while Smurfit resigned as chairman of Telecom, which eventually got only £5.6 million for its hot property. Desmond became a tax exile domiciled in Monaco, following in Smurfit's footsteps, though he retained his appetite for high-risk deals, often netting millions of pounds in the process. When in Dublin, he operates from a Master of the Universe suite on the top floor of the IFSC south block, which he bought in 1990 for £25 million, with glass walls that can be made opaque at the flick of a switch and a small gym with a lancet window and breathtaking view westwards over the Liffey Quays.

Desmond's scheme for George's Dock, drawn up in 1996 by a US firm of theme-park designers, was opposed by the DDDA on planning grounds and by the Department of Finance, which doubted the financier's contention that his ecosphere would become a destination in its own right, and feared that the Exchequer might have to pick up the tab if it failed. There was another problem, too. As long as the Government dithered over the proposal, seemingly unable to say 'no' to the powerful financier, little progress could be made on slotting the last element of the Custom House Docks into place – finding a viable, crowd-pulling new use for the early 19th-century Stack A warehouse, scene of the Crimea War banquet in 1856 – because it formed part of Dermot Desmond's *grand projet*. Stack A had been earmarked for the Irish Museum of Modern Art, but that plan was scrapped after it was cast out to the Royal Hospital by Charlie Haughey, at the instigation of Anthony Cronin, his cultural adviser, and Padraig Ó hUiginn, the extremely shrewd mandarin who then ran the Taoiseach's department. The fate of Stack A remained unresolved when the joint developers of the IFSC – Mark Kavanagh's Hardwicke Ltd and the British Land Corporation – walked away from the site in 1997 with millions of pounds in profit from their ten-year contract. Not long before it was wound up, the Custom House Docks Development Authority used a small part of its share of the proceeds to renovate and plant trees on the Custom House Quay campshire, while Ireland's leading charity fund-raiser, Norma Smurfit, commissioned a Famine memorial on the quayside by Rowan Gillespie. His gaunt, wraith-like figures, carrying their pathetic few possessions towards an unseen coffin ship, stand in telling juxtaposition to the power-dressed blocks of the IFSC.

As if to remind everyone that it still existed, the DDDA scheduled two media briefings in August 1999 – one on its annual report for 1998, which curiously made no reference to the Spencer Dock saga even though it had caused the authority so much grief, and the second to launch its draft master plan for the Grand Canal Docks area. Its message, orchestrated by PR grand master Jim Milton of Murray Consultants, was that the authority was continuing to make steady progress. The development of the IFSC extension would create an additional 650,000 square feet of office space, a 200-bedroom hotel, 190 apartments, a crèche and more retail facilities. Ronnie Tallon, Ireland's most revered and dec-

Frank McDonald

Rowan Gillespie's gaunt, wraith-like figures, carrying their few possessions towards an unseen coffin ship, stand in telling juxtaposition to the power-dressed blocks of the IFSC.

The Citibank office block on Custom House Quay, largest of an austere assembly of refined grey buildings designed by Scott Tallon Walker, in the twelve-acre extension to the IFSC, just west of Spencer Dock.

Frank McDonald

Paddy Whelan / *Irish Times*

Terry Durney, the DDDA's cautious planning director, who laid down uniform parapet heights for the IFSC extension. The result seemed too low-rise, even flat, compared to the first phase of the IFSC.

orated architect, stole a march on rival practitioners by garnering the commissions to design most of the new office blocks on the site from such prestige clients as Citibank and A&L Goodbody, later capturing the hotel, too. What Scott Tallon Walker produced was an austere assembly of refined grey buildings, a sort of urban business park, with uniform parapet heights laid down by Terry Durney, the DDDA's cautious planning director. The result seemed too low-rise, even flat, compared to the first phase of the IFSC, which was designed by Burke-Kennedy Doyle & Partners to a concept devised by US architects Benjamin Thompson & Associates. Plans for the twelve-acre site had also been chopped and changed to accommodate the hotel, as well as a BKD scheme for the National College of Ireland, which purported to meet one the key objectives of the Docklands master plan – a 'Saol Scoil' to provide opportunities for life-long learning in the area. The driving force behind the project was Prof Joyce O'Connor, president of the former National College of Industrial Relations in Ranelagh, and she persuaded the DDDA to allocate a free 1.3 acre site for it before her brother, Seán Fitzpatrick of Anglo-Irish Bank, was appointed to its executive board. But the whole idea was greeted with deep scepticism by the Department of Education, mainly because of a £31 million estimate for the building with its dramatically glazed entrance, translucent Teflon canopy over a central courtyard, and beacon-like circulation drum. Still, at least the DDDA could point to its new Community Training Workshop on Seville Place as a concrete step towards achieving its social objectives, even though FÁS felt that it needed to be fortified against unruly natives.

The authority's master plan for the Grand Canal Docks was billed by Lar Bradshaw as the blueprint for a 'world-class city quarter' that would help to shift the city's centre of gravity towards Docklands, which would, of course, be good for the DDDA if not for Dublin. The plan – drawn up by Urban Initiatives, Urban Projects, Hamilton Osborne King and Anthony Reddy & Associates – was contingent on decontaminating the gasworks site through the systematic removal of its toxic residues, a process that would take twelve months or more. Development guidelines specified six to seven-storey commercial buildings and seven to eight-storey apartment buildings on the main frontages, with lower-rise housing in the middle of the site, laid out along a network of new east-west and north-south streets. Inevitably, perhaps, the consultants identified two sites for slender high-rise buildings – one at the eastern end of Sir John Rogerson's Quay and the other adjoining the former IMP meat plant site on Grand Canal Street Upper, where Ken Rohan was completing a large office development, designed by BKD. The ink was barely dry when a consortium led by canny Clare-born builder Bernard McNamara lodged plans for a major office and residential development, ranging in height from six to thirteen storeys, on the former Dock Milling site of 1.5 acres beside Barrow Street station, which they had purchased by tender from IAWS for £8.8 million, fighting off strenuous efforts by Treasury Holdings to get their hands on it. This BKD scheme included ten large loft-style apartments in one of the listed stone-built grainstores on the waterfront. Other listed buildings around the dock basins, including Harry Crosbie's home on Hanover Quay, were to be

What the Custom House Docks site was meant to turn out like. An aerial view of a model of the winning scheme from 1987, designed by US architects Benjamin Thompson & Associates, which promised an 'exciting people place' around the IFSC.

Irish Times

retained under the Grand Canal Docks master plan, even where they stood in the way of developing the campshires as dockside amenities. But while Peter Coyne stressed the critical importance of Dublin Corporation taking early ownership of the master plan, there were mutterings in the higher echelons of the Civic Offices that the DDDA was becoming somewhat superfluous. Its *raison d'être* resided in its powers to make a Section 25 planning scheme for any part of the 1,300-acre Docklands area, thereby triggering a package of tax incentives, subject, of course, to Government approval. Some senior Corporation officials wondered aloud why they weren't getting a crack at it, using the 1999 Planning Bill's provisions for the designation of 'strategic development zones' and their own powers to draw up Integrated Area Plans (IAPs), but the City Manager insisted that he was quite happy to let the DDDA get on with it.

Though the Corporation had long been urged by An Taisce, among others, to draft detailed action plans for run-down areas of the city, it was not until 1996 that its first IAP was unveiled, covering a land area of some 270 acres stretching westwards from O'Connell Street to Collins Barracks. Known as HARP (Historic Area Rejuvenation Project), it divided the area into four zones – the established retail district of Henry Street / Mary Street, the Markets area, Smithfield, and a new 'museum quarter' centred on the National Museum's decorative arts and folklife collections in Collins Barracks – and put forward proposals to upgrade them. Smithfield, however, saw most of the action. This long-neglected civic space, with dimensions similar to the Piazza Navona in Rome, had suddenly grabbed the attention of developers, led by Terry Devey of Heritage Properties, who purchased the former Jameson Distillery from Hugh O'Regan, the pub transformation wizard with a string of trendy bars to his credit, including Thomas Read's, the Bailey and Pravda. O'Regan, who netted at least £1 million on the deal, had bought the 2.2-acre distillery site from Duffy's scrap dealers, who in turn purchased it from the State in 1991 for only £560,000. Devey subsequently developed the property as Smithfield Village, injecting some 220 apartments into the area as well as a new Irish Whiskey Visitor Centre, Chief O'Neill's hotel and an Irish traditional music museum, all within a geometric envelope designed by A+D Wejchert. Overall winner of the 1999 Guinness Living Dublin Awards, its centrepiece is the distillery's tall chimney stack, now transformed into an attractive public amenity with glazed pod on top offering panoramic views of the city. Seamus Brennan TD was so impressed by the pod that he promised funding of £250,000 from the National Millennium Committee, though the money never materialised.

This substitute for Nelson Pillar, albeit some distance to the west, rather undermined the argument for a rival 'landmark' on the opposite side of Smithfield, where Fusano Properties had paid £8 million for Duffy's scrapyard and the adjoining Linders car showrooms. In terms of price per acre, this worked out at more than fifteen times the figure paid for the distillery site just seven years earlier. The company, a consortium involving Joe Linders and two property developers, Paddy Kelly and John Flynn, jolted the property world in August 1999 by unveiling plans for a £100 million mixed development of apartments, offices, shops and cultural facilities, with a slender 23-storey residential tower as its focal point. Designed by Blackrock-based architects Horan Keogan Ryan, Fusano's daring tower would dwarf the renovated Jameson chimney, offering residents of the very spacious flats on its upper floors an even more stunning 360-degree panorama of Dublin. It would be clad in glass, stone and terracotta panelling similar to some of the new buildings on Potsdamer Platz in Berlin, and was intended by the architects to be a modern interpretation of the campanile so characteristic of Italian urban squares, such as the main piazza in Sienna. Even without this tower, the Fusano scheme was substantially taller than Smithfield Village, with a central spine up to nine storeys high, though this was not meant to be visible from the square. It also required the demolition and replacement of Brú na bhFiann on Queen Street, which had been built less than ten years earlier for retired members of the Defence Forces. Though anxious to encourage development in Smithfield, with area manager Jim Keogan plugging for it daily, the Corporation played it by the book and exercised its discretion to seek an EIS before making its decision on Fusano's planning application.

Meanwhile, the rectangular ground plane of Smithfield itself was remade to a competition-winning design by McGarry Ní Éanaigh, serious Drogheda-based architects who had been involved in Group 91, the influential consortium of eight practices responsible for the Temple Bar Architectural Framework Plan. Their scheme, which was seen as a central element of the overall HARP plan, included the erection of twelve sensational gas brazier 'beacons', each 26 metres (86 ft) high, like giant galvanised flamingos preparing to launch themselves into flight. Gone were the days when two- and three-storey Corporation houses represented the apex of civic achievement in the area. In 1986, when there was nothing happening, the Office of Public Works made an act of faith in the future by commissioning a new Juvenile Court on the east side of Smithfield. It was designed by John Tuomey, then an OPW architect (who later established O'Donnell & Tuomey, the multiple award-winning practice which also went on to join Group 91). Much later, the OPW bought a site nearby to rehouse the Land Registry, and Seán Benton, the commissioner responsible for State property, was delighted to receive an enthusiastic response from the new Director of Public Prosecutions, James Hamilton, to a suggestion that he might consider locating his much-enlarged office in Smithfield rather than in Dublin 2. It made a lot of sense. Lured by urban-renewal tax incentives, barristers had already extended the legal quarter around the Four Courts by providing themselves with purpose-built offices on both sides of St Michan's Church, backing onto Bow Street. With the Tallaght Luas line planned to run right through it, and hundreds of new apartments already built in the vicinity, Smithfield was at last emerging from the decades of decay when all it was good for was a rather dubious monthly horse fair held in the middle of a wasteland.

Increasingly, prospective developers eschewed the idea of erecting modest buildings on individual sites, and concentrated instead on the assembly of large blocks of property, often at enormous cost. Some of them followed the example of Cosgraves and Treasury Holdings in talking to big-name international architects who were perceived to have the expertise to realise massive schemes. Even Trinity College became embroiled in one such venture after it had been hatched by two of Dublin's movers and shakers – CIÉ's Jim Gahan and developer Bernard McNamara. What they came up with in mid-1999 was a mega-project for Pearse Station and adjoining properties owned by Trinity. Earlier plans to reinstate the corner of Westland Row with a building by Robinson Keefe and Devane, and to locate a long-delayed college sports centre, designed by Henry J Lyons & Partners, for the cleared site formerly owned by An Post, were peremptorily dropped, and three stellar names – Norman Foster, Richard Meier and IM Pei – were requested to provide concept designs in a frenetic limited competition. Harry Cobb, long-time partner of the Chinese-American architect, whose most celebrated scheme was the Grand Louvre in Paris, recalls that they were given just ten days to gather their thoughts together. He himself had not been to Dublin for thirty years, and spent two days here trying to get a sense of the site and its place in the city. Pei Cobb Freed & Partners, who won the contest, proposed a truncated glazed cone for the northwest corner of Westland Row, a huge high-rise hotel on the corner of Pearse Street and Erne Street, on a cleared site formerly owned by An Post, and more than a million square feet of high-tech offices above and beside the railway station. It even envisaged the demolition of Murray O'Laoire's Goldsmith Hall, built just five years earlier, and the glazed pedestrian bridge connecting it to the college. In return, Trinity was to get an additional two hundred student residential units, and anything else it wanted. But if the triumvirate of interests involved in this audacious scheme thought they they could get it through the planning process because it carried IM Pei's signature, they were wrong. An Bord Pleanála's decision on George's Quay and the struggle for Spencer Dock gave everyone pause – including the city's planners. Trinity's Director of Buildings, Tim Cooper, wisely put the high-rise plans on hold, pending the outcome of the skyline study, and sought permission for the less contentious elements on the north-west corner of Westland Row, including a vast underground sports complex designed by HJL and topped by Harry Cobb's glazed cone.

Few would agree with Martin Pawley's verdict that the Corporation's 'constructive dismissal' of Kevin Roche's plans for Spencer Dock suggested that Dublin had 'turned its back on a native son and a chance for prosperity', as he put it in the *Architects Journal*, arguing that the row also illustrated the 'great planning dichotomy between art history and economics'. On one side, the art-

Few places in Dublin have been so transformed in recent years as Smithfield, with its sensational lighting masts and an observation pod crowning the chimney of the old Jameson Distillery. In March 2000. the new-look Smithfield was the venue for U2 – as well as the Burmese opposition leader, Aung San Suu Kyi – to be conferred with the Freedom of the City.

Matt Kavanagh / *Irish Times*

Dave Meehan / courtesy of Dublin Corporation

historical view measured the value of a city 'according to its ability to provide vistas and skylines that delight the eye, along with streets of a pleasing homogeneity interspersed with public spaces and buildings that are said to be masterpieces'. On the other side, under the economic value system, 'streets and buildings are the circuit boards of the economy, so none of this is worth a light if the buildings are empty and the streets full of people selling the *Big Issue*.' This theme was taken up by Pawley's clients in a full-page newspaper advertisement on 22nd December 1999 – the first in a series – featuring a bleak aerial shot of the southern portion of the Spencer Dock site. In big capital letters, it declaimed: 'Look at this picture: Can you see the canal walk, the conference centre, the museum, the street theatre, the restaurants or even one of the 500,000 trees?' Though the site was currently an expanse of derelict dockland, over the next seven years it would be transformed by 'the most far-reaching and exciting urban regeneration project undertaken in Ireland since the redevelopment of Temple Bar', the developers said. It would become 'the heart of Irish financial and business life ... a thriving and vibrant community ... an entirely new Dublin neighbourhood for all of us to take pleasure and pride in'. That very day, after months of negotiations, the European Commission finally approved a deal with the Irish authorities under which rent and rates reliefs in the IFSC – seen in Brussels as 'operational aid' inimical to free competition – would be phased out over four years for those already in receipt of them. This was another body blow to the Spencer Dock project, because the developers' calculations presumed that the same package of incentives would be available to their prospective tenants. A spokesman conceded that the outcome left them facing a significant financial problem, especially as the Department of Tourism had just decided to seek the withdrawal and reallocation of the promised £26 million in EU aid. Though it pledged that this would be replaced with a straight Exchequer grant, the sum amounted to less than one-quarter of the inflated cost of an oversized project, and with serious doubt over the availability of capital allowances, the sums no longer stacked up. Unless the Government was prepared to put in 'some other sort of subvention', the developers warned that it would not be possible to finance the NCC. Whatever An Bord Pleanála's decision, and barring some miracle, it seemed that their vaulting ambitions were not going to be realised.

The tide was turning against Richard Barrett and Johnny Ronan. A wellspring of resentment had built up against them, particularly among fellow developers, over Treasury's apparent arrogance and nakedly monopolistic tendencies. This surfaced in Parnell Street, where the company had acquired a triangular site on Moore Lane and an even smaller site on Moore Street. which could be used as bargaining chips to gain slices of the action in two major developments being planned in the area – a hotel and retail scheme for the long-derelict site at the corner of Moore Street and Parnell Street, and a shopping mall and cinema complex on the former Carlton site and adjoining properties in O'Connell Street. Their strategy was to put the other owners under pressure to sell out to Treasury or, at

Paul Clinton, project manager of the Carlton Group (left), with Richard Quirke, the group's chairman, and Michael Ryder, chairman of the Dublin City Centre Business Association, with the plans for O'Connell Street.

The famous minutes of a fateful meeting between representatives of the Carlton Group and Treasury Holdings at the United Services Club in September 1997.

CONFIDENTIAL MINUTES

Meeting in H U S Club, Stephen's Green
Saturday 20th September 1997

Re: Millennium Masterplan

Present -   D. Quirke : Carlton.   J Ronan   Treasury
            P. Clinton : Carlton.   R Barrett Treasury

Treasury requested the meeting so a co-ordinated plan could be produced for the authorities and also to propose a joint venture which would also avoid unnecessary counterbidding. Carlton obviously have established property in the area and enquired what property Treasury could put into a joint venture

Apart from Treasury concluding negotiations on a share of the Ilac, they also own a small part of the Parnell Street site which has a strategic nuisance value. They have no other ownership's but are in discussions with the Parnell hotel site, the Fingal offices and Hanlons of Moore Street. (Carlton noted that they have a commitment on the Fingal block so it was not freely available to anyone else.) Treasury were aware that Carlton were also in negotiations on Hanlons

Treasury explained that there was an urgency as they along with Irish Life are meeting the City Manager the week after next. Treasury and Irish Life in partnership have jointly commissioned plans for the entire four acre development

Treasury are confident that there will be a substantial profit, well in excess of 50 million pounds for the right designated scheme once it is agreed with the Dept' of Finance that it is an Exchequer neutral scheme. Treasury also consider it is ill-advised to include the Ilac Centre in the Dept' of Finance discussions as it would definitely jeopardise our four acre designation. Treasury also consider multi-storey parking of 1000 to 2000 cars is crucial for the success of the scheme as it hijacks the cars as they come around from O'Connell street before they get to the Ilac carpark

Carlton explained that if they did not buy the Parnell site or the Fingal building themselves Carlton were prepared to enter a pro-rata joint venture with the present owners. This has already been discussed with the Fingal owner, who may well any way. The alternative of the pro-rata joint venture has not yet been mentioned to the Parnell site owner, as it was premature due to his difficulties

Carlton concluded that they were prepared to enter a joint venture with Treasury, if Treasury acquired and contributed ONLY either the Parnell site or the Fingal building (or both) to the masterplan (or a share of the Ilac). Co-ordinated strategies have to be agreed on these properties as Carlton may be in a better position to front the joint venture with a view to purchasing both, using Treasury funds whichever company is finally used Treasury are presently torturing the current Parnell hotel site owner and Treasury also recently injuncted the purchase by the present Fingal owner and brought it to court

...h Life act as mediator and holder of the Parnell
...venture is formally binding. Treasury thought that
...gree that Irish Life are informed of the principles

...her property owner in the area without Carlton
...discussions are terminated.
...anteous looking people with suits, shirts, ties
...Moore Street
...ed immediately preferably in the next few
...al sites, which are necessary for the joint

...l. Treasury are not to even tell their
...ent anyway in the project, if the joint
...ill nominate the Design Team and
...h Carlton will have a veto

Treasury Holdings
24/9/97

MILLENNIUM MALL PROJECT
O'CONNELL STREET, DUBLIN 1.

least, to enter joint venture deals with the company. After all, Barrett and Ronan reasoned, they were big players in Dublin's property development sector whereas the others involved had no real track records. The Carlton group had been left in a quandary after its plans to locate the National Conference Centre on the disused cinema site came to nought, while the prospective Parnell Street hotel developer, Garret Kelleher, was also something of an *ingénu*. Only Treasury Holdings, as Barrett and Ronan saw it, had the vision to see the bigger picture – and the muscle to make it a reality. Little did they expect that they would paint themselves into the black corner, with their 'small fry' opponents scoring an unqualified public relations victory at Treasury's expense.

The initial approach was made by planning consultant Frank L Benson, who telephoned the Carlton group's chairman, Richard Quirke, in July 1997 suggesting that it might be beneficial if Quirke met his clients, Treasury Holdings. Subsequently, the group's project manager, Paul Clinton, an architect who had been the right-hand man of cigar-chomping developer Finbarr Holland, received a number of phone calls from Johnny Ronan proposing lunch 'so that we could get to know each other better and to enable us to chat about a few ideas that might interest us'. Carlton eventually agreed to have lunch, not least because its principals were anxious to avoid making powerful enemies, if at all possible, as Clinton puts it. Confidential minutes of this meeting at the United Services Club in September 1997 noted that Treasury's site in Moore Lane had 'a strategic nuisance value', and said the company was 'presently [sic] torturing the current Parnell [Street] hotel site owner'. Garret Kelleher had recently returned to Dublin from Chicago, where he made a fortune on a number of loft-style apartment schemes, and this was his first major Dublin venture, though he had earlier made a cool £1 million on a quick turn involving the Belgo building in Temple Bar. He is still gobsmacked by what happened. At his first meeting with Barrett and Ronan in May 1997, after he had assembled the Parnell Street site with the help

Property developer Garret Kelleher, who is still gobsmacked by the tactics employed by Keelgrove to obstruct his hotel and retail development in Parnell Street.

opposite

The shopping centre and multiplex planned for the Carlton cinema site and adjoining properties in O'Connell Street that was held up by objections, appeals and a threatened judicial review by Keelgrove Ltd, a Treasury Holdings vehicle.

Marc O'Sullivan, Collins / courtesy of the *Irish Times*

of estate agents McNally Handy, he maintains that Barrett threatened to run him out of town – an allegation which the Treasury director denies. Kelleher was later offered, and admits he was minded at one stage to accept a take-out deal, much to the relief of Anglo-Irish Bank, which had lent him funds for his buying spree.

Treasury's game plan was to ease Kelleher out and consolidate control over a four-acre site, in partnership with the Carlton group, confidently expecting that the entire site would be designated for urban renewal tax incentives and that its redevelopment would yield a profit 'well in excess of £50 million'. The joint venture proposed by Treasury was to be organised in a 'most tax-efficient manner', with the details of how this would work being revealed after the deal was agreed. In the meantime, acquisition of further properties in the area was to continue with the utmost discretion, and there were to be 'no consultants or business-looking people with suits, shirts, ties and mobile phones floating around Moore Street', according to the minutes, which were composed by Clinton and signed by Barrett. With the active collaboration of Irish Life, which had agreed to act as a mediator, Barrett and Ronan commissioned Andrej Wejchert, whose office had prepared a massive renovation scheme for Irish Life's ILAC centre, to design a complex that would have been up to twelve-storeys high, with four lev-

Perspective of Treasury Holdings' plan for the Carlton site on O'Connell Street, designed by A+D Wejchert Architects.

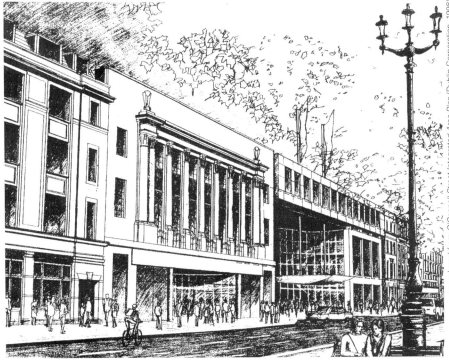

reproduced from *O'Connell Street Integrated Area Plan* (Dublin Corporation, 1998)

els of basement parking for almost 2,300 cars. Trading on Treasury's already formidable reputation, their aim was to convince senior Corporation officials that they were the boys who could deliver the Millennium Mall, which was seen in the Civic Offices as a vital element of the O'Connell Street Integrated Area Plan. And they clearly succeeded, because the plan itself, published in February 1998, included an image of Wejchert's bold scheme. Furthermore, although the Corporation had been initially enthusiastic about Kelleher's project, he maintains that he found it impossible to contact any senior official in the weeks before he lodged his planning application for a hotel and retail scheme designed by Ambrose Kelly's Project Architects. He was also astonished to discover that Treasury had made an elaborate presentation of its plans for the two sites in October 1997, while his own application was still 'live'. It was only after the proposed joint venture with Carlton collapsed in considerable acrimony, when Treasury discovered that its putative partners had gone 'freelance' to acquire one of the target properties, that it became clear the company hadn't much of a leg to stand on. Kelleher, who had invested at least £5 million in acquiring more than thirty property interests on the Parnell Street site, certainly felt 'tortured' when Keelgrove Developments Ltd, a Treasury vehicle, engaged Frank L Benson & Partners to object to and appeal against his plans. After An Bord Pleanála upheld the Corporation's decision to grant permission, Keelgrove, as the nominal owner of Treasury's Moore Lane site, sought a High Court judicial review. And when this action was struck out because it was filed too late, its lawyers BCM Hanby Wallace had the matter referred to the Supreme Court on a point of law revolving around the issue of when a decision is actually made. Richard Barrett also initiated enforcement proceedings under Section 27 of the 1976 Planning Act against Kelleher's company, Shelbourne Developments Ltd, challenging the legality of a surface car park it was operating on the derelict Parnell Street site without planning permission. More than three years after plunging himself into it, Kelleher had seen not a brick laid on a brick, largely because of Keelgrove's tactics. (Though wounded by this setback, the youthful-looking developer managed to shrug it off, and in April 2000 he shelled out £5.3 million for an Edwardian home in Herbert Park. The price, not surprisingly, was the talk of Dublin 4.)

Keelgrove took a similar route in pursuing its opposition to the Carlton group's Millennium Mall project, with Barrett telling Kelleher in June 1998 that he would 'tie them up in such legal knots that they would never be able to do anything with the site'. As in his own case, the company was determined to get even with its opponents for 'welshing' on what it insisted were enforceable joint venture deals. Again, Benson was engaged to object to and appeal against Clinton's proposal for a Milan-style galleria linking O'Connell Street with the ILAC centre, topped by a fifteen-screen multiplex. The plan was certainly ambitious, incorporating the former Carlton Cinema as well as the adjoining derelict site once owned by hotelier Noel O'Callaghan; Dr Quirkey's Good Time Emporium, owned by Richard Quirke; Carrolls of Dublin, one of a chain of trinket shops in the city centre owned by Colm Carroll; and the Fingal County Council office block, owned by another hotelier, Jim McGettigan, who had thrown in his lot with the development consortium. The fact that McGettigan had managed to purchase this crucial piece of real estate in 1996 for £4.55 million was a matter of deep regret to Johnny Ronan. He had sought to buy the building when it was offered for sale by tender by the Irish Airline Pilots Pension Fund and, according to his own affidavit, he was expecting 'a steer ... either directly or by means of hints' from the pension fund's agents, Jones Lang Wooton, on the amount of money which Treasury would need to offer if it wished to secure the property. When this 'steer' did not materialise and Ronan's late bid of £4.585 million was not accepted, Treasury lodged a *lis pendens* on the property and sued both the pension fund and JLW for breach of contract. It lost this High Court action, the *lis pendens* was lifted, and McGettigan kept the office block. After Benson's pleadings failed to deter either the Corporation or An Bord Pleanála from granting permission for the £175 million Carlton project in August 1999, Keelgrove took its case to the High Court for judicial review, ironically citing the mall's height and 500-space car park as 'excessive'. This action, perhaps unwittingly, opened the floodgates. In a lengthy affidavit, running to eighty-six numbered paragraphs and backed up by numerous appendices, Paul Clinton detailed the history of Carlton's dealings with Treasury Holdings... and it did not make pleasant reading. Barrett and Ronan knew they were in trouble. The Corporation wanted them out of O'Connell Street, and so did Bertie Ahern, who made it plain that he regarded them an obstacle to its long-postponed rejuvenation. In late 1999, they asked Noel Smyth, canny chairman of Dunloe Ewart plc, if he would be prepared to take them out by acquiring Keelgrove and he agreed, on the clear understanding that, once in control, the legal proceedings against both Garret Kelleher and the Carlton group would be dropped – as indeed they were. Senior Corporation officials – who had twice failed to make compulsory purchase orders for Treasury's properties in the area – warmly welcomed Smyth's involvement as well as the interest of Morrison Developments, a Scottish company, in Kelleher's site. Now there would be some chance of securing both schemes, after Barrett and Ronan were off the pitch. But the pair remain convinced that they could have delivered a much better development on the four-acre site had the proposed joint venture deals not come unstuck, and that the Corporation had invidiously singled them out as the only culprits.

Treasury found itself in hot water on other fronts, too. It transpired that the company was juggling thirty-eight separate litigations, many of them involving other developers, and this revelation merely served to underline the growing unease about its modus operandi. 'You were nobody in town unless Treasury was suing you', one of their targets commented later. In May 1998, two months after vanquishing Lancefort in the High Court, Barrett wrote to Paul Clinton, saying: 'Certain opponents of ours have underestimated our ability to cause legal chaos to their detriment.' But that was before their relations had soured over the proposed joint venture. In January 1999, after Clinton disclosed the minutes of the United Services Club meeting at a Bord Pleanála oral hearing on Keelgrove's appeal against Kelleher's plans for Parnell Street, Barrett and Ronan instituted libel proceedings seeking £20 million in damages. The *Sunday Business Post* quoted Barrett as saying of Clinton, 'I will sue the pants off him.' He also threatened to go all the way to the Supreme Court to challenge the constitutionality of the Special Amenity Area Order designed to protect Howth because it would devalue a large tract of land on the East Mountain, purchased by Allenspark Ltd – one of a bewildering array of Treasury-related companies – from Christopher Gaisford St Lawrence. Treasury suffered another serious reversal when An Bord Pleanála overruled Dun Laoghaire-Rathdown County Council and refused permission for an overarching plan by Andrej Wejchert to double the size of Stillorgan shopping centre, reversing the planning inspector's positive recommendation. Wejchert resigned the commission almost immediately, and his clients reverted to a more site-sensitive scheme by Gilroy McMahon, who had been runners-up in an architectural competition for the £50 million project.

But worse was to come. Treasury had diversified into alternative energy, largely because of the lucrative tax incentives available, and using a number of front companies, managed to secure more than half of the wind power franchises distributed in the last round under the Alternative Energy Requirement scheme. This brought Barrett and Ronan to the brink of an even bigger coup. They had managed to persuade Mary O'Rourke to amend the 1999 Electricity Regulation Bill so that privately run CHP (combined heat and power) plants would be classified under the 'alternative or renewable' energy heading, with full access to the electricity market in competition with the ESB. They had decided to build their own CHP plant at Spencer Dock after being informed by the ESB that it would not be in a position to provide an electricity sub-station to serve the north docks area in time to meet the deadline for drawing down the promised EU grant for the National Conference Centre. The ESB also saw the amendment as inimical to its own goal of curtailing the effects of liberalising the electricity market by limiting access to as few competitors as possible. A furious round of lobbying ensued, during the course of which the State company's secretary, Larry Donald, described Treasury's claim that it was unable, or unwilling, to supply power for the NCC as 'palpably false, misleading and ... clearly designed to promote another agenda'. Richard Barrett responded by characterising the ESB as 'a clubby band of corporate thugs' in a private letter to Labour Party leader Ruairí Quinn, subsequently read into the Dáil record by Emmet Stagg, the party's spokesman on public enterprise. Senior ESB officials so enjoyed this taunt that they had 'Corporate Thug' tee-shirts printed, but O'Rourke took such grave exception to it that she withdrew the amendment, much to the ESB's delight and Barrett's and Ronan's chagrin. In her view, the row suggested that 'everyone is out of step but our Johnny'. According to one acute observer: 'The Treasury boys were showing all the signs of being invincible and paranoid at the same time, which is always a volatile combination.' Even they would concede that the 'corporate thugs' taunt had been injudicious and deeply counter-productive, especially with Spencer Dock still unresolved.

Underlining the scale and complexity of SDDC's plan for Spencer Dock, An Bord Pleanála appointed three inspectors with expertise in architecture, planning and transport to deal with the eight appeals, including one from the developers seeking to have the full quantum of six million square feet reinstated. Before the oral hearing opened in the Gresham Hotel ballroom on 21st February 2000, it seemed almost inconceivable that they would get anything more from the appeals board than they had extracted from Dublin Corporation – and, in all probability, they would get even less. After more than three weeks of argument, it appeared that they would be lucky to get anything at all. Even as the inquiry was under way, SDDC's ambitions suffered two potentially killer blows. Firstly, the Government decided – on the recommendation of the Department of Finance – that there would be no tax incentives at all for further developments in the Docklands area, including Spencer Dock. Then, just ten days into the hearing, Bertie Ahern described the scheme as 'a monstrosity', in what was said to be an 'unguarded' remark to his driver which just happened to be captured by an in-car RTÉ camera and microphone. Although he wrote to An Bord Pleanála stressing that he had been speaking in a personal capacity, and urging that no account should be taken of it, nobody who knew Bertie Ahern thought this off-hand remark – an unprecedented intervention by a serving Taoiseach during a live planning appeal – was anything of the sort. Not only was he sending a clear message to his Docklands constituents that he was on their side, he also seemed to be indicating to everyone involved that there was no longer any high-level support for the Spencer Dock project. Whatever political capital the Treasury boys once had, they had squandered in O'Connell Street – right opposite the Gresham – and in their do-or-die battles with the DDDA and the ESB. Richard Barrett, Johnny Ronan and Harry Crosbie were on their own. If they sank in Spencer Dock, it was clear that no lifebelts would be thrown out to save them.

Their chances were also undermined, perhaps fatally, by Dermot Desmond. His intervention transformed David v Goliath into Goliath v Goliath, with David cheering from the sidelines. On one of the 140 days per year that he is entitled as a tax exile to be in Ireland, he chose to spend part of it in the Gresham throwing everything bar the kitchen sink at the massive development proposed for Spencer Dock, and then left his *chef de cabinet*, Roger Conan, and a team of professional advisers to prosecute his case. Deeply tanned from his current preoccupation with redeveloping the exclusive Sandy Lane resort in Barbados, and immaculately turned out, as usual, Desmond read a trenchant statement, fielded some barbed questions, and then departed from the room, dematerialising like hypermobile global capital. You could almost hear the whoosh of money as he swept out, casting a sideways glance at SDDC's table where there was no sign of Richard Barrett, Johnny Ronan or Harry Crosbie.

They were not going to dignify the appearance of their chief opponent by turning up to hear him. What they missed was quite a performance, an event that became the talk of the town. The financier argued that the 'overwhelming bulk and density' of the development would blight the Docklands area 'to the detriment of Dublin and its people'. And while he was not opposed to high buildings as such, he didn't want to see a 'concrete jungle' or 'a bit of Manhattan' – which bit he couldn't say – imposed on Spencer Dock. Asked at one stage by the presiding inspector, Des Johnson, if he had any views on the architectural quality of the NCC, he said its cylindrical atrium was so large that Liberty Hall would fit inside it, 'and the Central Bank, too'. The developers' team, led with gritty determination by planning consultant Tom Phillips, hit back by unveiling a huge montage of his 'Gorillas in the Mist' project which showed that it

Dermot Desmond leaving the Gresham Hotel after giving evidence at the Spencer Dock oral hearing.

would have risen even higher than most of the buildings they were planning. The Kaiser was not even slightly fazed. Anticipating this low blow, one of his assistants plucked out a short, surreal promotional video of the ill-fated scheme and showed it to the hearing. As for what had prompted him to make the appeal, Desmond said, 'we've all got a little bit of ownership of Dublin', which, in his case, includes a house in Ailesbury Road and a penthouse flat in the Custom House Docks. It was also part of his case that if planning permission was granted for 2.7 million square feet of office space at Spencer Dock, the developers would acquire a ten-year 'put option' on the commercial property market in central Dublin by mopping up most of the likely demand. He might also have mentioned that they were taking an each-way bet on the Edge City through the Clyde Road Partnership's plan for 1.71 million square feet of offices on the Legionaries of Christ land in Leopardstown.

Architecture critic Martin Pawley, who joked privately that he was 'supping with the devil' by giving evidence on SDDC's behalf, talked at length about the global forces driving developments such as Spencer Dock, about buildings as 'instruments of commerce' and about 'the spirit of free enterprise which sees history as something that has to be *made*, rather than something that has to be *kept*'. In his view, Spencer Dock would 'constitute an aesthetic as well as an economic breakthrough for a city for too long held back by its own past' and it should be seen as 'a rite of passage ... a step towards the world city that the Dublin of the future must become'. As for the 'chorus of complaint' that the proposed buildings were too tall, too bland, too overpowering or simply too international in style, he told An Bord Pleanála's inquiry that this was inevitable because of the requirements of global capital. They were the type of buildings to be found everywhere these days. But if this 'anywhere architecture' was being driven by an economic imperative, Cllr Ciarán Cuffe should have been allowed to expand on his attempt to counter it by suggesting that cities such as Dublin needed to assert their own identity in negotiating with global capital. Instead, he found himself cut short by Des Johnson, in what was the only lapse in the presiding inspector's otherwise exemplary conduct of the inquiry.

By the time Kevin Roche flew in from the US to present – and defend – his master plan for Spencer Dock, it seemed as if the whole project was going down in flames. For one-and-a-half hours, the 77-year-old architect held an extra large audience spellbound as he took them through the evolution of the scheme, explaining its elements in detail, and then capped it all by showing slides of his firm's extraordinary achievements in North America, Asia and Europe. Here was a living legend setting out his stall with a 'magisterial' presentation, as eco-architect Paul Leech termed it, which deservedly won a round of applause. Nearly everyone with questions to ask over the next three-and-a-half hours treated this architect-hero with due deference. Karl Kent, one of the inspectors, thanked him for his 'excellent presentation', saying it had been 'terrific'. Roche also struck a chord with many in the audience when he decried the destruction of much of Georgian Dublin, saying he would have 'no problem' reducing the height of his scheme if its impact on the vista down Fitzwilliam Street was regarded as catastrophic. 'I am not a height freak', he declared. And though he showed signs of tiredness as the day wore on, this was virtuoso stuff from a vintage architect, and it left his clients rubbing their hands with glee. But nobody apart from SDDC, its consultants and *per diem* supporters, agreed with Roche's vision – not the local residents, nor the conservation bodies, nor the principal public authorities – Dublin Corporation and, more forcefully, the DDDA. The real question was: How could such a nice man have designed such a terrible scheme? In his *Irish Times* column the following day, Fintan O'Toole wrote: 'What really denigrates the well-merited reputation of Kevin Roche is the way the Spencer Dock scheme turns his genius into a bland, placeless, identikit mediocrity.' If he was the architectural equivalent of James Joyce, as a great modern Irish artist in exile, what he had served up in Dublin was 'a John Grisham thriller that just happens to be set on the Liffey'.

Colourful metaphors abounded. Fr John Wall of St Laurence O'Toole's Church, whose spire would be dwarfed by the scheme, said it would be like 'a

A computer-generated montage of the huge glazed 'ecosphere' proposed by Dermot Desmond for the Custom House Docks site shown in juxtaposition with the proposed National Conference Centre at Spencer Dock. The aim was to demonstrate that Desmond aimed even higher.

massive mountain plonked in the middle of the parish', with local residents facing the grim prospect of 'living at the foot of the Grand Canyon or the Cliffs of Moher with windows'. Another critic suggested that Spencer Dock would 'make Liberty Hall took like a telephone kiosk', an apparently outlandish claim that contained a real grain of truth. Arguments about the plot ratio notwithstanding, the sheer scale of what SDDC had in mind was dramatically illustrated for all to see on a 1:1,000 scale model of the entire swathe of Dublin from Liberty Hall to the Point Depot, extending southwards to Merrion Square and northwards to Mountjoy. This model, showing every building in block form, had been requested by the appeals board to assess the huge scheme for Spencer Dock in the context of Dublin's generally low-rise skyline. What it did was to answer the fundamental question: 'How big it is, or how big is it in relation to everything else?' as Dublin's most famous architect, Sam Stephenson, once wrote about Kevin Roche's work. The model was supplemented by a strip elevation of the north quays from Butt Bridge to the East Link, which also illustrated the extraordinary bulk and scale of what was being proposed for the most pivotal site in Docklands. Yet, at least 50,000 square metres of it had been grossed up thanks to the Minister for Arts and Heritage, Síle de Valera, agreeing to the inclusion of the Royal Canal water-body within the developers' red line. And though the Waterways Division of Dúchas, the Heritage Service, was pleased with their pledge to restore the final stretch of the canal, it still had 'grave reservations' about aspects of the scheme, including the overshadowing of Spencer Dock by the NCC's largely blank gable wall, 43 metres high. The fact that Bord Fáilte, as commissioning agency for the conference centre, declined to give evidence suggested that it was not prepared to defend a building more than twice the size of what its brief had specified. Des Johnson, the presiding inspector, described this as 'unfortunate and unhelpful'. It also emerged that Dublin Corporation's ceiling of 427,350 square metres (4.6 million sq ft) had been based less on qualitative criteria backed up by a realistic assessment of what the site could carry, than on 'giving more value' to the developers, as its architectural adviser, Michael Lowe, disarmingly conceded. This made Brian Hogan's eloquent defence of the scheme all the more puzzling, given his role as an objector to SOM's plan for George's Quay and his long-held view that Dublin should develop as a series of urban villages or neighbourhoods. Spencer Dock and the projects it would spawn in Docklands could ultimately produce 'the grand enclosure that Anna Livia deserves' on the last leg of her journey to the open sea, he argued. In his view, seeking to impose a traditional street pattern on Kevin Roche's master plan would be 'another kind of unworkable pastiche papering over the fear of the new'. Sam Stephenson, whose name will forever be associated with the ESB in Fitzwilliam Street, the Central Bank, and the first phase of the Civic Offices, also rowed in behind Spencer Dock. In an unscheduled appearance at the inquiry, he described Roche as 'a master of development and design'. Paraphrasing WB Yeats, he said we would be disgracing ourselves yet again if we did not give him the opportunity to leave his mark on Dublin.

But there were too many imponderables about the scheme. For a start, most of the twenty-six buildings had not been designed, other than in outline, so there was a legal question mark over whether the developers had the right to seek full planning permission for it in those circumstances. In fairness, this was not

The Spencer Dock development would make Liberty Hall look like a telephone kiosk, according to one local resident. This strip elevation showing its scale in relation to the Custom House and Liberty Hall was adapted by Reid Associates, Dermot Desmond's planning consultants, from SDDC's environmental impact statement.

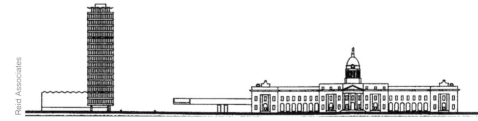

Reid Associates

entirely their fault. Because an EIS was required under the Planning Regulations, they had to make an application for full permission, but there wasn't enough time to flesh out the design because of the looming EU deadline. There was also the critically important strategic issue of the cross-river rail link southwards from Spencer Dock. In question here was whether CIÉ had any fallback position if the Government rejected the latest plan to run it underground to Westland Row, rather than Barrow Street, and then onwards to Heuston Station. Attempting to get a clear answer on this point from Ray Byrne, who appeared for CIÉ, was 'like trying to pick up mercury with a fork', according to the presiding inspector. At one stage, as the normally unflappable Byrne kept digging, project manager Dermod Dwyer was overheard telling him to 'sit down and shut up'. Relations between the partners sank so low that a heated argument later in the privacy of their suite at the Gresham almost came to blows. In fairness, Byrne was on a sticky wicket because of a seismic shift in transport thinking over the previous nine months, which left CIÉ running to catch up. In June 1999, the company told Dublin Corporation that it favoured an overground rail link between Spencer Dock and Barrow Street. Four months later, this had been supplanted by an underground link running in the same direction. And by the time An Bord Pleanála's inquiry got under way in February, CIÉ executives – if not their board – had come to the conclusion that the right route should run to Westland Row. As Ray Byrne noted, this was in line with a strategic review of suburban rail services by Ove Arup & Partners, as well as the latest thinking in the Dublin Transportation Office, which saw the Spencer Dock link as one the key elements of a future public transport network for the metropolitan area. Given the huge cost implications, it would have been presumptuous of him to second-guess a Government decision on the matter. What Byrne's uncomfortable cross-examination did indicate, however, was that the resolution of public transport issues revolving around Spencer Dock had taken second place to CIÉ's goal of maximising its real estate value.

One of the other questions both Johnson and Kent kept returning to throughout the inquiry was whether a developer-led scheme, driven by commer-

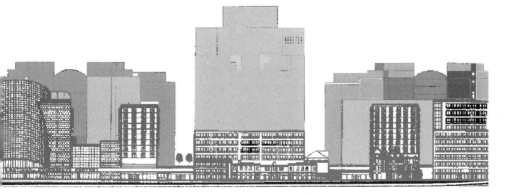

119

cial considerations, was the right way to go about planning the most important publicly owned site in Docklands. After all, the 'great leap forward' that the developers would have us take represents such a radical departure that it requires a municipal consensus, and this can only be achieved by preparing a publicly owned master plan for this mainly publicly owned site. The city skyline study commissioned by Dublin Corporation might well conclude that the Spencer Dock site could take a few high-rise buildings, even a tower or two that would be glimpsed from the Georgian Mile. But such an outcome would be very different to the great wall of tall bulky buildings proposed in Kevin Roche's master plan, about which the Corporation had so many reservations that the question the presiding inspector had on his mind was why it didn't simply refuse permission. The DDDA, ably represented at the inquiry by its planning director, Terry Durney, warned that if the present overblown scheme was approved by An Bord Pleanála, it would 'irrevocably and irredeemably prejudice the ability of the authority to achieve its policies and objectives in relation to the Docklands area as a whole'. It was, and is, that serious. If, on the other hand, the DDDA was to prepare a master plan for Spencer Dock, in consultation with the Corporation and the public in general, the cleanest way of preparing the ground for it would be a straightforward refusal by the appeals board. Thus returned to a blank canvas, it should then be possible to find a better location on the site for the National Conference Centre – addressing a public square rather that presenting a cliff-like gable to the Royal Canal – flanked by buildings with a scale more appropriate to Dublin. Meanwhile, the wider public got a chance to see Kevin Roche and his range of work over half a century in a remarkable one-hour TV documentary, broadcast by RTÉ a week after the oral hearing came to an end. The developers could hardly have hoped for a better presentation, as it bombarded viewers with stunning images of his architecture in an almost wholly uncritical fashion. Whether it would sway members of An Bord Pleanála to permit Roche to proceed with his bold plan for Spencer Dock was another question entirely.

By comparison with Spencer Dock and George's Quay, the millennium monument proposed for the site of Nelson Pillar in O'Connell Street would have a minimal environmental impact. Yet it became the focus of a much more intense controversy from the moment it was first unveiled at the Mansion House in November 1998. Designed by Ian Ritchie, a cockily self-confident London-based architect-engineer, the soaring stainless steel needle, twice the height of Liberty Hall, was chosen from 205 entries in an international competition to find an appropriate symbol of Dublin for the new millennium. His £3 million 'conical mast', tapering to a light at its pinnacle, would rise to a height of 120 metres (396

Ian Ritchie, the cockily self-confident London architect-engineer who designed the *Monument of Light*, otherwise known as 'The Spike'.

overleaf

The *Monument of Light*, a soaring stainless-steel needle twice the height of Liberty Hall, chosen from 205 entries to find an appropriate symbol of Dublin for the new millennium.

courtesy of Dublin Corporation

ft) from a base of just 3 metres (10 ft) and would be clearly visible from many parts of the city, dramatically defining the location of Ireland's main street. Light would be projected upwards from inside the hollow cone, spilling out through 12 metres of perforated stainless steel at the top and an apex made of optical glass. Former RIAI President Joan O'Connor, who chaired the competition jury, said it would be 'a wonderful wand ... a brave and uncompromising beacon' that reaffirmed the status of O'Connell Street. Ritchie himself described it as 'a pure symbol of optimism for the future', a modern interpretation of standing stones, saying he 'just knew' within twenty minutes of sketching it that he had a winning project 'designed for this site, for this city, for this moment in time'. Almost immediately, the Corporation received offers of up to £1 million to franchise images of this sensational structure.

The Lord Mayor, Senator Joe Doyle, who served on the competition jury, anticipated that it would in time become a 'familiar and well-loved' landmark, just like Anthony Gormley's *Angel of the North*, the remarkable winged metal figure standing above the A1 near Gateshead. Doyle's predecessor, John Stafford, who had initiated plans for the rejuvenation of O'Connell Street, was also very positive. 'It's extremely high, but I like the idea of it being tall. It could have been tall and gruesome, but it's not. It's tall and slim.' And Dick Gleeson, Deputy City Planning Officer, said it was 'absolutely the right thing' for Dublin, even though the competition brief had called for a monument that would 'relate to the quality and scale of O'Connell Street', as represented by its architecture and civic design. 'It's understated, yet magnificently radical and powerful at the same time. Really, it's a work of art which will reinvent the public domain.' Still, there was no shortage of begrudgers to lambaste the Corporation for its effrontery in backing the erection of something so high in the middle of O'Connell Street. Immediately on seeing a model of Ritchie's project, Cllr Eamonn O'Brien (Labour) said: 'It's a huge hypodermic needle, an eternal eyesore and symbol of

a drug city.' Dublin's legendary wits seemed to click into overdrive to devise derogatory nicknames, in rhyming doggerel, such as A Pinnacle for the Cynical, The Jab in the Slab, The Stiletto in the Ghetto, and others of that ilk, or, in shorthand, 'The Spike'. One beer company, cashing in on the public controversy, even produced a promotional postcard grossly exaggerating its bulk, with the slogan, 'Lucky we've got one ... A Good Sense of Heineken'.

Ritchie's needle, officially known as the *Monument of Light*, was bound to be controversial because it was so gobsmackingly tall, rising, indeed, three times the height of long-lost Nelson Pillar. But then, huge controversies had also swirled around the Eiffel Tower, the pyramid at the Louvre and London's Millennium Dome before they, too, won the admiration of the public. And we in Ireland have the added disadvantage that most of us seem unable to visualise what something will be like until it is actually built. Some opponents criticised the 'faceless' nature of the adjudication process, arguing that ordinary people should have had a role in it. But in the 1988 Pillar Project ideas competition, what the public voted for was a huge triumphal arch, perhaps not quite realising that it would have been twice the height of the GPO and bulky enough to sever O'Connell Street. Ian Ritchie's 'spike' had the elegance of simplicity, an elusive quality that is actually quite difficult to achieve. The best ideas are almost always simple, and there was a Yosser-like sense when the model was unveiled that 'I could do that'. The same was true of the pyramid form chosen by IM Pei for the Louvre – a project that Ritchie himself had worked on in partnership with Peter Rice, the late Dundalk-born structural engineer whose sheer brilliance had also made the Sydney Opera House stand up.

Where the millennium monument fell down was on the issue of public access. Dublin Corporation's brief was silent on this, even though one of the great advantages of Nelson Pillar was that anyone could pay sixpence at the entrance and climb its spiral staircase to enjoy an intimate panoramic view over the rooftops of O'Connell Street. But given that any contemporary monument providing public access would have to be accessible to all, including disabled people, this necessarily implied a much bulkier structure, incorporating both a staircase and a lift shaft. Nonetheless, Ian Ritchie's soaring spire would put O'Connell Street on the map because the beacon at its pinnacle, gently swaying in the wind, would be visible from such distant vantage points as Howth and Killiney. In this way, it addressed not only its immediate context, but also Dublin as a whole by redefining the city centre and people's perceptions of where that is, as well as providing a new icon. It is also intended to be the lynchpin for the renaissance of O'Connell Street, as envisaged in Dublin Corporation's £35 million integrated area plan, published in February 1998, because it would almost certainly inspire confidence in anyone planning to invest in the north inner city.

It was also avowedly contemporary, unlike many of the entries for the two-stage international competition which harkened back nostalgically to more familiar, even hackneyed forms. And because the competition was open to architects, landscape architects, urban designers, artists, sculptors and, indeed, anyone else who cared to enter, the standard was inevitably quite uneven. Indeed, it produced some wacky, weird and wonderful ideas, ranging from an enormous tattered Tricolour seemingly shot through by machine-gun fire, to a 'Love Elevator' featuring the romantic musings of Irish poets, plus lots of objects in the shape of obelisks, sails, rockets, spires or spirals. Interestingly, only one of the 205 entries had an overtly nationalist theme – a 'Liberty Fountain', with a wall fronted by the seven signatories of the 1916 Proclamation, all lined up waiting to be shot, the wounded James Connolly sitting in a chair. The sea change in the culture of Irish nationalism was mirrored by a paucity of monuments with a religious theme, with only a couple of giant Celtic crosses. Pagan imagery was much more popular, exemplified by several columns with a phoenix on top being born again in the legendary flames. There was also a bell tower in the shape of a bell, a huge slab inscribed in Ogham script, a hurdy-gurdy that might have escaped from Funderland, a 'writer's monument' as grim as any mausoleum, something that looked like a peat-fired power station, and even one strangely familiar icon which resembled a giant penis with a knot in it.

Much attention focused on the two runners-up in the final stage of the competition – Hunt McGarry Architects from London, with their monument to the information age, and Dublin-born Jonathan Bennett, whose proposal consisted of a memorial to the absence of Nelson. The adjudicators were concerned that a pair of out-sized electronic billboards at the base of Hunt McGarry's proposal would inevitably become commercial, thereby debasing the whole idea. There was also a fear that, because it was very much a monument to the electronic era, it could become dated very quickly. As for Bennett's scheme, Deputy City Planning Officer Dick Gleeson, who also served on the jury, felt that although the idea of hollowing out the core of a layered glass obelisk to reveal the profile of the old Pillar was 'quite hypnotic', it would be lost on younger people with no memory of Nelson's monument. In his view, nothing could match the 'pure abstract power' of Ian Ritchie's winning design, which was very much a 'young people's statement about the future', as City Architect Jim Barrett put it.

In January 1999, when all of the entries were on public exhibition in the Civic Offices, there was every expectation among senior Corporation officials that Ritchie's 'spike' would be erected in time for the new millennium. They had decided on a fast-track route to approve the project, using Part 10 of the 1994 Planning Regulations, under which the scheme would be exhibited for a month, submissions would be invited, and then the City Council would vote on it. They were so confident, indeed, that a slot had been provisionally booked in British Steel's production schedule for rolled stainless steel to ensure that the sections would arrive in Dublin in plenty of time to be assembled in place before the end of December 1999. Everything was going according to plan. A public notice was placed in the *Irish Times* inviting people to inspect the proposal and make written submissions, which would be taken into account by the City Council before it voted on the issue. A total of eighty-four such submissions were received, the overwhelming majority of them negative. Objectors argued that it would cost too much, that the money should be spent on social causes such as housing the homeless, that the monument itself was 'meaningless' or 'nihilistic', that it defied Feng Shui principles by creating 'negative vibes', that it should be erected somewhere else with broad open spaces such as the Phoenix Park, that a Nelson Pillar-style column should be built instead, with a statue of Robert Emmet, Padraig Pearse or Noel Browne on top, or, alternatively, that a free-standing statue of Christ the King should be erected on the site – or on Howth Head, in Rio de Janeiro style – to represent 'Ireland's Christian values'.

On 1st March 1999, after a lengthy debate – one of its most intelligent in living memory – the City Council decided to proceed with the project by an overwhelming majority of thirty-four votes to fourteen. Passionate views were expressed on both sides of the argument, but what swayed most councillors was the conviction of senior Corporation officials that the millennium spire would provide an appropriate focal point for the O'Connell Street Integrated Area Plan, which aimed to attract quality new uses into the street and to upgrade the whole public domain. The IAP, one of the most impressive planning documents ever issued by the Corporation, had been drawn up by an inter-departmental team headed by Dick Gleeson, with the estimable assistance of Mitchell & Associates, landscape architects. Unveiled in February 1998, its objective was to turn Ireland's main street into a Dublin version of the Champs Elysées in Paris, with the footpaths widened on both sides by reducing the number of traffic lanes, the installation of high-quality street furniture, and the creation of a civic plaza in front of the GPO, defined by a formal arrangement of trees and 'sculptured lighting'. An international design competition to find a suitable replacement for Nelson Pillar was always an integral part of the overall plan.

Outside the Mansion House, where the councillors were meeting while the City Hall was being renovated, an unforgettable siren was wailing. Mary Duniyva, a Russian émigré artist who described herself as the Ultimate Woman Poet, was telling anyone who cared to listen that the millennium monument would be 'an anorexic and alien body – alien from every angle in material, size, shape and symbolism'. She herself had entered the design competition and was distressed to finish among the also-rans. What she had proposed was to rebuild the Pillar, but with the sun – a sculpted sphere of bronze – rather than Nelson on top of it. Fixed beams in gold, silver and copper radiated from her 'Sun Pillar of Dublin', and at its base there was a poem 'cast on four silver plaques in burnished gold letters'. The first verse read:

> I, the Sun, am descending upon you
> to remind you that
> the Earth moves around me to warm you people up
> and even when I am in hiding behind the clouds
> I am there for you.

One of the also-ran entries in the competition, designed by Mary Duniyva, a Russian émigré artist, who subsequently took legal action to challenge the result. Her proposal was to rebuild Nelson Pillar, but with the sun – a sculpted sphere of bronze – on top.

The competition entry by Micheál Ó Nualláin. A 'skypod' mounted on a hexagonal column rising from a glazed foyer, he claimed that this 'sculpted Flying Saucer' would give Dublin as powerful a symbol as the Statue of Liberty or the Eiffel Tower.

opposite

A daytime view of the *Monument of Light*, as seen from North Earl Street.

According to its author, the Sun Pillar would be 'an act of catharsis to help Irish people to go onwards and up-wards in life, being a beacon of light and a symbol of hope and peace for this island'.

Obsessed with the belief that her proposal was the right solution for the site, she decided to take Dublin Corporation to the High Court, claiming that the winning design did not relate to the scale of O'Connell Street and that its 'cold mass' of stain-less steel would have the effect of 'negating the friendliness and warmth of the citizens of Dublin'. A month earlier, in April 1999, the High Court had granted leave to appeal to another disappointed also-ran, Mícheál Ó Nualláin, a 71-year-old artist, inven-tor, and brother of Brian O'Nolan, alias Flann O'Brien, alias Myles na gCopaleen. He told the High Court that he was shocked to discover that the adjudicators had made their deci-sion on the short-list in just two days and could not, therefore, have ade-quately considered all 205 entries, including his own. What he proposed was a 'skypod' mounted on a hexago-nal column which would rise from a three-storey glazed box at street level. It would, he argued in his competition entry, give Dublin a sculpted Flying Saucer, as powerful a symbol for the city as the Statue of Liberty in New York or the Eiffel Tower in Paris. At night, the column would create a ghostly reflection of Nelson Pillar, and while the skypod restaurant above it could be made to revolve, this would be a costly venture. 'It is more impor-tant for patrons to revolve (good

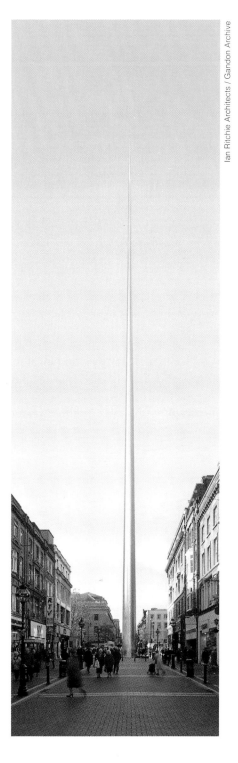

Ian Ritchie Architects / Gandon Archive

Peter Thursfield / *Irish Times*

Micheál Ó Nualláin, the artist, inventor and brother of Brian O'Nolan (alias Flann O'Brien / Myles na gCopaleen), who successfully challenged the result of the competition in the High Court.

wine)', he said. Future development might include underground toilets, 'flooded with daylight (courtesy of the present Japanese technology)' to permit flowers and plants to be grown naturally, 'thus making these toilets unique and pleasant'.

O Nualláin was encouraged to take his legal action by Michael Smith of An Taisce and Lancefort, himself no stranger to the Four Courts. Though Smith insisted that he was well disposed towards the millennium monument, he believed that the project was being 'bulldozed' through the system without adequate public consultation. It was Smith who identified to Ó Nualláin the weak point of the Corporation's position – it had 'deemed' that an environmental impact statement was not necessary. Smith argued that the project would have a significant effect on the environment due to its nature, size and location, even though it fell well below the two-hectare threshold for an EIS. He also put Ó Nualláin in touch with solicitor David Soden and barrister Colm MacEochaidh, both of whom had acted for Lancefort in the past. With their professional assistance, the Monkstown-based plaintiff went to court armed with an affidavit by Sam Stephenson, who maintained that Ian Ritchie's design would affect buildings of artistic, architectural or historical interest on O'Connell Street, particularly the GPO. Dublin Corporation countered with an affidavit by Arthur Gibney, Stephenson's one-time partner, president of the Royal Hibernian Academy, and former president of the Royal Institute of the Architects of Ireland, who argued the reverse.

The action was heard in May 1999 by Mr Justice TC Smyth, who had previously been a senior counsel specialising in planning law, and it dragged on for a week. Dick Gleeson was in the witness box for four hours of relentless cross-examination by MacEochaidh, who raked over every aspect of the adjudication process and the decision to proceed under Part 10. Two months later, Judge Smyth quashed the City Council's March 1st decision to proceed with the project, upholding Ó Nualláin's contention that an EIS was required before 'this bold beacon', as he described it, could be erected 'in the middle of the principal street of the capital of the country'. For that reason, the Corporation should have used Part 9 of the 1994 Planning Regulations, which requires an EIS and final approval by the Minister for the Environment. The judge said the decision on how to proceed was a very important matter and not merely a routine administrative issue because it had 'profound consequences'. It should have been taken by the City Manager or, at least, by some official with the appropriate delegated functions. In fact, he found, it had been taken by Gleeson, who did not have formal authorisation giving him the power to do so. 'If I had to make an order every time someone with an idea pops his head around my door, the place would be littered with them', Fitzgerald commented, showing his frustration at the outcome. What the judge's ruling meant, a victorious Ó Nualláin declared, was that the Corporation 'can't just contemplate its own navel and then decide to do what it likes'. He told the *Irish Times* that he actually liked Ian Ritchie's monument, but believed it would 'stick up like a sore thumb' in O'Connell Street. He was also not gloating over the fact that his successful legal challenge meant that 'The Spike' would not be erected in time for the millennium celebrations. 'I take no pleasure in holding up anything other than a pint of Guinness', the retired school inspector declared, as if in character for the part of *The Brother*.

It was, as Joan O'Connor noted with regret, 'the first time an EIS has been required for something as ephemeral as a slim and beautiful object'. However, according to Michael Smith, that was not the point. The proposed monument, he said, 'breached national and European law', which demanded an EIS for 'any urban development project which is likely to have a significant effect on the environment', as well as the terms of the competition which required it to relate to the scale of the buildings on O'Connell Street. 'An EIS is all about impact, not whether it is good or bad. Railroading the scheme in the absence of a clear assessment of its impact and in the teeth of so many objections was both arrogant and illegal', the unforgiving conservation champion declared. Smith also believed that the High Court judgment could open up to legal challenge other millennium projects, such as the Liffey boardwalk along Bachelors Walk and Ormond Quay Lower, and the remaking of Smithfield. But the City Manager was still 'very confident' that other projects would be unaffected, though he made it clear that the Corporation would 'have to take account of the judgment in this case' in planning new schemes. Though disappointed by the outcome, Fitzgerald insisted that an anticipated delay of six months in the delivery of the millennium monument for the Pillar site was 'not the end of the world'. He was much more embarrassed about the condition of O'Connell Street, and said he would 'continue to be embarrassed' about it until the Corporation's £35 million rejuvenation programme was completed. McHugh Consultants, veterans of George's Quay, were later appointed to produce a thorough EIS, in line with the High Court judgment, and the fate of the *Monument of Light* was left to the Minister for the

Environment, Noel Dempsey.

The Corporation also got on with the long-promised skyline study to put some flesh on the bones of its more relaxed guidelines on high buildings. DEGW, the respected London firm of architects and urban designers, got the job with a team headed by John Worthington, himself a regular visitor to Dublin. The brief, given to them in November 1999, noted that the city's low-rise character was 'part of its charm as a European capital', and said that any change in such a 'fundamental aspect' of this character 'can only be allowed to take place within a well-directed and controlled framework'. In the course of their study, DEGW would have to consider 'critical views across the city skyline', as well as where landmark buildings might be located, bearing in mind such issues as geography, transportation nodes and visual composition, as well as existing skyline features and neighbourhood centres. The consultants would have to look at the policies pursued by other European cities of similar architectural importance and ensure that the views of interested organisations and individuals, both citywide and locally, were taken into account. It was also necessary to 'widen the debate and recommendations beyond the scope of civic design/aesthetic arguments to a consideration of economic and social matters', the brief said. 'Many of those promoting the idea of higher buildings in Dublin argue that they are necessary for economic reasons, to maximise the development potential of urban land. Alternatively, it is

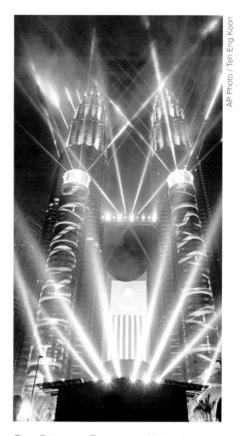

AP Photo / Teh Eng Koon

The Petronas Towers in Kuala Lumpur, Malaysia.

opposite

A model of Dunloe Ewart's tower for Sir John Rogerson's Quay, designed by O'Muire Smyth Architects.

argued that substantial increases in intensity of development can be achieved by marginal additions to existing building heights.' The consultants were required to examine these arguments in the context of Dublin's traditional form of development, the City Development Plan zonings and plot ratios, and also Government guidelines on density. And given the mounting pressure from developers to erect massive buildings on random individual sites, such as the new Four Seasons Hotel in Ballsbridge – then under construction to a design by international leisure architects Wimberley, Allison, Tong and Goo – the study was to be carried out 'as expeditiously as possible' with a view to presenting the final policy to the City Council in mid-2000.

Noel Smyth, the meticulous solicitor who shopped Charlie Haughey, couldn't wait. In December 1999, as chairman of Dunloe Ewart plc, he sought planning permission for a major development on the Hammond Lane works between Sir John Rogerson's Quay and the Grand Canal Docks, including a 'signature' office tower, 92 metres high – 12 metres taller than what the Corporation was prepared to permit at George's Quay and nearly twice the height of Zoe's apartment tower at Charlotte Quay. Dunloe, which had been set up originally by Smyth's friend and confidant Ben Dunne, had merged with Belfast-based Ewart, and was now spearheading a number of major developments, including a science and technology park at Cherrywood, in the Carrickmines Valley. One of Dunloe's earliest projects in Dublin was the completion in 1996 of twenty-four apartments in a badly guntered Georgian terrace opposite Government Buildings, but it established a new standard of excellence in Beresford Street, just north of the Markets area, with a very fine 177-unit courtyard scheme by O'Muire Smyth, jointly headed by Toal O'Muire and Noel Smyth's younger brother John. They had won their spurs on the urban-renewal front by designing what is still one of the most intelligent pieces of Liffeyside infill in Dublin, at Merchant's Quay, in the early 1990s. The plans for Sir John Rogerson's Quay were in a dif-

Dara MacDónaill / courtesy of the *Irish Times*

Noel Smyth, chairman of Dunloe Ewart plc, pictured here with his client, friend and confidant, Ben Dunne, leaving the Moriarty Tribunal at Dublin Castle in January 1999

ferent league, however, because they included a dynamic, tapering tower with a sail-like external glazed screen that would make quite a statement on Dublin's skyline. Noel Smyth himself had purchased the Hammond Lane site for £4 million, and cashed in on soaring property values in Docklands when he sold it on to Dunloe Ewart for £7.5 million in 1998. Given its pivotal location at the confluence of the Liffey and the Dodder, it was hardly surprising that the site had been earmarked for a landmark building in the DDDA's plan for the Grand Canal Docks area. Smyth, who has shed his legal practice to concentrate on property development in Dublin, London and Belfast, gave his brother the luxury of time to develop the scheme, which would provide 231 generous-sized apartments as well as almost 600,000 square feet of offices, with shops, restaurants and leisure facilities at street level. It was not 'something that has just mushroomed', John Smyth insisted.

Two months before Dublin Corporation commissioned its skyline study, *World Architecture* magazine carried a sceptical feature on high buildings by Frank Duffy, senior partner of DEGW. 'All architecture is to do with money, but supertowers are to do with entire global economic movements. If enough high-level economic activity concentrates itself in any one place for long enough, the towers shoot up', he wrote. 'If supertowers are an expression of financial success, then cities have to have them. There is no option, even if there are more obviously economic ways to achieve the desired floor area' and the towers themselves were 'ecologically disastrous'. The pressure to reach for the sky is, of course, most acutely felt in world capitals such as London, Tokyo and New York. Dublin was never in that league. The demand for office space in our little metropolis was fuelled by multi-national corporations seeking 'back offices', rather than 'front offices' or headquarters. Thus, it would never be required to scale the dizzying heights of Manhattan. The real danger was that it would lose the run of itself. In his article, Frank Duffy quoted salutary research by Dresdner Kleinwort Benson suggesting that, for the past one hundred years, the construction of the latest 'world's tallest building' had always been followed by an economic crisis in its region. Most notoriously, the Petronas towers in Kuala Lumpur, currently the world's tallest, were just being completed when Malaysia's 'Asian Tiger' economy collapsed.

3. Getting Around

There was something depressingly definitive about the shocking statement issued in October 1987 by John Wilson, then Minister for Transport. With no advance warning, it came as a bolt from the blue that the Government had decided to ditch twelve-year-old plans to extend the DART to Tallaght and Clondalkin, with an underground connection between Heuston and Connolly stations, and to tell CIÉ that it was to concentrate on less ambitious proposals for bus-based solutions and diesel rail services on existing lines. Not only that: less than twelve months after it had been set up by the previous Fine Gael-Labour coalition, the fledgling Dublin Transport Authority was abolished, and its chief executive, Phil Murray, who had just begun grappling with the issues, summarily dismissed. Viewed alongside the Fianna Fáil minority Government's earlier decisions to abolish the Metropolitan Streets Commission, An Foras Forbartha, and the Eastern Regional Development Organisation (ERDO), it was clear that 'the whole idea of planning in the most important region of the country is being abandoned', as the DTA's outspoken chairman, Peter Kelly, declared at the time. 'We may have First World trappings but, institutionally, we're lurching towards the Third World.' Indeed, with the DTA forced out of the frame, what passed for transport planning in Dublin was back in the hands of the same mishmash of bodies whose lack of co-ordination in the past had led to its establishment in the first place. The downgrading of plans to provide the city with the bones of a public transport system also ran counter to the Corporation's new development plan, then being drafted by a team headed by Pat McDonnell. 'It had a certain symmetry. But then the roof fell in, followed by the walls and, finally, the floor. What we're left with is little

Suddenly, it is possible to see how Dublin could develop a public transport *system*, with the metro-style Circle Line as a unifying organiser, intercepting every route leading into the city centre, including DART, Luas, suburban rail lines and QBCs. It would also extend the central business district to the east and west, knitting the inner city together in a quite remarkable way.

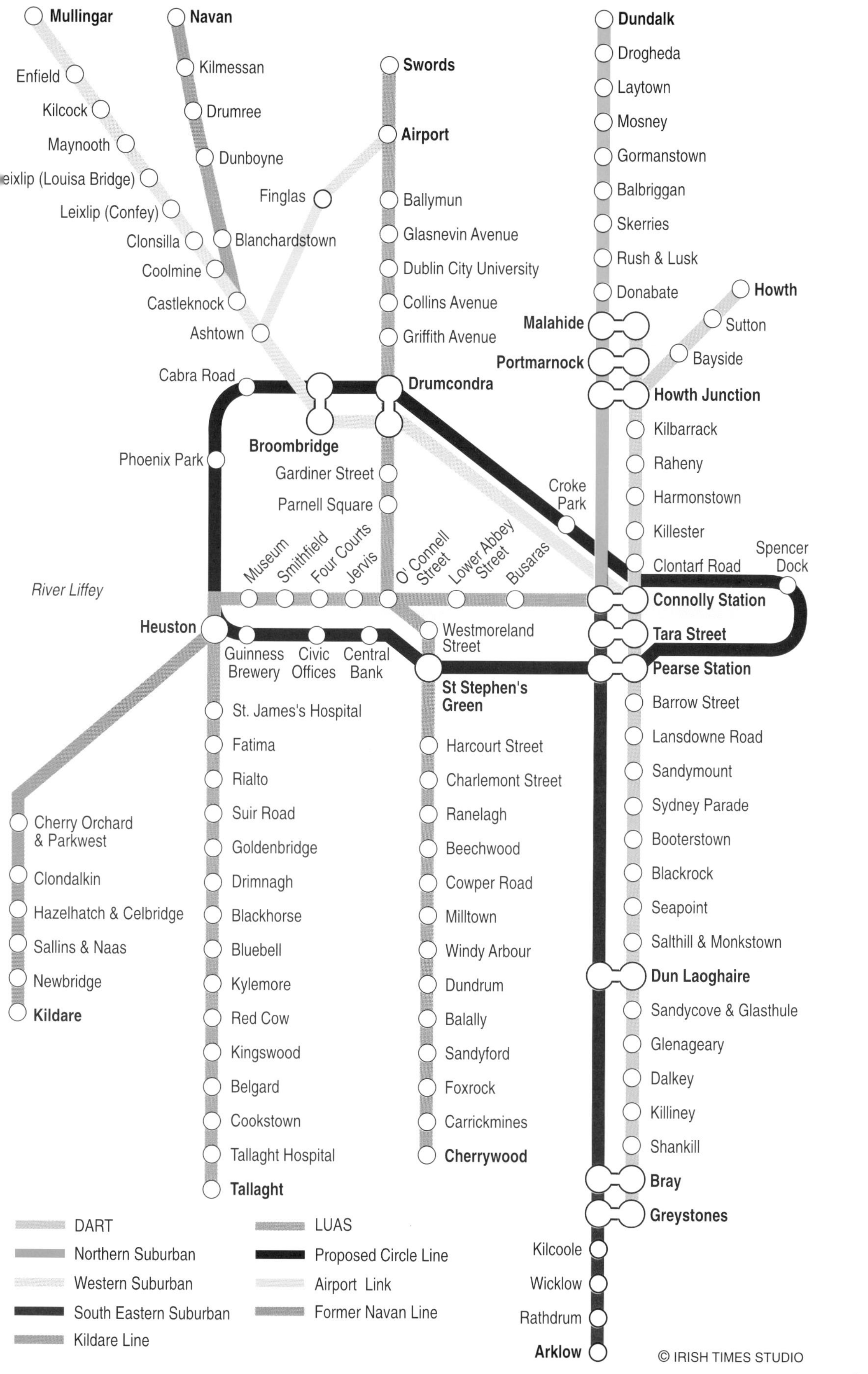

Mullingar
Navan
Dundalk
Enfield
Kilmessan
Drogheda
Kilcock
Drumree
Laytown
Swords
Maynooth
Dunboyne
Mosney
Leixlip (Louisa Bridge)
Airport
Gormanstown
Leixlip (Confey)
Finglas
Balbriggan
Clonsilla
Blanchardstown
Ballymun
Skerries
Coolmine
Glasnevin Avenue
Rush & Lusk
Castleknock
Dublin City University
Donabate
Howth
Ashtown
Collins Avenue
Malahide
Sutton
Griffith Avenue
Portmarnock
Bayside
Cabra Road
Drumcondra
Howth Junction
Broombridge
Kilbarrack
Gardiner Street
Raheny
Phoenix Park
Parnell Square
Croke Park
Harmonstown
Killester
Museum
Smithfield
Four Courts
Jervis
O'Connell Street
Lower Abbey Street
Busaras
Clontarf Road
Spencer Dock
River Liffey
Connolly Station
Heuston
Westmoreland Street
Tara Street
Guinness Brewery
Civic Offices
Central Bank
Pearse Station
St. James's Hospital
St Stephen's Green
Barrow Street
Fatima
Harcourt Street
Lansdowne Road
Rialto
Charlemont Street
Sandymount
Suir Road
Ranelagh
Sydney Parade
Cherry Orchard & Parkwest
Goldenbridge
Beechwood
Booterstown
Clondalkin
Drimnagh
Cowper Road
Blackrock
Hazelhatch & Celbridge
Blackhorse
Milltown
Seapoint
Sallins & Naas
Bluebell
Windy Arbour
Salthill & Monkstown
Newbridge
Kylemore
Dundrum
Dun Laoghaire
Kildare
Red Cow
Balally
Sandycove & Glasthule
Kingswood
Sandyford
Glenageary
Belgard
Foxrock
Dalkey
Cookstown
Carrickmines
Killiney
Tallaght Hospital
Cherrywood
Shankill
Tallaght
Bray
Greystones
Kilcoole
Wicklow
Rathdrum
Arklow

DART
LUAS
Northern Suburban
Proposed Circle Line
Western Suburban
Airport Link
South Eastern Suburban
Former Navan Line
Kildare Line

© IRISH TIMES STUDIO

better than a derelict structure', McDonnell complained later. A more jaundiced observer, remarking on how difficult it was to get things done in Dublin, said: 'We had a choice whether to pee or get off the pot. We chose to get off the pot.'

The only ray of hope at the time was that there would be a 'feasibility study' on the prospects of developing an integrated development plan for Dublin, largely aimed at winning more money from Brussels. Few were encouraged by this news. After all, Dublin was already one of the most studied cities in Europe, with a plethora of plans and – mercifully, in many cases – very little to show for them. They included the 1965 Schaechterle traffic plan, which endorsed the Corporation's destructive road-widening schemes; the 1967 Myles Wright Advisory Regional Plan, which led to the development of the three western 'new towns' of Tallaght, Lucan-Clondalkin and Blanchardstown; the 1971 Dublin Transportation Study, which delineated a motorway network to serve them and the wider city; the 1974 Travers Morgan study which, had we been able to afford it, would have driven motorways right through the inner city; the 1975 Dublin Rail Rapid Transit Study, which was ultimately binned by the Government's October 1987 decision; the 1980 Transport Consultative Commission report, which poured cold water on the DRRTS and advocated a more minimalist approach; and the 1985 ERDO settlement strategy, which was essentially a technocratic blueprint for yet more low-density suburban sprawl strung out along new motorways.

Given this grim background of failure and wrong-headed planning, there was not much confidence in the 1990 announcement by Padraig Flynn, then Minister for the Environment, that a steering committee of officials had been set up to oversee yet another transportation review. However, against all the odds, what started out as a bureaucratic exercise ultimately turned into something quite unexpected – the Dublin Transportation Initiative. And what characterised the DTI, by contrast with the previous studies, was that it drew together all strands of the public debate, from the Living City Group and the Dublin Cycling Campaign on one side of the argument, to the Automobile Association and the Chamber of Commerce on the other. With Pat Mangan, then principal officer in the Department of the Environment's roads division, as its enlightened chairman, and London-based Steer Davies Gleave as consultants, it began to look as if the DTI might actually provide some new signposts to point a way out of Dublin's transport planning mire – and even achieve a wide measure of consensus on the right way forward. The consultants' London-Irish project manager, Peter Ryan, was one of the main driving forces, and he let it be known that he was very dubious about the notion of throwing roads at the traffic problem. A committed anti-Thatcherite, he had also taken part in the mass picket of Rupert Murdoch's new printing plant at Wapping in the early 1980s.

Light rail transit (LRT) was almost bound to form part of the package of measures recommended by the DTI. Though Dublin had followed most British cities by abandoning its rickety old trams in 1949, LRT had become the flavour of the month, with a lot of enthusiastic talk among transport buffs about the 'new generation' tramways then being installed in the French cities of Nantes and Grenoble. But what made some politicians sit up and take notice was Manchester's emergence as the first city in Britain to embrace LRT. The fact that this was happening just across the Irish Sea, in a country from which we still borrowed so many of our approaches to urban planning, turned trams into a real prospect for Dublin. Indeed, in 1990, long before the DTI had completed its deliberations, an Italian engineering company called Ansaldo Transporti made proposals to the then Minister for Transport, Seamus Brennan, for an LRT network linking Tallaght, Dundrum and Dublin Airport with the city centre. Nearly everyone who attended the company's presentation at Trinity College in June 1990 was convinced that light rail had become 'a serious runner in Dublin', as Prof Simon Perry, one of its most stalwart advocates, said afterwards. There was also something in it for Galway-born Brennan. As far back as 1981, he had commissioned his own feasibility study on reopening the Harcourt Street line as a pre-election ploy to gain his Dáil seat in Dublin South. (The line had been closed in 1959 by Todd Andrews, then chairman of CIÉ. He maintained later that it was only being used by 'a few Protestant solicitors from Carrickmines'.) And in its manifesto for the 1991 local elections, Fianna Fáil explicitly promised that the city would get a light rail system.

This was the party's response to a campaign for the early construction of a mass transit system, which had steadily gained momentum as the traffic problem worsened. The People First initiative involved Prof Perry, along with the Dublin City Centre Business Association, An Taisce, the Irish Planning Institute, the RIAI, and even representatives of Iarnród Éireann and Dublin Bus. One of its subsidiary planks was to challenge the view, then being heavily canvassed by the roads lobby, that an Eastern Bypass linking Whitehall with Booterstown – as recommended in the 1971 Dublin Transportation Study – should be the principal

Seamus Brennan TD. As far back as 1981, he commissioned his own feasibility study on reopening the Harcourt Street line as a pre-election ploy to gain his Dáil seat in Dublin South.

Matt Kavanagh / *Irish Times*

priority. The Corporation's road engineers had always been in favour of it, but failed to get it through the City Council in 1980 because the original plan would have demolished over a hundred houses to provide a fast-track route for car commuters. They worked hard to have it reinstated, eventually commissioning Ove Arup & Partners to carry out a feasibility and environmental impact study of what was then called the Port Access and Eastern Relief Route. Though this study suggested that some of it could be tunnelled to avoid demolishing houses and that all of it should be tolled to deter car commuters, the issue remained highly divisive and the City Council decided in November 1991 not to include it in the new City Development Plan.

The Eastern Bypass also dominated much of the debate at the DTI's Consultative Panel in Dublin Castle over the following twelve months, until an extraordinary event happened – the arrival of a messenger from the Custom House at lunchtime one day in November 1992 with a statement from Michael Smith, then Minister for the Environment. In it, he announced that the Government had decided to abandon the controversial motorway, then costed at £300 million, in order to 'end the uncertainty' about whether it was on or off the agenda. The real reason for the shock announcement, in the middle of a general election campaign, had more to do with Fianna Fáil trying to take an extra seat in Dublin South East. By that stage, the main elements of the DTI package were already known, and, inevitably, they included a three-branch light rail network serving Tallaght, Dundrum and Dublin Airport (via Ballymun) – a 'flagship project' aimed at changing attitudes to public transport by providing a safe, reliable and efficient alternative car use. An MRBI opinion survey commissioned by Steer Davies Gleave found that nearly 90% of Dubliners favoured LRT, though there was also strong support for the Eastern Bypass. The overall package unveiled by the consultants in their interim report in October 1992 recommended completing the 'C-ring' to the north, west and south of the city, no major new road schemes within that ring, ten 'quality bus corridors' on main roads leading into the city centre, and a range of other measures aimed at managing Dublin's traffic. It was all meant to be a 'seamless garment', in the words of Pat Mangan, with only the issue of port access remaining to be resolved. Further work by the consultants examined a variety of options, including an imaginative proposal by Ciarán Blair, engineering director of National Toll Roads plc, for a £100 million east-west Liffey Tunnel linking the port with Islandbridge, before they recommended a north-south route from Whitehall (later refined as the Dublin Port Tunnel) in the DTI's final report, published in October 1994.

Even by then, Pat Mangan's 'seamless garment', priced at £1.2 billion, was already unravelling. The Fianna Fáil-Labour coalition, at Bertie Ahern's instigation, decided to double the capacity of the port tunnel, turning it into a four-lane dual carriageway on the basis that this would do more to relieve traffic congestion on existing roads. It was clear that the engineering imperative behind the Eastern Bypass had not been killed off by Michael Smith's bombshell announcement. In the words of Liz O'Donnell TD, it had become 'the serpent that refuses to die'. Furthermore, it appeared that the arrangements being put in place to implement the DTI's overall strategy and its coherent vision of Dublin* – dreamed up by Jim Steer and Peter Ryan – were too weak to prevent further cherry-picking by rival agencies or interests with their own narrow agendas. A 1995 by-election in Wicklow, for example, prompted Michael Lowry, then Minister for Transport, to announce approval with some fanfare for the proposed DART extension to Greystones, while saying nothing of the DTI's recommended extension to Malahide. The previous Government, in cobbling together its National Development Plan (1994-99), had also decided that only the Tallaght and Dundrum LRT lines would proceed – at an estimated cost of £220 million – as they were the most likely to be completed within the period of the plan. Yet again, the northside – and Ballymun, in particular – was left out in the cold. There was another reason, too. Because light rail was designed to entice commuters from their cars and there were many more car owners along the old Harcourt Street line, the DTI's narrow cost-benefit analysis favoured Dundrum over Ballymun. A subsequent review, carried out by Oscar Faber for the European Commission, which had pledged £114 million for Dublin's LRT project, endorsed this approach but stressed the urgency of proceeding with the northside line as quickly as possible.

CIÉ's newly appointed chief executive, Michael McDonnell, tore himself away from its boardroom strife to coin the name Luas – 'speed' in Irish – for the proposed tramway network being planned by an in-house project team headed by Donal Mangan. Veteran of the DTS and DRRTS exercises in the early 1970s, Mangan had been out of Dublin for years as a regional manager of Bus Éireann, after giving up hope on transport planning in the capital, and he was delighted to be back in the fray with a real project that seemed as if it was about to happen. But then, at the planning equivalent of two minutes to midnight, heavyweight critics emerged from the woodwork to challenge what Michael Lowry had trumpeted as 'the biggest and boldest public transport project since the foundation of the State'. Whatever the DTI had decided, they were determined that Luas would not run through the heart of Dublin on its street surfaces. The Transport Users Support Group, led by Tommy Newton, a Dublin Bus driver, had a bizarre plan to put it on the central median of the M50, with rail links to the city centre and

---

* DTI Vision of Dublin:
– Dublin as a leading European city: Competing and co-operating successfully, civilised, literate and vibrant.
– The National Capital: Proud of its history and heritage, its unique character conserved, a fit setting for Government and national centres of excellence.
– A Metropolitan Region: with a strong, growing and diverse city, town and rural economy, based on a skilled and adaptable workforce.
– A Living City-Region: on a human scale, accessible to all. At its heart a city to serve its people and communities and to meet their aspirations for an improving quality of life.

a surface line from Heuston to Connolly. A rival group set up by two engineers, Cormac Rabbit and Rudigger Monahan, lobbied relentlessly in favour of their Unified Proposal scheme, which called for a an even more extensive metro-style system, with a central station in Temple Bar, not dissimilar to what CIÉ itself once had in mind. Estimating its cost at £2 billion, including major roads, Donal Mangan said: 'To propose plans which involve expenditure of significant resources, usually the taxpayers, without some assessment of how much money can reasonably be made available is pointless.' The Chamber of Commerce, which essentially represents the suburban managerial class who have guaranteed off-street parking in the city centre, also beavered away behind the scenes and in public to undermine the project, seizing on premature reports of the alleged failure of Sheffield's Supertram as a salutary lesson. The success of new tramways in Grenoble, Strasbourg and Manchester, to name but a few, was dismissed on the basis that they were not valid comparisons. Scare stories about the likely scale of disruption during the construction period were used to mask the chamber's real agenda, which was to preserve valuable road space in the city for private cars. Its *Vision 2010* document, published in mid-1997, repeatedly voiced the concern that on-street Luas would result in 'unacceptable levels of congestion for other road users', particularly in Dawson Street. One part-time chamber executive even mused that Dublin's real problem was that it hadn't been extensively bombed during the Second World War, and, therefore, did not have the wide boulevards which he thought were necessary to accommodate a street-running light rail system.

Senator David Norris, heavily briefed by the Unified Proposal group, sought to exploit the Government's precarious position in the upper house to demand an independent study of the underground option as the 'price tag' for his support of the 1996 Light Rail Bill. The Bill had already been defeated in the Dáil because of a pairing cock-up, though it was subsequently steered through both houses by Minister of State, Avril Doyle – without the support of Norris. Hysterical commentary in some sections of the media, such as a *Business & Finance* magazine cover story entitled 'Light Rail Lunacy', raised the temperature still further. The most vociferous critic was former Taoiseach Garret FitzGerald, who penned a series of articles in the *Irish Times* arguing that Luas would not have sufficient capacity to cater for passenger numbers, that its frequency would block cross-city traffic along its routes 'on average once a minute', and that thirty or forty-metre trams could not be coupled to operate on-street. He had drawn

---

Diagrammatic map of the original first phase of Luas, showing the lines connecting Tallaght with Dundrum, via the city centre, with the proposed extension to Ballymun.

left Donal Mangan, the Luas project director. After being out of Dublin for years he was delighted to be back in the fray with a real project that seemed as if it was about to happen.

right Former Taoiseach Garret FitzGerald, who became the most vociferous critic of the Luas project, arguing that it would not have sufficient capacity to cater for passenger numbers.

Luas Project Team

courtesy of CIÉ

Irish Times

this conclusion after measuring the tight radius at the junction of Dawson Street and Nassau Street before 7 o'clock one morning, ignoring the fact the such vehicles are usually articulated and mounted on flexible bogeys which make them quite capable of turning corners. He gave no percentage to the proven ability of on-street light rail systems to civilise a city, aid urban renewal and calm road traffic. It was an underground or bust as far as he was concerned. Obviously, he had forgotten his closing address to the Dublin Crisis Conference ten years earlier, when he said the 'extremely low density' of our suburbs made the city 'quite unsuited to mass transportation', and, as a result, we would have to rely on buses rather than mass transit. But his espousal of the underground option was influential. It was immediately endorsed by Robert Molloy of the Progressive Democrats, and by Seamus Brennan·of Fianna Fáil, both of whom were being lobbied daily by the anti-Luas coalition. Neither were they prepared to accept the findings of a report by CIÉ's French transport consultants, Semaly, along with Ewbank Preece Ó hEocha, which perhaps not surprisingly endorsed the on-street project. There was also strong local opposition from residents of Arran Quay Terrace, off Smithfield, whose artisan homes would be demolished for the Tallaght line, as well as business interests in Inchicore, whose noisy campaign succeeded in having the line diverted away from the village, via Davitt Road, consigning it to backwater status in the future. Among the politicians claiming credit for this turnabout was Bertie Ahern, who told everyone he had made 'intense representations' on their behalf, and Jim Mitchell, who had previously been in favour of the 'exciting' prospect of running Luas through Inchicore. By the time local residents woke up to what was happening, it was too late.

Even CIÉ conceded that the positive message it was trying to convey about light rail was not getting through. At an endless round of public meetings, organised by local groups or by Eamonn Brady, the unflappable Luas information officer, every concern under the sun was raised, from the visual impact of the overhead wirescape to the alleged need to 'screen' nearby housing from tram lines. People also had worries about security, maintenance of existing parking facilities, noise and vibration, integration with other public transport services, park-and-ride capacity and access to LRT stops. But rational discussion of these issues was almost impossible in some cases because of the hysteria whipped up by rival lobbies, turning the public consultation process into a nightmare for the Luas project team. At one meeting in Mount Brown – described by Bernard McHugh, the project's planning consultant, as 'one of the nastiest public meetings I've ever attended' – Donal Mangan was required to sit in front of a 'No to Luas' banner while opponents video-taped him and other members of the team. Highly inaccurate and inflammatory claims were made. In Inchicore, for example, elderly women were told that they wouldn't be able to cross the road to go to Mass if Luas went ahead as planned. At every meeting, the Luas project team was dogged by representatives of the Unified Proposal group and others who fundamentally disagreed with the light rail plan, despite its fulsome endorsement by the DTI in 1994. 'No matter what we did, we were wrong', McHugh recalled. They were forced to cut their losses. One of the most unfortunate compromises involved St James's Hospital, where the project team originally planned to go straight through the grounds, following the same route as many car commuters making a short-cut between James's Street and South Circular Road. But this ran into unexpected opposition from the Department of Health, on the basis of 'let's not do anything here that could pre-empt anything else in the future', as one Luas source put it. Ray Byrne, CIÉ's head of programmes and projects, assured the Department that he would sort it out, so Luas was re-routed around the back-lands of the hospital at an estimated additional cost of £500,000. And South Dublin County Council, though ostensibly in favour of Luas, successfully resisted a plan to bring the trams into Tallaght's planned Millennium Square.

As if all of these problems weren't enough, the project suddenly lost its political head when Michael Lowry was forced to resign in December 1996 after the *Irish Independent* revealed that the lavish refurbishment and extension of his period house near Holy Cross, Co Tipperary, had been funded by Ben Dunne in part-payment for Lowry's refrigeration engineering work for Dunnes Stores. In writing this exposé, journalist Sam Smyth had unwittingly opened a can of worms which led to the unmasking of Charlie Haughey, and much else besides. Alan Dukes, Lowry's successor as Minister for Transport, then had to satisfy himself that running Luas on-street was the way to go, and the rather surprising oracle he turned to was Maurice Doyle, former Governor of the Central Bank. In May 1997, fortified by his verbal report, Dukes announced an allocation of £100 million for the first phase of Luas from Tallaght via the city centre to Dundrum, with a commitment to extend it to Sandyford Industrial Estate, plus further funding for design work to begin immediately on the Ballymun line. He made it clear that putting Luas underground in the city centre 'isn't an option', largely on cost grounds, and he accused Fianna Fáil of 'trying to ride two horses' by calling, on the one hand, for Luas to proceed and, on the other, for yet another study of the underground option. 'This would stop the project dead in its tracks – not just parts of it, but the whole project', he warned sternly as the June 1997 general election loomed. 'The people of Dublin have a very definite choice – either action from the Government on the present proposal or paralysis from Fianna Fáil', he declared.

CIÉ had presented Dukes with a mammoth environmental impact statement on the project, compiled by McHugh Consultants, which conceded that there would be significant disruption and inconvenience over a period of two years in the Markets area, Abbey Street, College Green, Dawson Street and St Stephen's Green during the construction phase of the project. However, it pledged that 'unpleasant effects' would be minimised as far as possible by 'a high degree of project management and co-ordination' in relocating under-street gas, water, sewerage, electricity and telecommunications lines and, later, installing the cushioned trackbed and overhead cables for Luas to operate. It helped enor-

Luas Project Team

Photomontage showing the dramatic cable-stayed structure proposed to carry Luas over Lower Churchtown Road, which would become a significant landscape feature in the Dundrum area.

mously that a large proportion of the route would be laid on the old Harcourt Street railway reservation, with new custom-designed bridges, including a dramatic cable-stayed structure spanning Lower Churchtown Road, which would become a significant landscape feature in the Dundrum area. Every on-street tram stop would have low platforms, no more than twice the height of existing footpaths, with ramps facilitating level boarding by all passengers to the low-floored Luas trams, as well as ticket machines and 'real time' information systems showing when the next tram would arrive. Each tram would have a capacity of 235 passengers – sixty seated and the rest standing – and the line would be capable of carrying 3,000 people per hour in each direction. 'This will cater for the maximum estimated demand', the EIS said. It also defended CIÉ's decision to opt for a more circuitous route to Tallaght than the most direct one, via Kimmage and Harold's Cross, because the latter had recently been blocked by a new housing estate in the grounds of Mount Argus. As passenger numbers increased over time, it could become a separate light rail line. As for building an underground

Luas Project Team

Photomontage showing one of the Luas trams at Heuston Station, with the former Dr Steevens's Hospital (now the Eastern Health Authority's headquarters) in the background.

instead, the EIS assumed – wrongly, as things turned out – that this issue had been settled by the DTI. Going underground, it said, would involve 'significantly greater levels of disruption and environmental impact', and the 'very considerable additional cost ... would not be justifiable given the level of demand and the financial resources available to Dublin'.

Nonetheless, Seamus Brennan ensured that a pledge was inserted in the Fianna Fáil election manifesto to carry out an independent study of the underground option. He even suggested that all three lines should go ahead, leaving the issue of how to join them up in the city centre to be decided later. The party's future coalition partners, the Progressive Democrats, made a similar commitment after Mary Harney became convinced of the need for it by her transport guru, Gerry Duggan, business development manager with ESB International, who strongly favoured sinking Luas out of sight in the city centre. And so, within a week of taking office in July 1997, the new Government decided to commission the promised study, in what this writer described at the time as a craven capitulation to the car lobby. In a bitter irony, the assistant secretary assigned to oversee it was Pat Mangan, former chairman of the DTI, which had emphatically rejected the underground option. As he knew, it had taken nearly three years of detailed work, involving CIÉ's project team and up to eighteen firms of consultants, to bring Luas to the public-inquiry stage, and any further delay would run the risk of losing EU funding. Alan Dukes had appointed Judge Seán O'Leary, a one-time Fine Gael handler in the FitzGerald era, to preside at the inquiry. All he could do in the wake of Mary O'Rourke's announcement of the latest study was to adjourn until it was completed. Trying to look on the bright side, Donal Mangan said the study should 'clear up the issue once and for all'. But he could not deny that, ten years after the idea of building an underground had been rejected, we were back looking into another hole in the ground.

The twelve-page brief given to the British engineering consultants, WS Atkins, in October 1997 was very comprehensive. It called on them to provide 'clear and objective advice' on two broad options – running Luas on-street or putting it underground, in terms of the contribution each of them would make to Dublin's overall transport needs, including long-term passenger demand. They were also asked to address such issues as traffic and land-use impacts, relative disruption during construction, transport integration, accessibility, capital and operating costs, socio-economic benefits, and likely implementation timetables. Clearly, all of this was going to take time, and with Commissioner Monika Wulf-Mathies already warning that 'all or part' of the EU's funding might have to be reallocated to other projects, Mary O'Rourke moved to mollify those who feared that Luas would never happen. Addressing the South Dublin Chamber of Commerce at a November power breakfast in Tallaght, she gave 'firm, unequivocal commitment' that it would go ahead, whether on-street or underground in the city centre. She was not 'hung up' on either option, but said she needed to have the 'fullest of facts' before the Government could make a final decision, even if it was two minutes to midnight in planning terms and Luas was already eighteen months behind schedule. If WS Atkins endorsed the CIÉ plan, it would be a case of 'away we go'. If it recommended going underground, it would be a case of 'away we go with further planning'. O'Rourke said she would also be reassuring the formidable Wulf-Mathies, at a 'frank' meeting in Dublin the following day, that 'I'm about my business', as well as confirming her own 'enthusiasm' for the Luas project and the Government's 'commitment' to proceed with it. As a Dubliner, Bertie Ahern was 'certainly not going to go down as the Taoiseach who did not bring in Luas', she declared confidently. Hailing from Athlone, O'Rourke herself did not have the same interest in Dublin. However, as a shrewd and pragmatic politician who was nobody's fool, she knew that she had to deliver on Luas.

The independent consultants' 200-page report, presented to her in April 1998, was not favourable to the undergrounders. In fact, they were almost apoplectic about its findings. Because what WS Atkins had concluded was that it would cost at least an extra £500 million to put Luas underground between the canal ring and O'Connell Street – a figure very close to the estimate provided by CIÉ's own consultants nearly two years earlier. Not only would the surface option, now estimated at £263 million, cost less to build and operate, it would also carry more passengers – based on the assumption that CIÉ would use longer forty-metre trams rather than the thirty-metre trams provisionally ordered from GEC-Alsthom in France. And contrary to Garret FitzGerald's central contention, the consultants said the Tallaght-Dundrum line would have 'sufficient capacity to carry forecast passenger demand for the foreseeable future, at least until the year 2025'. Of course, they conceded that its construction would have a much more significant impact over a wide area of the city centre, with lane closures on some streets, increased delays at junctions, and temporary bus routes, bus stops and footpaths. However, they also pointed out that building an underground would cause 'significant, but localised, disruption'. Dublin Corporation's traffic management strategy for the city centre, which included banning left turns from Dawson Street into Nassau Street, would also facilitate an on-street Luas line by reducing the flow of other traffic – a point ignored completely by Garret FitzGerald. 'Bearing in mind the need to ensure best use of scarce resources, the recommendation of the study is that the surface option is the most appropriate and cost-effective in meeting the transport needs of the city and providing capacity to meet long-term passenger demands', WS Atkins said.

Reaction to this recommendation was swift. The Unified Proposal group described it as 'a sad day for Dublin', saying the city would 'never recover' from the disruption of laying Luas on-street. Along with other critics, its spokesmen seized on the consultants' forecast that the Tallaght-Dundrum line would reduce the number of people travelling by car by only 1% and, therefore, it wasn't worth having. But this startling figure referred to total trips throughout the Greater Dublin Area. Obviously, the city's first Luas line was not going to attract car users from, say, Blanchardstown. In 2006, according to Atkins, it would account for 5% of all trips in the morning peak period and 15% of public transport trips. It would attract twenty-nine million passengers per annum, as against twenty-three million for the underground option, reducing peak-hour car use by 3,300 trips per day, compared to 2,800 for the alternative. But even though the Tallaght-Dundrum line would carry significantly more passengers than the seventeen million a year then using the DART service, it was the '1%' figure that transfixed Government ministers. They came to believe that if the benefits were so slight, the disruption of city centre streets over the two-year construction phase could hardly be justified, especially if it was to result in a significant political backlash. And as a Cabinet sub-committee met to thrash out the issues raised by Atkins, there was another intensive round of lobbying by the anti-Luas brigade, with the Chamber of Commerce, IBEC and the AA in the vanguard. They simply couldn't conceive of road space being 'sacrificed' for public transport. It didn't seem to matter that the on-street project still had solid support from the Dublin City Centre Business Association which, after all, represented the shopkeepers likely

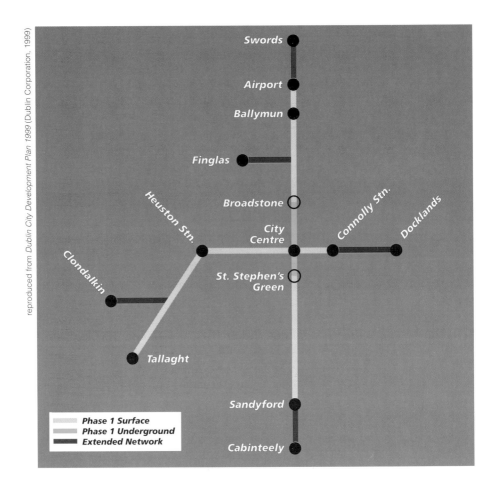

reproduced from Dublin City Development Plan 1999 (Dublin Corporation, 1999)

Joe St Leger / *Irish Times*

The Government's Luas plan, cobbled together by ministers in May 1998, after they had sent out for extra dry-ink markers to dress up their binning of the independent WS Atkins study.

Mary O'Rourke, Minister for Public Enterprise, who gave an estimate of '£400 million-plus' for the Government's revised Luas plan. When asked what this meant, she said, 'Plus means extra'.

to be most affected by the disruption, or that the City Manager, John Fitzgerald, had reiterated Dublin Corporation's view that it was 'the best option for the city and we're satisfied that it can be managed well'.

Despite her publicly stated position of neutrality on the issue, Mary O'Rourke had become convinced that Luas would have to go underground, at least between St Stephen's Green and the northside, if only to neutralise the opposition. So had Tánaiste Mary Harney, whose party had produced a policy document on the issue just two months earlier. With Bertie Ahern having no serious convictions one way or the other, so long as *something* was agreed, the two Marys set about ditching the Atkins report. The matter had to be handled carefully, however. They knew that the Government would not get away with simply disowning it, thereby delaying Luas for months on end while the CIÉ project team were sent back to the drawing boards. Even from a narrow public relations viewpoint, the decision would have to be marketed as a forward-looking package. And so, ministers pored over maps of Dublin at two Cabinet meetings and sent out for extra dry-ink markers to dress up their binning of Atkins by offering 'something for everyone in the audience', just like the good old days of Gay Byrne's *Late Late Show*. What they cobbled together was a crude schematic diagram showing an expanded Luas network, with lines in different colours running off to Connolly Station, Ballymun, Sandyford and Dublin Airport – and, of course, an underground link between St Stephen's Green and Broadstone. Hot off the laminator, this 'grand plan' was unveiled to the expectant media by Mary O'Rourke, in characteristic schoolmarm mode, on the evening of 5th May 1998, using a pointer to demonstrate that it was to be merely the first phase of the Government's 'longer-term vision' of a light rail network that would be extended in future to serve Swords, Finglas, Docklands, Cabinteely and Clondalkin. When asked how much it would cost, she quoted an elastic estimate of '£400 million-plus', which even then seemed ludicrously low. Pressed later in the Dáil by Ivan Yates, the Fine Gael spokesman on transport, about what she meant by '£400 million-plus', O'Rourke memorably declared: 'Plus means extra.'

But no amount of spinning by O'Rourke could conceal the fact that the Government's immediate decision to put Luas underground in the city centre was a gutless response to irrational fears about the disruptive effects of installing it on-street. Both Fianna Fáil and the Progressive Democrats were terrified that they would lose seats in the next general election if Dublin was in chaos because of the Luas construction programme, so they kicked for touch. Donal Ó Brolcháin, tenacious spokesman for the Drumcondra 2005 campaign, rightly characterised their cop-out as 'a triumph of prejudice over common sense, expertise and cost-effectiveness'. It showed that there was no political will to take the hard, potentially unpopular decisions required even to begin sorting out Dublin's traffic problems, especially if this meant trodding on the toes of powerful vested interests. Others saw it as a clever political move. By removing the most contentious aspect of CIÉ's original plan, the Government bought time for public inquiries on the Tallaght and Sandyford lines to proceed in a less poisonous atmosphere. But one way or the other, the Atkins report, intended to provide ministers with 'the fullest of facts', had been binned, and the EU's £114 million would have to be reallocated to other projects. Furthermore, by opting for a 'short tunnel' in the city centre, the Cabinet decided to proceed with a scheme which had been *specifically rejected* by the consultants. They advised that it would 'not offer any capacity advantages relative to the surface option', and, in any case, its key rationale was dubious because Dublin Corporation's proposed traffic management measures would remove much of the traffic conflict it was intended to avoid. But it had been recommended – for free – by Gerry Duggan in his PD policy document, 'Transport in Dublin: A City in Crisis', published just a few weeks earlier. In the light of the Government's decision to go for it, the £200,000 spent on the Atkins report was money down the drain.

The Dublin Transportation Office, set up in 1995 and given a half-hearted mandate to implement the DTI strategy, immediately began drafting a short-term action plan to alleviate growing traffic chaos in the city, proposing a number of public transport projects which could 'draw down' a sizeable proportion of the EU aid allocated for Luas. CIÉ made its own submission to Mary O'Rourke for £230 million to upgrade DART and other suburban rail services, and to renew track and signalling on the mainline rail network. Paradoxically, the political furore over the postponement of Luas had created a much more favourable climate for investment in public transport, with an increasing acceptance for radical steps to improve a notoriously underfunded service. Most of the money earmarked in the DTI's 1994 package had been spent on roads, and there were still schemes on the stocks with a ballpark value of £640 million – £100 million more than the estimate for a part-underground for Luas. This so undermined the DTI's 'balanced and integrated' strategy that the Dublin Cycling Campaign had already been moved to hold a mock funeral procession mourning its 'slow death', complete with white-faced pall-bearers carrying an empty black coffin through the city, before consigning it to the River Liffey in front of the Custom House.

Having ditched Atkins for tactical reasons, O'Rourke was desperately keen to be seen to make progress on implementing the Government's plan for Luas. 'She saw it as a chess game, with the queen still on the board', as one source acidly put it. Obviously, there was no point in Judge Seán O'Leary convening his scheduled public inquiry into the Tallaght-Dundrum line when there was still a major question mark over how the city centre section would be treated. So the inquiry was adjourned yet again to allow CIÉ to recast the project and then make separate applications to the Minister for two free-standing Luas lines – one from Tallaght to Middle Abbey Street and the other from Sandyford to St Stephen's Green. But though the judge had said there would be an opportunity to debate the underground issue in the light of Atkins' findings, the Government's decision that Line A would go ahead anyway effectively stifled public discussion. It also had the effect, more beneficially, of leaving the undergrounders with no leg to

Judge Seán O'Leary. Searing and pointed, considerate and witty, he so impressed senior officials with his expeditious handling of the Luas public inquiries that one of them wistfully commented, 'If only we could clone him...'

Irish Times

stand on. As if to prove that Luas was back on track, CIÉ applied for a light rail order for the Tallaght line less than three months later, and said a newsletter would be distributed to every household in Dublin informing the public of the Government's plan for an extended Luas system and giving an indicative time frame for its completion. Nonetheless, the application to proceed with 'Line A', as it was called, came exactly two years after the Dublin Light Rail Act became law and twelve months after Judge O'Leary had been forced to abort the scheduled public inquiry into CIÉ's original plan.

No wonder O'Rourke felt there was a need to establish a 'small but dynamic' Light Rail Advisory Action Group, chaired by Padraic White, former managing director of the IDA, to ensure that the project would be implemented as quickly as possible. Its membership includes the Luas project director, Donal Mangan, and Mary Harney's transport adviser, Gerry Duggan, as well as Pat Mangan, assistant secretary at the Department of Public Enterprise and former chairman of the DTI. Top brass in Heuston Station, who were used to being treated with contempt by a bossy Minister, opposed the creation of this task force because they saw it as a Trojan horse that could take Luas out of their orbit, both during its planning phase and, later, when it became operational. Their fears were confirmed when the Minister later commissioned Arthur Andersen and Steer Davies Gleave to produce a report suggesting that private sector interests should be invited to bid for a franchise to operate Luas and any rail link to Dublin Airport, in line with the Government's preference for public/private partnerships (PPPs). It emerged that the Department of Public Enterprise was particularly anxious to 'optimise risk transfer and cap costs in relation to the proposed underground section', effectively by getting the private sector to carry the can for it.

On 2nd November 1998, the Luas Line A public inquiry finally opened in the former Sugar Company offices on Earlsfort Terrace, and its star, undoubtedly, was Judge O'Leary. By contrast with the grey engineers who presided at road or motorway inquiries, he was searing and pointed, considerate and witty, and he also managed to deal expeditiously with all of the issues in just twenty days. At the end, Maurice Gaffney SC, for CIÉ, paid him a warm tribute, saying that everyone involved in the inquiry was 'overcome with admiration and gratitude at the way it was conducted'. Bang on time, the Cork-born judge submitted his report before Christmas, recommending that the project should go ahead, subject to twenty-one conditions – including compliance with a demand by the residents of Kingswood Heights, north of Tallaght, that a 2.5-metre wall would be built between them and the line, as if it was going to carry a belching 'iron horse' from the days of the Colorado gold rush. But while the judge recognised the 'depth of feeling and sense of loss' suffered by residents of Arran Quay Terrace over the inevitable demolition of their homes, he agreed that Luas would contribute to urban renewal and bring forward the day when cars would have only limited access to the city centre, in common with other European cities. O'Leary also emphasised the critical importance of managing the project to minimise disturbance to residents and traders during the two-year construction phase, particularly in the Markets area and Abbey Street. The Minister gave Line A her seal of approval on 1st March 1999, saying she thought the judge had done a 'splendid job' and he was subsequently appointed as inspector to preside at the public inquiry into Line B (Sandyford to St Stephen's Green), for which O'Rourke granted a light rail order in November 1999. In both cases, O'Leary's reports were crisp and clear, and written in such an unambiguous way that no lawyer who read them was able to find any grounds for judicial review. With so many other major infrastructural projects being planned, one senior official wistfully commented: 'If only we could clone him...'

By July 1999, in its first report, the Light Rail Advisory Action Group was able to report that the Luas project was 'substantially on schedule'. Preliminary work would start on Line A in October, underlining the transition from planning to implementation, and it would be open by February 2003. In the case of Line B, work could start even earlier than the autumn 2000 target in CIÉ's indicative timetable, with a view to completion in mid-2003 – and there was even the tantalising possibility that 'interim services' would be introduced on sections of each line as they were finished, given that CIÉ was scheduled to start taking delivery of the trams from GEC-Alsthom in October 2001. Consultations were proceeding on Line C, linking Middle Abbey Street with Connolly Station, and on six different options for Line D, serving Ballymun. All of this good news was designed to dispel widespread public scepticism about the project, an 'I'll believe it when I see it' attitude which had developed due to the endless delays. It was also intended to counter a cutting jibe from Earthwatch that Mary O'Rourke had become the 'Minister for Gridlock', as well as for aviation, electricity, telecommunications and much else besides.

Inevitably, there was 'some slippage' – as the action group termed it – in preparatory planning for the 2.5-kilometre underground link between St Stephen's Green and Broadstone. No final decision on this highly contentious proposal could be taken until after detailed geo-technical studies were completed. Even then, any scheme would be subjected to an environmental impact study, taking at least a year to complete, and this would have to examine alternatives such as the original on-street proposal. Ironically, the consultants chosen by CIÉ to examine underground route options for Luas were the very ones who had recommended proceeding on-street – WS Atkins. As part of this study, geo-technical specialists drilled forty-six boreholes along the potential routes during the autumn to assess the conditions for underground construction. These tests showed that tunnelling would present some problems in the north inner city, particularly near Broadstone, because of its variable boulder clay – 'more boulder than clay', as one of the Atkins engineers commented. The consultants were also grappling with such issues as how to handle the tunnel openings at either end, at St Stephen's Green and in the vicinity of Broadstone. There was also the question of cost. Running Luas underground in the city centre would add at least £300 million to the overall bill for the project, without offering any increase in its capacity to transport more passengers. 'Unless it's done in the context of a public-private partnership franchise to run the whole system, it's a non-runner', said one well-placed source. Indeed, the Department of Finance had become so sceptical about this element of the project that an initial draft of the National Development Plan 2000-2006 did not allocate any money to pay for it. Only later was a £300 million 'contingency fund' included in the plan, presumably at the insistence of Harney and O'Rourke. But some transport planners were still working on the assumption that a final, irrevocable decision on the underground option for Luas would not be taken until the Tallaght line started running in early 2003. Once people saw the trams running through the streets, they reasoned, there would be no question why any of it should 'go under'. There was some good news for CIÉ, too. The action group came out against procuring Luas by means of a PPP because this would only mean delaying it further due to the need for new legislation and contract procedures that had yet to be developed. Michael Sheedy, CIÉ's project manager, responded by announcing that the company intends to operate the light rail system 'on a 24-hour basis, 365 days a year if passenger demands so require'. CIÉ also believed it was 'essential' to build the first phases of the project to a high standard. 'A cheap and cheerful scheme would be seen as negative and take from the perception of a quality system which is essential to its high patronage', Sheedy said.

Other cities went through the same pain that Dublin was facing to acquire high-quality light rail systems, and none of them regret it. In Grenoble, for example, there was a similar outbreak of scepticism in 1983, when its modern on-street tramway was being planned. This was reflected in the results of a referendum, which approved the project by a slim majority of 53%. A year after the trams started running in 1989, public approval soared to 93%, and planning started

Frank McDonald

Grenoble in south-eastern France became the first city in Europe to opt for a modern, up-to-date tramway system. These photographs demolish two myths about light rail transit – that the 'wirescape' carrying its electric power is a major eyesore in the urban environment, and that a city needs broad boulevards to accommodate trams.

Frank McDonald

Strasbourg used its light rail project to lever major environmental improvements, such as the creation of a stylish pedestrian piazza on Place Kléber, the city's main square (pictured above), and high-quality street furniture, including ticket machines, seating, and emblematic modernist stations such as the one shown below.

immediately for extensions to the system. The same pattern was repeated in Strasbourg, where the most beautiful trams in Europe started gliding through its streets in 1994. And because the city's entire bus network was replanned to link up with the tramway, passenger numbers have doubled, with the trams alone carrying 60,000 people per day, boosting public transport use by 43% and reducing car traffic entering the inner city by 17%. The project was steered through by Mayor Catherine Trautmann, in typically determined French style, and easily achieved its central aim of 'reducing the hegemony of the car'. Though critics of Luas were quick to point out that part of Strasbourg's tramway runs underground (to serve its mainline station), the length of tunnel is only 1.7 kilometres and its proportion of the overall system will obviously decline over time as it is extended. They also ignored the fact that light rail was used as a lever to gain major environmental improvements in Strasbourg. No longer would traffic be permitted to criss-cross the city's historic core. Under the plan championed by Trautmann, it is allowed in on an access-only basis. Place Kléber, the main square, has been transformed. Once dominated by traffic – up to 50,000 vehicles used to pass through it every day – it is now a vast pedestrian plaza, with short-term parking for a thousand cars underneath. Similarly, traffic has been banished from Rue des Francs Bourgeois, Strasbourg's equivalent of Grafton Street, leaving it free for pedestrians and trams.

Manchester's privately run Metrolink light rail system has also been a 'roaring success', in the words of Pat Karney, a Dublin-born member of its Labour-controlled city council. Inaugurated in 1992, four years after it was planned, the first tram line between Bury and Altricham, running on-street through the city centre, carried more than fifteen million passengers in 1998 – double the number that used the disconnected suburban railway services it replaced – and had taken at least a million car journeys off the roads. By then, a second tram line was under construction to Eccles, via Salford Quays, and further lines were being planned to Rochdale, Didsbury, Manchester Airport and the 2002 Commonwealth Games site. 'We would have trams running all over the place if we had the money', Karney told the *Irish Times*. 'What's more, the disruption during the construction phase wasn't as horrendous as we thought. People knew what they were getting and went along with it because it would help sell the city.' Two mistakes were made. Firstly, opting for high-floored trams to avoid lowering station platforms on the old railway line meant having to build ugly platforms, a metre high, in city-centre streets. And secondly, resistance from property owners resulted in the light rail 'wirescape' – barely noticeable in Grenoble or Strasbourg – being suspended from thick black poles rather than from buildings on the street frontages, with so many of them littering Piccadilly Gardens that it became known as 'Pole Plaza'. Despite these drawbacks, Metrolink quickly became an icon of the city as the first 'new generation' tramway in Britain. According to the British government's Urban Task Force, chaired by architect Richard (Lord) Rogers: 'The experience of Manchester's Metrolink shows that a major new public transport scheme can help reinvigorate a city's transport system, taking cars off the street and enhancing the city's identity.'

Despite all of this evidence, the sniping at Luas continued. In mid-December 1999, the three-day inquiry into Line C – linking Middle Abbey Street with Connolly Station – heard claims by apartment residents in the Custom House Docks that they would become 'prisoners in our own homes' as a result of Luas halting in Harbourmaster Place beside a new entrance to the revamped station. Ignoring the record of high-quality public transport in boosting property values in the area it serves, as the DART experience shows, 222 owners – including absentee landlords living in Tralee, Hong Kong and the United States – objected to the proposed stop because it implied that the line would be extended along a narrow strip to the rear of the apartment blocks, raising fears that this would draw 'low life' into the area. Rather surprisingly, Judge Seán O'Leary took their side, saying that CIÉ had not properly considered the 'adverse consequences' of an estimated 20,000 passengers per day using the Harbourmaster Place stop. In his view, the quality of life of those living or working in the vicinity would be 'changed utterly' by the 'severe effect' of this large influx. Accordingly, he recommended that the Minister should only approve Line C as far as Store Street, leaving the Light Rail Project Team to come up with a more acceptable link to Connolly Station.

However, the most surprising salvo against Luas was fired by CIÉ's own top brass in Heuston. After it became the focus of public controversy, they sought to disown the whole scheme, describing it as a Government project for which CIÉ was merely acting as agent. Even as late as April 1999, its then chairman Brian Joyce expressed alarm about the escalating cost of Luas – estimated at £671 million, including the proposed underground link from St Stephen's Green to Broadstone – and suggested to Mary O'Rourke that this money 'could be used more effectively in solving the gridlock problem in Dublin' by investing it articulated buses, upgraded suburban rail services and a new airport rail link. Joyce's letter obviously irritated the Minister, particularly as it seemed to indicate that CIÉ wanted to change tack and abandon a key element of the DTI strategy which she had committed herself to deliver. 'I find it difficult to understand how your board can reconcile the reservations conveyed in your letter with its concurrent advocacy of the project before a public inquiry … and with its long-standing promotion of, and support for, light rail since the inception of the DTI process', she said in her response. Pat Mangan, who had presided over the DTI, wrote to Michael McDonnell asking what evaluation CIÉ had carried out to enable it to reach the conclusion that the Luas financial allocation should be diverted to other projects. 'Does CIÉ have a clear and measured assessment as to the order of its overall investment priorities?' he asked, pointedly. In his reply, McDonnell had to admit that CIÉ management had 'not specifically costed alternative public transport options', but he insisted that a bus-based solution using the Luas corridors would be 'operationally feasible' and would avoid the need for 'expen-

Pete Hanan

Mary O'Rourke first heard about the resignation of Brian Joyce as chairman of CIÉ while she was 'in the bath' listening to *Morning Ireland* on RTÉ radio.

opposite

A computer-generated perspective of the northern portals of the Port Tunnel. The fact that the M1 would run directly into it, with city-centre traffic consigned to slip roads, strongly suggested that this was indeed the first phase of the Eastern Bypass.

sive property acquisition, major utilities diversion and on-street disruption arising from construction work'. The thousands of hours of work put into designing and progressing Luas over the previous four years, it seemed, had no value at all. But there was another interpretation: the demented proposal to bury it, merely to avoid 'disrupting' traffic between St Stephen's Green and Parnell Square, had added immeasurably to the overall cost, threatening to devour half of the total investment allocated for public transport Dublin, even though Luas would carry only a tenth of all passengers. Mary O'Rourke's '£400 million-plus' had become a financial nightmare of unknown, and unknowable, proportions.

Despite an attempt by the Department of Public Enterprise to suppress it under the Freedom of Information Act on the grounds of 'commercial sensitivity and/or deliberative process of Dept', the embarrassing core issue in the exchange of correspondence found its way into the news pages of the *Irish Times*. A week later, on 6th March 2000, Brian Joyce resigned as chairman of CIÉ, citing fundamental differences with the Minister over Luas, the State company's autonomy and 'sub strata' interference by her in industrial relations issues which had completely undermined CIÉ management. On RTÉ's *Morning Ireland* radio programme the following day, O'Rourke said the first she heard of it was while she was 'in the bath' listening to the 7 o'clock news headlines. 'Within minutes, her office was on the phone to *Morning Ireland*, explaining how an audit of spending on rail safety, to be published that day, would not make happy reading for Mr Joyce', reported Mark Brennock, the *Irish Times* political correspondent. According to O'Rourke, the chairman had resigned because he 'couldn't face the music'. But the rail safety audit, which noted that 'a great deal has been done' by Iarnród Éireann and recommended additional management controls to speed up the programme, was hardly a resigning matter. O'Rourke's attempt to give it an alternative spin, said a hard-hitting editorial in the *Irish Times*, was 'mean-minded and self-serving' because it 'amounted to a denial of responsibility and a transference of blame'. Fortunately, the full text of Joyce's resignation letter had been published by the newspaper, allowing its readers to make up their own minds on where the truth actually resided.

Unlike Luas, the Dublin Port Tunnel was dogged by controversy right from its inception. In June 1996, a month before an EIS on the scheme was published, Britain's Health and Safety Executive implicated the New Austrian Tunnelling Method (NATM) in the 'catastrophic failure' of a tunnel at London's Heathrow Airport during construction of the express rail link to Paddington Station. As *New Civil Engineer* magazine said at the time, the HSE's 86-page report recited 'a tale of inadequacy and failure in concept, design, management and execution of NATM projects worldwide', and warned that all parties involved in their design and construction would have to take heed of its litany of ninety-seven safety recommendations. Of particular note in the Dublin context was the HSE's finding that twin-bore tunnels – as envisaged for much of the port access route – required thorough ground investigations to minimise the likelihood of 'meeting unexpected conditions of a critical nature'. Coincidentally, the Heathrow tunnel

courtesy of the Port Tunnel promoters

collapse happened in October 1994, a day after the Government here had sanctioned a twin-tunnel port access route using NATM, which was then regarded as
a cheaper option. Four weeks earlier, four people died in Munich when a bus
plunged into an enormous crater caused by another NATM failure. Unlike conventional tunnelling which relies on building a concrete structure to retain a tunnel as it is bored, the Austrian method involves spraying each section of a newly
excavated tunnel with quick-setting concrete to form a retaining shell. However,
the HSE concluded that the particular hazard with NATM was 'the absence of
any ready means of supporting the heading should ground collapse into the tunnel'. It didn't help that Geoconsult, the Austrian engineers involved in the
Heathrow project, were also acting as consultants for the Dublin Port Tunnel.

Not surprisingly, the HSE report cast a dark shadow over this improved
access route to the increasingly busy port, now catering for almost two million
trucks per year, in line with the Government's decision that its capacity should be
doubled. Consultant engineers Ove Arup & Partners and Geoconsult, who had
been advising Dublin Corporation on plans for a full-blown Eastern Bypass
motorway, were appointed by the National Roads Authority in 1995 to design the
scheme – a mainly tunnelled four-lane dual carriageway – and prepare an EIS. At
the time, it was envisaged that the route would link the M1 just north of
Whitehall with the port, and include one kilometre of twin 'cut and cover' tunnels and 2.4 kilometres of twin bored tunnels with associated interchanges,
including a new single-span bridge over the River Tolka. The cost was estimated
at £130 million – already significantly higher than the Fianna Fáil-Labour coalition had bargained for at £104 million. The fact that the M1 would run directly
into the tunnel, with city-centre traffic consigned to slip roads on either side,
strongly suggested that this was indeed the first phase of the Eastern Bypass.
Traffic projections indicated that a large proportion of the vehicles using the
route – over 80%, in fact —would be cars rather than trucks heading to and from
the port, and the study suggested tolling to ensure that it fulfilled its primary purpose of removing heavy-goods traffic from the Liffey Quays instead of merely
serving as a fast-track commuter route. Assuming that Dublin City Council sanctioned it and that a motorway order was approved by the Minister for the
Environment following a public inquiry, it was envisaged that work would start
in 1998 and the Port Tunnel would be open to traffic in 2001.

Almost immediately, residents of Marino rose up in revolt against the proposal. They were alarmed by the news that the tunnel would be bored and blast-
ed through limestone rock at an average depth of 16 metres (53 ft), directly
underneath almost three hundred houses in the area, causing noise, vibration and
even 'some ground movements', as the EIS put it. They were even more alarmed
about these conclusions because of the serious questions which had been raised
about the safety of using NATM, even though the consultants pledged that the
British HSE's recommendations 'would be fully considered and taken into
account where appropriate' in the design of the Dublin Port Tunnel, saying that

alternative tunnelling methods were not being ruled out. Residents of Whitehall and Santry were also alarmed that the tunnel would result in air pollution from traffic in the vicinity of its portals and along the M1 motorway, while those in East Wall were not looking forward to a predicted 39% increase in traffic in the north port area – something that would only be relieved by a full Eastern Bypass. It was also revealed that a trench measuring 150 feet wide and 66 feet deep would have to be dug right through Fairview Park to make way for the Port Tunnel. Spurred on by the Marino Development Action Group, they all got together to form the prosaically named Combined Residents Associations, and waged such a relentless campaign that even strongly pro-roads councillors, such as Fianna Fáil's Ivor Callelly and Seán Haughey, broke ranks to denounce the scheme.

Facing his first major challenge since taking office as City Manager in June 1996, John Fitzgerald quickly realised that a decision on changing the City Plan to facilitate the scheme would have to be deferred to allow more time for public consultation 'in the interests of promoting the democratic process'. If it had been put to a vote, he feared that it would have been defeated. The Corporation's project manager for the Port Tunnel, engineer Gerry Murphy, conceded that the fact that people were afraid of it was a matter of serious concern, and he repeatedly stressed that the tunnel was safe because it would be bored through hard limestone rather than soft boulder clay. But there was no assuaging the residents. Since this was the first bored tunnel ever proposed in Ireland, they had a natural fear of its environmental impacts and were not prepared to accept the assurances of 'experts' at face value. 'Bluntly, they don't trust us', one senior engineer conceded. So they picketed City Hall as councillors met in stormy sessions and John Fitzgerald worried that the whole project might be lost because of what he bluntly described as a 'political cop-out'. Meanwhile, the National Roads Authority had nothing to say about the fact that one of its board members, Peter Langford, was chairman of Ove Arup & Partners, consulting engineers for its biggest single project, the Port Tunnel, and other major road schemes, such as the Arklow by-pass. Langford himself said he took no part in any NRA meeting dealing with projects in which his own firm was involved. It was one of those conflicts that are almost inevitable in a relatively small country with a limited pool of civil engineering expertise.

Those who opposed the Port Tunnel from a principled position, such as the Green Party, argued that the project was a misguided response to the tightening traffic noose around the port, and that it was only being pursued as a Trojan horse for the Eastern Bypass. After all, it would create a north-south connection between the port and the M50, following exactly the same alignment as Arups-Geoconsult had proposed for the northern segment of their Eastern Relief Route just three years earlier. The Greens argued that an east-west route would be more logical, given that so much port-related traffic uses the quays, and called for a re-examination of the Liffey Tunnel scheme proposed by National Toll Roads plc in 1992. They also pointed to plans by Harry Dobson, a Canadian multi-million-

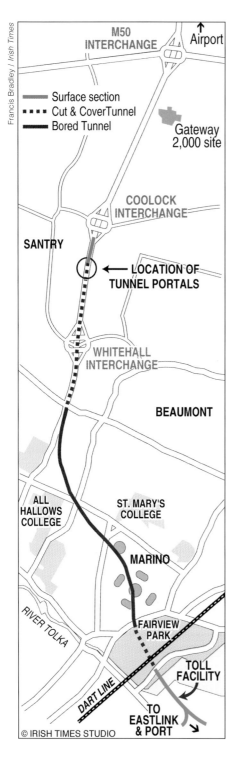

Francis Bradley / Irish Times

M50
INTERCHANGE
↑ Airport

— Surface section
■■■■ Cut & CoverTunnel
▬▬ Bored Tunnel

Gateway
2,000 site

COOLOCK
INTERCHANGE

SANTRY

← LOCATION OF
TUNNEL PORTALS

WHITEHALL
INTERCHANGE

BEAUMONT

ALL
HALLOWS
COLLEGE

ST. MARY'S
COLLEGE

MARINO

RIVER TOLKA

FAIRVIEW
PARK

DART LINE

TOLL
FACILITY

© IRISH TIMES STUDIO

TO
EASTLINK
& PORT

aire, to create a national freight distribution centre in Clondalkin with a rail link to Dublin Port. This imaginative proposal was the brainchild of estate agent Fintan Gunne, but his premature death in 1997 and the absence of a real commitment to the concept by CIÉ meant that it was not realised. Despite its significant job creation potential, there was also strong opposition to the project among Clondalkin residents who feared that their roads would bear the brunt of all the heavy-goods traffic it would inevitably generate. Under fire, Dobson withdrew his planning application for his 'logistics centre', and subsequently sold half of his equity to Dunloe Ewart plc, chaired by Noel Smyth, the extraordinarily successful entrepreneur-solicitor who had played a leading role behind the scenes in the controversial Ballsbridge bakery site transaction in 1990. Inevitably, an office park is now being considered for the Clondalkin site. But even while Fintan Gunne's concept was still on the table, the Port Tunnel juggernaut was in motion, and there was no willingness on the part of the NRA or anyone else involved in the project to look at alternatives of any kind. And there could be no doubt that they had chosen a north-south alignment for the port access route, rather than an east-west one, to keep the Eastern Bypass option alive. In this, they had some powerful allies, including the AA, Dublin Chamber of Commerce, IBEC, the road haulage sector, the DTO, and residents of Drumcondra – Bertie Ahern's own people – who believed the Port

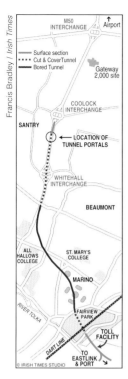

Juxtaposed maps of the Port Tunnel and its extension southwards via Sandymount Strand show the master plan for a full Eastern Bypass.

opposite

Map showing the revised route for the Port Tunnel, with the northern portals relocated from Whitehall to Coolock Lane.

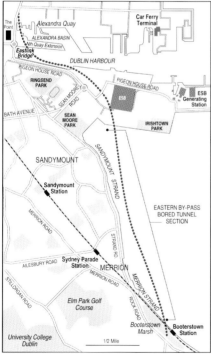

Tunnel would bring some relief from intolerable levels of through-traffic.

But the opponents were not entirely defenceless in the face of this phalanx. Their allies included Adrian Phillips, professor of geology at Trinity College, who warned that the southern part of their area lay in a geologically unstable fault zone, with no guarantee that the tunnel would not run into problematic buried rivers – a thesis he later defended at the public inquiry. Prof Ian Clayton of Surrey University, who had been retained by the Marino Development Action Group, also challenged the geological assessment carried out by the consultants, generating a fractious argument about how many test boreholes had been drilled. By then, relations were so strained that the action group would only communicate with the project team through its lawyers. Describing the scheme as 'not just imperfect, but totally wrong', the group said: 'A major infrastructure project such as a port access route must be 100% right in terms of viability, health and safety, value for money and soundness of construction. All concerned parties, including residents, must have a proactive involvement.' It also condemned six councillors for taking part in a 'junket' to view similar tunnels in Oslo and London, and, worse still, returning to Dublin apparently quite impressed by what they saw. But with the 1997 general election looming on the political horizon, one thing was certain – the City Council would not take any decision to sanction the Port Tunnel until after it was over.

More studies and public consultations followed, as a result of which the scheme was amended to make it more saleable politically. Though the 'A6' alignment was reaffirmed, the project team made substantial concessions by agreeing to relocate the northern portals on the M1 from Whitehall to a largely industrial zone north of Coolock Lane, and to dig the tunnel deeper beneath the houses in Marino, at an overall extra cost of £30 million. Even though this did not go far enough to satisfy all of the objectors, it was enough to persuade the City Council to confront what John Fitzgerald had called 'the single most important decision facing the city'. And so, with the general election safely out of the way, councillors adopted the revised scheme by thirty-one votes to twelve. The additional cost of the project didn't matter to them because most of the money was coming from somewhere else, mainly Brussels. Yet it was becoming apparent that the price of the Port Tunnel was escalating out of control, with Prof Simon Perry of Trinity College warning that it could exceed £200 million – roughly double what the Government thought it would cost in 1994. By the time a motorway order had been prepared by the project team in 1998, the estimate had already reached £178 million, and few doubted that it would continue to rise from this new base figure. The Port Tunnel, in other words, was becoming a black hole that threatened to devour the funds allocated for other DTI projects, such as Luas.

It also seemed to be jinxed. In February 1999, a few weeks before the public inquiry was due to start, Geoconsult was convicted at the Old Bailey in London of safety failures over the 1994 Heathrow tunnel collapse and fined £500,000 sterling. Mr Justice Cresswell described it as 'one of the worst civil engineering disasters in the United Kingdom in the last quarter of a century', saying the huge crater it created could have 'unzipped' the Piccadilly underground line and crushed people to death. He imposed a record fine of £1.2 million on Balfour Beatty, the main contractors, after hearing evidence that they had been running a self-certification system which gave them control of construction and design. Geoconsult was responsible for the design and supervision of the Heathrow tunnel, but only one engineer was employed to monitor soil shifts and interpret the data, leading the judge to brand the Austrian consultants as 'the watchdogs who didn't bark'. Balfour Beatty and Geoconsult had denied charges of failing to ensure the safety of both employees and members of the public, and it was argued on behalf of the Austrian consultants that they were being scapegoated for the defects in the contract, but the judge concluded that both parties had fallen 'seriously short' of health and safety regulations. This damning verdict had implications for the Dublin Port Tunnel, as the NRA's intention from the outset was to put it out to tender as a 'design and build' scheme. In its wake, the project team was at pains to stress that it would be properly designed and that detailed day-to-day monitoring would ensure the required level of safety.

Everyone had their say at the six-week public inquiry – the longest for any road scheme in the Republic. All of the arguments, both for and against, were fully ventilated, including the Marino Development Action Group's claim, repeatedly stated by its spokesman Fintan Cassidy, that the A6 route had been chosen by the project team without any prior consultation and presented as a fait accompli. Even after it was thrown back into the melting pot, as a result of MDAG's campaign, it re-emerged as the preferred route simply because, as Cassidy said, it was 'the top half of the Eastern Bypass' – though the Corporation's engineers had always maintained that they were designing a 'stand-alone' project. Inevitably, their opponents highlighted the safety record of NATM and challenged the credibility of Geoconsult in the wake of its Old Bailey conviction. They also claimed that the British HSE's ninety-seven recommendations had not yet been fully factored into the cost of the Port Tunnel, should NATM be chosen as the construction method. Prof Adrian Phillips expanded on his concerns about ground conditions along the route, but the project team had its own geological consultants, headed by Irmina Poeschl, another Austrian, and she argued that it was a question of interpretation. What faults there were could not be regarded as an engineering impediment, though they might have implications for the cost of the project. There was also the outstanding issue of tolling. In October 1998, the National Roads Authority confirmed a toll of £3 per car (index-linked), with trucks travelling free of charge, making it unlikely that residents in Drumcondra and other areas would get much relief from 'rat-running' commuters. The two inspectors who presided at the inquiry – Anthony O'Connell, a retired engineer from the Department of the Environment, and Dr Vincent O'Malley, of Forbairt – submitted their report to the Minister in early September 1999, by which time the cost estimate had been revised upwards to £204 million. However essential Noel Dempsey regarded the Port Tunnel, he had to tread carefully because the MDAG had reconstituted itself, using an off-the-shelf company called Zuband Ltd, and retained a team of lawyers to pursue a judicial review of his decision, if necessary. Dempsey approved the plan with some minor amendments just before Christmas 1999, but the announcement was made by Bertie Ahern, underlining the importance which he attached to it, or, perhaps, showing that he couldn't resist playing to the gallery of his Drumcondra home-base. 'For too long', the Taoiseach declared, 'our capital city has been strangled by articulated trucks and other heavy-goods vehicles trundling to and from Dublin Port.' Marino residents and other opponents of the scheme were 'disgusted' by the decision, according to Fintan Cassidy, because it seemed to confirm that nobody had listened to their concerns. But they did not follow through on their threat to take the case to the High Court – 'we ran out of time and money', Cassidy said – and resorted instead to direct action against further test borehole drilling until they received an assurance that the work would be independently monitored. Six months before Dempsey's decision, Dublin Corporation's project manager, Gerry Murphy, found a new job with the NRA in charge of developing public-private partnerships.

There was, of course, an alternative solution to the port traffic problem, but it was so radical that the authorities could not even bring themselves to consider it, even for a moment. Put forward out-of-the-blue in 1989 by consultants

ESB International, it would have involved relocating most of Dublin Port's activities to a purpose-built container port near Loughshinny, in north County Dublin. The nominated site could not have been better located because it was less than a mile from the Dublin-Belfast railway line and just a couple of miles from the planned M1 motorway, making it accessible to everywhere in Ireland. All 'lo-lo' (load on, load off) and 'ro-ro' (roll on, roll off) freight could have been processed through this new facility, leaving the old port to deal with passenger ferries and the odd cruise liner, while simultaneously opening up a vast acreage of land for commercial and residential development conveniently located to the city centre. But ESBI's exercise in lateral thinking found no favour with the then Dublin Port & Docks Board, which dug in its heels against the Loughshinny option with such determination that the DTI's consultants, Steer Davies Gleave, were expressly forbidden even to consider it. Others in positions of power had a different reason for keeping the port in the middle of Dublin Bay; come hell or high water, they were determined that nothing would get in the way of a north-south port tunnel route and, ultimately, a full-blown Eastern Bypass.

L ike other major pieces of infrastructure planned for Dublin, the Port Tunnel is at least four years behind schedule and is now unlikely to be finished until mid-2004, at the earliest. It was among the projects cited by the Cross-Departmental Team on Infrastructural Development in its September 1999 report to the Government, which recommended ways of speeding up the legal process by establishing a special division of the High Court or perhaps even amending the Constitution to curtail the rights of objectors. In some cases, certainly, major schemes have been held up by no more than a handful of people exercising their legal right to seek a judicial review of ministerial decisions following completion of the full process of environmental impact assessment, public consultations and inquiries. The Southern Cross section of the M50, linking Firhouse with Sandyford, was approved in August 1992 by the then Minister for the Environment, Michael Smith, and should have been open to traffic by the end of 1997. But it was held up for three years by the Select Vestry of Whitechurch and two local landowners, Edward Fitzachry and Major TB McDowell, chairman of the Irish Times Trust. Their legal action, settled at the doors of the High Court on terms which have never been disclosed, resulted in the creation of a huge artificial mound – what one engineer described as 'the largest earthworks to be carried out in this country since Newgrange' – to screen the properties of those involved from the sight and sound of the motorway. Meanwhile, its cost leaped from an estimated £55 million in 1992 to £90 million in 1999 – and that may not even be the final figure. Similarly, after Noel Dempsey approved the last leg of the M50 – the South

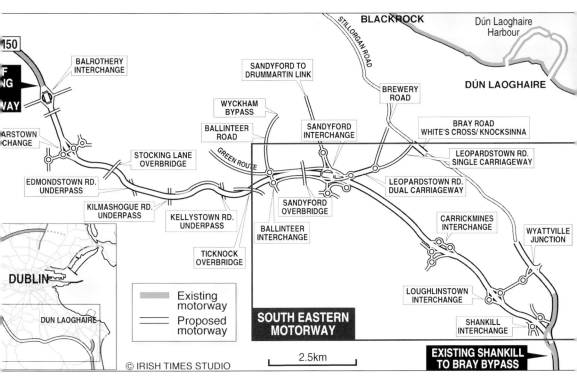

Map showing the Southern Cross Route and the South Eastern Motorway, both of which were held up by legal actions by affected landowners.

Eastern Motorway linking Sandyford with Shankill – in October 1998, his ministerial order was challenged in the High Court by Birmingham-based Jackson Way Properties, on the grounds that its 106 acres of development land in Carrickmines would be severed by the eleven-kilometre route. The action was unsuccessful, and, in December 1999, an appeal to the Supreme Court was settled, again on undisclosed terms. Soaring property prices also meant that the estimated cost of the South Eastern Motorway had to be revised sharply upwards from £161 million to £300 million – or a whopping £27 million *per kilometre*. Dempsey's department was even more irritated by a major challenge to the £65 million Kildare bypass, especially as this involved a probing investigation by the European Commission. In March 1999, An Taisce made an official complaint to the Commission that the design of this bypass, which includes a 1.5 kilometre cutting south of the traffic-choked town, could result in the de-watering of Pollardstown Fen, an important natural habitat northeast of Kildare designated as a Special Area of Conservation under EU legislation. According to Tony Lowes, then chairman of An Taisce's natural environment group, the Commission, which would be providing most of the funding, said the documentation submitted was 'the most devastating ever seen in support of an environmental complaint'. As long ago as 1993, the Office of Public Works drew attention to the potential impact of the by-pass cutting on the water-table in the Curragh, including Pollardstown Fen, from where Guinness draws spring water for its Dublin brewery. However, its strong reservations were not sufficient to persuade those designing the by-pass to eliminate the cutting, apparently because of a determination to protect the nearby National Stud. But the Kildare county planning officer, Philip Jones, later appointed as a senior inspector with An Bord Pleanála, told the 1993 public inquiry into the by-pass scheme that if it came to a choice, Pollardstown Fen was more deserving of protection. The National Stud could be relocated. Tony Lowes, who wears several hats in the environmental arena through his involvement in An Taisce, Lancefort and Friends of the Irish Environment, was equally mystified about why the engineers were 'going to such lengths to keep the road in a cutting when the simplest and cheapest solution would be allow it to run along the surface'. Having toyed with a proposal to line the cutting with a special plastic membrane to prevent the Curragh aquifer draining into it, the National Roads Authority finally plumped for a Dutch system known as 'tanking' to control groundwater drainage, adding £5 million to the cost.

A much more famous battle was fought for the Glen of the Downs, one of the most picturesque valleys in Ireland. It started in March 1997 after Brendan Howlin confirmed Wicklow County Council's compulsory purchase order for a stretch of woodland on either side of the N11 to enable the road to be turned into a dual carriageway. The problem was that the primeval forest was in State ownership and had been designated as a nature reserve in 1980, giving official recognition to the importance of this almost unspoiled glen. It was precisely to stop similar schemes in Britain that 'Swampy' and his fellow eco-warriors set up camp on targeted sites, occupied threatened trees, and dug tunnels in the earth to frustrate construction gangs and the private security firms and police who protected them. For more than two years, a plucky band of Swampy's Irish cousins maintained a constant presence in the Glen of the Downs, while one of their number – Dermot Murphy, a computer programmer – pursued a legal action against the county council, claiming that it had no right to destroy part of the nature reserve merely so that motorists could save a few minutes on their way to the next traffic jam. Public reaction was mixed. Sympathisers honked their horns or brought them food, while opponents accused them of doing more damage to the woods than the road ever would. It was clear they did not have the type of widespread local support enjoyed by their counterparts in the English shires. Unfortunately for those occupying the glen, the judicial review was confined to narrow procedural issues, and even though the High Court found that the county council had erred on this score, it ruled that the road scheme should be allowed to proceed – a verdict upheld by the Supreme Court in December 1999.

Though desperately disappointed, the eco-warriors gave no indication that they would give up their fight. They were clearly unprepared for the arrival, just four days after the judgment, of a chainsaw gang which proceeded to rip through scrub and trees on the east side of the N11. As the *Irish Times* reported, 'white crosses hung from the trees on both sides of the road while a lone bugle player added to the funeral atmosphere. The sign declaring the area a nature reserve looked incongruous beside the felled trees.' Bryan Doyle, the Wicklow County Secretary, pointed out that ten years had passed since the decision was taken to widen the road, and he pledged that the council would plant 5,000 trees elsewhere from Glen of the Downs seedlings. Murphy went back to the courts and obtained a temporary injunction to prevent further tree-felling, on the basis that the glen had been designated as a Special Area of Conservation under the EU Habitats Directive. But he was accused by Michael Looby, the County Engineer, of deliberately holding back this point for the sole purpose of delaying the road works. After Murphy lost his latest legal action to block the project, Síle de Valera, the Minister for Arts and Heritage, waded in with an absurd order closing the Glen of the Downs to the public, on the grounds that 'structures, devices and tunnels' had been installed there, causing 'damage to the nature reserve'. Obviously, the order did not apply to the chainsaw gangs, because, backed up by gardaí, they continued to hack down the remaining trees standing in the way during the first weeks of the new millennium. Subsequently, thirteen eco-warriors were jailed for contempt by the High Court after they refused to give undertakings not to trespass on lands in the glen owned by the county council. After

For more than two years, a plucky band of eco-warriors maintained a constant presence in the Glen of the Downs in protest against the existing N11 road through this designated nature reserve being turned into a dual carriageway.

Matt Kavanagh / *Irish Times*

Irish Times

Liam Connellan, chairman of the National Roads Authority. He claimed in 1999 that spending almost £1 billion a year on national roads would relegate traffic congestion 'largely to the domain of an unhappy memory'.

spending more than a week in Clover Hill Prison, nine of them 'purged' their contempt to gain their freedom, but the more recalcitrant chose to remain behind bars for longer periods, and were soon joined by two more. The NRA defended the scheme on the basis that the road through the glen was already carrying 18,000 vehicles a day in 1997 – 4,000 more than the threshold at which a dual carriageway should be considered for safety reasons. But it could not say whether this torrent on the N11, which had increased to 25,000 by the end of 1999, was national traffic or commuter traffic emanating from the dormitory suburbs spreading across north Wicklow, because, incredibly, it had not carried out an origin-and-destination survey. The estimated cost, meanwhile, had shot up to £35 million.

The NRA, set up in 1994 under the chairmanship of Liam Connellan, former director general of the Confederation of Irish Industry, is such a champion of road-building that it even plans to run the N4 as a dual carriageway right through the centre of Sligo, demolishing dozens of houses along the route. Its headquarters are in St Martin's House in Waterloo Road, where almost half of its 68-strong staff, including all of the top executives, have free off-street parking spaces. In its 1998 *Road Needs Study* – a wish-list of all the road schemes it wanted to pursue – the NRA showed that it was still firmly locked in a 'predict and provide' mode. This was the simple rule of thumb which informed road planning in Britain since Ernest Marples opened its M1 motorway in 1959, promising motorists freedom of the road. The main task of transport planners was to forecast how much traffic there would be, and then build enough road space to cater for it. They didn't realise at the time that building more roads would simply generate more traffic. 'Predict and provide' became so entrenched that traffic forecasts could not even be challenged by objectors at public inquiries into major road schemes. It reached its apotheosis in 1989 with the Tory government's policy document, *Roads for Prosperity*, and Margaret Thatcher raving about the 'great car economy'. Ben Elton, in his scathingly anti-car novel *Gridlock*, summed it up by having his fictional Minister for Transport, Digby Parkhurst, address the Tory party's annual conference in these terms: 'I shall tell you what we are going to do. We are going to build roads! We are going to build roads, roads and then more roads! We are going to build roads to tunnel under roads, roads to fly over roads, roads to fly over roads flying over roads. Roads, roads, roads, roads, roads!'

Growing public protest at the damage being done to the English country-side prompted a critical review in the mid-1990s of the whole idea of throwing roads at the traffic problem. John Gummer, then Environment Secretary, became the first senior Tory to disown Thatcher's 'great car economy' when he declared in 1994 that the policy of catering for cars on an open-ended basis 'cannot go on'. His conviction was reinforced by the British government's Trunk Road Assessment Group, which explicitly recognised in 1997 that the volume of traffic was not inexorable and could be influenced by policy choices. 'Different policies will result in different forecasts', it said. And so, 'predict and provide' became 'predict and prevent'. Though mass car ownership had offered us control over time and space which no previous generation ever had, it had become self-defeating. 'Liberating our minds from the assumption that solving congestion depends on building more roads has been an important step in allowing us to consider alternatives', said Prof Phil Goodwin, the British government's transport policy adviser. Its 1998 White Paper, *A New Deal for Transport*, envisaged the introduction of road pricing measures, such as electronic tolling, with deputy prime minister John Prescott pledging that the revenue they raised would be used to fund improvements to public transport. Prescott, whose fondness for Jaguars was notorious, also planned to impose a tax on workplace parking to discourage car-commuting, though lobbying by supermarkets and shopping centres saw off plans for a similar parking levy on their turf. Just fifteen months later, he appeared to change gear by assuring the road lobby that local authorities would have to hold referendums before moving to introduce congestion charging, and that funding would be provided for thirty-seven major road schemes, including a possible widening to ten lanes of the busiest section of London's notoriously congested M25 orbital motorway. The red flag had been raised by Tony Blair, who feared that some of Prescott's more radical proposals would aggravate his party's recently acquired middle-class supporters in the suburbs. Even Blair could not conceal his amusement at William Hague's taunting of 'Two Jags' Prescott as 'someone whose idea of a park-and-ride scheme is to park one Jaguar in order to drive away in the other'.

However lukewarm, the change in Britain's transport planning philosophy – always influential here – seemed to go unnoticed by our National Roads Authority. Left to its own devices, it would mimic Ben Elton's transport minister by building flyovers at every defective roundabout interchange on the M50, turning them all into triple-decker affairs. Using the US Highway Capacity Manual as its bible, the NRA's *Road Needs Study* estimated that £6.14 *billion* was needed to finance further road improvements to national primary and secondary routes over twenty years to cater for anticipated traffic growth. Yet even after all of this money was spent, it admitted that traffic would probably have reached saturation levels, and may then, in the year 2019, require to be 'attenuated' – engineering-speak for reduced, thinned out or made leaner. Despite this prognosis, the Government decided to double road investment to almost £1 billion a year under the National Development Plan, telescoping implementation of most of the projects in the NRA's twenty-year plan to just seven years. Contradicting the findings of its own study, Liam Connellan claimed that this would relegate traffic congestion 'largely to the domain of an unhappy memory'. Normally, ministers would defend enormous expenditure on roads because, rightly or wrongly, they carry so much freight and can thus be seen as 'the sinews of economic development'. However, this is what Noel Dempsey had to say on the day the NDP was published: 'The number of private cars has risen by 40% since 1992 and stands at 1.2 million. But we still have a considerable way to go before reaching European ownership levels. In a nutshell, the case for investing heavily in national roads is compelling.' In other words, predict and provide.

Though funding for the Eastern Bypass is not included in the NDP, the realisation of this Holy Grail of Dublin's road engineers for thirty years was brought a step closer in March 1999 when it was inserted into the current City Plan – six years after being officially ditched by the Government. The initiative to reintroduce it came from a cross-party triumvirate of councillors – Senator Joe Doyle (FG), Deputy Eoin Ryan (FF) and Cllr Dermot Lacey (Labour) – representing the Pembroke ward, which includes traffic-plagued Strand Road in Sandymount. According to the City Manager, it was no more than 'a concept, a line on a map' and further detailed studies would have to be undertaken before a final decision was taken. But he said it would be 'crazy to deny ourselves the option', especially as there was considerable demand for it among Dublin's business community. Neither Dublin Corporation nor the NRA, which later commissioned another study of the Eastern Bypass, could say what it might cost to run a four-lane dual carriageway in a tunnel beneath Sandymount Strand and Booterstown Marsh, but it was obvious that the 'serpent that refuses to die' would not come cheap. Its price tag would be at least £500 million, and probably a lot more. What it had going for it was the almost inescapable logic of extending the Port Tunnel southwards, to connect up with the South Eastern Motorway, thereby encasing the city in a 'motorway box' – one of the key objectives of the road engineers since it was first articulated in the flawed DTS report of 1971. Instead of the M50's C-ring, Dublin would get a full orbital ring road, and thus a neat equation in engineering terms. A 1998 public opinion survey commissioned by National Toll Roads plc (NTR), which wants the franchise to build and operate it, found that 76% of Dubliners thought the Eastern Bypass would relieve traffic congestion in the city centre. But the Corporation's disarmingly frank chief roads engineer, Tim Brick, said that although it would undoubtedly bring relief to the Sandymount area and make Dublin Airport much more accessible to southsiders, 'anyone who thinks that it will remove a solitary vehicle from St Stephen's Green is living in cloud-cuckoo land.' (To his immense credit, Brick was also responsible for ditching forty-year-old plans to turn Cork Street and North King Street into dual carriageways. The revised Cork Street scheme, costing £12 million, was even redesigned primarily as a public transport corridor, with separate bus and cycle lanes and just one traffic lane in each direction.)

Whatever its proponents say, it seems certain that the Eastern Bypass would exacerbate a trend that threatens to turn Dublin into a small-scale version of Los Angeles, sprawled out around its motorways. Ironically, Los Angeles used to have the most extensive tramway network of any city in the US – at least until 1926 when it was bought up by a consortium comprising Firestone Rubber, General Motors and Standard Oil, which closed it down and decreed that the city should be developed to cater for cars. As a result, it is now about half the size of Belgium, with two-thirds of its land area given over to road space and parking. Similarly, Chicago has consumed a staggering 440 square miles of farmland since 1970 for low-density 'edge city' development – including a stray 31-storey skyscraper, with underground parking, some twenty-five miles from the city centre. There is already ample evidence in Dublin that a US-style, car-dependent 'edge city' is in the making along the curved spine of the M50. Industrial estates, office parks and shopping centres are increasingly locating in its catchment area, creating a counter-magnet to the city centre in a weird world – almost a parallel universe – of interchanges, slip roads, drive-in eateries and colour-coded parking zones. This is also generating a whole new pattern of travel, mainly by car. No longer are commuters driving from a suburb to the centre, but criss-crossing the wider metropolitan area from one suburb to another. It is not just a problem for commuters. As more companies move further and further out, doing business with them often involves writing off a morning or afternoon, because even off-peak traffic has become so horrendous on the outskirts of the city. And while there is some prospect of improving access to the city centre, where commerce once clustered because everyone could walk to each other's premises, it seems unlikely that outlying business parks can be well served by public transport.

A 1997 survey by the National Roads Authority on the M50, which was intended to cater primarily for *national* traffic, found that commuters account for nearly 70% of all journeys during the morning peak, with four out of every five cars occupied by one person. It was also being clogged, particularly on Saturdays, not by cars seeking to bypass the city but by an army of motorists flitting between shopping-centre 'experiences'. Traffic volumes increased five-fold from an average daily flow of 13,000 vehicles in 1990, when the first section of it opened, to 64,500 in 1999. This was good news for NTR, which had built the West Link bridge, because it boosted the company's annual toll revenue to £21 million-plus, a quarter of it going in licence fees to the Department of the Environment. With just two sections completed – the Western Parkway and the Northern Cross – the M50 was already so congested at peak times that the NRA dusted down plans to widen it to six lanes, including the construction by NTR of a second West Link bridge over the Strawberry Beds, mirroring the form and profile of the original structure so sensitively designed by the late Morgan Sheehy. But unlike the continuing controversy in London over a succession of proposals to widen its even more congested M25 motorway, there has been no public debate about the NRA's proposed improvements to the M50. It is known, however, that the Dublin Transportation Office would be opposed to new flyovers on the woefully designed roundabout interchanges because of the danger that this would smooth the path, at least temporarily, for more car commuters to gain access to the city. There is also a long-term plan for an Outer Ring Road, beyond the M50, with the ostensible purpose of linking the three western 'new towns' of Tallaght, Lucan-Clondalkin and Blanchardstown, though its future function is more likely to be an M50 bypass, particularly if Dublin continues to sprawl. And land is already being speculatively acquired along this route, too, even though it has been dropped from the Fingal County Plan, largely because it would run through Luttrellstown Golf Club. But if Baldonnel is developed as a second airport for Dublin, it will need not just the Outer Ring Road, but also a new Luas line.

Given the level of congestion throughout the metropolitan area, it seems almost inevitable that steps will have to be taken to 'attenuate' traffic, at least at peak periods. Among the early advocates of road pricing to achieve this goal was Garret FitzGerald. During a 1989 Dáil debate, he said something would have to be done to curtail the free availability of road space. 'If champagne were free, it would be over-drunk', he said. 'If a valuable product is made available free of charge, people will use it and abuse it to the point of grossest economic distortion.' Ten years later, the Department of the Environment commissioned British transport consultants Oscar Faber to assess the potential for introducing road pricing in Dublin to deal with 'the growing gap between travel demand and transport supply'. Its economic rationale is that every driver using the roads in congested conditions imposes delays on everyone else, and these delays have a cost not taken into account in his or her personal choices. The aim of road pricing is to tweak these choices and change travel patterns by charging motorists for the use of finite road space. It was pioneered as far back as 1975 in Singapore, where charging tolls to enter the city centre is now fully automated. Electronic surveillance cameras monitor compliance as the tolls are deducted from prepaid cash cards in units fixed to the dashboards of all cars. Combined with the provision of an efficient public transport system and a deliberate policy of making cars relatively expensive, this has reduced traffic levels in Singapore by 17% and raised its average speed at peak periods to an astonishing 60kph. Oslo has become the first European capital to introduce electronic tolling for cars entering the city centre, using the same system as Singapore. Motorists in the Austrian city of Salzburg, birthplace of Mozart, must pay a hefty fee to enter its historic core, levied at a necklace of more basic checkpoint/barriers. If it delivers freeflow traffic conditions, as it seems to do, perhaps road pricing is something even Dublin's car lobby should be campaigning for.

But even before the Oscar Faber study was completed in autumn 1999, the Automobile Association's very vocal spokesman, Conor Faughnan, was condemning road pricing as 'a seductively easy approach' that would 'damage the economic health of the city' by deterring the use of cars – 'the most efficient mode of transport that we have'. Charging motorists would do nothing to reduce traffic jams, he maintained. 'We have one of the worst public transport systems in the civilised world, yet our Government wants to slam motorists instead of sorting it out.' It transpired, however, that there was nothing imminent about the imposition of a £3 charge for, say, crossing the canal cordon or using the M50 at peak periods. John Henry, director of the Dublin Transportation Office, made it clear that there would have to be 'a big improvement in public transport' before such a charge could be justified. Although the AA claimed to be in favour of better public transport, it almost always has a problem with specific proposals, such as running Luas on-street in the city centre or going ahead with the Stillorgan Road Quality Bus Corridor before 'park-and-ride' sites had been provided. The latter was 'an insult to motorists', it said. 'AA goes OTT about the QBC', said the headline over an opinion piece in the *Sunday Tribune*, in which Ann Marie Hourihane amusingly suggested that it was a mistake for the AA (and, indeed, the *Irish Times* and RTÉ broadcaster Pat Kenny, who is so enthusiastic about cars that he gave three away as a single prize on his *Late Late Show*) to treat the arrival of Dublin's third QBC 'as if it were the Normandy landings – seen from a German perspective'. In the run-up to its introduction at the end of August 1999, according to another *Tribune* columnist, Diarmuid Doyle, the *Irish Times*, through its daily, in-depth coverage of the issue, had reacted 'as though the world as it knew it was about to end', and proved itself to be 'the house journal of the car-owning residents of south Dublin'. The fact that there had been no similar media flap over the introduction a year earlier of a QBC on Malahide Road merely served to underline its lowly status. Unlike Stillorgan Road, it is not one of the main conduits used by Dublin's decision-makers to drive into town. But the AA, which had whipped up much of the hysteria, fell uncharacteristically silent when Dublin Bus, which had 'pulled out all the stops' to make it work, revealed that the Stillorgan Road QBC had more than doubled bus passenger numbers in the first month, and the new service was even attracting plenty of 'suits'. The DTO had calculated in advance that there were 7,500 commuters with access to cars living in its immediate catchment area (500 metres on either side) whose destinations were served by it. In other words, they could easily walk to the nearest bus stop rather than hop into their cars. They didn't need a park-and-ride site.

The introduction of the Stillorgan Road QBC was an acid test for the traffic authorities in their efforts to reallocate road space in the city in favour of more efficient modes of transport, putting the emphasis on moving people rather than vehicles. The gradual creation of 'environmental traffic cells' to exclude through-traffic from large parts of the city centre could also be seen as restraint measures

In Salzburg, cars are only permitted to enter the central area for limited periods on payment of a £10 charge. Its deterrent effect has dramatically reduced traffic in the city's historic core.

The roads lobby and its supporters in the media treated the arrival of the Stillorgan Road Quality Bus Corridor in August 1999 'as if it were the Normandy landings – seen from a German perspective', as the *Sunday Tribune* put it.

aimed at managing the traffic problem – and all the evidence showed that they were working. As part of the O'Connell Street Integrated Area Plan, two traffic lanes are to be removed from the street to allow the footpaths on both sides to be widened. The ultimate aim is to dedicate the thoroughfare to buses, pedestrians and cyclists. In order to achieve this, the Corporation intends to reduce the volume of traffic 'presenting at O'Connell Bridge' by banning the much-used left-turn from Dawson Street to Nassau Street, thereby reducing the flow by half. Traffic would have to turn right and on towards Westland Row, Pearse Street and Tara Street to cross the Liffey at Butt Bridge. In the medium term, the installation of two additional bridges at Macken Street and Blackhall Place, both designed by Santiago Calatrava, would form part of an inner bypass of the city centre to the east and west of the O'Connell Street area. This ambitious exercise in traffic management is a grander version of the measures gradually introduced in recent years throughout the inner suburbs to prevent commuters 'rat-running' through residential areas. Contrary to expectations, these measures have not led to huge congestion elsewhere. What happens, it seems, is that motorists change their trip patterns fairly widely to take account of a new regime. This was borne out by a UK study, which found that on average 20% of the traffic that uses a particular road seems to evaporate after it has been closed. In 1994, for example, structural problems forced the closure of Tower Bridge in London. Yet four years after it was reopened, the traffic had still not returned to its original level. The findings of the study – by Prof Phil Goodwin of University College London – cast doubt on traditional assumptions about driver behaviour, and earned a provocative headline in *New Scientist*: 'If you want to ease traffic congestion, there's a simple solution: Shut a few roads.'

An EU-funded research project by the sociology department at Trinity College said Dublin had focused on 'putting intelligence into the road network' with the use of a sophisticated system of computer-controlled traffic lights, known as SCATS. Such measures, it found, had increased road capacity, 'thus generating more traffic in exactly the same way as would building more roads'. But the creation of environmental traffic cells in the city centre should at least ensure that through-traffic is confined to the main corridors, leaving the 'rooms' off them relatively traffic-free, with more street space for pedestrians and cyclists. The pursuit of such radical traffic management measures represents a sea change in the whole philosophy of Dublin's transport planners since the late 1980s. Then, the Corporation was pursuing destructive road-widening schemes to increase traffic capacity, as in Clanbrassil Street. Now, many of its engineers are involved in road-*narrowing* schemes to constrict it, as in South William Street. But despite this new enlightenment, there was an unreconstructed minority who were marking time for the latest philosophy to fail, when they would, as one councillor remarked, be 'given buckets and spades' to build the Eastern Bypass. Meanwhile, the Corporation's traffic department, headed by Owen Keegan – a cyclist himself – was developing an up-to-date traffic simulation tool called

courtesy of Dublin Corporation

Dublin Corporation's supercool Traffic Control Centre at the Civic Offices is a metaphor for the way Owen Keegan does business.

Owen Keegan, Dublin Corporation's Director of Traffic. His modern-thinking, pragmatic approach and sense of humour did much to establish the credibility of this post.

The introduction of wheel-clamping freed up numerous spaces in the city centre previously hogged by commuters, and doubled the annual revenue from parking to £7 million.

Dave Meehan / courtesy of Dublin Corporation

courtesy of Dublin Corporation

Paramix, which physically digitises the city's street network and 'drives' individual cars, trucks, buses, bicycles and Luas trams along the various routes, to gauge the effect of making changes. Even driver behaviour is programmed into it, so that the traffic planners can see how an aggressive driver will behave compared with a tame driver. An estimated 10% of drivers are aggressive and these are responsible for 90% of problems, according to John Henry, the DTO's director.

Both Keegan and Henry, in their different ways, are prime examples of the new breed of officials in charge of traffic and transport in the city. Keegan had been an economist with consultants Davy Kelleher & McCarthy before he became an assistant city manager in 1994 – an appointment that rocked the local government system. Nobody from the private sector had ever been taken in at such a high level. He performed impressively in housing and planning before landing the job of Director of Traffic in 1996, much to the chagrin of the Corporation's senior engineers. His modern thinking, pragmatic approach and sense of humour did much to establish the credibility of this new post. The supercool traffic control centre in the Civic Offices, with its bank of forty television screens fed with real-time footage from a network of high-level cameras around the city, is a metaphor for the way Keegan does business. The only thing it can't do is zap the cars. Wheel-clamping was another feather in his cap. Though run at a loss to the Corporation of £500,000 in the first

Dara MacDonall / *Irish Times*

John Henry, Director of the Dublin Transportation Office. More radical than Owen Keegan in his approach, he created a cadre of highly motivated, like-minded professionals in the DTO.

The SIMI leaflet distributed at car showrooms and petrol stations in autumn 1999 which accused the authorities of pursuing policies to 'stifle' traffic, with 'disastrous consequences' for the economy. One senior official described its contents as 'Neanderthal, Jurassic Park stuff'.

year – after Control Plus, the US-owned franchisee, made an operational profit – its powerful deterrent effect doubled the annual revenue from on-street parking to around £7 million, 'ring-fenced' for investment in further traffic-management measures. One of the principal benefits of wheel-clamping and the imposition of time limits on parking is that it freed up numerous spaces in the city centre that were previously hogged by commuters. It is quite easy nowadays to find casual parking around Merrion Square and St Stephen's Green.

Soft-spoken John Henry had been a senior roads engineer with Dublin County Council before he was appointed as director of the DTO in 1995. If anything, more radical than Keegan in his approach, he bought into all the latest European thinking on urban transport planning, and created a cadre of highly motivated, like-minded professionals in the DTO's offices on Stephen's Green. Henry, distinguished by his 'patriarch's beard' – as long-distance commuter Eileen Battersby described it – even moved house from Blessington to Dundrum so that he could make more use of public transport and thereby earn some 'street cred' in taking on the car lobby. What seems to have influenced him most was a two-year stint as a young engineer with the Connecticut Highways Department in the late 1960s, when all he had to do as a member of a think-tank was to devise innovative transport solutions with a fifty-year horizon. His mission at the DTO is to facilitate and develop public transport in Dublin so that it becomes a real alternative to travelling by car. If it was left to him, the Stillorgan Road QBC would have been carried right through Donnybrook, instead of vanishing, reappearing, vanishing again and reappearing again. 'We are not interested in the capacity for cars. What we want is a straight run-through for the bus. Let the cars suffer', John Henry said once, in a Marie Antoinette phrase that was seized on by the car lobby as evidence of his 'bias'.

Inevitably, there has also been bureaucratic friction between Keegan and Henry. Keegan's office sometimes interprets what the DTO says and does as an implied criticism, and resents its apparent search for an executive role both in strategic and detailed transport planning. In turn, the DTO was often frustrated by the Corporation's more cautious approach and its rush to claim the kudos for various initiatives, such as pre-Christmas park-and-ride sites. However, both sides had signed up to a unifying code, the Strategic Planning Guidelines for the Greater Dublin Area, which state bluntly that there is 'no alternative to a public transport-based solution and that failure to implement the appropriate measures could seriously prejudice the economic and social growth of Dublin'. Not everyone agreed on this central thesis. The self-styled Society of the Irish Motor Industry – which, in reality, is an association of car dealers selling £3 billion worth of imported vehicles annually – was, if anything, more strident and hysterical than the AA. In a leaflet distributed at car showrooms and petrol stations in autumn 1999, the SIMI accused the authorities of pursuing policies to 'stifle' traffic, with 'disastrous consequences' for Ireland's ability to operate as a modern economy. 'The official excuse for gridlock is that we have too many cars. Not true. Ireland has one of the lowest car ownership rates in Europe', the leaflet said, ignoring the crucial distinction between ownership and use. It wanted cars carrying three or more people to be allowed to use bus lanes, contraflow systems to ease bottlenecks at peak hours, underpasses in congested areas, the Eastern Bypass motorway (of course) and, lastly, 'better public transport options', including an underground rail system. It was 'Neanderthal, Jurassic Park stuff', one senior official commented. 'They're just amazingly off-course. The ordinary punters have a much better understanding of the situation. They say they mightn't like what we're doing, but they understand that it has to be done.'

Though sensitive to criticism from the car lobby, not least because it is still so influential politically, the authorities got on with the job of sorting out Dublin's traffic chaos. And they could point to the fact that policies aimed at restraining cars and encouraging people to use public transport work very well elsewhere. The common aim of these policies is to make commuting by car a 'sunset industry', as Owen Keegan once termed it. 'If you ask the inhabitants of a town which transport policy should be followed, they will not choose the car', according to Ernst Joos, deputy director of the Zurich transport authority. 'They are much more intelligent than politicians believe and have higher values than merely standing still in a traffic jam.' Delivering a DTO-sponsored lecture in Dublin in June 1999, he warned that cities could not expect to solve their traffic problems by building more roads and car parks. And he pointed to Zurich as 'living proof' that the economy of a city does not suffer from a transport policy based on restraining car use. Over the past twenty years, in a series of referendums, its citizens defeated plans for an underground metro system in favour of reallocating road space for the benefit of buses, trams, pedestrians and cyclists. This also showed that people were 'ahead of the politicians' on the issue. And contrary to the fears of Garret FitzGerald that trams would block junctions, Zurich's traffic lights are programmed to detect oncoming trams and let them pass, virtually in the blink of an eye. After each tram goes through a junction, the lights immediately revert to their previous sequence to facilitate other traffic. Zurich has also progressively reduced the availability of city centre parking to a maximum of ninety minutes, forcing commuters to park at the edge of the city and take a bus or tram instead. On many streets, the speed limit has been reduced to 30kph (18.6mph).

Incredibly, traffic volumes in Copenhagen are down by 10% on their 1970 levels. Apart from roads associated with the Oresund link to Sweden, the city's road infrastructure is no larger than it was then. What has made the difference is public transport and a lot of cycling. Copenhagen's planners are determined that the total level of road traffic in the city does not increase. So, all the time, they are working to improve the public transport system and provide better facilities for cyclists, including covered secure parking at every rail station. Traffic calming and reduced speed limits are being introduced in the city centre, not only to reduce traffic levels but also to make the streets safer for pedestrians and

Frank McDonald

Zurich has one of the most extensive public transport systems in Europe. Pictured is one of the city's suburban railway stations, designed by Santiago Calatrava.

One of the eight Brutalist-style 'parking houses' built in the centre of Stockholm during the 1960s and early 1970s. They are to be demolished to make way for apartment buildings, with shops at street level.

Frank McDonald

cyclists. On-street parking – none of it available for commuters – is gradually being replaced by underground car parks. There is no traffic congestion in Stockholm either. The Swedish capital has an excellent public transport system, based on a metro with 102 stations, ninety-nine of which are disabled-accessible, supplemented by suburban rail, buses and, lately, a light rail line looping around the inner suburbs. It is also starting to demolish city-centre 'parking houses' built in the 1960s. They are to be replaced by apartment buildings with retail uses at street level. In Amsterdam, too, there is no sense of a city dominated by cars. One of its main streets, Damrak, is slightly wider than Westmoreland Street with a potential five traffic lanes. Instead, it consists of two wide footpaths, two wide cycle tracks, two tram lines and a single lane for cars. This is the kind of con-scious choice about the allocation of space on urban streets made by a country – the Netherlands – which has a population of fifteen million and no less than *six million* cars. The Dutch have chosen not to allow their cars to dominate their cities and the civilising effect of this choice is evident for all to see, even in the body language of people in Amsterdam.

All over Europe, cities are increasingly pursuing similar policies. 'They realise that unbridled use of cars for individual journeys is no longer compatible with easy mobility for the majority of citizens', according to the former EU Environment Commissioner, Ritt Bjerregaard. She said traffic was having 'a

Amsterdam has long been a cycling paradise, with cycle lanes on every street and facilities to park bicycles always within easy reach. Traffic congestion is low despite – or perhaps because of – the minimal space provided for cars, particularly in the central area.

Frank McDonald

detrimental impact on the way of life of about 80% of European urban residents, with multiple harmful effects on their local environment increasingly confirmed by the results of scientific studies on the health effects of air pollution'. Under the EU air framework directive of 1996, local authorities are required to implement action plans to improve urban air quality where it does not comply with pollution limits. It also obliges cities and towns with more than 250,000 inhabitants to keep them informed about ambient air quality, to adopt improvement plans to deal with thirteen pollutants, mainly from traffic, and to ban traffic should the authorised limits be exceeded. By affirming the right of citizens to quality air, the directive has prompted local authorities to take alternative measures, including the promotion of cycling and public transport. In France, any renovation or construction of urban thoroughfares must include provision for cyclists. France has also led the way in developing modern tramways, starting with Nantes and Grenoble. Valenciennes, near the Belgian border, has become the thirteenth French city to join that club, following the successes achieved elsewhere – notably in Strasbourg. Montpelier's light rail system, planned at the same time as Dublin's, was due to open in June 2000. La Rochelle, where the Luas trams are being manufactured, has pioneered the use of electric cars, scooters and vans. In 1997, it held an experimental 'car-free day' in the city centre, an idea that was adopted by thirty-five French towns the following year, and even more in 1999.

The bicycle is also making a comeback. 'Bicycles cause no pollution. They are silent, economical, discreet, accessible to all members of the family, and, above all, faster than a car over short urban distances', according to an excellent, easy-to-read handbook published in 1999 by the European Commission. *Cycling: The Way Ahead for Towns and Cities* not only says the promotion of cycling is 'one of the key features of sustainable transport systems' in urban areas, but also sets out to demolish some of the prejudices associated with bicycles. One of the oldest canards, as it notes, is that bicycles are 'dangerous' in urban areas. And while cyclists are relatively slow and somewhat vulnerable compared to heavier road users (cars, buses and trucks), statistics in fact show that the most dangerous mode of transport in an urban environment is the car. The handbook cites numerous studies across Europe which show that a reduction in speed limits to 30kph 'would benefit all urban dwellers and would encourage the use of bicycles', as well as reducing the accidents attributable to cars involving pedestrians, cyclists and motorists. 'A speed limit of 30kph is compatible with all of the many activities which have to co-exist in a town. At this speed, trips in cars hardly take any longer, but motorists are better able to perceive their environment, can react more swiftly to unexpected events, traffic accidents are less serious, and the traffic is altogether calmer.' It also points out that more than 30% of trips made by car in Europe cover distances of less than three kilometres, and 50% are less than five kilometres. For such journeys alone, bicycles could easily replace cars, contributing directly to cutting down traffic jams 'without any significant difference in journey time door-to-door'.

Dublin architect Paul Keogh believes that anyone who lives in the city's inner suburbs and drives into town is 'absolutely mad'. He and his wife Rachael Chidlow cycle to work from Rathmines almost every day, while their two daughters walk to school. 'Only occasionally would we take them somewhere by car, but usually that's only if there is some other reason for doing so', Keogh says. He himself cycles because he finds it so convenient. 'The sheer hassle of parking in the city centre is unbearable. But with a bike, you can leave it outside the office door and then use it to get to wherever you want to go within the central area in five or ten minutes ... I know lots of people who cycle to work, use their bikes to get around town, and think nothing of it.' Keogh and his wife use the car for site visits outside Dublin, supermarket shopping, weekend trips down the country, and for carrying bulky items. For him, sitting behind the wheel of a car in heavy traffic is a huge waste of time. 'Even cycling in wet weather is better than walking, waiting for a bus or sitting in a car.' However, he would not let his two daughters cycle to their schools in Rathgar and Kildare Place. 'I would just be nervous about it because of the absence of any provision for cyclists in the city.'

Concern about the safety of children of all ages is so widespread that more than half of them are chauffeured to school by parents. According to the DTO, school runs account for at least 20% of morning peak traffic during term-time, adding significantly to the levels of congestion. The problem is exacerbated by the decisions made by parents to shun the local community school or college in

Paul Keogh and his wife Rachael Chidlow cycle to work from Rathmines almost every day, while their two daughters walk to school. The family car is usually left parked in their driveway.

Alan Betson / *Irish Times*

185

favour of sending their children to a more socially acceptable fee-paying school, which might be located several miles away from where they live. But the most insidious aspect of the school run is the car dependency culture it creates. Chauffeured children come to believe that there is no other way of getting around. Some of the posher schools have had to provide parking spaces for sixth-formers with their own cars. In the US, where car dependency is extreme, one out of every five children suffers from obesity because of the lack of physical exercise, and 33% of the total population is obese, compared with 10% in Europe, according to the European Commission's cycling handbook. In Britain, too, the trend in car use for school journeys is sharply upwards, nearly doubling over the last ten years, according to the final report of its Urban Task Force. Germany, by contrast, has experienced only a small fraction of that increase in school runs.

Initiatives to deal with the school run phenomenon here are part of the DTO's short-term action plan, which provides for the creation of safer walking and cycling routes to schools. In August 1999, it announced a pilot programme to promote the idea of 'walking buses', whereby groups of twenty children in each area would be walked to school by two adults. 'The concept is meant to be fun', said Michael Ahern, of the DTO. 'Often, the children put on little jackets, and when they are "getting on the bus" they are given a sticker which they can exchange for sweets at school.' They also enjoy being with friends. Similar collective 'pick-ups' are increasingly common abroad and seem to work well, but as soon as the 'walking bus' idea was mooted here, it was rejected as 'impractical' by the National Parents Council (Primary). It lacked an understanding of the practicalities and logistics of two adults accompanying a large group of children aged four to twelve, the council said, adding that there was also a question of public liability insurance. For John Henry, it was another depressing example of how 'we always seem to be looking for reasons why things won't work'. But if children are to be encouraged to walk or cycle to school, it would help to reduce the general speed limit to 30kph in urban areas. In 1998, that safer limit was introduced in Graz, Austria, on the very day the kids went back to school.

One of the main obstacles to a more pro-cycling policy in cities and towns, according to the European Commission's handbook, is a fear among politicians that they will come up against 'massive opposition' from well-organised motoring pressure groups. But it says that, in fact, traffic authorities which ignore their protests quickly gain support from the population. Even the AA in Britain is now 'wholly in favour of persuading its members to step up their use of bicycles', declaring that cycling is 'an environmentally friendly mode of transport ... and constitutes an appropriate alternative to the car for some trips'. The handbook points out that cycling is also healthier, citing a British Medical Association report which 'refutes the tired old excuse which is often trotted out by those in power – that cycling should be encouraged if it weren't so dangerous, because its advantages for public health far outweigh its disadvantages and the risk of accidents'. Noting that the risk of coronary heart disease for a person who takes no regular physical exercise is equal to that of a smoker on twenty cigarettes a day, the handbook says that cycling is as beneficial as swimming and much easier to do. 'Two trips of fifteen minutes by bicycle a day are enough to guarantee a healthy heart.' A study in Washington of six hundred men and women found that the rate of cardiac problems among regular cyclists was only 42.7 per thousand as against 84.7 per thousand for non-cyclists. Equally remarkable reductions were noted in cyclists for high blood pressure, bronchitis, asthma, orthopaedic problems, varicose veins and diseases of the sebaceous glands.

The Commission's handbook suggests that a 'relatively low cycling rate' of up to 10% of all trips is 'without doubt within the reach of most European towns', with rates of up to 25% 'quite possible'. Delft and Groningen in the Netherlands have already reached bicycle-use rates in excess of 30%. Ireland has one of the lowest number of bicycles per thousand inhabitants at 250, compared to 900 in Germany, 980 in Denmark, and a staggering 1,010 per thousand in the Netherlands – more bicycles than people! Only Spain and Greece have lower numbers than us. Yet, throughout the EU, bicycles notch up an overall mileage of seventy *billion* kilometres a year. As for the perceived disadvantages, such as steep gradients, strong winds and heavy rain, the handbook says that objective conditions favourable to cycling 'are in fact met more often than is usually imagined', with car drivers trying out cycling to work for the first time 'often pleasantly surprised by the qualities of the bike'. Sweden is a cold country, yet 33% of all journeys in Vasteras (pop. 115,000) are made by bicycle. Switzerland is not a flat country, but the equivalent figure for Basel (pop. 230,000) is 23%. Even in Britain, described by the EU as 'a wet country', 27% of all journeys in Cambridge (pop. 100,000) are still made by bicycle. In London, no less than 100,000 commuters regularly use the bicycle as their preferred mode of transport – though this represents a mere 2% of the commuting population. Cycle lanes in the British capital are patchy at present, but when the full network is in place by 2005, it will cover more than 3,000 kilometres at a cost of £70 million.

Under its action plan, the Dublin Transportation Office expects that its 180-kilometre network of cycleways in the city and suburbs will be completed by 2001, at a cost of £10 million. The objective is to double the use of bicycles, which accounted for a mere 3.3% of peak-hour trips in the Greater Dublin Area in the 1997 traffic census, though it is fair to point out that the DTO's area includes parts of Meath, Kildare and Wicklow. In the 1999 census, the Dublin Cycling Campaign was heartened that the figure for cyclists was increasing at last. Within the canal ring, the proportion of commuters cycling to work is much higher, at around 10%. In 1960, it would have been five times that figure, but we were poorer then and owning a car was the luxurious exception. To help change the picture, planning conditions now specify that a much larger proportion of the more limited parking space attached to new office buildings in the city must be allocated to bicycles. Great strides are also being made by Dublin Corporation and other local authorities in providing new cycle tracks and a multitude of secure on-street parking, including stylish stainless steel stands in the city centre. Though motorists who have never considered cycling will only be persuaded by active promotional campaigns, the European Commission says a large number of car drivers are already thinking about switching to cycling. All they are waiting for is 'a sign from the public authorities' that proper facilities will be provided.

Meanwhile, the DTO embarked on a major review of the whole DTI strategy to take account of the greatly altered circumstances of the city and its booming economy. With travel demand in the Greater Dublin Area increasing by 7% per annum, the challenge facing transport planners is to increase the capacity of its public transport network by an equivalent percentage year by year. Otherwise, traffic congestion will only get worse. Since travel demand is linked to economic growth, and with the first phase of Luas still three years away, the only short-term solution to the traffic problem involves providing more buses and trains and persuading more people to cycle or walk to work. 'There is no other way', according to John Henry. The Government showed that it was also coming around to this view. After years of maintaining CIÉ on a famine-relief diet, suddenly a lot of money was made available for public transport improvements. These included twenty-six extra carriages for DART, to increase its capacity by 25% and help relieve unpleasant overcrowding at peak periods. Incredibly, despite a near doubling of passenger numbers since the service was inaugurated in 1984, not one extra carriage had been added to it in the previous fifteen years. DART extensions to Greystones and Malahide were completed, in line with the DTI strategy, though the opening of a full service to both towns was delayed for months on end because of an industrial relations problem in CIÉ. Almost fifty Arrow-style railcars were ordered from Japan for the other suburban lines and steady progress was being made on the installation of a double-track between Clonsilla and Maynooth on the Dublin-Sligo line, where commuters had to put up with a congested, clapped-out, Bombay-style train service for years. Dublin Bus, which still receives the lowest level of subsidy of any city bus service in Europe at just 4% of its running costs, began taking delivery of nearly two hundred new double-deck buses and testing other low-floored, wheelchair-accessible models, as well as seeking tenders for an initial fifteen articulated single-deck buses with something of the ambience of a modern tram.

The ability of Dublin Bus to deliver a much higher quality service is critical to the success of QBCs in particular. With a total of eleven planned under the DTI strategy, the traffic authorities repeatedly stressed that sufficient buses have to be provided at peak times on each route as it comes on stream so that motorists switching to public transport are not put off it for life by long waits in queues as full buses sail past. But the AA was quite right when it pointed out that what Dublin is now getting falls short of the high specifications which the DTI had in mind. A QBC was meant to be 'a single, direct unambiguous alignment upon which investment in a high-quality operation can be focused'. Apart from providing a continuous frequency of buses, each stop on the route was to have a shelter equipped with timetable information, lighting and seating. 'Wherever possible, additional service facilities like telephones, vending machines, etc, should be incorporated in the shelter, turning bus stops into attractive focal points and ensuring that even the minimal wait for a bus on a QBC alignment is not an unpleasant experience', in the words of the DTI's final report. QBCs were also to be served by secure park-and-ride sites, where motorists could leave their cars and switch to public transport. However, the authorities were not prepared to concede that progress on implementing the QBCs should be delayed until all of these facilities were in place. 'The situation is so bad that we couldn't wait for that', said John Henry. At the time of writing, the acquisition of two sites on the south side of the city, large enough to park a total of 1,000 cars, was under negotiation, and the likelihood was that these would be developed in partnership with private sector interests, with an emphasis on design and security 'to create the right image'. But with buses coming along at three-minute intervals at peak periods and travelling into town up to 50% faster than other traffic, many motorists began asking themselves whether it was time to get out of their cars.

However, one of the aggravating factors in Dublin's traffic chaos is that so many employees have guaranteed off-street car-parking spaces at or near their workplaces – some 25,000 of them, in fact. The availability of these spaces, usually free of charge, is a sure-fire guarantee that the employees who have them will drive their cars – often also supplied free – to work. One AIB executive who had been using the DART to get to work complained to the DTO that, after he had been given the 'perk' of a company car and a designated parking space at Bankcentre in Ballsbridge, a more senior manager warned him that he would run the risk of losing both if he didn't make use of them. Though otherwise quite happy to continue using public transport, he felt he had no option but to drive to work. 'Company cars are generally viewed as status symbols, which gives companies an incentive to provide them and their drivers an incentive to use them, even when alternatives are available', according to a 1998 paper for Earthwatch by Sadhbh O'Neill. And typically, company cars 'carry only the driver, without any passengers'. They are also generally larger and less fuel efficient than other private cars, quite apart from encouraging unnecessary driving. A 1997 study of seventeen UK cities found that 43% of off-street parking was provided free to drivers of company cars, and that four out of every five cars coming into London at peak hours were company cars. In the Republic, company cars account for a staggering 40% of new car sales. Dishing them out is one of the most convenient ways for an employer to reward valued executives, given our still relatively high income-tax burden; and though benefit-in-kind (BIK) tax is charged, the DTO has calculated that the real cost to company car users works out on average at just £1,000 a year. In his 1999 Budget speech, the Minister for Finance, Charlie McCreevy, said consideration would be given to the possibility of extending BIK to off-street parking spaces, and he set up a working group to look into it. Referring to the fact that many civil servants in his own Department and in the

Revenue enjoy the perk of free parking, he remarked sardonically that they would be looking forward to this task with 'very obvious delight'. A year later, in his 2000 Budget speech, he had no progress to report. McCreevy's only positive step was to allow employers to give their staff free public transport travel passes, exempt from BIK.

Figures obtained by the *Sunday Tribune* under the Freedom of Information Act in September 1999 showed more than 4,200 civil servants enjoy the perk of free, off-street parking spaces in the centre of Dublin, with by far the largest number (780) held by the Revenue. Tourists wishing to visit the Chapel Royal at Dublin Castle must negotiate their way through banks of Revenue staff cars in the Lower Castle Yard, while Dublin Tourism not only parks its own staff cars in the grounds of St Andrew's Church, but also rents spaces to other commuters. Hundreds of apartment owners in the city centre who paid an extra £7,000 to £12,000 for parking spaces in their schemes have also cashed in on this handy little earner. At Mountjoy Prison, the first phase of its current development programme was a multi-level car park for warders who, by definition, do not need to use their cars during working hours. Most hospital car parks are full not with the cars of anxious relatives visiting patients, but with those of their commuting staff. Indeed, the Coombe has even managed to poach midwives from Holles Street with offers of free on-site parking. The grounds of every third-level college are also choc-a-bloc with parked cars, and a peremptory move by Trinity in mid-1999 to slash on-site parking from 520 to 260 spaces led to a staff revolt. Even the Garda Siochána, who are charged with enforcing the traffic regulations, still park three abreast in front of Pearse Street Garda Station, despite an informal agreement with the Director of Traffic that they should limit this parking to a maximum of two rows. The Department of Education also showed that it might benefit from remedial classes in mobility management when it leased about eighty parking spaces in the multi-storey public car park on Marlborough Street from Irish Car Parks Ltd, and provided them free to staff, pending completion of a two-year programme of development at its headquarters nearby. 'You will appreciate that the rent incurred for these spaces is substantial and the facility represents a valuable concession which requires to be fully utilised to derive maximum benefit', a circular letter told staff. 'As the demand for spaces exceeds the supply, you are reminded that should the facility be underutilised by you it will be necessary to review your particular situation.' A spokesman for the Department told the *Irish Times* that it had already reduced on-site car-parking from two hundred-plus spaces to less than one hundred, for traffic management reasons. 'If we hadn't provided an alternative when spaces were lost because of the current building programme, it would have raised an industrial relations issue which would have cost a lot more to sort out', he said. But then, much of Leinster Lawn had been paved in mid-1998 to provide 'temporary' car-parking for TDs and Senators while building work was under way at the Houses of the Oireachtas.

There was also evidence that the proliferation of multi-storey car parks in

The former Ansbacher Bank on the corner of Lower Leeson Street and Adelaide Road, where the gardens of four houses were joined together to provide white-lined parking spaces in front of a listed, but decaying, Regency mews.

Much of Leinster Lawn was paved in mid-1998 to provide 'temporary' car-parking for TDs and senators while building work was under way at the Houses of the Oireachtas.

the centre of Dublin had encouraged car-commuting. A survey by Dublin Corporation in 1996 estimated that up to half of all the spaces in these car parks were probably being used for all-day parking by commuters, contradicting the whole thrust of transport planning in the city. Until 1990, Dublin had only four multi-storey car parks, which provided a total of 2,165 spaces between them. But a generous package of tax incentives, introduced in 1994 by Bertie Ahern, fuelled a construction boom and a further eighteen were built on the back of it, bringing the total number of spaces in the city centre to just over 9,100. The package was so juicy, allowing investors to write off half of the capital cost and operators to claim double rent allowances against their tax liability, that Irish Car Parks Ltd found itself out-bid for new developments by well-heeled private investors seeking quick-yielding tax shelters. Some of these 'high net worth' individuals had used such devices so extensively that they did not pay any tax at all, for years. Ostensibly, the new multi-storey car parks were to be available 'wholly or mainly ... for members of the public generally', but the restrictions were so woolly that the Revenue Commissioners – dab hands at looking after their own parking needs – accepted that the term 'mainly' was satisfied if no more than 49% of the spaces were contracted to commuters. Thus, at least 120 of the 391 spaces in the Temple Bar multi-storey car park on Fleet Street were 'spoken for' even before it opened in 1995, because they had been allocated to Telecom Éireann staff who previously occupied a surface car park on the site of Temple Bar, as well as to staff of the ESB and Bank of Ireland.

The indiscriminate nature of Bertie Ahern's tax incentives also ran counter to the declared policy of Dublin Corporation to 'provide for short-term shopping and business requirements and to strictly control the quantity and distribution of long-term commuter parking facilities' in the city centre. The DTI's final report also recognised that the provision of adequate short-term parking in the city centre was critical to its ability to compete successfully with out-of-town shopping centres such as Tallaght, Blanchardstown and Quarryvale. At the same time, the DTI said it would be 'essential' to set a target of reducing the total number of commuter parking spaces in the city centre, both to relieve traffic congestion in the morning and evening peaks, and to encourage motorists to use public transport. Failure to address this issue, it warned, could undermine the DTI strategy and lead to 'a waste of scarce resources'. Had the tax incentives been targeted at the provision of park-and-ride sites at DART stations, proposed Luas stops and major bus termini in the suburbs, they would have been fully in line with public policy. Because they were not, they had the opposite effect, leaving Dublin Corporation with the thankless task of implementing, insofar as it could, a licensing regime and tiered scale of charges to ensure that multi-storey car parks catered adequately for shopping, business and leisure trips to the core area. Plans for new car parks would also have to demonstrate that there was actually a real need for them in the areas proposed.

This put Owen Keegan on a sticky wicket. Not only did the Corporation have 350 staff parking spaces on two levels beneath the Civic Offices, but also an overflow car park in the Coombe. If it was to retain any credibility as the city's traffic authority, it could no longer justify providing off-street parking for all of its staff members who drive to work. With the overflow car park due to close to make way for the Cork Street-Coombe bypass road, staff unions naturally insisted that it would have to be replaced. Keegan, who cycles in from Stillorgan, went public on the issue saying the Corporation had to lead by example on this issue and, at his instigation, a working party was set up to deal with the matter. The unions came up with all sorts of excuses why staff needed to use their cars, but Keegan's view was that, if they felt cheated of a valued perk, they should go to the Labour Court to make a case for some compensatory payment, 'and if they get £1,000 or £2,000, good luck to them'. In the meantime, he got on with the business of eliminating free on-street parking spaces in and around the city centre, and replacing some 3,800 meters with 430 multi-bay 'pay and display' machines. Some commuters driving in from the southern suburbs to offices in Ballsbridge were incensed when the Corporation imposed a two-hour limit on non-residential parking in the area. They had come to regard the places where they parked as their own property. Now, they were at the mercy of unscrupulous residents who started renting out their gardens for parking.

From mid-1999, in dealing with planning applications for major commer-

A car emerging from the two-level car park beneath the Civic Offices. If Dublin Corporation was to retain any credibility as the city's traffic authority, it could no longer justify providing off-street parking for all of its staff members who drive to work.

Frank McDonald

cial developments, local authorities began to impose conditions requiring the developers to draw up 'mobility management plans' to reduce car commuting by their staff, and thereby contribute to achieving a more sustainable transport system. Such a requirement was incorporated in the Corporation's planning decision on Spencer Dock, specifying that targets must be set for each mode of transport – rail, bus, bicycle and car – and a 'mobility co-ordinator' appointed to implement 'sustainable commuter plans' for each building or company operating there. Dun Laoghaire-Rathdown County Council laid down similar conditions for a huge motorway office park in Leopardstown, on lands formerly occupied by the Legionaires of Christ. Private companies were also responding. Citibank, which leased a very large office block in the IFSC extension, realised that it had a problem on its hands because there were only 130 parking spaces on-site for 1,200 staff, so it was the first to commission a firm of transport consultants to prepare a commuter plan. Other major inward investors, particularly from mainland Europe, are moving in the same direction. Somewhat alarmed to find that it can take as long to travel from Dublin Airport to, say, Ballsbridge as it does to fly in from Amsterdam or Brussels, they wonder how their future employees will get to work, and are increasingly turning to agencies such as the DTO for some help in solving this puzzle.

In line with European practice, the DTO's long-term objective is to 'get rid' of commuter parking spaces, according to John Henry, though how he can hope to do so when so many of them have become real property is a moot point. In August 1999, the *Sunday Business Post* revealed that nine commuters had paid £50,000 apiece for parking spaces in the rear garden of a house on Fitzwilliam Square. Mad as this seemed, it showed just how determined some motorists are to secure off-street parking, what with free on-street spaces disappearing at the rate of two to three hundred per month. The EU Commission estimated that the cost of providing off-street parking works out at £3,000 for an open-air parking space, £6,000 per space in a multi-storey car park, and £12,000 per space underground. Thus, the savings to companies that take steps to reduce the number of workplace parking spaces are quite considerable. 'Compelling companies to provide a mobility plan for their employees is one way of inducing them to promote cycling among their staff', the Commission said, adding that some employers now offer 'an entire panoply of incentives' to encourage employees to cycle, including mileage allowances, showers and changing rooms. RTÉ may become the first major employer in Ireland to follow their example by giving an annual allowance to staff who use bicycles for work-related trips, following an initiative spearheaded by journalist Tom Kelly. Its radio and television complex at Montrose was beginning to look like a series of buildings in a huge surface car park, with no less than eight hundred designated spaces, plus up to two hundred illegally parked cars at any given time. But then, even the Custom House is flanked by car parks. Brendan O'Donoughue, former Secretary of the Department of the Environment, confessed that one of the most difficult problems he had to confront while there was to achieve a reduction in staff parking so that James Gandon's masterpiece would not be compromised by the clutter of cars.

The DTO has drawn up a template showing how to organise 'green commuter plans', with the aim of promoting public transport, cycling and walking as alternatives to private car use. Another initiative, called the 'Way to Go' project, which also focuses on car-pooling and telecommuting, involves the Irish Energy Centre, Intel, Irish Life, Dun Laoghaire-Rathdown County Council and two Government departments – Environment and Public Enterprise. The National Development Plan also briefly mentions the need to achieve 'sustainable transport' in the Greater Dublin Area, saying that this 'must involve a wide and shared responsibility. Key players – central and local government, business organisations, the ports and airport authorities, trade unions, educational interests as well as communities and individuals – must assume a greater onus and initiative in relation to good transport practice.' If the Government is serious, transport planners in Dublin expect some move to increase BIK on company cars and extend it to parking spaces, to reduce their attractiveness as perks. They reason that if the tax take is increased and companies are confronted with the full cost, more and more of them will say: 'This is costing us so much. Why don't we just give you the money and a free public transport pass?' But even if the company car is here to stay, John Henry sees nothing wrong with it – 'provided it's left at home'.

The general approach being taken by the DTO to transport planning is almost a carbon copy of the findings of the British government's Urban Task Force in its final report, *Towards an Urban Renaissance*, in 1999. 'Over the last fifty years, the planning of development has been dictated primarily by the demands of the car user. This, not surprisingly, has had the effect of encouraging car use, even for journeys which would be much better made by walking or cycling', it said. 'In many parts of urban England, walking is a dreadful experience of trying to negotiate obstacles, moving and non-moving, which prevent you from getting where you want to go.' And, on parking, Lord Rogers and his task force firmly endorsed charges, saying: 'We cannot go on as we are. Providing parking space for vehicles uses up vast tracts of our urban land. Much of this could be put to far better use, to accommodate housing development or to create new squares and parks, reversing the car's erosion of our urban space ... Private, non-residential parking is an even bigger problem, because it fuels traffic growth. The planning system has allowed private developers to get away with demand-based provision, often on the basis of exaggerated demand. We must therefore change the way in which the planning system influences the design of commercial facilities, so as to maximise access for pedestrians, cyclists and public transport.' It also highlighted the failure of public transport systems to provide people with 'the choice and the incentive to get out of their cars', saying that they had not kept pace with changing commuter patterns, with few orbital routes, for example.

One of the most obvious gaps in Dublin is the absence of a rail link to the airport. Though passenger numbers were growing almost exponentially, Aer

Rianta paid little attention to this glaring deficiency, concentrating its efforts on expanding terminal facilities and car-parking. Cynics even suggested that its apparent disinterest in a rail link was at least partly coloured by the revenue it made from parking – a claim that Aer Rianta denied, of course. But it was certainly lukewarm towards the idea of a Luas line via Ballymun, as the DTI had originally suggested. When the State-owned airports authority finally did pay some attention to the issue, its first instinct was that any rail link should extend westwards from the Dublin-Belfast railway line, not least because this might attract more passengers from Northern Ireland. Eventually, CIÉ and Aer Rianta set up a working group to consider the matter, and in 1998 it recommended a spur to the airport from the Dublin-Sligo line. This was seen as a more technically feasible proposition because the Belfast line was relatively congested because it had to accommodate the Enterprise service as well as DART and northern suburban trains, whereas the Sligo line was underutilised and could easily absorb an airport link. But when it came to deciding the precise alignment, even CIÉ could not make its mind up, submitting three alternatives to Fingal County Council and leaving its planners to decide which reservation to accept for inclusion in the county plan. All CIÉ seemed to be clear about was that the city-centre terminus should be at Spencer Dock, where it had a huge vested interest in the redevelopment of its North Wall rail freight marshalling yards. The National Development Plan also failed to clarify the issue. Indeed, it added to the confusion by proposing that among the options to be evaluated would be 'a new rail link from the Belfast line through Swords and Dublin Airport to the Western lines', which might include a reinstated inland line to Navan, and 'a new rail link east of the current Loop Line in Dublin city centre'.

The Strategic Planning Guidelines for the Greater Dublin Area, published in March 1999, also identified the need for a high-capacity heavy rail link to the airport, in preference to a Luas line, and an additional cross-river rail link between Spencer Dock and the new DART station at Barrow Street, adjoining the Grand Canal Docks. But this document, too, was tentative about the alignment of an airport line, saying it 'could be provided through a branch from the Maynooth line', with a possible city terminus at Barrow Street, or, alternatively, mainline trains on the Belfast line 'could be routed via Swords and the Airport, possibly to the former terminus at Broadstone, which might be connected to the LRT network'. It was, in other words, all up in the air. Clearly, what Dublin needed was a strategic blueprint for the development of its regional rail services. CIÉ, whose transportation input into the plans for Spencer Dock was quite incoherent, knew that it needed some good advice, and in mid-1999, the company commissioned consultant engineers Ove Arup & Partners to examine all the options and come up with a package of firm development proposals that would make rational sense. It was during the course of this exercise that the Arup team, headed by Michael Grace, began considering the thorny issue of the new cross-river rail link between Spencer Dock and Barrow Street. Making that connection was not as simple as it might have seemed. For a start, there was an obvious problem regarding its vertical alignment. If the rail station at Spencer Dock was underground, as proposed, the line would have to tunnel beneath the Liffey and then rise up to reach Barrow Street DART station, two storeys above ground level, on a gradient too steep for trains to negotiate. The only other option, it seemed, was a high-level bridge, and this was opposed by Dublin Corporation because of its 'detrimental effects' on the riverscape. Potentially, the planners feared that it would be another ghastly mistake, on a par with the Loop Line.

While CIÉ's consultants were wrestling with this problem, somebody had a brainwave. Instead of making the cross-river connection between Spencer Dock and Barrow Street, why not take it underground to Pearse Station (Westland Row), and, having got there, why not continue on to Heuston Station to link up with the Phoenix Park tunnel and loop around the north side back to Spencer Dock? This was lateral thinking at its most brilliant, because what it offered to Dublin was the prospect of a Circle Line in and around the city centre. Westland Row would be transformed into a major hub, with escalators/lifts connecting the DART and underground lines. Further stations along the route would include St Stephen's Green, offering a link with the Sandyford Luas line, the Central Bank in Dame Street, the Civic Offices at Wood Quay, Watling Street or thereabouts and Heuston, where the Arrow service on the Kildare line terminates and the Tallaght Luas line would stop right outside the front door. On the north side, along the existing but largely disused railway line, stations might include Marlborough Road, off the North Circular, giving access to the Phoenix Park. Cabra Road, Croke Park and Drumcondra, in addition to Broombridge, where there

Detail of the integrated rail-network map (reproduced in colour on page 135) showing how a rail-based public transport system could extend the central business district east and west.

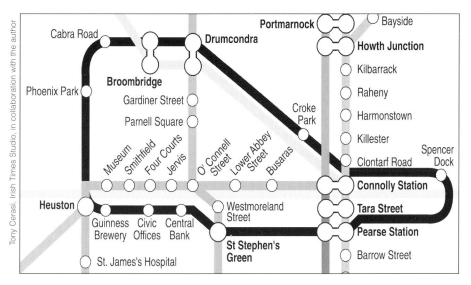

Tony Cerasi. Irish Times Studio, in collaboration with the author

would be a connection to the Maynooth and Navan lines. Even the rail link to Dublin Airport could be plugged into the Circle Line, so that passengers could travel by train from St Stephen's Green, for example, to the airport in less than half an hour.

Suddenly, it was possible to see how Dublin could develop a public transport *system*, with the metro-style Circle Line as a unifying organiser, intercepting every route leading into the city centre, including DART, Luas, suburban rail lines and QBCs. It would, of course, require a pair of single-track tunnels from Spencer Dock to Heuston. But as the WS Atkins report on Luas indicated, these would only be 5.4 metres (17.8 ft) in diameter – somewhat larger than the Grand Canal drainage tunnel, dug without much difficulty in the late-1970s, but considerably smaller than the twin-bore Dublin Port Tunnel carrying four lanes of traffic, including very tall juggernauts. More substantial excavations would obviously be required for the six underground stations on the south side, possibly involving disruption at street level while they were under construction. As for fears that such stations would be inaccessible or even dangerous – both issues that were raised in the debate on undergrounding Luas – Atkins said the first problem could be solved by providing lifts to the platforms, while underground stations 'can be made safer through good design, excellent lighting, the visible presence of station staff at all times and a high level of passengers travelling on the system'. The cost is estimated at £300 million – coincidentally, the contingent sum allocated in the National Development Plan to put Luas underground between St Stephen's Green and Broadstone. Mitsui, the Japanese conglomerate, might be interested in a contract to build and even operate the Circle Line. It had already expressed an interest in a similar deal for the underground section of Luas, working in close collaboration with the Unified Proposal group. The geological tests carried out on foot of the Government's May 1998 Luas decision would not go to waste either. They could be used as inputs to an environmental impact and feasibility study of the Ove Arup proposal. The Arup review also envisaged that the Sandyford Luas line could be upgraded to a metro in the longer term, entering a tunnel in Ranelagh to run northwards beneath St Stephen's Green and the core area of the city centre towards Dublin Airport. Garret FitzGerald was among the first to welcome this change of tune, saying that it would overcome the capacity problem with Luas which he had been highlighting since 1995. It also offered Dubliners the prospect of a public transport system that they 'will be able to enjoy rather than endure'.*

The incredible symmetry of the Circle Line in transportation terms is mirrored by its spin-off benefits for land use and planning in the city. A straight connection between Spencer Dock and Barrow Street, as proposed originally by the Chamber of Commerce, would serve to reinforce the south-easterly drift of the city's centre of gravity, with potentially damaging long-term consequences for

* *Irish Times*, 18th March 2000

Dublin's historic core. The Circle Line, on the other hand, would have the opposite effect by extending the central business district to the east and the west, knitting the inner city together in a quite remarkable way. For example, a station in the vicinity of Watling Street would inevitably open up Victoria Quay and adjoining areas for redevelopment, including large tracts of redundant land at Heuston and on the Guinness brewery site. Combined with the Tallaght Luas line, which would run through St James's Hospital and down Steevens's Lane, it would rescue the south-western sector of the inner city from its benighted isolation as the city's most neglected quarter – a lowly state in which it has been languishing for two hundred years. The argument for routing the Circle Line through Spencer Dock rather than Connolly Station is equally compelling because it would transform the relationship between Docklands and the rest of the inner city, as well as making use of the existing North Wall railhead. Conversely, a counter proposal by the DDDA, tabled in October 1999, for a circle line springing from Connolly to Pearse and on to Heuston would bin this strategically located railhead for all time. Its only advantage is that it would connect the two mainline railway stations by heavy rail, but they are to be linked anyway by Luas, under the Government's plan, and this light rail line will inevitably be threaded through the north Docklands area as far as the Point Depot.

The DDDA's most useful suggestion was that Luas could be extended to make use of the Broadstone railway alignment, branching off the Tallaght line at Church Street to serve Phibsboro, and join the Ballymun line at Dorset Street. Further Luas extensions have been recommended by the DTO, such as a separate line to Clondalkin and a spur to serve City West and Baldonnel from the Tallaght line where it crosses the Red Cow interchange of the M50. The latter would become particularly important if Casement aerodrome was developed as a second airport for Dublin. Transport planners were also examining such issues as whether the airport line should offer an express service into town or stop along the way, and what implications this would have for land use in its potential catchment area. They were also trying to reach agreement on the most suitable alignment for the future Navan line, and looking at plans for quadruple tracks on existing lines to eliminate conflicts between mainline and commuter services.

As all of this work continued on the infrastructural side, the Corporation got on with all the 'non-sexy stuff', as one senior official put it, in an effort to manage the traffic. Parking enforcement was already having a dramatic impact, at least in making more space available for short-term use, but it needed to be set in the wider context of 'street management'. For example, nobody in central government had foreseen that telecommunications deregulation would multiply the number of road openings in the city, with no less than thirty-six companies vying to install new lines. Here again, the Corporation was left to pick up the pieces. Its requirement that each company digging up a street would have to provide ducts with sufficient space to accommodate the cables of its rivals even landed senior officials in the High Court. Trying to impose some order on all the chaos, they moved to introduce a new regime requiring the telecom companies to carry out roadworks at night-time, charging builders for temporary road closures and restricting deliveries to off-peak periods. And though new clearways were also designated, facilitating car commuters in the short-term, Owen Keegan insisted that these would accommodate more QBCs over time. Much more money was also being made available for traffic management in Dublin, some £200 million altogether under the National Development Plan, within an unprecedented allocation of £1.58 billion for public transport. Whatever about the failings of the DTI in terms of forecasting, it was clear that the philosophy behind it – of achieving a major switch from car use – had endured. Certainly, John Henry felt that the Government had finally taken this agenda on board.

The most intractable problem on the transport front in Dublin – its abysmal taxi service – had nothing to do with the expenditure of public money and everything to do with the failure of successive ministers to tackle politically powerful vested interests. As TCD economist Seán Barrett has pointed out, it started in the mid-1970s when the late Jimmy Tully was 'persuaded' by a taxi blockade of Butt Bridge not to issue new licences. This myopic policy was continued by his successors in the Custom House, with the result that taxi plates acquired a scarcity value, rising steadily from £3,500 in 1980 to a peak of £80,000-plus in the mid-1990s. Some of those who bought plates were investing their money in a new career, while many others were not themselves taxi drivers but business people seeking a convenient vehicle to stash 'hot money' away from the prying eyes of the Revenue. They included bookmakers, barristers and other professionals as well as criminals and even some politicians, who were careful to mask their identities through the use of front companies. Some of the investors owned more than twenty plates, renting them out to 'cozys' for up to £400 per week. Against this background, it is hardly surprising that any move to increase the number of taxi plates ran into entrenched and sustained resistance, with some Fianna Fáil councillors, in particular, openly taking the side of the existing licence-holders against the clear public interest in securing a better taxi service. Perhaps they never had to stand in line with up to a hundred others on a cold or rainy night at the rank in College Green waiting, in effect, for Godot.

Despite continuing political opposition and militant action by taxi owners and drivers, including an infamous blockade of the city centre, Dublin Corporation made steady progress in liberalising the market by granting new licences for disabled-accessible, van-type taxis, and even secured agreement to their use for a remarkably well-organised venture into taxi-sharing in December 1999. And though the existing licence-holders staged a strike in protest against Junior Environment Minister Robert Molloy's pledge that the number of plates would be doubled by end-2000, it seemed that the artificially restricted taxi trade in Dublin was finally on its way to deregulation, even if the ludicrous distinction between 'taxis' and 'hackneys' was being preserved. 'The Government owes them [taxi plate owners] nothing. We don't pay out on losing National Lottery tickets.

Nor do bookies pay out on the also-rans in racing', Seán Barrett wrote in the *Irish Times*. 'If the Government weakens its resolve to deregulate the sector totally, the scarcity value of a taxi licence will begin to rise again and the whole sorry saga of the past three decades will repeat itself.' Apart from seeking to preserve their investment, the plate-owners and their political supporters did not seem to recognise that taxis play a vital role in any urban public transport system. 'The major problem has been this lack of belief in the taxi service itself', according to Owen Keegan. 'There is a huge potential demand for taxis in Dublin. More taxis will mean more business, so it can be a success for everybody, including the operators.' Taxis are permitted to use bus lanes, with or without passengers on board, and this means that they can get around much easier than other traffic – a lesson that was not lost on a certain tycoon living in Killiney, who became hugely enthusiastic about the Stillorgan Road QBC even though he drives a top-of-the-range Mercedes. Just when you think you've heard the last dodge in a country full of dodgers, it transpires that he invested £75,000 in a taxi plate for his car and now zips into town on the bus lane.

How many Councillors who openly back existing licence-holders against the clear public interest in securing a better taxi service ever had to wait on a cold rainy night at the rank in College Green?

Cyril Byrne / *Irish Times*

4. Spreading Out

Montpelier Hill, crowned by the ruins of the Hell Fire Club, offers one of the best vantage points to observe what has happened to Dublin over the last thirty years or so. Beneath it, as far as the eye can see, the city is spread out like an irregularly shaped carpet, with a few lumps here and there. The nearly identical twin striped stacks of Poolbeg power station, with their plumes of water vapour, provide the most obvious orientation point. On a clear day, with the aid of a good pair of binoculars, it is possible to pick out some of the domes and spires in the haze over the city as well as the towers of Ballymun on the northern horizon and even the planes flying into and out of Dublin Airport. In the foreground, there are still green fields just below the slopes of Kilmashogue... but for how long? Beyond them lie Tallaght, Lucan and Clondalkin, three historic villages now swamped by a vast sprawl of featureless low-density suburban housing, nearly all of it built within the past three decades.

If this was Myles Wright's vision, the Liverpool University professor of town planning was miles wrong. But it is too easy to blame Wright and his Advisory Regional Plan of 1967 because the truth is that the 'four fingers' of development he proposed, extending westwards from the city, were turned into three formless blobs by the Dublin local authorities. They ignored alternative proposals that development should be concentrated on the coastal strip between Balbriggan and Bray, where new housing areas would at least have been served by a railway line, and opted instead for a motorised city, in which every family would have at least one car and public transport would play no more than a residual role. The 'new towns' they created were also designed around drains, their water and sewerage infrastructure, and an engineering straitjacket of roads wide enough for cars to travel at high speeds, presenting a danger to children and older people, in particular. Instead of following the British example of taking all the

Model of MacCormac Jamieson Pritchard's 1997 master plan for Ballymun's new main street.

land required into public ownership and setting up a development commission to plan the 'new towns', what happened in Dublin was largely developer-led. Speculators would acquire options on parcels of land and persuade the county council to rezone it, netting enormous sums of money for themselves at the stroke of a planner's broad-brush or a vote by the elected members. Land values multiplied, generating a hothouse environment in which corruption flourished. With millions of pounds to be made, it is hardly surprising that some councillors accepted and even solicited bribes for their championship of particular rezonings, though the libel laws and the obvious difficulties of proving such transactions prevented the media from exposing those involved. Successive governments of all political hues showed no willingness to probe this murky area where politics and planning are entwined, probably because of a visceral fear that the can of worms was so large that they dared not prise it open. It might have been plugged had any of them implemented the 1974 Kenny Report on Building Land, which recommended that development land should be compulsorily acquired by the local authorities at a small margin above its existing use value. Though Judge John Kenny was one of the foremost constitutional lawyers in Ireland, the oft-repeated excuse for doing nothing about his committee's majority report was that it might be unconstitutional – an issue never tested in the courts.

Over the years, allegations of corruption were contemptuously denounced as 'shameful' and 'outrageous' even by councillors who were up to their brass necks in it. In 1993, the then Minister for the Environment, Michael Smith, raised the hackles of his Fianna Fáil colleagues when he denounced land rezoning in Co Dublin as a 'debased currency', saying that many of the decisions being made at the time indicated a 'frightening level of irresponsibility'. Meetings of Dublin County Council to deal with successive county development plans, held in a soundproofed chamber intended as a retail premises on the ground floor of its O'Connell Street headquarters, took on the atmosphere of a noisy real estate agency or pork belly futures market. You could almost smell corruption in the air. The tiny public gallery was often packed beyond capacity by landowners, speculators, developers and their agents waiting for favourable rezoning decisions, often involving hundreds of acres of land. In the corridor and lobby outside this curious democratic assembly, they could be observed in huddles with friendly councillors about whether the numbers were present to pull off whatever coup was planned. At least one agent, Frank Dunlop, was observed doing a head count himself. Asked how he felt after losing a crucial vote, he quipped: 'What you need in this business is a spine of steel and balls of iron, and if we can't make a shilling here we'll make it somewhere else.' (He was commenting on the outcome of his own scheme to redevelop chunks of the greenbelt between Baldoyle and Portmarnock, where he had acquired an option on four hundred acres of land owned by John Byrne, the veteran developer and Haughey crony. It fell at the last fence, when councillors who pledged to support it lost their nerve under a media spotlight.) Afterwards, if things went well, the councillors and their clients would repair to Conway's pub on Parnell Street for several rounds of celebratory drinks. Dunlop's bill on the night Quarryvale was finally rezoned after a seven-hour marathon debate in 1992 came to £900, because some of them were 'trousering' bottles. This writer could name at least twelve members of the 78-strong council who were irredeemably corrupt and should long since have been imprisoned in Mountjoy. I was also aware, long before he retired as Dublin County Manager in 1989, that George Redmond was 'on the take'. Sources estimated that he had received more than £1 million in kickbacks over the years. But none of this could be reported at the time because the only evidence available was circumstantial, even hearsay. Ray Burke, of Fianna Fáil, was one of the very few politicians to be directly implicated. In 1974, the *Sunday Independent* reported that he had received a payment of £15,000 – then a very substantial sum – under the heading 'Planning' from a company controlled by house-builders Brennan & McGowan, with whom he had a close relationship. As a county councillor, he sponsored rezoning motions for lands they had speculatively acquired, particularly in the Swords area. As an auctioneer, he would later sell the houses they built on these

courtesy of the *Irish Times*

Ray Burke, pictured in 1990 at the launch of a book by Tom Reddy, then an *Irish Independent* journalist and, more recently, press officer for Fianna Fáil. The racy book dealt with famous Irish murders.

overleaf

Front-page story introducing a six-part series by Mark Brennock and Frank McDonald on land rezoning in the *Irish Times* in July 1993. It quoted one developer's agent as saying that some councillors 'put a value on their votes', and could bring others with them 'depending on how they're looked after'.

lands. A Garda investigation was ordered, during the course of which Burke was reportedly interviewed twenty times, but no action was taken. Further Garda inquiries into land rezoning corruption in Co Dublin on foot of allegations made in 1989 very extensive, and focused on an alleged 'ring' at the heart of planning. The man who headed those inquiries, Detective Superintendent Brendan Burns, came to the conclusion that what they were dealing with was nothing less than 'a nest of vipers', though his report on the outcome of the investigation was considerably less critical.

THE I[

PRICE 85p (incl. VAT) 75p sterling area

'Cash in brown pap

**By Mark Brennock
and Frank McDonald**

LANDOWNERS and developers have offered, and in some cases paid, sums of money to Dublin county councillors who supported controversial land rezoning schemes in Co Dublin, a property developer, a developer's agent, a councillor and a former councillor have confirmed to *The Irish Times*.

The payments were in the form of election campaign donations, financial assistance for specific purposes and sometimes straightforward personal cash gifts. Sources have indicated the identity of some of the recipients, but

they cannot be named for legal reasons.

However, *The Irish Times* has established that a former Fianna Fail chairman of the council, the late Mr Sean Walsh TD, had almost £250,000 in bank and building society accounts after his death in December 1989. Mr Walsh, who was a full-time public representative, had been one of the most active councillors in earlier rezoning controversies.

These revelations come as the changes made by the current councillors to the draft development plan for Co Dublin are on public display. Since the latest rezoning blitz got under way 15 months ago, a total of 2,640 acres

of agricultural land has been designated for housing or industry, as well as 300 acres of green belt — multiplying its value by a factor of 20 or more.

On
spoke
dition
fied,
the va
counc
dedica
peopl
their
Howe
indivi
times
assist

On
The I
fered
occas
excha
cific
clined

The gardaí were called in again after the *Irish Times* ran a week-long series of articles on the rezoning blitz in July 1993, researched and written by myself and Mark Brennock. It was provocatively introduced by a headline across the top of the front page, 'Cash in brown paper bags for councillors'. Our story quoted one developer's agent as saying: 'There is a certain number of people in that council chamber who put a value on their votes. They are the power-brokers who can bring five votes with you, or five votes against you, depending on how they're looked after.' The system worked on the basis of 'straight cash in brown paper bags'. Later in the week, a businessman came forward to tell us that he had personally handed a white envelope containing £2,500 to a named councillor in a successful effort to persuade him to change his vote on a key rezoning decision. He also offered the same amount to another councillor, who turned it down because 'his fee was higher'. Another informant said his son, who owned a site in Tallaght which he wanted to have rezoned for industry, had been told to deliver £10,000 in a brown envelope to a man outside Holles Street Maternity Hospital, to overcome the unexpected opposition of one particular councillor. Other allegations in the *Irish Times* series came from a councillor who had been offered

SH TIMES

NDAY, JULY 12, 1993

bags' for councillors

who
n con-
denti-
f that
county
rking,
ch of
n't do
ears."
of key
some-
ns of

s told
as of-
on one
er, in
r spe-
ne de-

A current Dublin councillor has revealed that she was approached by two property developers in advance of last November's general election and offered "assistance" in meeting campaign expenses. She also declined this offer. Other councillors spoken to in the past week say, however, that they have never been offered, nor have they solicited, any such assistance.

According to the developer, payments to the small number of councillors involved could be as little as £500, but could also amount to substantially more, depending on the circumstances. Some councillors involved are regarded as "key individuals" who can influence the votes of a significant number of others.

Another developer's agent said: "There is a certain number of people in that council chamber who put a value on their votes. They are the power-brokers who can bring five votes with you, or five votes against you, depending on how they're looked after." The system worked on the basis of "straight cash in brown paper bags", he added.

In some cases, payments have not been made until a scheme has been successfully shepherded through all stages of the rezoning process. The money is then paid as a "success fee" rather than as an initial incentive.

The leader of the Fianna Fail group on the council, Ms Betty Coffey, said that she was aggrieved by allegations that some councillors received "incentives" to influence their vote. "I don't know of any, I don't see any, I don't agree with it, and if developers are doing that, I'd like to see them, and the person receiving money, put in jail."

The Minister for the Environment, Mr Smith, has already attacked the council's record, saying that zoning in Co Dublin has become a "debased currency" and that many of the decisions indicate a "frightening level of irresponsibility".

See also page 5

money by two developers, purportedly for election expenses, and a former councillor who had been offered an apartment on one occasion and money on another. All of the newspaper's informants agreed to speak on condition that they would not be identified. The only one who was named, Seán Walsh, had died in 1989, leaving cash totalling almost £250,000 in bank and building society accounts. Walsh had for years been one of the leading rezoners on the county council, but the newspaper was excoriated by former Tánaiste John Wilson, among others, for traducing his reputation when he was no longer in a position to defend himself. It was a neat Irish equation – one couldn't speak ill of the dead, because that ran counter to a long-established tradition, and one couldn't tell the truth about the living because they would sue for libel. The Garda investigation – headed by Detective Inspector Michael Guiney – got nowhere either, mainly because it could not guarantee immunity from prosecution to informants with first-hand evidence.

There seemed to be no way of breaking through the wall of silence and denial armed only with antiquated laws against corruption, some dating back to the Victorian era, notably the Public Bodies Corrupt Practices Act of 1889.

Another vehicle would have to be found – and it came from a quite unexpected source. In July 1995, a most unusual and intriguing advertisement appeared in the *Irish Times*. Placed by a Newry firm of solicitors, Donnelly Neary & Donnelly, it offered a £10,000 reward for information leading to the conviction of anyone involved in land rezoning corruption. The Newry solicitors were acting for anonymous clients – later revealed as Michael Smith and Colm MacEochaidh – who had become incensed about the continual rezoning of amenity and agricultural land and the persistent allegations that much of this was corruptly arranged. 'It is widely believed that the rezoning process is influenced by those who stand to become multi-millionaires if the tracts of land they have assembled are rezoned', the solicitors said. 'Those behind the reward believe it is regrettable that the State has never sought a prosecution in this area.' Indeed, the sponsors of the £10,000 offer had to go outside the State and engage the Newry firm to act for them because several firms of solicitors in Dublin had declined to do so. Not only was their initiative seen as quite unorthodox; its very subject was regarded as too 'hot' to handle. Within weeks, Donnelly Neary & Donnelly had been contacted by thirty individuals, all with stories to tell about corruption in the planning process. They included James Gogarty, an elderly and disgruntled former managing director of Santry-based Joseph Murphy Structural Engineering Ltd. He alleged that he had been present in Ray Burke's Swords home (built, incidentally, by Brennan & McGowan) in June 1989 when brown envelopes containing a total of £80,000 were handed over to the then Minister on behalf of JMSE and Bovale Developments in return for helping to iron out planning difficulties on a range of sites dotted around north Co Dublin. Bovale, run by Roscommon-born brothers Mick and Tom Bailey, was one of the most active firms of housebuilders in Dublin at the time, with numerous housing estates already built and a substantial land bank assembled for future development – often with the benefit of 'material contraventions' of the county plan, pushed through by its supporters on the council. Staunch Fianna Fáilers, the Baileys knew Burke well, and one of the purposes of Mick Bailey's attendance at that fateful meeting in Briargate, the then very powerful TD's home, was to introduce him to James Gogarty.

With this explosive timebomb ticking away behind the scenes, the sponsors of the £10,000 reward issued a lengthy statement two months after the newspaper advertisement appeared, condemning 'official inertia' and calling for a public inquiry into the as yet unpublicised allegations, which were later drip fed to the media. 'This is not blackmail', they declared. 'It is the resort of persons forced to take action in an arena, which outside of a banana republic, should be the realm of government.' But Brendan Howlin, then Minister for the Environment, said that while he was 'totally committed to rooting out corruption' in the planning process, he was 'not prepared to do so on the basis of threats from anonymous sources'. He also declined to meet Smith and MacEochaidh after they had put out 'feelers' seeking to engage his interest in the matter on a confidential basis. His Fianna Fáil shadow, Noel Dempsey, also criticised the still-anonymous sponsors, saying it was 'very difficult to accept' their bona fides when they continued to issue 'veiled threats about "outing" public officials and politicians without producing any evidence of wrongdoing'. He also said that the only thing that would come out of it was gratuitous publicity for a hitherto unknown firm of Newry solicitors. The then Minister for Justice, Fine Gael's Nora Owen – herself a former Dublin county councillor – was also made aware of the principal allegations by Tommy Broughan TD (Labour), who had interviewed Gogarty. But she, too, was unenthusiastic about establishing a public inquiry into the matter. In any case, as Willie O'Dea TD (FF) pointed out at the time, obsolete laws on bribery and corruption made it 'virtually impossible' for the State to mount a successful prosecution against corrupt politicians or officials. And with the media hamstrung by the libel laws, Gogarty's allegation about Ray Burke took a long time to surface in print, even though journalists had been aware of it from an early stage. In the United States, the whole story could have been published at the outset under the press freedom guarantees in the First Amendment to the US Constitution. That's what enabled the *Washington Post* to get to the bottom of the Watergate scandal in the early 1970s. The joke in Doheny & Nesbitt's pub during the 1980s was that if Watergate had happened here, Nixon would still be president and Deep Throat would be in jail.

Even though Burke had still not been named by the media, Bertie Ahern, who never misses a thing, was

courtesy of the *Irish Times*

James Gogarty, the disgruntled former managing director of Santry-based Joseph Murphy Structural Engineering Ltd, who became a star of the Flood Tribunal.

The intriguing advertisement placed in the *Irish Times* on 3rd July 1995, which ultimately led to the Flood Tribunal.

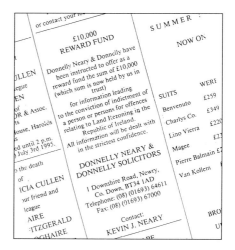

well aware of the Gogarty timebomb before he appointed this Fianna Fáil stalwart as Minister for Foreign Affairs after the June 1997 general election. He later memorably declared that he had been 'up every tree in north Dublin' to see if there was any truth in Gogarty's claims and had asked the then party whip, Dermot Ahern (no relation), to undertake a pro-forma 'investigation'. Extraordinarily, he did not interview the former JMSE managing director. After the *Sunday Tribune** finally named Burke in July 1997, claiming that he had received £30,000 from Bovale Developments, perhaps confusing the firm with JMSE, it was clear that his position was becoming untenable. Three weeks later, Burke issued a statement saying he had 'done nothing illegal, unethical or improper', and accusing the former JMSE executive of conducting a vendetta against him. He also threatened to sue the *Sunday Business Post*[†] after it carried an interview with Gogarty by journalist Frank Connolly, who had doggedly pursued the story. But it was not until *Magill*[°] published a 1989 letter from Mick Bailey telling Gogarty that he could 'procure' a majority of Dublin County Council to support the rezoning of lands held by JMSE that the Government finally agreed to establish a tribunal of inquiry headed by Mr Justice Feargus Flood. That same month, October 1997, Burke resigned as Minister for Foreign Affairs and as a Dáil deputy, still insisting that he had done nothing wrong. Though over eighty, clearly frail, and motivated to get even with his former employers in a convoluted dispute over his pension, Jim Gogarty emerged as a public hero during his four months in the tribunal's witness box. On the way to Burke's house in June 1989, he recalled asking Mick Bailey if they would get a receipt for the money. 'Will we, fuck!', he quoted the Roscommon man as saying. Throughout, his evidence was stridently contested by lawyers acting for JMSE and the Bailey brothers, both of whom persistently denied that they had ever given Ray Burke any money for anything. The tribunal was told that Bovale maintained an unorthodox record of under-the-counter cash payments to a variety of people, including employees; it was know as the Pussy Book because it had a picture of a kitten on the cover. JMSE's accounts showed that the money it gave to Burke was listed under two headings – 'planning permission' and land 'enhancements'. It also emerged that the former Dublin North TD had been collecting money from sources that had nothing to do with land rezoning. In February 2000, concert promoter and one-time Century Radio boss Oliver Barry admitted to the Flood Tribunal that he had given Burke £35,000 in cash in May 1989, after ill-fated Century had secured the national commercial radio licence. Burke was Minister for Communications at the time.

Though initially established to investigate a series of land transactions in north Dublin involving JMSE and Bovale Developments, the Flood Tribunal's terms of reference were widened, allowing it to trawl through unconnected alle-

---

* *Sunday Tribune*, 20th July 1997   ° *Magill*, September 1997
[†] *Sunday Business Post*, 17th August 1997

gations that money had changed hands in relation to other planning decisions – in effect, a fishing expedition to find out 'who gave what to whom', as Paul Cullen, of the *Irish Times*, succinctly put it. By far the most sensitive area to which the tribunal lawyers turned their attention was whether there was any link between donations to Fianna Fáil in 1994, when Bertie Ahern was Minister for Finance and Honorary Treasurer of the party, and the designation of areas for urban renewal tax incentives. It was during this period that Fianna Fáil's debt was miraculously reduced from more than £3 million to just £500,000, and not just by running a series of 'golf classics'. At the time, there were reports that developers had come under pressure to subscribe to the party if they wanted their sites in Dublin and elsewhere to end up 'on the right side of the line'. At one stage in mid-1994, according to Emmet Stagg TD (Labour), then Minister of State for Housing and Urban Affairs, sensitive files relating to urban renewal designations 'disappeared' from the Department of the Environment. On inquiring after their whereabouts, he was told that the files had been requisitioned by the Department of Finance. He was also informed that they could no longer be found there, because they had been taken somewhere else. In a detailed statement by Stagg, the Flood Tribunal 'was told where they had allegedly gone', according to the *Sunday Tribune*,* Indeed, Stagg took such a serious view of the situation at the time that he travelled by car to Roscrea, Co Tipperary, to inform the Minister for the Environment, Michael Smith, who subsequently declared that developers who thought that they could gain advantage by making political donations would be doing themselves no favours. On their last day in office following the collapse of the Fianna Fáil-Labour coalition in November 1994, Smith and Ahern signed orders designating the Golden Island site in Athlone for urban renewal tax incentives, paving the way for this part of the Shannon floodplain to be developed as a major shopping centre. According to the *Sunday Times*,[†] what the tribunal is investigating was whether there was any connection between this belated move and a £100,000 contribution to Fianna Fáil from Cork-based Owen O'Callaghan, one of the developers involved in the Athlone project. It had been solicited by Des Richardson, a close associate of Ahern who had been appointed by him as the party's chief fund-raiser, operating from an office at the Berkeley Court Hotel.

The Flood Tribunal's biggest catch – so far, at least – was George Redmond, who had spent his entire working life in the service of Dublin Corporation and Dublin County Council. Redmond was drawn into the net by Gogarty's claim that he had met him a number of times and, on one occasion, had given him £15,000 over tea in Clontarf Castle. According to Gogarty, Redmond was to become a consultant to JMSE after he retired as county manager in June 1989, and the money was given to him in compensation when this offer was not pursued. Flood's star witness also claimed that Redmond was paid £12,000 after he

---

* *Sunday Tribune*, 19th March 2000   [†] *Sunday Times*, 12th March 2000

had arranged to have the duration of a JMSE planning permission in Swords extended, thus saving the company more than £100,000 in new fees and development levies. All of this appeared to confirm the rumours circulating for years that this crusty former official had been feathering his nest. But much worse was to come. On the afternoon of Friday, 19th February 1999, Redmond was arrested at Dublin Airport by the Criminal Assets Bureau, having just returned on a flight from the Isle of Man. He was carrying almost £300,000 in cash and cheques, which he had apparently withdrawn from banks in Douglas – less than a week after denying, in an exculpatory interview with *Ireland on Sunday*,* that he held any overseas accounts. (The other explanation was that he had brought this stash to the Isle of Man and was dismayed to discover that no bank there would take it becuase of tighter rules on money laundering.) His arrest and subsequent interrogation at Harcourt Terrace Garda Station was the most shocking event in the history of Irish local government, though it certainly spread a ripple of glee among many of his former subordinates.

This was the man who, with his deep tan and arms usually folded, had sat like a lord on the left-hand side of successive chairmen of Dublin County Council, delivering his views with an authoritative air and proving more than a match for councillors who disagreed with some of the actions he took. This was the man who, while he was serving as assistant city manager in charge of Dublin Corporation's planning department in the late 1970s, had the say-so about who got planning permission in the city and subject to what conditions. This was the man who had gone to the same school as Charlie Haughey, St Joseph's CBS in Marino, and joined the local authority's service as a clerk in 1941, at the age of eighteen. He was typical of a whole generation of senior local authority officials, in that he never worked in the private sector and effectively spent all of his 48-year career in the same organisation. But he differed from most of them in that he received cash for some of the actions he took. Asked by the Flood Tribunal to account for his accumulation of money, Redmond said he was a 'heavy saver'. He might have added that he was also notoriously tight, rarely if ever paying for his lunch in the canteen, according to those who worked with him, and driving around in a twelve-year-old car. Apart from his arrest at Dublin Airport, Redmond's most dramatic moment came in March 1989, just months before he retired, when he told the council he had earlier signed a cheque for £1.9 million in planning compensation to Grange Developments Ltd, a Brennan & McGowan company, after it had threatened to have the County Council put into receivership over a planning refusal to develop land at Mountgorry, near Swords. But there was something deeply squalid about the revelation that while he was county manager, he had an interest in an amusement arcade in Westmoreland Street – where he was known as 'JR' – and that he used to saunter down there every week to collect nearly £500 in cash. When this handy little earner was reported by RTÉ's

---

* *Ireland on Sunday*, 14th February 1999

Charlie Bird in March 1999, Redmond denied owning a share in the premises, saying the money was repaying a loan he had advanced to the proprietor, Jim Kennedy, a friend and associate for many years. In February 2000, Redmond reached a settlement with the Revenue Commissioners to pay tax debts totalling £875,000, in the hope of avoiding imprisonment. He was lucky to get away with a fine of £7,500 after pleading guilty to charges of failing to file tax returns for ten years. And despite the fact that he is in receipt of an index-linked local government pension of £27,000 per annum, his counsel, Paddy McEntee SC, described him as 'effectively destitute'. Subsequently it emerged that he had just sold his detached house on the Deerpark Lawns estate in Castleknock for £750,000, and his wife had purchased a more modest £260,000 home in the the same area. Asked how he felt after being fined, the former county manager said he was 'very contrite about the whole thing'. The

George Redmond, former Dublin county manager, whose arrest at Dublin Airport in February 1999 was the most shocking event in the history of Irish local government.

Marc O'Sullivan, Collins, Dublin / courtesy of the *Irish Times*

extent of this contrition will be measured by what he tells the Flood Tribunal.

In September 1988, nine months before he retired, Redmond was among the senior Dublin officials, led by Frank Feely, who were summoned by the dreaded Haughey to Government Buildings for a meeting to discuss the Government's dismay at the absence of construction activity in the city. It has since emerged that one of the main purposes of this ninety-minute 'open and frank' exchange, at which Haughey was accompanied by Ray Burke, Padraig Flynn and Ray McSharry (but no civil servants), was to underline the need to facilitate major retail projects planned by Tom Gilmartin. The Sligo-born developer who spent most of his life in England, had clearly been inspired by such Thatcher-era megaschemes as the Metro Centre on Tyneside, and he was the first to spot the strategic significance of Quarryvale, 'where the M50 meets the N4'. Though the first phase of the M50 was only under construction at the time, he was busily assembling a 180-acre site to realise his dream of a massive motorway shopping centre, comparable in size to any of the out-of-town retail magnets in Britain. Leinster House records show that Flynn had already met Gilmartin, and was to meet him

Irish Times

Map showing the strategic location of the Quarryvale (Liffey Valley) site on the M50 in relation to rival shopping centres in Tallaght and Blanchardstown.

opposite

Tom Gilmartin, the Sligo-born, Luton-based property developer, with a model of the huge shopping centre (foreground) he was planning in 1990 for the strategically important Quarryvale site, 'where the M50 meets the N4'.

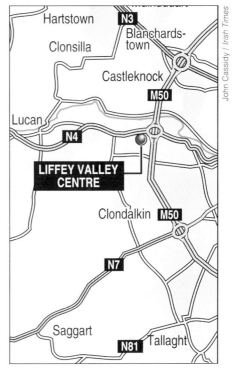

Main entrance to the Liffey Valley shopping centre. The Grosvenor-O'Callaghan consortium was shell-shocked by An Bord Pleanála's decision to refuse planning permission, mainly on traffic grounds, for a scheme to double its size to 500,000 square feet.

on at least four other occasions in 1989. He was made well aware of the Luton-based developer's plans both for Quarryvale and for Bachelors Walk and Ormond Quay Lower where Gilmartin was planning another major shopping centre, twice the size of the one on St Stephen's Green, with parking for 1,400 cars at basement level and a city bus station on the roof. As the poll-topping TD for Dublin Central and Minister for Labour, Bertie Ahern was also aware of the Luton-based developer's plans. He too had met Gilmartin on a number of occasions in 1988-89, and one of his runners, ex-councillor Joe Burke, had also been in touch with him, allegedly to outline the planning problems posed by his shopping centre / bus station concept. In a Dáil statement in January 1999, Ahern was adamant that neither he nor Burke had solicited any donation for Fianna Fáil.

Meanwhile, in order to complete his acquisition of the Quarryvale site, Gilmartin had to get his hands on a 69-acre holding owned by Dublin Corporation and zoned for industrial development. At first, it seemed that this could be done by private treaty, without bothering to go to public tender. According to a memorandum in October 1988, a few weeks after the 'summit' at Government Buildings, the then deputy city manager, Paddy Morrissey, who was also at the meeting with Haughey et al, issued instructions to dispose of the Quarryvale site to Gilmartin for a price equivalent to just over half of what he eventually agreed to pay for it six months later. According to the Corporation's files on this transaction, the only reason why it didn't go ahead was that a rival developer, the Green Property Company, had also expressed an interest in acquiring the 69-acre site. John Corcoran, Green's managing director and veteran of the 1969 battle over Hume Street, had become aware of Gilmartin's scheme, and he was understandably concerned about its impact on Green's plans for Blanchardstown. With Redmond's active support, Corcoran had secured planning permission to develop its designated town centre, including 750,000 square feet of retail space – twice as much as originally planned. Asked at the time why Green had now got double the floor area, the county manager said: 'These fellows have done their sums and this is what they believe will work. Who are we to say it won't?' The last thing 'these fellows' needed was a rival shopping centre, more than twice the size again, at two million square feet, to be developed a few miles away – and it was Redmond who tipped them off about Gilmartin's cunning plan. After Corcoran wrote to the Corporation to say that Green Property would be interested in acquiring its Quarryvale holding for industrial use, a public tender became inevitable – though the very small notice advertising it was buried at the bottom of the antiques page in the *Irish Times*. In April 1989, two tenders were received – one for £4.4 million from Green Property, and another for £5.1 million from Gilmartin. Green's offer to pay an extra £7 million if the site could be rezoned for retail was deemed invalid by the Corporation, as it was in no position to guarantee such an outcome. The following month, it signed a contract with Gilmartin, fully aware of his plans for a huge out-of-town mall, with potentially damaging impacts on the city centre and its own commercial rates base.

The Luton-based developer, his Sligo accent undiluted after three decades in England, was hoping that Quarryvale might get a similar package of urban renewal tax incentives as the one that magicked Tallaght town centre out of the ground for Phil Monahan and Monarch Properties. But it soon became apparent that he was walking into a hornets' nest, encountering people along the way who told him that he would have to pay out a lot of money – a sum of £5 million was mentioned, according to him – if his ambitions for Quarryvale were to be realised. In June 1989, Gilmartin decided to make a substantial donation to Fianna Fáil, and gave Padraig Flynn, then Minister for the Environment, a blank cheque for £50,000, which Flynn asked him to make out to 'cash', and which he then lodged in his own bank account at the Bank of Ireland on College Green. Flynn was 'not the worst of them', he told the *Irish Times** in December 1999. 'I was being held to ransom by boys a lot cuter than him. The donation was paid because I was told it would help to curb the activities of these boys.' According to the 1989-90 Garda investigation, as revealed by Catherine Cleary in the *Sunday Tribune*,[†] Gilmartin outlined some of the pressure he was under to the then City Manager, Frank Feely, and the then Assistant City Manager, Seán Haughey (Charlie's brother). Both of them took detailed notes of his allegations during a meeting in February 1989 that lasted three hours. Although it is clear from the report that he did not tell them everything, the matter of George Redmond joining Green Property after he retired in mid-1989 was discussed. Feely later told the gardaí that he was concerned at the timing of Green's interest in purchasing the Corporation's sixty-nine acres at Quarryvale and Gilmartin's allegation that Redmond had been offered a job with the company. The gardaí later telephoned Gilmartin at his Luton home, but while he made unspecified allegations against unnamed people, he never put these in writing.

Meanwhile, his hopes that fiscal benefits could be conferred on the Quarryvale site were dashed for a reason that had nothing to do with him. The same benefits had been denied to Green Property in Blanchardstown, apparently after a vengeful Haughey took umbrage on being informed that John Corcoran's very forthright wife, Anne, had made some disparaging remarks about the Taoiseach at a horsey-set dinner party. 'That fucker Corcoran won't get tax incentives for Blanchardstown – not today, not next week, not fucking ever', Haughey is reported to have fumed when he was told about the faux pas. Blanchardstown never did get a tax deal, and neither did Quarryvale. With or without the prospect of tax incentives, Gilmartin still had a mountain to climb if he was to make a return on the money he had already sunk in his *grand projet* to create Ireland's biggest-ever shopping mall. The basic problem was that the Quarryvale site had never been intended for such a development, even at a much smaller scale. Since 1972, successive Dublin county plans had zoned another site in Neilstown, adjoining the Dublin-Cork railway line, as a 'town centre' for the

---

* *Irish Times*, 30th December 1999   † *Sunday Tribune*, 23rd April 2000

Lucan-Clondalkin agglomeration. But this site was relatively isolated, with very poor road access and a marked absence of development in the vicinity. It was for that reason that the shrewd Cork developer, Owen O'Callaghan, had concluded that it was not viable, and decided to throw in his lot with Gilmartin. O'Callaghan, who was involved in developing shopping centres at Merchants Quay in Cork and Arthur's Quay in Limerick, had acquired an option on the designated Neilstown site in 1988, but he soon became aware that Government ministers favoured Quarryvale instead. At one stage, he was even asked by Padraig Flynn to reconsider his Neilstown scheme to let Gilmartin's project go ahead. Like him, O'Callaghan could see that the strategic location of Quarryvale at the fulcrum of the M50 could not be beaten. In time, it would become a magnet for well-heeled shoppers within a 30-minute 'drive-time' radius, including those in the affluent southern suburbs. But unlike Gilmartin, he realised that plans for a mega-mall would not travel the distance. If there was to be any chance of making progress, they would have to be scaled down to 500,000 square feet. He also came up with the brilliant wheeze of offering to build a 40,000-seater football stadium, with a retractable roof, on the Neilstown site, just to show that it could be used for something. (Needless to say, though full planning permission was granted for this project in 1993, nothing ever came of it.)

With £15 million racked up on the Quarryvale site, and AIB, which was bankrolling it, becoming increasingly worried about the prospects, O'Callaghan was encouraged by the bank to buy out the Luton-based developer's equity in 1991. In fact, AIB had given Gilmartin an ultimatum – either he agreed to make way for the Cork developer or the bank would put his venture into liquidation. Its confidence in O'Callaghan's ability to make Quarryvale pay was confirmed when he immediately set about the task of having the site rezoned once in the driving seat. Working closely with him on this problematic project were two of the most experienced hands in the business – lobbyist Frank Dunlop and archi-

Michael McSweeney / courtesy of the *Irish Times*

Owen O'Callaghan, the developer who first threw in his lot with Tom Gilmartin on the Quarryvale site, then bought him out with AIB's encouragement.

tect Ambrose Kelly, both past masters in the application of emollients. It was suspected at the time that Dunlop was also the 'bagman' for Quarryvale. Their game plan was to sell the scheme as a much-needed amenity for the deprived communities of north Clondalkin, and in no time at all, they managed to recruit almost every significant local group to O'Callaghan's cause, as well as the area's four councillors – Colm McGrath (FF), who admitted in January 1999 that he had received substantial financial contributions from Barkhill Ltd, the Cork developer's vehicle, John O'Halloran (Ind), Therese Ridge (FG) and Colm Tyndall (PD). McGrath suffered the indignity of being 'de-selected' by Fianna Fáil for the June 1999 local elections, but ended up romping home in Clondalkin as an independent. It also emerged, via the Flood Tribunal, that Frank Dunlop had been paid a total of around £700,000 to cover the onerous costs of running the Quarryvale campaign. At least £175,000 of

Paddy Whelan / *Irish Times*

Frank Dunlop, the PR consultant, lobbyist and strategist who opened the floodgates of corruption in Dublin County Council with his dramatic statement to the Flood Tribunal.

this money was deposited with Shefran Ltd, a company run on his behalf by two directors in the Channel Islands, and a secretary in the Isle of Man. Barkhill's investment certainly yielded dividends. In May 1991, just a month before that year's local elections, Dublin County Council voted by a large majority (29:13) to relocate the 'town centre' zoning from Neilstown to Quarryvale on the northeastern extremity of the 'new town' it was meant to serve, despite a warning from the planners that this would be 'seriously detrimental' to the realisation of the long-established county development plan. Every Fianna Fáil councillor, with the honourable exception of Anne Brady, an architect and town planner who could see the implications, voted in favour of the rezoning. Then, quite unexpectedly, the temperature was raised by John Corcoran, who held a dramatic press conference in the middle of the election campaign to denounce the council's 'irresponsible' decision, warning that it could result in Green Property's long-standing plans for Blanchardstown being cancelled. A huge political storm blew up. Councillors who supported Quarryvale were 'eaten alive' on the doorsteps, and twelve of the most prominent rezoners lost their seats, including Liam Lawlor

TD (FF), who admitted years later that he had acted as a £3,500 per month consultant to Tom Gilmartin. In the south county, where the battle to save Carrickmines Valley was already under way, public awareness was raised by an ad hoc Campaign for Honesty in Politics, set up by a young man called Michael Smith, who would later play such an important role in flushing out the truth. The group circulated thousands of leaflets headed 'Politicians on the Fiddle – Vote Them Out', arguing that councillors 'should represent the people of Dublin, not party bosses and shady developers'.

All of this had happened long before Frank Dunlop momentously took the stand at the Flood Tribunal in mid-April 2000 to face a searching examination by Patrick Hanratty SC, one of its leading lawyers. 'For once, the tables were turned on the suave, assured public relations guru. The basic operating principle of a lobbyist is anonymity, but here was Dunlop in the full glare of the media searchlight [with] no time for off-the-record briefings or delicate spin-doctoring', wrote Paul Cullen in the *Irish Times*.* 'No amount of damage limitation or carefully prepared mantras could hide the basic facts: Dunlop hid £175,000 from the taxman for up to seven years, and he was unable to account in any detailed way for what he did with this money'. He had withdrawn large sums of up to £40,000 in cash from Shefran's account at the AIB in College Street, and said he had spent this stream of income from Barkhill on ponies for his children, a caravan, holidays in the US, and the refurbishment of his home near Dunboyne. 'Shefran was, to all intents and purposes, me', he admitted. He also described the work he had done on Barkhill's behalf in relation to Quarryvale as 'voluminous and monumental'. There were strategy meetings at his offices in Upper Mount Street, attended by Owen O'Callaghan, architect Ambrose Kelly, and several key councillors, meetings with local community groups, and an endless round of 'schmoozing' sessions with individual councillors 'over pints in a local pub, dinner in the Gresham Hotel, or, for the lucky ones, lunch in one of Dublin's top restaurants', as Cullen put it. The most dramatic revelation came right at the end of Dunlop's first day in the witness box when Hanratty queried whether he had ever been asked for money by any of the councillors in connection with their support for the Quarryvale rezoning. 'Yes, I was', the lobbyist replied. He then wrote down a name on a sheet of paper and handed it to the tribunal. Three days later, in the *Irish Independent*,† Sam Smyth revealed that the councillor in question was the late Tom Hand of Fine Gael, who had requested a 'fee' of £250,000 for his support for Quarryvale, and even gave Dunlop the number of an offshore account in the Isle of Man, where the money was to be lodged. Dunlop was so gobsmacked that he mentioned Hand's alleged demand later to several other Fine Gael councillors, and even, he claims, to the party leader, John Bruton, who has vehemently denied that he was ever told about it. One of Hand's colleagues, the transparently honest Mary Muldoon, resigned from Fine Gael because she was so 'sickened' by

---

* *Irish Times*, 15th April 2000   † *Irish Independent*, 14th April 2000

Gandon Archive

The Fingal County Council building on Upper O'Connell Street, George Redmond's headquarters for ten years, and former Augean stables of Dublin County Council

Conway's pub, around the corner on Parnell Street, the most favoured 'castpoint' for corrupt county councillors, and odd choice of venue for John Bruton to lecture the Fine Gael group on their rezoning activities in 1993.

Frank McDonald

what was going on around her. In the *Sunday Business Post*,* she recalled that Bruton had summoned the Fine Gael members of Dublin County Council to a meeting in 1993 to tell them bluntly that they had become 'a laughing stock' over land rezoning, and that this must stop, which, of course, it didn't. The meeting, ironically, was held in the upper room of Conway's pub, the most favoured 'cash-point' for corrupt councillors, including Tom Hand. What surprised Dunlop was not that Hand, who died in 1996, had asked for money in return for his vote; it was just that his 'fee' was so stratospheric, far above the going rate.

That became evident when the noticeably less chirpy lobbyist resumed giving his evidence to the tribunal a week after his first appearance. He was asked about another mysterious bank account held by him at the AIB branch in Rathfarnham, from which there had been substantial withdrawals of cash, amounting to almost £250,000, and these runs on the bank coincided with the county council's votes on Quarryvale. Dunlop at first denied that this money had been used for any 'illicit or improper purposes'. But Mr Justice Flood intervened to say that it was 'a most unusual account', and he suggested that the lobbyist, who was now on a very sticky wicket, should reflect overnight on what its real purpose was. The following day, Dunlop was back again to face the music. His whole demeanour had changed, with some observers commenting that this now chastened man, a one-time Government press secretary, looked as if he had aged ten years. There was certainly no sign of the 'spine of steel and balls of iron'. Led by Patrick Hanratty, he then began detailing his relationship with a 'core group' of Fianna Fáil and Fine Gael councillors, and the money he had paid them in lieu of their 'assistance' with the rezoning of Quarryvale. Suddenly and sensationally, the wall of silence and denial that surrounded corruption on Dublin County Council for so long was being breached by an insider who had decided to 'come clean'. Dunlop wrote down a list of payments, with names attached, and recounted the circumstances under which each wad of cash was disbursed. The sums ranged from a piddling £500 at the lower end of the scale to a remarkably avaricious £48,500, which was paid to one 'powerful individual' who had played a key role in the affair. Other less significant members of the 'core group' received more modest sums of £2,000, but some benefited to the tune of £12,000, £15,000 and £20,000. Some of these 'bundles of joy', as Frank McNally called them in the *Irish Times*, were given to corrupt councillors in Conway's pub on Parnell Street, a favourite venue for them and for fathers celebrating happy events at the Rotunda Hospital just opposite. Other payments were made by Dunlop in the Dáil bar, in his office, or in the recipients' homes, and he told the tribunal that his entire outlay amounting to £112,000 was reimbursed later by Owen O'Callaghan. After getting all of this off his chest, the lobbyist was overcome by a strong weakness, and asked to be excused. The overwhelming trauma of facing the awful truth had obviously taken its toll. He emerged ashen-faced, walking

---

* *Sunday Business Post*, 30th April 2000

slightly stooped behind his lawyers before being ushered into the back seat of a black BMW to be driven away from his day of destiny at Dublin Castle.

Whatever his motivation, there could be no doubt that Dunlop had performed a sterling public service by deciding to tell all. He would go on to detail further contributions to councillors, ranging widely across the political spectrum, which included such thoughtful gestures as printing their election leaflets, for example. Aping Boss Croker's definition of an honest man, the ones who were bought stayed bought, and Dunlop, it seemed was prepared to tell all, about everything that went on. Though his courageous confession that he had been personally involved in bribing councillors was bound to boomerang on his own business, it represented a catharsis and set the stage for others – such as George Redmond – to make a clean breast of it in public before the re-energised Flood Tribunal. It also provided a valuable preface to the long-awaited appearance by Tom Gilmartin. He was said to have been delighted by Dunlop's performance and raring to go for his long-awaited stint in the witness box, to tell a colourful tale about what happened at Quarryvale. At last, as RTÉ's Charlie Bird put it, 'the genie is out of the bottle'. Dunlop's revelations opened a Pandora's box of bribery and corruption, and there was no telling where it would lead. Not for the first time since the Flood and Moriarty tribunals were established, politicians in Leinster House were transfixed by what was happening in Dublin Castle. After all, Quarryvale was just one of numerous controversial land rezoning decisions taken by Dublin County Council over the years, and if a 'core group' of councillors had put a price on their support for it, there was every reason to believe that the same gang had also taken money to steer through many other decisions that made fortunes for the developers involved. According to reliable sources, almost every major rezoning adopted by the council during the early 1990s was contaminated by corruption. In that light, there was something faintly ridiculous about announcements by Fianna Fáil and Fine Gael on the day Dunlop spilled the beans that they had both set up inquiries to establish whether any of their councillors had taken bribes. Had they been paying no attention at all to media reports over the years, not least the *Irish Times* series in 1993? Did they not even suspect that some of their members had climbed aboard the rezoning bandwagon to line their own pockets with ill-gotten gains as they made a pig's breakfast of planning in County Dublin?

The fire-wall of denial had been so well constructed that Trevor Sargent TD of the Green Party was verbally and physically abused in February 1993 when he brandished a £100 cheque he had received from a property developer – merely to *read* a rezoning submission – and asked other members to declare similar contributions. His intervention provoked uproar in the council chamber as the rezoning majority rounded on him, spitting out a stream of hysterical vituperation. Sargent found himself gripped in a headlock by one Fianna Fáil councillor who tried to grab the cheque, and the meeting was adjourned in disorder by the Cathaoirleach, Therese Ridge (FG). Some days later, Joan Burton (Labour), then

Minister of State at the Department of Social Welfare and former member of the council, delivered a speech at the AGM of the Ballynacargy branch of the Labour Party in Co Westmeath. She was sued for libel by *forty-two* of her one-time colleagues from Fianna Fáil and Fine Gael. Burton had referred to the unseemly sight of property developers and their agents 'crowding the council's ante-chamber and gallery, ticking off lists of councillors as they arrive and vote for decisions that multiply at a stroke the value of lands they own or control'. Bravely, she went on to say that the public was 'entitled to know from each and every councillor what campaign contributions, what hospitality and what assistance, direct or indirect, in recent elections or at any other time, they or their parties received from these developers, landowners, associated builders and their agents'. Within days, she herself was in receipt of nearly twenty letters from Gallagher Shatter, solicitors, on behalf of every Fine Gael member of Dublin County Council, and one from Frank Ward & Co, on behalf of all the Fianna Fáil councillors. They also sued the *Irish Independent*, which had reported her speech. Ward's letter called on the newspaper to publish an immediate retraction, making it clear that there were 'absolutely no grounds to suggest bribery or corruption in Dublin County Council', apologising to the Fianna Fáil councillors 'for the distress and embarrassment caused to them, their families, friends and associates' and affirming that they had 'always dealt with rezoning applications ... with the utmost integrity and having regard only to appropriate planning criteria'. Commendably, the *Irish Independent* declined to publish such an obsequious and, as we now know, untrue statement, but Joan Burton found herself out-of-pocket by £400 or £500 to cover her legal costs in responding to the law suits, even though they never got to the door of the Four Courts. Yet all she had done was to raise questions about the murky business of land rezoning on Dublin County Council. Eithne FitzGerald, another former member of the council who had repeatedly clashed with the rezoning majority, found it extraordinarily difficult as Minister of State in Tánaiste Dick Spring's office to steer new ethics legislation through the Dáil during the mid-1990s. Attacked by opponents for adopting a 'holier than thou' stance, she had to defend the Bill line by line, and with no enthusiasm for it among the major parties, the Ethics in Public Office Act 1995 did not go half as far as its sponsor had hoped. Warning that landowners still stand to make 'stratospheric profits' from the unrelenting expansion of Dublin, FitzGerald has more recently proposed that a Development Land Commission should be established to designate land for development, purchase it for marginally more than its agricultural value, as the Kenny Report recommended in 1974, and then install the necessary infrastructure before releasing sites to private developers.

On Easter Sunday, in the immediate aftermath of Dunlop's bombshell statement to the Flood Tribunal, Frank Connolly reported in the *Sunday Business Post* * that the tribunal has been investigating even more sensational allegations

---

* *Sunday Business Post*, 23rd April 2000

– viz, that two senior Fianna Fáil politicians, one still in Government, had received cheques for £50,000 each in September 1989 'in return for their assistance with the development of a major retail project in Dublin'. (Jody Corcoran, who has also been to the fore in probing political corruption, had a similar story in the same day's *Sunday Independent*.) In an affidavit sworn for the *Business Post*, an unnamed businessman claimed that he had paid the politicians on behalf of the developer involved, using cheques drawn on an Irish Nationwide Building Society account in Patrick Street, Cork. The cheques were in white envelopes, and in both cases, their recipients 'opened the envelopes and examined the contents in his presence', according to the businessman. One of these encounters, with the still serving politician, took place in the car park of the Burlington Hotel in Dublin on the night of the All-Ireland football final in Croke Park, while the other, involving another minister who has since retired from active politics, was at a function in the Silver Springs Hotel in Cork. After the businessman first told his shocking story to Flood Tribunal lawyers, the tribunal made an order in February 2000 seeking access to the cheque journal and other records held by Irish Nationwide. Its delay in handing over the relevant documentation landed the society's managing director, Michael Fingleton, in hot water, with Patrick Hanratty SC describing his attitude to the order as 'cavalier in the extreme'. During a number of uncomfortable appearances on the witness stand, Fingleton insisted that the society was 'not hiding anything'; it was just that the transactions which the tribunal was interested in had taken place eleven years earlier and that Irish Nationwide had a policy of destroying 'certain things', such as bank statements and cheque counterfoils, after six years. After being warned that he could be committing an offence for failing to comply with the order, Fingleton was told to provide whatever documentation he could and to sign a letter authorising access by the tribunal to records held by the society's clearing bank AIB, to establish how the two cheques were cashed.

But it was the *Business Post's* contention that the latest allegations were so serious as to provoke a general election that set political tongues wagging. It seemed as if a dam was about to burst, engulfing the Government, as a spokesman for the Progressive Democrats warned of 'immediate and swift action' if the allegations proved to be true. Bertie Ahern moved just as swiftly to set the record straight. Speaking on the 'hallowed ground' of Arbour Hill after the annual Fianna Fáil 1916 commemoration on Easter Monday, he identified himself as the currently serving senior politician mentioned in newspaper reports and categorically denied receiving money from Owen O'Callaghan 'or anyone else' in the car park of the Burlington Hotel 'or in any other car park in 1979, '89, '99, or any other time'. O'Callaghan had made 'a good number of contributions over the years' to Fianna Fáil, but he said these had gone through party channels and not through him, and they had all been notified to the Flood Tribunal. 'I'm a straight, honest person, and if I had received the money I would say I did', Ahern declared, to cheers from party members. As for the former senior politician who was also alleged to have received £50,000, the Taoiseach said this man had made it clear that if anyone published his name in this connection, he would sue. His own theory was that the unnamed businessman 'must have some gripe' with the Cork-based developer. The *Irish Times* referred to the weekend reports in a sulphurous editorial:* 'A sophisticated game of bluff and deception, backed up with hidden threats and undoubtedly with secret promises, is being conducted in and around the business of the Dublin Castle tribunals. The stakes are as high as they can be in this society's structures of advantage and privilege. Senior political figures stand to lose their reputations and their grip on power. Influential business interests stand to be exposed as manipulating political and civic authority. And in between are to be found a variety of murky figures – tanglers and fixers, each on a percentage or with a profitable hand in the pork barrel ... Media spinning has reached new heights. The most elaborate ploys are being used to lead journalists away on false scents ... It is a time to be careful – very careful – about what one reads and where one reads it.' O'Callaghan, too, had smelled a rat. In a statement issued on April 23rd, he said that a 'concerted attempt' was being made to 'derail' his company's £320 million Mahon Point project in Cork, which was the subject of 'binding contracts' with Cork Corporation. Referring directly to Frank Dunlop's evidence the previous Wednesday, he said that he would be telling the Flood Tribunal 'in the most emphatic way' that he 'never instructed or authorised anyone' to pay money on his behalf to any politician for his or her vote on Quarryvale. The man who claimed he had paid off the two senior Fianna Fáil politicians was later revealed[†] as Denis O'Brien, a little-known Cork businessman and former chairman of Glen Rovers GAA club, who had been involved with litigation with two banks, Anglo-Irish Bank and the Ulster Bank, over loan repayments; a High Court judge, Mr Justice Barr, concluded that he had directly or indirectly forged a letter in one of these cases. Earlier, Liam Lawlor had effectively conceded that he was the 'powerful individual' alluded to by Dunlop, say-

Liam Lawlor TD, who said that he would 'never condone any payments being made to politicians in return for their vote'.

* *Irish Times*, 25th April 2000
† *Sunday Business Post*, 30th April 2000

ing that 'whatever financial support' he received had been used for legitimate electoral purposes and to help run his very busy constituency office. 'I have never and would never condone any payments being made to politicians in return for their vote', he declared. One of his Fianna Fáil colleagues observed that Lawlor had 'perfected the technique of hiding while in full public view'.

Way back in 1990, suspecting that there was something afoot, Pat Rabbitte TD (Labour) had called for a Dáil inquiry into the sale of Dublin Corporation's holding at Quarryvale to Tom Gilmartin, but quite predictably there was no willingness on the part of a Fianna Fáil-led government to turn over this particular stone to see what class of maggots might crawl out. There was also very little public discussion, other than in the *Irish Times* property supplement, about the implications of providing three competing regional-scale shopping centres within a few miles of each other at Tallaght, Blanchardstown and Quarryvale on, or just off, the merry-go-round of the M50. Nonetheless, the political fall-out from the 1991 local elections had a sobering effect. After a marathon seven-hour meeting in December, Dublin County Council unanimously decided to cap Quarryvale's retail element at 250,000 square feet – half of what it was before the electoral debacle and one-eighth of what Gilmartin had in mind. But although the zoning cap was spelled out in the council's last county plan, adopted just before it was wound up twelve months later, everyone – including Owen O'Callaghan – knew that this was 'just for openers', and that Quarryvale would grow like Topsy. Why else would no less a personage than Gerald Grosvenor, Duke of Westminster, have agreed to take a 50% stake in it? The fourth richest person in Britain, he was certainly not lured to west Dublin by a mission to meet the needs of deprived communities, but rather by the alluring prospects inherent in the pivotal location of the site.

And so, even before the first phase of the 'Liffey Valley Experience' (marketing name for Quarryvale) opened its doors in October 1998, South Dublin County Council had already decided to lift the zoning cap on its retail content, allowing the developers to double its size. Frank Kavanagh, the Wexford-born county manager, defended this unilateral decision on the basis that 'more flexibility' was required in the context of the EU single market, and denied that the council had been influenced by such squalid considerations as the extra rates revenue it would rake in from a substantially larger shopping centre at Quarryvale. Plans to extend it would, of course, be subject to a retail impact study which would have to take account of the 'metropolitan interest' as well as ministerial guidelines on major retail schemes, he said in March 1998. Frank Dunlop, who had been engaged by O'Callaghan to lobby for the the 'cap' to be lifted, was handsomely rewarded with a 'success fee' of £300,000 when the County Council agreed to go along with it. In the past, the Dublin City Centre Business Association would have been to the fore in objecting to such aggrandisement on the periphery, but its fervour in defending the city's retail core has been dulled over time by globalisation of shopping and the fact that many of its more important members now have large outlets in suburban malls. The only obstruction to Quarryvale's progress came from another unilateral decision – this time by the Minister for the Environment, Noel Dempsey, when he imposed a ceiling on the size of 'superstores' in June 1998. Both RGDATA, representing independent retailers, and SIMI, representing car dealers, had lobbied for this restriction, fearing the consequences of Tesco's plans for a chain of superstores, each with its own cut-price petrol station, including a major outlet at Quarryvale. Further plans for the elevated Liffey Valley site included a 'motor mall', more retail warehousing, a four-star hotel, a library and other community facilities, as well as a newly constructed 'heritage trail' to commemorate historical places or figures in the area, including William (sic) Sarsfield. The Grosvenor-O'Callaghan consortium had no problem persuading South Dublin County Council to grant permission for a doubling of the shopping centre's floorspace to 500,000 square feet, including a Tesco supermarket, fronted by surface parking for 6,000 cars. But the developers could barely have imagined the outcome of appeals to An Bord Pleanála by RGDATA and the Irish Hardware Association. In a decision strongly contested by their planning consultants, Reid Associates, the board requested the Dublin Transportation Office to submit its observations on the proposed development, and the DTO's director, John Henry, had no hesitation in blowing it out of the water. Having considered the matter in detail, the board – in an order signed by Lewis Clohessy, who once worked for An Taisce – refused planning permission for the project in March 2000, on the grounds that it would create serious traffic congestion and undermine established retail outlets in the Lucan/Clondalkin area. Even though the decision left the developers shell-shocked and Liffey Valley without a major food anchor, it sent out a clear signal that planning policies really meant something.

Based on the UK experience, there was every reason to believe that huge out-of-town shopping centres were having an adverse impact on high street retailing. In 1996, ten years after Tyneside's Metro Centre opened malls lined with more than two million square feet of shopping space, John Gummer used his powers as Environment Secretary to impose new planning rules designed to make it difficult for developers to get planning permission even for relatively modest schemes. At home, RGDATA director general Michael Campbell continually pointed to evidence that 42% of villages in the UK no longer had a local shop because of ruthless competition from superstores, usually in out-of-town shopping centres. 'Ireland has the opportunity to avoid repeating the planning errors there, and this opportunity should be grasped', he declared in March 1998. For him, it was galling to see Tesco trying to introduce the same sort of developments that had proved so problematic just across the Irish Sea. Dempsey's imposition of a limit of 3,000 square metres (32,300 sq ft) on the size of superstores was a response to this concern. So was the publication of a draft set of Retail Planning Guidelines in April 1999. 'The experience in other European countries is that these developments have had quite damaging effects on existing urban centres and have not been in line with the principles of sustainable development', Dempsey said. In future, the preferred location for retail development would be within town centres, especially on sites served by public transport, and there would be 'a presumption against' large retail centres adjacent to national roads – including, presumably, 'where the M50 meets the N4'. But before a final version of the Retail Planning Guidelines could be confirmed, Mary Harney, a one-time environmentalist herself, intervened to express concern about their possible impact on competition policy, and so yet another consultancy study had to be commissioned.

As elsewhere, shopping followed people out of the city and showed a marked tendency to concentrate in middle-class areas, such as Blackrock, which is unique in Ireland for having two shopping centres facing each other across a busy public road. Since the Stillorgan centre opened in 1966, at least thirty more have been built throughout the Dublin area. With shopping centres mushrooming in the suburbs, the city centre fought back, first with the suburban-style ILAC centre and later with more upmarket, urban equivalents in St Stephen's Green and Jervis Street. Dublin Corporation, with its eyes firmly focused on urban renewal (and the future of its commercial rates base), did everything it could to facilitate these enclosed retailing machines – even allowing developer Paddy McKillen to stack five levels of car-parking on the roof of the Jervis Centre. But even in the late 1980s, at least some of its senior officials recognised that Tom Gilmartin's scheme for Bachelors Walk and Ormond Quay Lower was typical of the kind of development which had 'wrecked the hearts of English cities like Sheffield and Birmingham', in the words of then City Architect Chris Dardis. Arlington Securities, Gilmartin's vehicle, was later acquired by British Aerospace, and went on to become one of the victims of Britain's economic recession. The site it had assembled on Bachelors Walk was sold in 1993 to Zoe Developments, and later developed for an architect-free residential and retail scheme. The Corporation was so concerned about the accuracy of its mock-Georgian detailing that it seemed to overlook the fact that the vast bulk of its 330-plus apartments had just one bedroom. As for what British Land should do with the St Stephen's Green Centre, an excellent guide to contemporary architecture in Dublin* suggested that since its Mississippi riverboat cladding had been bolted on, it could just as easily be bolted off.

Meanwhile, back in the suburbs, things were going from bad to worse because there seemed to be no limits on what the three new local authorities in

_____

*Dublin – A guide to recent architecture, by Angela Brady and Robert Mallalieu (Ellipsis, 1997)

Frank McDonald

The Stephen's Green shopping centre, designed by James Toomey for British Land. A recent guide to contemporary architecture in Dublin suggested that since its Mississippi riverboat cladding had been bolted on, it could just as easily be bolted off.

The Jervis Centre, as seen from a vantage point in Temple Bar. Dublin Corporation was so anxious to facilitate this major retail development in the city centre that it allowed developer Paddy McKillen to stack five levels of car-parking on the roof.

Frank McDonald

Co Dublin would permit. In Crumlin, right on the edge of the city boundary, South Dublin's councillors voted for a 'material contravention' of the county plan in 1996 to permit a £30 million shopping centre to be erected on the site of the Submarine Bar. They did not have to concern themselves with the survival of Crumlin village, which is in the Corporation's area. A year later, the rezoning majority on Fingal County Council pushed through a new development plan for Swords, with Cathaoirleach Anne Devitt (FG) ruling out of order an attempt by Seán Ryan TD (Labour) to defer it pending further studies on sewage treatment, traffic management, and the route of a rail link. Devitt, who sponsored most of the rezonings in partnership with Cyril Gallagher (FF), maintained such a brisk pace in going through the motions that Michael O'Donovan (Labour) pleaded with her to 'give us a chance to think between votes'. As for the previously agreed development boundary for Swords, Gallagher paraphrased Parnell: 'I've never put a boundary to the onward march of a nation and I never will.' Throughout the council meeting, members of Swords Community Council picketed its offices in O'Connell Street, with placards reading 'Town planning, not town cramming', and 'Swords – soon to be twinned with Alcatraz'. Week after week, more agricultural land on the city's periphery was falling prey to this frenzy of land rezoning, done by councillors at the behest of those who stood to make massive windfall gains, and leaving the public to pick up most of the tab for new roads, schools, sewers and water supplies. Many of the councillors who sponsored or supported such land rezonings did so for purely ideological reasons. They did not need to have brown envelopes slipped their way. They believed, fundamentally, that their role was to facilitate development, whatever the planners had to say about the wisdom of their developer-led approach. Corruptly driven or not, it was becoming more and more apparent that if this type of 'planning' prevailed, we would start hitting the outskirts of Dublin in or around Kinnegad. Yet its engine has been driven by a virtual coalition of Fianna Fáil, Fine Gael and Progressive Democrat councillors, all of whom represent parties which say they are in favour of controlling public expenditure – in the case of the PDs as an article of faith – with the support of some more self-seeking independents. This pattern is mirrored in Kildare and Wicklow, particularly around their historic towns and villages. Clane is threatened with having its population trebled in five years, while Delgany may have a suburban estate of three hundred houses tacked onto it. The danger is that Co Kildare will end up with the worst of both worlds – continuing overdevelopment in the towns of Celbridge, Clane, Leixlip, Kilcock and Maynooth, all within easy commuting distance of Dublin, *as well as* a new concentration in the Naas-Newbridge area. This is the 'pick and mix' approach favoured by its power-brokers, a 'strategy' described by one of whom – Paddy Power, a former Minister for Defence – in 1997 as being 'as good as any other'. The same sort of laissez-faire approach threatens to coalesce Greystones, Delgany and Killincarrig in north Wicklow.

Under its 1999 county plan, Fingal substantially redefined its greenbelts to permit development opportunities for 'integrated leisure complexes', so that these visual breaks between swathes of the proverbial concrete jungle would be more available to the general public. Permitted uses include hotels, conference centres, golf courses, fitness centres, equestrian centres, tennis academies, and even low-density housing. It seemed to mark a resigned acceptance by the planners that these areas, mostly in private ownership, would continue to come under development pressure and might be better protected by giving them an economic use. Fingal's attitude to Dublin Airport is so fawning that the county plan actually describes the council as 'the guardian of this national resource', with a 'unique role in facilitating its development potential'. The fact that Aer Rianta pays £5 million a year in commercial rates presumably had no bearing whatsoever on the council's decision in July 1998 to grant planning permission, subject to just four conditions, for a new Pier D, which will obscure the only remaining airside view of the airport's original terminal building. Though this masterpiece of 20th-century architecture, designed by Desmond FitzGerald and completed in 1940, is listed for preservation in the Fingal county plan, the council saw no problem in Aer Rianta tacking on the new pier, over 90 feet wide and nearly 700 feet long. It didn't even bother to consult the Heritage Council, An Taisce, or the Fingal County Architect, David O'Connor. It also ignored a plea from the architect's grand-daughter, Catherine FitzGerald, to protect what remains of the original terminal's setting instead of adding yet another discordant element to the 'general morass' of buildings at the airport. When she appealed to An Bord Pleanála, it not only confirmed Fingal's decision – against the advice of Stephen Dowds, the planning inspector who dealt with the case – but reduced the number of conditions from four to two, neither of which related to visual matters. Anyone building a bungalow in north Co Dublin would have to comply with much more numerous conditions. The indulgent treatment of Aer Rianta reflects the pressing need to provide more terminal facilities at an airport that is bursting at the seams, with passenger numbers reaching 13.5 million in 1999. This loyalty to the State airports authority at least partly explains why both Fingal County Council and An Bord Pleanála rejected plans for Huntstown Air Park, a privately run terminal on the west side of the airport promoted by brothers Ulick and Des McEvaddy.

Other landowners around the airport and elsewhere in Fingal were more fortunate. By the time its latest county plan first appeared as a draft in October 1998, they were almost hysterical about the prospects of having their green fields turned into gold. Peter Coyle (Labour) said so many of them had been lobbying him that he barely had time to eat his dinner. These were usually the ones who had scanned the draft prepared by the planners, been horrified to find that their particular patches were not being zoned, and got on to their councillors straight away. The County Manager, Willie Soffe, who steered the preparation of this draft plan, insisted that he had not met a single landowner prior to proposing that hundreds of acres of land throughout Fingal be rezoned for housing, includ-

Gandon Archive

The original terminal building at Dublin Airport. Aer Rianta's plans for a new Pier D will obscure the only remaining airside view of this masterpiece of 20th-century architecture.

The main terminal at Dublin Airport, centrepiece of the general morass of buildings that now engulfs the original terminal.

Alan Betson / Irish Times

ing large chunks of the greenbelt between Baldoyle and Portmarnock. This came as very good news to John Byrne, who had made a number of failed attempts to develop four hundred acres there over the previous twenty-five years. Baldoyle Racecourse would now be covered in new homes, as he had long intended. The owners of the Phoenix Park Racecourse, home turf of successive British viceroys, were also delighted to have it rezoned for housing, as this enabled them to sell the 100-acre site to house-builders Flynn and O'Flaherty for a whopping £37 million. The substantial profit made on this transaction more than adequately compensated Norman Turner and Robert White for the years of effort they put into their failed Sonas Centre project. Even with thirty acres reserved to provide a 'visual break' between Castleknock and the city, it was clear that the racecourse site could accommodate at least 1,000 houses and apartments, much to the distress of Pat Allison and others involved in a spirited campaign to preserve it.

The entire north fringe of the city from Castleknock right across to Baldoyle Estuary is being opened up to development by a £33 million drainage scheme, with a capacity to cater for 20,000 new homes, some likely to be served by temporary sewerage facilities pending its completion in 2002. One of the major beneficiaries of this public investment is developer Gerry Gannon, who owns or has acquired options on large tracts of land in the area, and has plans for huge housing schemes in what Fingal County Council refers to as the 'south Fingal fringe'. With vastly higher population targets set for almost every town in Fingal and so much land rezoned by the planners to meet these new targets, lucky landowners stood to make fortunes for themselves – and at a reduced 20% capital gains tax, thanks to Charlie McCreevy. There was no question of deferring crucial decisions until the Greater Dublin Area Strategic Planning Guidelines were finalised. But then, why should Fingal wait when none of the other local authorities in the region had stayed their hand? The shortage of housing, and the shocking prices people had to pay to put a roof over their heads, simply meant that they had to get on with it. Though the firebrand Socialist Party councillor, Joe Higgins TD, pointed out that almost 2,000 acres of residential-zoned land in Fingal had yet to be developed, the housing crisis had become a mantra to justify yet more land rezoning. Those who opposed it, such as 'people who have a house and a job and don't want anyone else coming to live in their area', would have to be 'faced down', according to the County Manager. However, the need to cater for first-time house-purchasers could hardly be used as an excuse for rezoning several small, isolated parcels of land between Malahide and Kinsealy for luxury low-density housing, or indeed isolated fields right up to the boundary with Meath, all done against the planners' advice. Whatever shadow the Flood Tribunal was casting, it did not seem to penetrate Fingal's council chamber – the former Augean stables of Dublin County Council. But it was the planners who paved the way for Charlie Haughey to put 9.7 acres of his Kinsealy estate on the market in April 2000, with the expectation that it would raise as much as £5 million as a handy hedge against future tax bills from the Revenue Commissioners. In 1998, they zoned this sliver of land on Abbeville's road frontage with the aim of consolidating the rather formless village of Kinsealy as an alternative to bungalow blitz; similar zoning changes were made in nine other villages in the north county area. If Haughey had any shame, he would have handed over his Kinsealy estate to the nation, and accepted the position of life tenant to atone for his sins.

With residential land fetching as much as £1 million an acre, even the British Government cashed in. Glencairn, its long-time embassy residence on thirty-five acres in deep south County Dublin, was sold in December 1998 for just over £26 million to Park Developments, netting a huge return on a country house purchased for just £35,000 in 1956. It, too, looked set to be covered in more 'luxury' commuter belt homes, just like the sprawl of suburban housing which crept up to its gates like Birnam Forest to Dunsinane. Park Developments, founded by Frank McInerney and now run by Michael Cotter, trumped itself just over a year later by agreeing to pay £36.5 million for forty-nine acres of the Grimes family farm between Carrickmines and Cabinteely, with the intention of developing it as an office park linked to the South Eastern Motorway. A nearby 31-acre site in Carrickmines, much of which was required for a motorway interchange, was rezoned for industry at the behest of the Fianna Fáil group on Dun Laoghaire-Rathdown County Council. All this meant was that the council would end up having to pay its English owners, Jackson Way Properties, ten times as much to buy the land it needed for the road scheme. Another questionable change made against all planning advice involved the rezoning of a 21-acre field for low-density housing right in the middle of the greenbelt separating Shankill from Bray. It was sponsored by Larry Butler (FF), who subsequently became chairman of the council's strategic planning committee. Elsewhere in the double-barrelled 'county', there was outrage when the council abandoned ceilings on residential density in the old borough to consolidate the built-up area – denounced as a 'recipe for disaster' by Labour councillor Jane Dillon-Byrne, who lives in leafy Silchester Road – and rezoned almost two hundred acres of farmland between Stepaside and Kilgobbin.

The same pattern was repeated in South Dublin. In Lucan, residents associations formed a coalition called ALARM (All Lucan Against Rezoning Madness) to campaign against the rezoning, on Frank Kavanagh's initiative, of 530 acres south of this sprawling built-up area for more housing. But although ALARM lodged more than 3,000 objections, it was 'faced down'. What had galvanised them into action was the contemptible rezoning of Laraghcon, one of the most controversial proposals in the early 1990's rezoning spree. It involved eighty-five acres of farmland on an elevated site overlooking Lucan village, some of it owned by a supporter of the Progressive Democrats. It should have been covered by an extended Liffey Valley Special Amenity Area Order; instead, the council voted down two motions which sought to preserve it. Casting aside the advice of the planners who warned that any development at Laraghcon would intrude on the Liffey valley, the four Castleknock area councillors – Seán Lyons (Ind), Tom Morrissey (FG), Sheila Terry (PD) and Ned Ryan (FF) – proposed that Laraghcon be rezoned for low-density housing. Since then, An Bord Pleanála has three times refused permission to Shannon Homes for up to 355 houses on the lands, citing the effect such a scheme would have on the Liffey valley. The South Dublin county plan also rezoned a strip of two hundred acres along the southern rim of Tallaght, running up to the foothills of the Dublin Mountains, as well as extensive tracts of farmland around the historic villages of Newcastle, Rathcoole and Saggart. Because of the absence of any regional planning framework, all of this amounted to 'making it up as we go along', as the council's Labour chairman, Eamonn Walsh, conceded when the draft plan was published in April 1998. It flowed from the notion that South Dublin was a viable economic and social area in its own right within the Greater Dublin region. Tallaght was being branded as the place 'where Ireland does business with Dublin', a sort of shining city on a hill. Its spatially exploded core became the focus of imaginative plans to transform a random collection of free-standing buildings, each surrounded by surface car-parking and palisade fencing, into a real town centre laid out in streets and squares. The effervescent County Architect, Brian Brennan, clashed with the more conservative Planning Officer, Enda Conway, over whether it shouldn't also have a few tall buildings, or 'architectural spikes', as Brennan calls them. With the aid of tax incentives to lever an estimated £250 million worth of private sector investment, he foresees a time when the area will be buzzing with bars and restaurants, and the pointless artificial mounds obscuring Tallaght Hospital are replaced by substantial buildings to house nurses, medical consultants, or whoever.

By contrast with the rezoning mania in the county, particularly in Fingal, Dublin city councillors were more hesitant in their approach to changing the status of land, mainly because so much of the city was already built-up and inhabited by their constituents. In November 1998, when the Corporation's planners proposed that the last remaining tract of agricultural land within the city boundary at Pelletstown, off the Navan Road, should be rezoned the move was deferred amid indications that it might be defeated. One of the most compelling arguments for rezoning it for residential development was that the 105-acre site, wedged between the Royal Canal and the River Tolka, has a railway line 'on its doorstep' and could be serviced quite quickly for housing, according to deputy city manager Seán Carey. But Labour and Green Party councillors, and even one or two from Fianna Fáil, referred to the area as an 'oasis' or 'green lung' with a 'real rural character', and said local residents wanted to see it developed as a 'millennium park' featuring a city farm, organic garden, picnic areas and pony-trekking trails. After adjourning the matter for a week, the council was still so divided that the rezoning was finally adopted on the casting vote of the then Lord

courtesy of O'Mahony Pike Architects

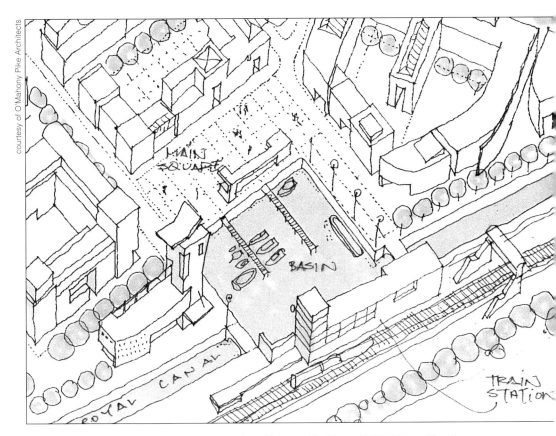

Sketch designs by O'Mahony Pike (in association with Dusseldorf-based O'Neill Consulting) for a major residential development at Pelletstown, between the Royal Canal and the River Tolka. The scheme marks a radical departure from the conventional form of suburban housing, with a distinct urban character and strong sense of place.

Mayor, Senator Joe Doyle (FG), subject to a firm assurance that the Corporation would acquire enough land to develop an 'ecologically sensitive' linear park in the Tolka valley. This followed intensive negotiations between senior Corporation officials and two developers, Ballymore Homes and Castlethorn Construction, which had acquired options on the Pelletstown land. The council was also assured that a detailed action plan would be prepared for the area, based on the principles of sustainable development.

The Pelletstown action plan, drawn up by a team headed by deputy chief planning officer Dick Gleeson, in collaboration with Kelvin Campbell's Urban Initiatives, took nearly a year to emerge, but it was worth waiting for. Delivered to the City Council as a draft in October 1999, it marked a radical departure from the conventional form of suburban housing. Instead of serried ranks of two-storey semi-detached houses, the action plan envisaged the creation of 'a vital, viable and sustainable community with a distinct urban character and strong sense of place ... using the most up-to-date environmental policies and planning guidelines'. Liberally illustrated with images from European cities, it called for buildings of up to five storeys in height, laid out along tree-lined boulevards on the Royal Canal frontage, adjoining the railway line. With the existing Ashtown station at the western end of the site and the prospect of a new station at its eastern end, the plan provided for two 'village nodes' at these points, with shops, crèches, own-door offices, pubs and restaurants at street level. In order to sustain such a range of community facilities, the density of residential development would have to be as high as 150 homes per hectare (62.5 per acre) – way above suburban norms – to accommodate a target population of up to 10,000. Not all of Pelletstown's new residents would be living in apartments. Under the action plan, there would also be some detached and semi-detached houses in a parkland setting. As in Temple Bar, the Corporation said it was anxious to promote 'contemporary and innovative' architecture on the site to complement new public spaces, which would include a crescent-shaped park, two urban squares, pedestrian bridges across the canal, and an informal linear park along the Tolka. It was all very radical stuff, consciously intended by the planners to provide a new, more European model for Dublin's suburbs.

Higher housing density, particularly in town centres and along good public transport routes, is one of the common themes of the latest development plans adopted by all four Dublin local authorities. This welcome departure from 'prairie planning' is in line with sustainable development principles, Government guidelines and the Bacon reports on house prices. Developers were reputedly slavering at the mouth over the prospect of being able to cram double the number of units on every site, but this was just one example of a lot of woolly thinking on the subject. Ordinary people seem to equate higher-density housing with high-rise buildings, conjuring up nightmare images of Ballymun. But it needs to be stressed again and again that Ballymun, the most notorious Irish experiment in high-rise living, is actually a *low density* housing estate of system-built towers and slabs, laid out in a windswept parkland setting. It is about to be demolished. What's on the agenda now is somewhat more sophisticated. And while the primary objective is to deliver an increased supply of housing from the available bank of zoned and serviced land, building at higher densities should also improve our quality of life by cutting down on travel. Many trips on the road network are made by people hopping into their cars to go to the nearest shop or pub or to drop their kids off at a distant school. If everything can be made more compact and located within easy reach of public transport, so the theory goes, it can be a 'win-win' situation for everyone. But according to Eoin Ó Cofaigh, former president of the Royal Institute of the Architects of Ireland, the design spend on standard suburban housing estates works out at just £400 per house, 'or about the cost of a decent washing machine'. Architects are not involved in designing many of these estates, which at least partly explains why the resulting residential environments turn out to be so woeful. If higher-density housing is to be successful, as the Department of the Environment has repeatedly emphasised, a much higher level of design input will be required.

The DoE first indicated that it favoured higher housing densities in March 1997 in its strategy to achieve 'sustainable development', and a circular letter encouraging local authorities to promote the new policy was issued a year later. In effect, they were being told to re-examine provisions in their own development plans which have an impact on residential density – not just in terms of the maximum number of housing units permitted per acre, but also car-parking standards, minimum lengths for front and back gardens, and the provision of public open space. Simultaneously, the whole issue of higher housing densities and how they might be achieved was being thrashed out by a joint working party set up by the RIAI and the Irish Planning Institute, representing those who would find themselves at the 'coal face' of change in this area. The first Bacon report on house prices, in April 1998, endorsed the new approach, and was followed almost immediately by the appointment of consultants to draw up a comprehensive set of Residential Density Guidelines. Part of the brief given to planning consultant Fergal MacCabe, in association with architects McCrossan O'Rourke and chartered surveyors Jones Lang Wooton, was to consider the safeguards required in promoting greater residential density generally, and, in particular, to ensure that it did not result in an 'unacceptable amenity cost' to the existing houses in any neighbourhood or to the residents of a proposed higher-density housing scheme. The Department had to be careful that the new regime it was promoting would not produce another batch of planning disasters as appalling in their own way as the low-density sprawl spawned by the standards applied over the past thirty years. 'A higher quality of design and layout and a good quality living environment, including the availability of proper shopping, transport and leisure infrastructure, are essential if increased densities are to be acceptable', the consultants concluded. So if the new guidelines were to be properly implemented, developers would have to seek out the best possible professional advice, and the local author-

courtesy of the Irish Times

Standard suburban estates consist of rows of houses usually full of young working couples, probably with two cars, which they spend half the day sitting in. And because the housing is built at such low densities, these estates are difficult to serve by public transport.

ities would have to deploy the expertise they had available to them to 'work up' plans for new housing areas so that there would be some chance of producing the right result. It was not simply a question of building twice or three times as many housing units on any given site. The whole effort had to be 'design-led'.

This message was driven home at two major conferences organised jointly by the RIAI and the IPI. Under the banner of 'Stopping the Sprawl', the most recent gathering in November 1999 was a high-density event, with nearly three hundred participants squashed into a dark, makeshift hall in the horrible barn of the RDS Simmonscourt 'pavilion'. Disturbingly, however, there was only one TD present (Eamon Gilmore) and two councillors, but no county managers, senior civil servants or roads engineers. As IPI president Philip Jones conceded, the the planners and the architects have yet to convince this wider body of interests that higher residential densities 'can be made to work effectively to create good quality environments that people will want to live in'. The cultural problem, as he noted, is that Irish people 'expect to be able to have their own house, their own hall door, their own patch of garden in which to hang out the washing, play with the cat (if not actually swing it) and sit out if the sun comes out'. In Cork city, as its highly respected chief planning officer John O'Donnell once said, what the average person wanted was a bungalow on a half-acre in Patrick Street, preferably with a view of the sea, 'and they're compromising from that point onwards'. The challenge facing all planners – 'the gatekeepers of the building boom', as Jones called them – is to attempt to change this anti-urban culture and meet the demand for housing at the same time. This battle will be won or lost not in the inner city, but 'out there in suburbia', he told the RIAI-IPI conference. Local authority managers, engineers and other officials – 'including, let it be said, some planners too' – must be convinced that higher-quality residential developments 'can come about in suburbia if we change the design philosophy'.

According to Patrick Clarke, technical director of Llewelyn-Davies in London, most suburban housing estates have been planned on a 'worst-case scenario' for car use, with almost a third of their site area given over to roads and parking. If the requirement for off-street parking was replaced by on-street parking, the number of dwellings could be doubled and, contrary to popular belief, this would produce a significantly better residential environment. The lesson was that developers 'must be prepared to invest in tailor-made designs rather than rolling out a carpet of standard housing types'. David O'Connor, the Fingal County Architect, said this meant a lot more than 'putting on brick fronts' to make new houses more attractive. To illustrate his point, he showed an image of two-storey houses with half-brick fronts standing opposite each other across a distributor road flanked by slip roads, with an aggregate width exceeding O'Connell Street. Why do we make roads like that when we could be making streets like those in the Drumcondra area of Dublin? he asked. Nobody would regard Iona Road or Lindsay Road as undesirable, yet they were built at a density of up to twenty-eight houses per acre – nearly four times the density of many

Brian Brennan

Cheeverstown Road in west Tallaght, with low-density, terraced two-storey houses backing onto it. 'If we build prairies, why are we so surprised to find that they attract wandering horses?', asks Brian Brennan, the South Dublin County Architect, who took this bleak photograph.

Tree-lined Griffith Avenue, widely acknowledged as one of the finest achievements of 20th-century town planning in Ireland.

Pat Langan / *Irish Times*

suburban housing estates of much more recent vintage – with schools, churches and shops all within walking distance. David Taylor, of Alan Baxter & Associates, a London-based firm of cutting-edge consulting engineers, showed images of new housing in Poundbury, near Dorchester, which was developed to a master plan by Leon Krier for the Duchy of Cornwall estate, owned by the Prince of Wales. Though the style struck some as twee, at least it had the merit of placing houses in a traditional street setting, creating very strongly defined spaces where it would be safe for children to play. 'Imagine that,' commented Eddie Conroy, deputy county architect in South Dublin, 'houses facing onto streets. What will they think of next?' And yet the idea seems revolutionary because we have so lost our way over the past thirty years.

Conroy, a noted housing expert, is not only convinced that the newer suburbs ringing Dublin do not work, he also believes that people are getting bad value for their money. 'What we have are rows of houses full of young working couples, probably with two cars. Inside each home, they've got the big dining room that's never used, because they eat at a little Habitat table in the kitchen and then watch the telly in the front room. Upstairs, there's the room they sleep in, as well as a second bedroom that's full of their wedding presents and a tiny third room that has the computer in it, because a bed won't fit. What they have is an inflexible house where they can't do ordinary things like eat in the kitchen with their friends or work in a living room. Outside, there's a big front garden that they can't do anything in because everyone can see them and, eventually, it's paved over for parking. As for the long back garden, they're working so hard that they don't have time for gardening, so the easiest thing is to cover it with grass. Yet at a time when they should be questioning the whole idea of the semi-detached house and spending half the day sitting in a car, we have this phony housing crisis that is forcing people to buy the same sort of houses further and further out. The Government expects the local authorities to provide more serviced land, but there's enough serviced land available in Dublin to build something like 39,000 houses, based on a density of only twelve houses to the acre. So there is no actual supply crisis. The problem is that land is being held.' Conroy's thesis was supported by the ICTU, in a research paper by Jerome Casey, published in March 2000, which argued that much of the housing land bank in the Dublin area was held by seven or eight major property developers who had been slow to release it. And though the ICTU paper did not name them, the *Sunday Tribune* did, in an investigative article by its editor, Matt Cooper, titled 'Who Owns Dublin?'* According to Cooper, 'industry experts believe that Manor Park Homes, Castlethorn Construction and Ballymore Properties probably hold the largest amounts of land.' Others named in the article included Flynn & O'Flaherty, Martin Lydon, Bovale Developments, Gannon Homes, Park Developments, Drumlish Homes and Kelland Homes. But no convincing evidence has

---

* *Sunday Tribune*, 20th February 2000

been produced that any of these companies, or their smaller-fry competitors, are deliberately hoarding land. With house prices very high and signs that the boom would not continue indefinitely, it could be argued that they had every reason to make hay while the sun shined.

Many architects and planners agree with the question posed by David O'Connor at the most recent RIAI-IPI conference: 'How can we continue building remote low-density satellite suburbs when we haven't consolidated the existing ones?' Indeed, throughout Fingal and South Dublin, there are vast areas of useless open space, known as 'SLOAP sites' (an acronym for Space Left Over After Planning), which could be developed for higher-density housing to provide a more urban edge for distributor roads in particular. As built, these roads are usually fronted by the rear ends of two-storey houses on either side, with their breeze-block garden walls and random collection of sheds evoking images of shanty towns. Between this ragged boundary and the road, wide linear green strips serve no purpose other than, perhaps, to provide a convenient cover for sewerage mains. They are certainly not pleasant places for a stroll. 'If we build prairies, why are we so surprised to find that they attract wandering horses?' asks Brian Brennan. He regards these bleak, windswept open spaces as 'opportunity sites' for private sector housing, built at higher densities, and even takes bets that Cheeverstown Road in West Tallaght, a particularly grim example of the genre, will be transformed into something resembling tree-lined Griffith Avenue, widely acknowledged as one of the finest achievements of 20th-century town planning in Ireland. It also happens to be the only suburban road in Ireland designed by a planner – Patrick Abercrombie – under his inspired plan for Dublin in the 1920s. (Griffith Avenue Extension, built since the 1960s as an afterthought, is a squalid mish-mash by compared to the grandeur of the original.)

But the message about higher housing density can become so garbled and misinterpreted that South Dublin's planners, confronted with an apartment scheme at the edge of Bushy Park in Terenure, actually defined the park as a 'semi-rural area', even though it is located three miles from the city centre and on a QBC too. Their insistence that the developers would have to screen the new buildings with forest planting led to open warfare with their more radical colleagues in the architects' department. Not only would future residents of the apartments be denied a view of the park, but the very idea of screening suggested that the planners could not bring themselves to accept that Terenure is an integral part of the urban area. Bushy Park belongs to Dublin Corporation, and it saw no problem in having apartments overlooking this 'semi-rural area', especially as the scheme had been designed by O'Mahony Pike Architects, who were responsible for the splendid development by Sheelin Homes on the Johnston

The splendid development by O'Mahony Pike Architects for Sheelin Homes in Ballsbridge. A strikingly successful feature is the strong relationship which it establishes with Herbert Park and the River Dodder.

Mooney & O'Brien bakery site in Ballsbridge. Its most strikingly successful feature is the strong relationship which it established with Herbert Park, creating a new axis between its bandstand and the bridge and a six-storey apartment building, serpentine in plan, that pleasantly overlooks both the park and the River Dodder.

Other examples of woolly thinking on housing are not hard to find. In 1998, when Wicklow County Council proposed to rezone more than seventy acres of land near Greystones at a density of just one house per acre, it got a well-deserved reprimand from Noel Dempsey who, quite reasonably, took the view that such a move would be unsustainable with the DART being extended to serve the area. In another case, involving the sixteen-acre Mount St Anne's site between Ranelagh and Milltown, well-heeled local residents led by Brendan Gilmore, an associate of Tony O'Reilly, engaged a team of consultants to oppose plans by Park Developments for an ambitious scheme – also designed by O'Mahony Pike – of three hundred apartments, up to five storeys in height, as well as 158 houses and such welcome social facilities as a crèche and leisure centre, incorporating a gym and two squash courts. Residents pointed to the dwindling amount of green space in the area, and called on Dublin Corporation to acquire the pleasantly wooded convent site as a public park. From their side of the fence, the developers maintained that it was an ideal site for a relatively high-density residential scheme because of its location beside the Sandyford Luas line – an argument accepted by the Corporation's planners. However, in April 1997, just weeks after the DoE said it favoured higher-density housing on public transport routes, An Bord Pleanála refused permission on the grounds of overlooking, overshadowing, visual obtrusion and density. Eighteen months later, after another appeal by the residents, the board gave its approval for a revised version of the Mount St Anne's scheme, which has a density of twenty-five units per acre, with 22% of the site dedicated to public open space.

In Dartry, too, shocked residents rose up in revolt against Trinity College when it planned to increase by a factor of five the number of students housed at Trinity Hall, just south of Palmerston Park. The ten-acre wooded site and its main buildings had been in the ownership of the college since 1869 – longer, indeed, than the age of most of Dartry's houses – and it had obvious potential for development. Located just four kilometres from College Green, Trinity Hall is within easy cycling distance, as well as being well served by bus routes and the future Luas line from Sandyford, due to start running in 2003. Dublin Corporation, in its 1999 City Development Plan, seeks to maximise the benefits of Luas by facilitating higher density residential development along its routes, with the additional objective of reversing population decline in the outer city. Developing new halls of residence at Trinity Hall was also in line with the Strategic Planning Guidelines and Government policy, as expressed in the 1999 Finance Bill, which sought to address the acute shortage of student accommodation by providing tax incentives for its construction. The Residential Density Guidelines, issued by the

DoE in September 1999, also make it clear that 'a balance has to be struck' between protecting the amenities and privacy of adjoining dwellings and the established character of areas – such as Dartry – and the need to provide residential infill at higher densities.

But when Trinity College lodged its plans to increase the number of student bedspaces at Trinity Hall from two hundred to nearly a thousand, even Des O'Malley, former leader of the Progressive Democrats and long-time resident of Palmerston Road, joined the ranks of local objectors. The scheme, designed by Murray O'Laoire Architects, attempted to rationalise the site by providing new halls of residence laid out on both sides of a formal avenue on the axis of Sunbury Gardens, terminating in a five-storey central tower containing such facilities as a shop, launderette and restaurant with seating for four hundred. Apart from an unlisted gate lodge and some nondescript additions, it was proposed to retain and refurbish the existing buildings on the site, integrating them with the new development. The density, at seventeen apartments per acre, was less than Mount St Anne's, and since the nearest house is 35 metres (115 ft) away, there were no issues of overlooking or overshadowing. Yet the Dartry & District Preservation Association maintained that Trinity's plan would be 'detrimental to the visual amenity and character of the area', harming its 'sense of place', that the alleged 'floodlighting' of buildings on the site would have an 'intrusive effect' (no such floodlighting was proposed), that the influx of so many students would have 'a profound impact in terms of social behaviour', that it would 'give rise to serious noise nuisance within a tranquil suburban setting and therefore depreciate the value of property in the vicinity' (the 'students with ghetto-blasters' argument), that the additional traffic generated would 'adversely affect the use of major roads in the vicinity', and that the open parkland at the front of the site should be preserved. Fergal MacCabe, Trinity's planning consultant and principal author of the Residential Density Guidelines, pointed out that only 5% of Trinity's students use cars, and said 'the suggestion that open, zoned and serviced land proximate to quality public transport should be sterilised is contrary to the principles of sustainability.' He also noted that the main student halls of residence for Queens University in Belfast, comprising four ten-storey towers and three other blocks, with a total of 1,720 rooms, did not appear to have any discernible impact on property prices in the vicinity of Malone Road. Having requested an environmental impact statement (EIS) on the plans for Trinity Hall, Dublin Corporation granted permission in November 1999, subject to fourteen conditions, and the local residents then took their case to An Bord Pleanála.

Even the Corporation has double standards on the density issue. At the same time as its planners were producing their radical action plan for Pelletstown, laying down the ground rules for a major private sector scheme well served by public transport, its housing department was seriously entertaining plans to demolish Fatima Mansions and clear the site for suburban-style two- and three-storey houses right next to the Luas line from Tallaght. Here, the running was

courtesy of Murray O'Laoire Architects

Residents of Dartry rose up in revolt against Trinity College when it planned to dramatically increase the number of students housed at Trinity Hall. These photomontages show views of the proposed scheme by Murray O'Laoire Architects.

courtesy of Murray O'Laoire Architects

made by Principal Officer Brendan Kenny, who had forged a relationship with the local people, as he had done with many other marginalised communities in the city, sitting in draughty meeting halls, seeking out the local heroes and working closely with them to build up the social infrastructure. He knew that if he talked to them about architecture, density and achieving a more balanced housing mix, 'he would be told to feck off', as one of his colleagues put it. Kenny argued that there were some areas such as Fatima Mansions where, in order to deal with the mistakes made in the past in managing a Corporation estate, the only solution was to start afresh by giving the people what they wanted. 'We're caught in a cleft stick between implementing what we all believe and what the Government says is its policy, on the one hand, and the reality of "public consultation" on the other', said one dispirited senior official. 'The way it works is that people say, "we're telling you what we want, so the consultation is now over", and the simple thing to do is to give in to them. Yet Ireland is the last country in Europe building local authority housing, and the National Development Plan says we will build another 35,000 units over the next seven years. But because we're atrocious at estate management, the easy way out is to give everyone two-storey houses, which they will ultimately purchase and then the management problem is solved.' And if Fatima Mansions were demolished, wouldn't other soundly built flat complexes from the 1950s and early 1960s, such as Dolphin House and St Theresa's Gardens, inevitably end up in a skip, too?

Surprisingly, the City Manager sided with Kenny against the advice of Jim Barrett and Dick Gleeson, both of whom strongly favoured an alternative approach, based on achieving an appropriate level of urban development. In their view, only six of of the fourteen blocks in Fatima Mansions should be demolished, with the remaining residents rehoused on the site in a tight high-density housing scheme, and the rest of the blocks sold off for refurbishment as private sector apartments. 'If the site is covered in two storey houses, the opportunity cost to the Corporation would be up to £50 million', one senior official warned. There were also problems with the redevelopment plans for St Michael's Estate in Inchicore and Swan's Nest Court in Kilbarrack, both system-built schemes like Ballymun, but on a smaller scale. Though the Inchicore estate, built in 1970 on the site of a notorious slum, Keogh Square, is also located near the Tallaght Luas line and the City Architect's department had prepared plans to turn it over to the private sector and build new housing for its residents at zero cost, the Housing Department's preferred option – again dictated by its tenants —was to redevelop the estate for suburban-style housing at a cost of £24 million, with taxpayers footing the bill. And when it came to Kilbarrack, located right beside the DART, even the idea of replacing the seven-storey blocks of flats with a medium density scheme of three-storey housing, designed by Gerry Cahill Architects and Derek Tynan Architects, ran into an unexpected obstacle. Whatever the DoE's guidelines said, some of its own senior officials would have preferred two-storey houses, at least until they were persuaded otherwise. John Fitzgerald agreed that, in

Terry Thorp / *Irish Times*

One of the seven 15-storey towers of the system-built Ballymun scheme, flanked by an 8-storey spine block. When it was completed in 1969, nobody imagined that 'Ireland's greatest housing scheme', as it was billed, would become the State's worst planning disaster.

courtesy of Ballymun Regeneration Ltd

general, new housing schemes should not 'go against the grain in terms of achieving the right architectural and planning solutions'. But in some cases, such as Fatima Mansions, 'you go out there and walk around and look at kids who are three years old and realise that they'll probably be fifteen before you get to the end of that process.' The conditions were so appalling and the need so urgent that compromise was inevitable. Otherwise people would say 'we're not listening to them or dealing with their problems', he said.

The last thing any of them wanted was to be used as guinea pigs for another 'brave new world' solution, handed down like tablets of stone by architects and planners, as happened in Ballymun during the 1960s. Though this hideous experiment in high-rise living was pushed through by Neil Blaney, then Minister for Local Government, there can be no doubt that there was an architectural imperative to build it. After all, prefabricated system-building was all the rage at the time, particularly in Britain. It was an idea whose time had come, offering a fast and cheap answer to Dublin's housing problems. The National Building Agency, set up with a mandate to oversee its construction, would provide a total of 3,068 dwellings in seven 15-storey towers, named for the signatories of the 1916 Proclamation, as well as nineteen 8-storey 'spine blocks', ten 4-storey blocks of 'walk-up' flats, and 452 terraced 2-storey houses, all laid out in a parkland setting on a 359-acre site at Ballymun acquired from Albert College. The density worked out at just 8.5 units per acre, about the same as the suburban norm. When it was completed in 1969, nobody imagined that 'Ireland's greatest housing scheme', as it was billed, would become the State's worst planning disaster. Although individual flats were quite commodious and mostly well cared-for, many residents complained about rubbish-strewn external spaces and graffiti-scarred stairwells and landings as well as the isolation of living at high levels. The lifts were often out of order. In one twelve-month period in the late-1970s, the Corporation had to deal with 2,425 complaints due to equipment failures, misuse or vandalism. By the mid-1980s, Ballymun had become a sociological 'sink' and a symbol of everything that was bad about public housing. 'I see seven towers, but I only see one way out', Bono sings on one of U2's earlier albums, *The Joshua Tree*. The only way out for too many young people in Ballymun was via drugs. At least a thousand of the tenants were drug addicts, one in six were unmarried mothers, a further 10% were deserted/separated wives, unemployment was reckoned to be 45%, and up to a third of the estate's population of 12,000 was on the waiting list for housing elsewhere. In terms of facilities, this town, the size of Clonmel, had just one supermarket, two pubs, a part-time bank, and twenty-four container shops (i.e. operating out of disused 40-foot containers). No wonder Ballymun was declared the State's 'most disadvantaged area'.

All over Europe, local authorities – and governments, too – have been trying to come to terms with the appalling legacy of system-built, high-rise housing. What was seen in the 1950s and 1960s as a quick technical fix, even as a heroic response to housing needs, is now acknowledged as a disaster, not least for the people who have had to live with it. In Ireland, too, what used to be known as the working class was the subject of similarly crude experiments in social engineering – from the classic high-rise, low-density layout of Ballymun to the congested low-rise, high-density plan of Darndale, to the sprawling estates on the western outskirts of Dublin, all bereft of adequate facilities. Ballymun was recognised as a special case, and in 1993, one of its towers and two of the nineteen spine blocks were refurbished at a cost of £6.7 million. Three years later, following an evaluation of the estate by specialist consultants, the bill for an overall renovation was put at £144 million. Demolition and replacement of the towers and spine blocks, plus refurbishment of the four-storey blocks of 'walk-up' flats, was estimated at £170 million. In other words, it was nearly as expensive to refurbish the existing, fatally flawed high-rise blocks as it would be to demolish and rebuild. By the end of 1996, Brendan Howlin, then Minister for the Environment, became convinced that Ballymun should be redeveloped as a 'model town for the 21st century'. Though this solution was also favoured by community groups in the area, the scale of the task was so monumental that it would clearly require a full master plan and a dedicated agency to oversee its implementation. So in July 1997, just four months after the Rainbow Coalition Government accepted the demolition plan, Dublin Corporation set up a wholly owned subsidiary, Ballymun Regeneration Ltd, to take charge of the project, starting with an international design competition.

The competition was won by London-based architects and urban designers MacCormac Jamieson Pritchard, in association with O'Mahony Pike. After an extensive programme of public consultation, they produced a £261 million master plan in March 1998, painting a bright new future for the benighted estate. By then, BRL had decided to clear away every element of the late-1960s legacy, including the four-storey blocks. The whole estate was to be developed as five distinct areas – Sillogue, Balcurris, Poppintree, Shangan and Coultry – all with their own access from a new tree-lined 'main street' which would, in the words of David Pritchard, 'heal the rift' caused by the dual carriageway running through the middle of Ballymun. There was to be a Luas light rail line and a mix of public and private sector housing, such as Section 23 apartments above new shops on the main street targeted for renting to students from nearby Dublin City University. It seemed that the new town would be a recognisably urban place characterised by diversity – more like Rathmines than, say, Killinarden – and that it might even be reintegrated with surrounding areas which had turned their backs on it. The emphasis was on laying out new houses on traffic-calmed streets, thereby atoning for the aberration of the past. Open spaces throughout the area were to be rearranged into more formal circles, crescents and larger parks, surrounded and overlooked by more humane, low-rise housing of appropriate scale to replace the loathed flats complex. Subsequently, thirteen firms of architects, including several from Britain, were selected to design the first batch of 620 new homes – and that's when the real fun started.

Detail of model of MacCormac Jamieson Pritchard's 1997 master plan for Ballymun's new main street [colour photo, p203], and close-up view of proposed new housing by O'Mahony Pike.

BRL had 'bent over backwards', in the words of PR consultant Mary Murphy, to facilitate public involvement in the master plan process, and this policy continued in relation to the design of individual schemes. It facilitated local residents, with women to the fore, to set up their own design groups so that they would be able to tackle the architects on their own terms and spell out the type of housing they wanted to live in. Architects making presentations to public meetings found it tough going, and the process turned into something of a war of attrition. One of them recalls a meeting at which he outlined his ideas for duplexes above garden-level flats, each with their own doors onto the street. Shared access, such as common hallways, had already become a non-starter. After he was finished, a man sitting with folded arms in the front row said: 'That's all very well, but what the people around here want is two-storey houses with front and back gardens. All the rest is just shite.' There were bound to be problems of communication and understanding. One architect did the profession no favours by waxing jargonistically at another consultation session about 'the iconography of the chimney to denote a dwelling'. Attempts by BRL to wean people away from the obsession of having their own patches of land by showing them photographs of derelict front gardens gracing private houses in Glasnevin seemed to have no effect. The will of the people had to prevail.

Where did they get their ideas from? It would appear that the residents of Ballymun related everything back to what they knew (or what they thought they knew), what they had seen and what they were envious of. They also saw themselves as victims, and in this continuing state of victimhood they were not prepared even to think about alternatives that clashed with their mindset. Running through it all was an assumption, which the architects found amazing, that they were not sufficiently social to share a hallway, or even a flight of steps, with a neighbour. For them, as for the middle classes, the beginning of their private realm would be the back of the footpath on the street outside their homes. In this respect, their views were coloured by their own experience of endless problems with noisy neighbours, and common areas which were not properly maintained. For years, they had lived in a grim, even squalid environment, as victims of the system. Now they were in a position to demand the type of housing they felt they were 'owed', and their community leaders saw to it that they would get what they wanted. Thus, plans for the first phase of Ballymun's redevelopment were not particularly innovative or forward-looking. Two-storey houses with front and back gardens made up the bulk of what was planned, and some of the designs were so traditional that they might even be regarded as hackneyed. In general, they were laid out along wide suburban roads rather than tight urban streets. The scale was also suburban, never rising to more than three or four storeys in order to ensure that each dwelling had own-door access from the outside world, and there was also extensive provision for car-parking.

This reflected the relatively cautious approach taken by BRL in planning the 'new town'. Its own rules specified that back gardens must have a minimum length of 10 metres (33 ft), representing a significant tranche of land. Yet for what purpose? So that people would be able to grow their own vegetables, fulfilling the Garden City ideal? What if they had no interest in gardening? Ciarán Murray, the company's managing director, admitted that it was a 'difficult process', but he continued to insist that BRL was getting across its message that building more compact, easily managed neighbourhoods could address the problems thrown up by prairie-style planning. He also maintained that the redevelopment of Ballymun still complied with notions of sustainability because its density would work out at between sixteen and twenty housing units per acre. One of the major constraints on achieving a more urban scale related to the need to avoid overlooking existing low-rise housing in the area. At Shanliss Green, for example, architects McGarry Ní Éanaigh's scheme tapered down to single-storey height where it backs onto a private housing estate in Santry. Another scheme, designed by BRL's in-house architects, headed by Mick McDonagh, was reminiscent of mid-1980s Corporation inner-city housing, while O'Mahony Pike's effort, with curved brick projections in front of every house and both vertical and horizontal windows, was clearly Dutch-inspired. Levitt Bernstein also came up with an interesting mix of house types in their scheme for a new road linking Coultry and Shangan. But what all the schemes had in common was a suburban rather than urban character, offering what one of the designers called 'a more pretty architectural suburbanity', which, like the misguided scheme for Fatima Mansions, had more to do with ownership and ultimate sell-off. To that extent, the redevelopment of Ballymun represents a huge missed opportunity to point Dublin in a different direction.

Despite all the compromises, BRL believed that 'important new statements' were being made. In terms of its architecture, Ballymun would have more variety than any other Dublin suburb, public or private, according to Ciarán Murray, though he conceded that its density would be only 'around fifteen to sixteen units per acre'. One of the flagship projects is a £4 million community arts centre, which will contain a multi-purpose 220-seat theatre as well as a bar, restaurant, dance studio, crèche, training facilities and community offices. But Ballymun could only become 'the capital of northside Dublin', in Murray's imagination, if urban renewal tax incentives were made available to encourage private sector commercial development, thus giving it an edge over other, more sought-after locations in the city. That was guaranteed by the Ballymun Integrated Area Plan, one of six such plans for different areas of Dublin on which the Corporation had scored a double hat-trick, securing Government approval for the lot. 'All the big players have been out here, including Monarch and Green Property, and there's even interest from US and China because they see the Irish economy performing so well', Murray said in July 1998, long before the package was finalised. Assuming that the master plan was implemented in full and underpinned by tax incentives, he believed that Ballymun would become a 'valuable piece of real estate', strategically located between the M50 and the city centre, with economic regeneration proceeding in tandem with the housing programme. Indeed, the proximity of the M50 could be its salvation. A 105-acre site, strategically located beside the motorway's Ballymun interchange, carrying the benefit of juicy tax incentives, is to be developed as a 'technology park' by Green Property, in a joint venture with BRL. The promised Luas line will also open up the area.

Inevitably, the development programme generated opposition, mainly from outside Ballymun. The Willow-Cedar Action Group, representing people living in private housing estates directly to the south, vehemently objected to BRL's plan to build housing in part of Poppintree Park, reducing its size from sixty-five to forty-six acres. It wasn't that any of them actually used this park. They just didn't want public housing built on the northern side of their breeze-block garden walls. One of them, Vincent Reggazoli, even went to the High Court to challenge this element of the master plan, and though this action was later withdrawn, the loud protests of the Willow-Cedar residents soon had local politicians running for cover. Instead of trying to explain that the security of these private estates would actually be improved if new housing was built backing onto a portion of the park, some of them applied strong pressure to have the proposal dropped altogether. Fortunately, they failed. Two more spanners were thrown in the works in July 1999 just as Ballymun was about to become a colossal building site, with an 'extraordinary game of musical chairs', as David Pritchard put it, being played out as new houses were built in phases to replace the existing flats. The Willow-Cedar Action Group, in collaboration with Friends of the Irish Environment, cherry-picked three of the thirteen new housing schemes and appealed to An Bord Pleanála, arguing that there should have been an environmental impact assessment of the entire project, and a Breton musician, Robert Guillemot, sought a High Court judicial review. As a long-time resident of one of the tower blocks, he believed that the idea of razing them all to make way for a low-rise housing estate made no sense in terms of sustainable development, even if all the rubble was recycled to provide foundations for new houses and streets. Both actions were condemned by Róisín Shorthall, local Labour TD and councillor: 'Everyone was expecting that the JCBs would be on site this autumn, but now there's a danger that people could lose faith in the whole process because of the actions of a small group of objectors.' But FIE's Tony Lowes insisted that the Ballymun project was 'not being held up by raving foreign trouble-makers' for no valid reason. It was perfectly legitimate to call for an environmental impact statement because this would 'ensure that the mistakes of the past are not repeated'. Indeed, FIE felt so strongly about the absence of an environmental impact assessment that it made a formal complaint to the European Commission, forcing BRL to commission a separate EIS on each phase as there was no mechanism to review the entire project.

All of this cast 'a cloud of uncertainty' over the development programme, running the risk that Ballymun might be 'short-changed for a second time', as Ciarán Murray put it. If the new homes were held up by planning appeals and legal actions, some of the existing blocks could not be demolished to make sites available for development. And given that the latest scheme of urban renewal tax incentives is due to expire in 2002, there was a 'very narrow window of opportunity' to realise the BRL's plans. The new-look main street, in particular, was in danger. 'What went wrong with Ballymun when it was first built thirty years ago is that it never developed like a normal town', he said. The danger now was that continuing delays and uncertainty would 'seriously compromise' the social and economic regeneration of the area by deterring much-needed private sector investment. As if to demonstrate its own resolve, BRL pressed on with what it billed as Ireland's first design competition for higher-density residential development on a prominent 4.5-acre site at the entry to Ballymun. The contest, which attracted thirty-nine entries from Ireland, Britain and Europe, was won by Scottish architects ARP Lorimer & Associates, mainly for the sentinel quality of their pair of slender eight-storey apartment towers, intended to form a 'gateway' to the new estate. Terraced four-storey buildings would provide an appropriate edge to the new main street, and, to the rear, the winning architects envisaged a series of mews-like courtyards of two and three-storey houses, integrated with existing houses in Sillogue Gardens. Howley Harrington, architects of the millennium footbridge over the River Liffey, were the runners-up with a scheme which the jury saw as a microcosm of a walled city with its own plazas and bastion towers. BRL's intention was that the winning scheme would be built by pri-

Winning design of BRL's 1999 Ballymun Gateway competition by ARP Lorimer & Associates of Scotland. It features higher-density housing, student flats and some retail at street level.

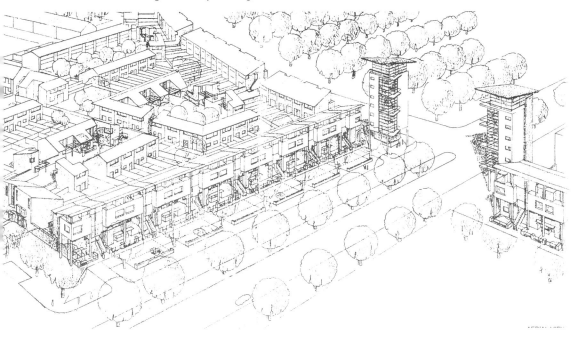

vate developers, providing a total of 172 homes at a density of forty units per acre. According to John Graby, director of the RIAI, one of the aims of the competition and of the institute's Housing 2000 initiative was to dispel apprehensions about higher-density living by demonstrating that it could offer the best option to solve the housing crisis. Two days before Christmas 1999, An Bord Pleanála rejected the three sample appeals before it and confirmed Dublin Corporation's decisions to approve them, citing among its reasons the master plan for Ballymun and the DoE's Residential Density Guidelines.

With the planning authorities reeling from the sheer horror of badly designed private sector proposals, sailing under the higher density flag of convenience – such as the appalling trio of barracks-like blocks at the Cherrywood junction of the N11 – good models were sorely needed. And though the floodgates had already opened, Fingal County Council committed itself to producing a design guide setting out detailed standards for housing layout, landscaping, roads, parking, open space and urban design. The council also allocated a 45-acre site in Mulhuddart, zoned residential for several years, for a development package competition to provide a mix of private and social/affordable housing, with bids being accepted only from builders and architects who showed that they could produce a high-quality scheme. The land was to be made available at the very modest price of around £15,000 per house site, and County Architect David O'Connor estimated that it could accommodate over six hundred homes. With IBM just up the road and a regional technical college going in next door, the winning scheme was bound to find a ready market. It would also provide a counterpoint to Castleheany, on the opposite side of the N4. This low-density housing estate, built less than ten years ago, is arranged around a series of cul-de-sac internal roads, much like the branches of a tree, with just one entrance onto the Navan Road. In the morning, car commuters must queue for up to half an hour to get out of the estate. Residents of numerous other estates all over Dublin's suburbs are similarly afflicted. As first-time house-buyers, they may have thought that the single set of Versailles-style entrance gates gave these corrals the cachet of exclusivity. Now most of them realise that it is a maddening nuisance. On RTÉ television's *Nation Building* series,* Joan O'Connor ridiculed the 'Stockbroker Belt' marketing image being used by estate agents to sell supposedly exclusive housing estates on the outskirts of Dublin, such as Alderbrook, a scheme of 189 four-bedroom homes in Ash-

_____

* Made by an independent production company, Making Waves, in association with the RIAI, with sponsorship from the ESB and the Heritage Council. Broadcast by RTÉ in early 2000.

bourne, Co Meath. It had been sold with images of golf clubs and the Ward Union hunt, yet as she pointed out, the hunt (master: Mick Bailey of Flood Tribunal fame) is very closed and under threat, while most of the golf clubs in the area are also private. What Alderbrook's image conjured up was 'Daddy the stockbroker's gone to the city with a bowler hat and a brolly and I'm taking the children to the pony club', she said. Yet it was remarkable that there were no children playing on the estate. 'There is nobody here during the day because the people who bought these lovely houses are working to afford the mortgages to pay for them', Ms O'Connor said, adding that she wondered whether we were creating 'uni-class ghettos' in such estates. 'Hopefully, this estate in time will become full of children, but the sad thing is, in twenty years beyond that, it will be empty of children. And unless we tackle the issue of diversity of housing type, this will become a ghost town of grandparents living in four-bedroom houses.'

Somebody once defined the suburbs as places where developers cut down the trees and call estates after them. Yet their lineage can be traced back to the Garden City movement of the late 19th century, with its notion that everyone would not only have fresh air but also a patch of ground large enough to grow their own vegetables. According to Brian Brennan, this ideal was 'something we've held onto like a soother, even though it no longer has any architectural vocabulary with hardly any change in house plans for nearly fifty years'. His view is echoed by the British government's Urban Task Force, chaired by Richard (Lord) Rogers: 'We seem to have lost the art of designing cities which was once part of our rich urban tradition ... With a few notable exceptions, such as the post-war Roehampton Estate in London, the remainder of the 20th century has failed to deliver spaces and places of similar architectural and urban distinction.' There had also been 'an over-reliance on rigid planning standards and controls on zoning, parking and density, which have stifled creativity, [and] a lazy over-use of off-the-peg designs and layouts'. Rogers and his task force found that things were different on the Continent. 'Well-designed suburbs, such as those in Stockholm or the German town of Freiburg, provide a high-quality living environment with a mix of uses, good local services and excellent public transport connections to the city centre.' The Stockholm suburb of Skarpnack, for example, consists of five- and six-storey apartment buildings laid out along urban-style streets, with not a single 'house' in the whole place. Developed in the 1980s at the edge of the city, it offers residents immediate access to the forest, as well as providing shops, crèches, and even primary schools on the ground floor of apartment buildings, and bus services to the local metro station with a fast link to the city centre. Innovative higher-density suburban housing, all of it 'design-led', is also the norm in the Netherlands, notably in the new town of Almeer, built in a polder near Amsterdam. If everyone wanted a two-storey house with front and back garden, especially in a country which has been largely manufactured by its own people over the centuries, it would be recipe for disaster. Architects working in the Netherlands are also designing new house types for people in their mid-fifties, with one large bedroom and lots of storage space for books and CDs, 'but we're still building the same box for everyone', as RIAI Director John Graby complained. The Dutch also have a very different definition of 'affordable housing', in some cases including households on 80% of national average income. As Rogers noted, this means that many of the people occupying 'social' housing are working households in reasonably paid jobs. 'By helping to bring about a more even distribution of wealth within a locality, it can work towards supporting viable neighbourhood facilities', according to his task force.

'One of our biggest problems', in Brian Brennan's view, 'is that we are obsessed with class distinctions between socio-economic groups instead of offering everybody a broader choice of housing.' Not everyone *needs* a three-bedroom semi-detached house with gardens front and rear. Members of the RIAI-IPI joint working party agree that there must be a mix of housing types on every new estate – single-bedroom and two-bedroom apartments, three-bedroom and four-bedroom houses, some in the form of duplex units over garden-level flats, and even bungalows designed for ease of use by elderly or disabled people. There is also a widespread consensus in favour of diversity of tenure, with some homes built for rent by local authorities, some by housing associations, as well as others built for sale as 'private' houses. This would have the full support of the four Dublin local authorities. Their current housing strategy, adopted in April 1999,

Skarpnack in Stockholm, is a good example of higher-density suburban development. Apartment buildings laid out on streets or enclosing pleasant green spaces with plenty of room for children to play. The area is also served by a local bus service and its own metro station.

Frank McDonald

pledges to explore 'innovative and creative' initiatives to promote different housing types, sizes and densities in a mix of public rented, shared ownership and private ownership tenures. In Britain, such a policy could be relatively easy to
achieve because most social housing is now in the hands of a strong and influential housing association sector, which produces homes that are indistinguishable
from those provided by the private sector, as well as being more innovative. In
Ireland, however, the housing association movement is still in its infancy, accounting for just 1% of the total output of 42,349 homes in 1998. Associations such as
Focus, Hail and Sonas had a tough time gaining recognition from the initially
very sceptical authorities, and then faced an uphill struggle to secure adequate
capital funding. Even the smallest schemes must go through the bureaucratic
wringer. And just when the voluntary sector's contribution to social housing
finally won acceptance, the Department of the Environment began courting
large, experienced British organisations, such as the St Pancras Housing Association, encouraging them to venture into the Irish housing market. Perhaps not
surprisingly, the new arrivals were met with a phalanx formed by NABCO, the
National Association of Building Co-Operatives. 'English developers' were not
welcome here. If they were, or if their fledgling Irish equivalents could get their
act together, there would be some chance of breaking through the rigid division
between private and public housing, as well as meeting the needs of a more

NABCO's housing at Allingham Street in the Liberties, designed by Gerry Cahill, works really
well even though there are no front gardens and small back gardens. Individual houses are also
flexible enough to cater for people of different ages, abilities and family circumstances.

courtesy of Gerry Cahill Architects

diverse market. Another alternative would be to subvent people rather that build-ings, but that would mean practically closing down local authority housing departments, which have a clear vested interest in the status quo. In 1998, South Dublin County Council made an operational profit of around £2 million from rents and the proceeds of sales of its housing stock, with the money all going into general revenue to be used for such projects as tree-planting in middle-class areas and the employment of more officials.

As for the form new housing should take, there are some useful models, even in Dublin. The mix of duplex units, single-storey flats, town houses and some flats with shared access at the corner of Bride Street and Golden Lane seemed to mark something of a departure when it was completed by the Corporation in 1996. An even higher density was achieved later at Jervis Street, where the housing is located above ground-floor shops, with access from Wolfe Tone Street to its own high-level courtyard. Father Kitt Court in Crumlin village is also a remarkably attractive and successful scheme, consisting mainly of shel-tered housing for the elderly as well as some family homes. NABCO's housing at Allingham Street in the Liberties, designed by Gerry Cahill, a skillful and com-mitted architect with wide experience of social housing, works really well even though there are no front gardens and only postage-stamp back gardens. Individual houses are also flexible enough to cater for people of different ages, abilities and family circumstances. Plans prepared by the City Architect's depart-ment for infill housing at Bridgefoot Street and Queen Street, locating the new blocks on reinstated street frontages previously exploded by the road engineers, are another step forward. The Queen Street scheme, designed by Shay Cleary Architects, ran into opposition from some local councillors, including Tony Gregory TD, who campaigned for houses to be built there instead because that's what the people believed they needed. If Gregory and other left-wing councillors had their way, Dublin would acquire more toytown housing in the style of City Quay, just 500 metres from O'Connell Bridge, or Seán MacDermott Street, less than 300 metres from the main thoroughfare. The Bridgefoot Street scheme, designed by Brian O'Brien who led Students Against the Destruction of Dublin in the late 1980s, will certainly provide an interesting counterpoint to the type of housing churned out by the Corporation in that period. Architects can design almost anything well, but unless the issue of managing common areas is addressed satisfactorily, there will only be fitful progress. Apartment buildings need a concierge and someone to look after the shared spaces which are 'designed out' under a Ballymun-type formula, because no such structure exists – despite the shining example, for almost a century, of the Iveagh Trust. 'You would imag-ine blocks of flats like that would be recipe for hell, but instead they turned out to be a recipe for endless accommodation, out of which came a community', as Eddie Conroy puts it. 'What we're doing now with all the houses set back from roads is pushing people away from each other.'

With the population now falling throughout much of the built-up area, most architects and planners agree that the city needs to be consolidated, not least to make use of existing social facilities such as shops and schools as well as sewers, roads and other physical infrastructure. Under the Strategic Planning Guidelines, however, the area administered by Dublin Corporation would account for just over 30% of the GDA's population in 2011, according to economist Colm McCarthy. By opting, in effect, for a policy of continued sprawl, the guidelines 'reflect a degree of contentment with the patterns which have given rise to today's problems', he told the RIAI-IPI conference in November 1999. 'If Dublin was a concrete jungle like Hong Kong, suffocated by its residents, you might say we should build a few dormitory towns. But this is the lowest density city of its size in western Europe. There are farmers mowing hay inside the M50, within eight kilometres of the city centre, and two abandoned racecourses growing weeds out there, with railways running right alongside them. We also have this strange trick of making sure that development takes place as far away as possible from the railway lines. Take any train to Maynooth and you're out in open country in jig time.' Outside the GDA, McCarthy expects that the population of south Louth, as well as Laois, east Offaly and Westmeath, will show big increases in population in the forthcoming census. In Arklow and Carlow too, the authorities are said to be only too anxious to facilitate their transformation into outer commuter-belt dormitories. 'They see Dublin people as the genesis of a new kind of renewal', says Gold Medal-winning architect Seán O'Laoire, just as other provincial towns have welcomed with open arms whatever droppings they can gather from successive 'decentralisation' initiatives. The arrival of a new batch of civil servants does wonders for property prices and the fortunes of local retailers. 'There's lot of people in Dublin who don't really want to live in a city', McCarthy maintains. 'They want bucolic isolation, with lots of green fields around them, and the place to go for that is the Styx. If they want to live in the middle of nowhere, they should shag off down the country. But if they're living in the middle of a big city, and someone wants to turn a building into a hotel or to develop an abandoned racecourse, that's rock and roll. It's what happens in a city.'

The Strategic Planning Guidelines are unlikely to have much impact on the economic engine fuelling Edge City development along the M50 corridor. Brian Hughes, lecturer in urban economics at the DIT in Bolton Street, has noted that Sandyford Industrial Estate, together with the developing areas around it, is becoming a major employment locus on the southern outskirts of the city, as significant as Dublin Airport on the northern outskirts. Steadily, as land values in the area soar, sheds that were thought sufficient less than ten years ago are being replaced by office blocks of four, five and even six storeys, with extensive provision for car-parking. Hughes estimates that 25,000 people are employed on the Sandyford estate, plus 6,000 in the nearby Leopardstown Science Park, and, in the not too distant future, a further 8,000 in the huge out-of-town office scheme planned by Treasury Holdings and developer David Arnold for the Legionnaires of Christ land in Leopardstown. Trading as the Clyde Road Partnership, they

Frank Miller / *Irish Times*

Sandyford Industrial Estate, together with the developing areas around it, is becoming a major focus of development activity, with sheds that were thought sufficient less than ten years ago being replaced by office blocks of four to six storeys, with extensive provision for car parking.

In Park West business park beside the M50/Naas Road interchange, there could be more than 25,000 people employed by 2003.

courtesy of the *Irish Times*

bought this twenty-acre site in May 1998 for a hugely inflated price – in excess of £27 million – and then had to set about 'making the sums stack up' by maximising the quantum of office space they could build on it. One of the hurdles they faced was that the Dun Laoghaire-Rathdown County Plan, adopted two months later, specified that major office development with a gross floor area of more than 1,000 square metres (10,760 sq ft) would 'generally only be permitted in Dun Laoghaire town centre and Dundrum'. But with more liberal policies being pursued in both South Dublin and Fingal, Dun Laoghaire-Rathdown was obviously going to 'miss the boat' if this restriction remained in place, so its planners helpfully introduced a new category of 'office-based industry' – anyone sitting at a computer terminal, in simple terms – to cater for the Sandyford scenario, and this crucial amendment to the county plan was adopted in September 1999. An Taisce didn't object to the Clyde Road Partnership's plans for 1.75 million square feet of office space on the Legionaries of Christ site because it felt that the proposed buildings were not excessively high, and a three-paragraph appeal to An Bord Pleanála by two local residents was later withdrawn after an intensive round of negotiations with the developers. The fact that 'Central Park' would have two levels of basement parking, excavated at enormous expense to provide space for almost 4,000 cars, was neither here nor there. But while the potential of the £250 million scheme to become a huge traffic generator was ignored by the conservationists, it was not lost on the planners. They pared the volume of office space back very slightly to 1.71 million square feet and tied its phasing to the completion of both the South Eastern Motorway and a Luas light rail extension from Sandyford, as well as the preparation of a mobility management plan. They also argued that schemes such as Central Park and the redevelopment of Sandyford Industrial Estate were in line with the principle of sustainability, because they would provide alternatives to city-centre commuting. But there can be little doubt that some Dun Laoghaire-Rathdown officials were also conscious, at least in the back of their minds, of the rates revenue that would flow from all the new office blocks. Bertie Ahern has also given his personal endorsement to Edge City development. In October 1999, he was lined up by Donegal-born developer Pat Doherty to launch the 225-acre Park West business park beside the M50/Naas Road interchange, declaring that its 'state-of-the-art facilities' would make it 'the nerve centre of the IT industry in Ireland', employing no less than 25,000 people by 2003. Doherty and his partners in the enterprise, including broadcaster Mike Murphy, reportedly shared a profit of £20 million when the first phase was sold off – with the benefit of enterprise zone tax incentives – to various investors for a whopping total of £73.5 million. By the time Park West is finished in 2003, it is expected to contain two million square feet of office space, and as much again for warehousing and distribution. It will even have its own 'town centre' with a range of shopping facilities, as well as a crèche, gymnasium and swimming pool.

As for where Dubliners are going to live, Brian Hughes believes that the Strategic Planning Guidelines represent a reversion to the 1985 ERDO settlement strategy, 'dressed up in fancy clothes'. The time available for Brady Shipman Martin to carry out the study that led to the production of the guidelines was far too short, and it was overseen by a very tight steering committee driven by the DoE and the local authorities. And just as ERDO wrote off the inner city, both Hughes and McCarthy maintain that the latest blueprint allocates far too little of the region's anticipated population growth to the Dublin Corporation area. Between 1971 and 1996, as McCarthy points out, the city's share of the GDA's overall population fell from 53.5% to 34.3%, and it would fall still further to just 30.4% in 2011 under current planning policies, even after taking into account an expected increase of 25,000 in the number of people living in the Docklands area. As a result, 'Luas will be built mostly in areas with either a constant or falling population.' Such a scenario could be offset by increasing the density of established suburban areas by offering some incentive to middle-aged couples or widowed people whose grown-up children have left the family home to 'trade down' to smaller houses or even apartments, thereby making more houses available to younger couples at an earlier stage in the lifecycle. McCarthy believes that the simplest solution would be to abolish stamp duty on the sale of second-hand homes to encourage a much greater degree of residential mobility. The provision of more sheltered housing for elderly people would also help to release houses. Cllr Eamonn Ryan (Greens), who represents the Rathmines area, says his only concern on this score is that property prices throughout the inner suburbs will continue to rise at a faster pace than those on the periphery 'and the people living out there will not be able to afford to move back'. He is also not alone in believing that suburban sprawl will continue, if only because it is in the interest of the outer counties.

But if the Strategic Planning Guidelines were revised to favour urban consolidation, what are the consequences and is Dublin ready to stomach them? Clearly, the remaining fields that are still being mowed within the M50 C-ring, such as those at Pelletstown, would be the first casualties, along with redundant recreational land uses such as the former Baldoyle and Phoenix Park racecourses. However, McCarthy would go much further. 'If you look at a map of Dublin, there's an awful lot of green blobs', he says, referring to the fact that it reputedly has more public parks per capita than any other city in Europe. 'Some of the parks, such as Herbert Park in Ballsbridge, are used intensively, but others not so. St Anne's Park in Raheny is the size of a suburb, but it's so sparsely used that women, in particular, won't go for a walk there even during the day. It has a fine arboretum, but the park is so enormous that you could walk a mile before finding it. It's an empty quarter, there's just nobody there. Apart from the arboretum, the rose garden and the Red Stables, the rest of it should be built on. Of course, there should be some yardstick, such as the number of punters per acre per day, but if it's below a certain footfall, the park is not worth having.' Such clinical surgery on some of the city's green spaces would be very radical stuff, but McCarthy insists that the alternative of dispersing new housing further and further out,

with no public transport to serve it, conjures up a 'nightmare scenario' in terms
of traffic and car dependency.

'If the Dublin local authorities just sit there and adjudicate on planning
applications as they come in, it's pretty clear that the older suburbs will continue to lose population and the pace of infill development won't compensate for
that', he says. 'You have to break eggs to make an omelette, and those eggs might
include the likes of St Anne's Park. The local authorities should also be identifying derelict or underutilised sites, and using their compulsory purchase powers to
buy them for housing, public or private. For example, you could almost fit the
city of Limerick on the site of CIÉ's Inchicore works, and it's right beside a good
railway line. Some of the army barracks, such as Clancy at Kingsbridge or Cathal
Brugha in Rathmines, should also be sold off for housing. They were originally
built by the British to garrison the city against the natives – and since the natives
are no longer restless, the army should get out of these places. There are also lots
of open spaces in the suburbs with no use. Some fellow mows the grass there
every so often, and if he sees twenty kids arrive with four jackets for goalposts,
he tells them they're not allowed to play football there.' Many planners agree.
Even where pitches are provided, 'only a tiny proportion of the local population,
around 20%, actually use them', according to David O'Connor. He would favour
the alternative of purpose-built recreation centres, such as the very successful

St Anne's Park, Raheny, is the size of a suburb, but economist Colm McCarthy maintains that
it's so sparsely used that much of it should be built on as an alternative to dispersing new housing further and further out.

John Searle / Gandon Archive

leisure centres in Belfast, not only because they would cater for a much larger and more diverse range of users, but also because it would spare more land for housing. 'All-weather playing facilities, such as what we've agreed with the Corporation for Pelletstown, are worth ten pitches on grass', says James Pike, senior partner of O'Mahony Pike Architects. Where local authorities provide such community facilities, the 1999 Planning Bill allows them to recoup the cost by imposing a levy on house-builders in the area, though this, in itself, will not overcome chronic staffing difficulties. Alternatively, they could be built and operated by the private sector, but this would obviously mean charging user fees.

The 'densification' of established suburban areas might also involve developers buying up entire housing estates and demolishing them to make way for higher density, more urban schemes. This is already happening on a smaller scale. On the corner of Trees Road in Mount Merrion, one developer paid a large price to acquire a pair of semi-detached houses and later obtained planning permission to replace them with a small apartment block. Golf clubs such as Milltown and schools with land to spare like Blackrock College may also be tempted to cash in, particularly if they are located close to good public transport routes. But judging by the number of councillors coming out of the woodwork to denounce higher-density housing, the public remains deeply sceptical. Dun Laoghaire-Rathdown County Council had a tough time convincing local residents of the need for such an approach in Cherrywood and Stepaside. Their fear, based on personal experience, is that every household will have at least two cars. It just means that there will be more of them, causing horrendous traffic congestion. If housing was to be built at all, the locals had a preference for individual houses on their own sites or, at least, a very low-density pattern of development, rather than the fifteen units per acre adopted by the council. 'The planners really didn't sell the benefits of a more compact approach', according to John O'Sullivan, An Taisce's over-worked planning officer. 'And when it came to locating an extension of the Luas line, they put it right through the main open space in the area.' Until the line is extended, this reservation will serve as a dedicated bus route, feeding the Luas terminus at Sandyford. But at least Dun Laoghaire-Rathdown prepared an action plan for the Stepaside development area, albeit based on a quite conservative density of fifteen units of housing per acre, or thirty-six per hectare. Elsewhere, in general, planners have not been planning for housing at a scale of 10,000 to 20,000 units. Maynooth, for example, may have started out as a planned town, but it is now surrounded by haphazard, low-density sprawl because of the absence of any overall view of where it's going.

'The lower the density (say, twenty dwellings per hectare), the larger the amount of area that is occupied by buildings, roads and open space', as the Rogers report notes. 'It is, however, not just about the loss of land. The implications of unsustainable forms of development go much wider. It means more traffic on overcrowded roads, more energy use, further depletion of natural resources, fewer tranquil areas, loss of biodiversity, increased air pollution and intensified social segregation.' His task force cited a hypothetical low-density housing estate which could extend to nearly 1.5 kilometres in diameter, pushing over 60% of the houses beyond the acceptable 500-metre or five-minute walking limit. 'This form of layout promotes excessive car use and makes it difficult to justify a bus route. As density levels are increased, even to the moderate levels of forty or sixty dwellings per hectare, the land-take diminishes rapidly. More people are close enough to communal facilities to walk, and an efficient bus service can be made viable. Moreover, the critical mass of development contributes to the informal vitality of the streets and public spaces that attracts people to city centres and urban neighbourhoods as well as contributing to energy efficiency.' The great challenge facing architects and planners, according to Rogers, is to persuade people to reconsider urban living, recognising that needs change throughout an individual's lifetime. 'For many people, the crunch comes with having children. An urban environment previously perceived as diverse and stimulating starts to appear unsafe. Schools and health services become more important. While it is therefore accepted that, at this stage in their lifecycle, many people will continue to move to more suburban or small town environments, we must look to persuade more families to stay. This means looking beyond the design, planning and building of the urban environment at the role played by health, education, security and social services, amongst others. And just as we need to look at how we persuade people to stay, we need to understand how we can encourage people to move back to our urban heartlands once children have left home. As well as ease of access to work and a good mix of leisure attractions, childless households will want high-quality living accommodation and space for guests, including visiting children and grandchildren.'

This is not, of course, what anyone had in mind when the inner-city apartments boom started rumbling in the early 1990s. Then, the priority was to fill the holes in Dublin's architectural fabric with whatever the developers wanted to build – in effect, a crude form of urban dentistry, where anything was better than nothing. During the earlier phase of this movement, the inner city was used as a laboratory for a variety of hideous experiments, and some of the apartment blocks produced at the time seem destined to become the tenements of the 21st century. Purchasers got only the bare minimum – usually shoebox-size single-bedroom apartments laid out by the dozen on long, narrow, artificially lit corridors redolent of a budget hotel, with just one tiny lift to serve them. Balconies, where they were provided at all, were of the 'clip-on' variety with just about enough room for a few pot plants. Storage space was non-existent, with even the upper level of a hot-press fully taken up by a heavy duty PVC cold water tank. Kitchens usually consisted of small windowless galleys in 'alcoves' tacked on to the end of living rooms, while nearly every apartment was 'single aspect' – in other words, they looked out only in one direction, even to the north. And what estate agents described as 'landscaped courtyards' were merely surface car parks with some trees to take the bare look off the cobble-lock paving. Show flats were generally decorated in chintzy suburban style, often using scaled-down furniture to give the impression that there was more space, but bedrooms were still so small that one could only walk sideways to get past the end of the bed. Many of these shoeboxes were purchased by young first-timers seeking a tax-efficient foothold on the housing ladder, and by people from the country looking for somewhere to stash the kids when they went to college in Dublin. But most of them were snapped up by an army of investors availing of the Section 23 tax incentive, which allowed them to write off 100% of the capital cost against all rental income. Month after month, Hooke & MacDonald were able to claim another 'sales coup' as scheme after scheme sold like hot cakes to a public largely uneducated in what to expect of apartment living in a European capital city.

Even by mid-1993, the alarm bells had started ringing. The fact that so many of the new apartments under construction just about met the minimum standards laid down by the DoE suggested to critics that Dublin was being short-changed. However, when Cllr Ciarán Cuffe (Greens) tabled a set of twelve 'development principles' for new schemes on the Liffey Quays, in an effort to achieve real quality, his ideas were denounced by Ken MacDonald, managing director of Hooke & MacDonald, the estate agents who sold more inner-city apartments than any of their competitors. In a lengthy article published by the *Irish Times*, he described Cuffe's proposal to ban single-aspect flats with corridor access as 'an extraordinary design limitation which would push up the cost of apartment construction'. As for the notion that apartments should be 'commodious', with more two-bedroom and larger units in every scheme, MacDonald maintained that this would make them unaffordable. 'To place unnecessary obstacles on architects, builders and ultimately home-buyers would be very damaging to the entire urban renewal process,' he declared. Yet, as he himself knew only too well, the bulk of the apartments that went through his books at the time were architect-free. Hooke & MacDonald's principal client, Liam Carroll's Zoe Develop-

Marc O'Sullivan, Collins, Dublin / courtesy of the *Irish Times*

A rare picture of Liam Carroll, the managing director of Zoe Developments. Notoriously private and modest about his achievements, he became the main engine of urban renewal in Dublin.

ments, which built more apartments in the inner city than all other developers combined, did not employ a single qualified architect to design any of its earlier schemes. Instead, they were designed by the developer himself, and worked up by a team of technicians headed by his chief henchman, David Torpey. Architects, Carroll once ludicrously claimed, were 'only interested in designing penthouses for fellows with Mercs'. The city paid a high price for his prejudice. Zoe's lack of architectural advice and his own devotion to developing sites as quickly as possible were reflected in the quality of so much of the company's output. Yet Liam Carroll became the main engine of urban renewal in Dublin.

A Dundalk-born mechanical engineer with Jacobs International before turning his hand to building blocks of flats, Carroll is quite unlike most other property developers. He shuns such traditional trademarks as the fawn-coloured cashmere overcoat with black velveteen collar, expensively tailored suits and top-of-the-range cars. Though Zoe has made millions over the years, its managing director is practically indistinguishable from the workers on its building sites, with his tie-less checked shirt, sleeves rolled up, and blue jeans tucked into Wellington boots. He might, indeed, have just stepped down from the scaffolding after doing a bit of brick-laying to keep things moving along, and to get around town he drives an ordinary Toyota. Carroll's real strength over the years, apart from an ability to manage several building sites simultaneously, has been his extraordinary prowess at site assembly. Every single site he has developed, usually in run-down and very unfashionable areas where property could be acquired cheaply, was assembled by him personally, rather than at arm's length through estate agents, and he would often go back again and again to reluctant vendors until he clinched a deal. He has also rarely had to contend with a refusal from Dublin Corporation's planners, though he did run into problems over fire certificates. They saw him almost as a saviour, and welcomed him with open arms when he moved into the inner city after completing a number of schemes on its outskirts, such as Beaver Row in Donnybrook, Fisherman's Wharf in Ringsend, and Portobello Harbour, developed on the site of a 1930's neo-classical shed previously occupied by Brittain Motors. What replaced it had no design or functional integrity, consisting of two terraces of single-aspect 'town houses' laid out back-to-back on the spine of the building. Those on the Grand Canal frontage, itself a mock-Palladian travesty, are four storeys high, and each 'house' has one room on each floor and a staircase so constricted that it has proved difficult to get double beds in. Since then, Zoe has completed schemes on three sides of Mountjoy Square, on Arran Quay and Usher's Quay, on Bridge Street Upper, Francis Street, Newmarket, Werburgh Street and Cornmarket in the Liberties, on Ringsend Road, Brunswick Street, Dorset Street, Gardiner Street, Green Street, Great Strand Street, Abbey Street Upper and Charlotte Quay. In nearly every case, it was the architectural equivalent of Albert Gubay's bargain-basement retailing philosophy: 'Pile 'em high and sell 'em cheap'.

Even Bachelors Walk, arguably the most important site in the heart of the

Frank McDonald

Frank McDonald

Two early schemes by Zoe Developments – Portobello Harbour *(above)*, a mock-Palladian terrace of 'town houses', each four storeys high, with one room on each floor, and Newmarket Square *(left)*, where one block faces the gable wall of another.

opposite

Arran Quay before it was struck by 'urban renewal' *(top)*, and after Zoe Developments installed another block of flats, with a mock-Georgian façade and an interior redolent of a budget hotel *(bottom)*.

Frank McDonald

Frank McDonald

Frank McDonald

Bachelors Walk in 1990 after it had been reduced to ruin by twenty years of property speculation, with some of the surviving Georgian houses flanking the fire-damaged former headquarters of the Dublin United Tramway Company, one of the city's rare art deco buildings. It was demolished by Zoe Developments to make way for an offensive parody, with an Egyptian-style coved parapet mocking the original, as part of a barracks-style scheme of apartments dressed up in architectural wallpaper.

Frank McDonald

city, got the Zoe treatment. Behind mock-Georgian façades, which American tourists appear to think are the real thing, Carroll installed a scheme which consists of 335 apartments, of which 293 are single-bedroom units, all laid out along corridors 4'2" wide. 'Not just an apartment – more a way of life', trumpeted his agents, Hooke & MacDonald. Tragically for Dublin, Carroll had not managed to overcome his prejudice against architects by the time he acquired this critical two-acre site from Arlington Securities in late 1992 for the bargain-basement price of just under £3 million. Because what he produced there was mere architectural wallpaper, a pastiche of this and that, covering up a barracks-style scheme in which no more than five of the flats have three bedrooms. In fairness, Zoe did faithfully restore No.7 Bachelors Walk, one of the finest panelled houses on the Liffey quays. It had been vandalised while in the care of Arlington Securities, a British Aerospace subsidiary which lost a lot of money trying to realise Tom Gilmartin's mad shopping centre/bus station scheme for the site. But Zoe also needlessly demolished one of the city's few surviving Art Deco buildings, built in 1930 as the Dublin United Tramway Company's headquarters, to make way for a really offensive parody, with an Egyptian-style coved parapet mocking the original, and rehoused the Blessed Sacrament Chapel in a claustrophobic ground-floor space previously earmarked for low-ceiling shop units. Quite unexpectedly, Carroll went on to hire a Malaysian architect called Tong to design a muscular scheme of flats for the corner of Gardiner Street and Parnell Street. But it was only after Zoe had acquired a pivotally located coalyard site at Charlotte Quay in the Grand Canal Docks that he finally accepted the argument that good architectural advice was needed. And it really paid off. Why else would An Bord Pleanála have granted Zoe planning permission to reinstate four storeys that were lopped off the slender sixteen-storey tower by Dublin Corporation's planners? Carroll himself knew that this victory was won on design grounds because of his decision to hire O'Mahony Pike as architects for the project [see page 41]. Had he stuck to his old ways of doing things, it would probably never have risen above twelve storeys. And when Bono of U2 together with Harry Crosbie offered him a cool £1 million for two penthouse apartments, Dublin's most prolific builder had the luxury of being able to turn them down. He had decided to retain them himself.

But Charlotte Quay also turned out to to be Liam Carroll's nemesis. In November 1997, he was denounced in the High Court by Mr Justice Peter Kelly as 'a disgrace to the construction industry'. This followed the death of James Masterson, a 24-year-old building worker, who had fallen from a height on the Charlotte Quay site, and the recitation in court of a lengthy catalogue of other casualties as well as convictions for breaches of the health and safety code at this and other sites. Masterson was one of numerous victims of the Celtic Tiger boom in the building industry, mainly because too much was being built too fast. In two years, forty-seven construction workers had died on building sites. And although the Health and Safety Authority's prosecution of the case fell into a

What Grafton Architects produced at the corner of Church Street and North King Street is arguably Zoe's best scheme – a complex of six town houses and sixty apartments, rising to five and six storeys on the street frontages, with tall workshop units on the ground floor, sharply defined corners, and sliding cedarwood shutters at every level of its framed brick façades.

legal quagmire, it was the kind of publicity that Carroll could have done without. (Since then, safety on Zoe's sites has improved so much that the HSA brings other builders around to see them.)

Notoriously private and modest about his achievements, and always wary of media prying, he has never given a formal press interview. All of his quoted comments over the years were always gleaned from bearding him on sites. It was also in 1997 that something quite astonishing happened – Zoe's chief became a member of the jury for an architectural competition. Carroll had bought a site on the corner of Bow Street and North King Street, but couldn't get his hands on the site next door because it was owned by Dublin Corporation, and the Corporation, at Jim Barrett's instigation, wouldn't sell it to him until he agreed to co-sponsor the competition and build the winning scheme. This led to an unusual collaboration with Grafton Architects, a highly respected practice run by Yvonne Farrell and Shelley McNamara, who had won numerous awards for their buildings, such as the basalt cube that houses the Department of Mechanical Engineering in Trinity College. Carroll must have found it difficult to accommodate himself to their high architectural aspirations, referring to them as 'the girls'. But what they produced was arguably Zoe's best scheme, a complex of six town houses and sixty apartments, rising to five and six storeys on the street frontages, with tall workshop units on the ground floor, sharply defined corners, and sliding cedarwood shutters at every level of its framed brick façades. The building took an awful lot of time to complete because it had to be crafted to an intricate design, inspired by the idea that 'most people want a quality of lifestyle rather than just a place to live', in the words of project architect Phillipe O'Sullivan. Though its interior spaces were compromised by Zoe's 'steamroller' approach, the contrast between this project and most of its other schemes could not be more marked. At last, it seemed, Liam Carroll had grasped the concept of being involved in the creation of a permanent legacy to the city, and it might as well be a good one. But its sheer quality did not deter the Dublin City Association of An Taisce, which did nothing to stop Bachelors Walk, from appealing to An Bord Pleanála on the basis that a pair of derelict houses were being sacrificed. Fortunately for Dublin, the board rejected this myopic plea.

Zoe's standards undoubtedly improved as a result of the belated architectural input. But like other developers, it also had to comply with revised guidelines for apartment design, laying down somewhat higher minimum sizes as well as specifying a more varied mix of unit types in every scheme. The guidelines were issued by the DoE in 1995, two years after controversy had first erupted over its earlier, even more minimal standards. Apparently, some senior officials were afraid that the 'bubble would burst' if higher standards were applied. Six months later, Minister of State Liz McManus, a qualified architect who could see what was going on, commissioned a root-and-branch review of the urban renewal programme since its inception in 1986, with a view to redirecting it. This study, carried out by KPMG, Murray O'Laoire and the Northern Ireland Economic

Research Centre, estimated that the tax incentives available under the programme had levered some £2 billion worth of investment by the private sector, at a net cost to the Exchequer of around £400 million. The consultants were particularly critical of 'small and spatially repetitive' apartments, with small bathrooms and kitchenettes, 'many of them internalised with little natural light or ventilation', and also a lack of semi-public and private external space – though even the worst flats had increased in value, due to the property boom. They suggested that the DoE's guidelines and, more generally, the selection of designated areas 'could be more stringent', recommending changes on both counts. In future, tax incentives would be linked to area-based plans which take into account community development, employment, urban design and conservation considerations, as spelled out in what became known as an Integrated Area Plan. Local authorities were then required to draw up an IAP for any area they sought to have designated, with all these plans to be vetted by an independent panel of experts. No longer would it be a question of some minister sliding his index finger over a map, saying 'we'll designate that', as Robert Molloy once described the previous process. Disappointingly confirming An Taisce's worst fears, the consultants found that 'refurbishment' schemes, which often involved gutting historic buildings, accounted for only 11% of total output under the urban renewal heading, mainly due to cost, mismatch of use, and difficulties with the Building Regulations. In

Four of Dublin Corporation's project managers for the city's Integrated Area Plan zones – Ciarán McNamara (O'Connell Street), Paul Maloney (North East Inner City), Jim Keogan (HARP) and Michael Stubbs (Liberties/Coombe). Not included is Mary Taylor, who was later appointed to co-ordinate the Inchicore/Kilmainham IAP.

courtesy of Dublin Corporation

particular, a 'Living Over the Business' scheme, aimed at persuading shopkeepers to release upper floorspace for residential use, had 'failed to make a significant impact' because of the 'daunting' logistics involved. The review also noted the belief of indigenous local communities that urban renewal had 'not addressed issues which are central to the regeneration and sustainable redevelopment of these areas, such as unemployment, lack of public amenities, education, training and youth development'.

For all of its physical evidence of urban renewal, City Manager John Fitzgerald believes that Dublin would be 'building castles on quicksand if we don't address the social problems', with 'nice new developments' rapidly degenerating into 'slums'. In April 1999, after all six of the Corporation's IAPs had won Government approval, he held out the hope that they would generate a total investment of more than £750 million, two-thirds of it by the private sector. Announcing the appointment of project managers to oversee the most ambitious urban-renewal programme ever planned by the Corporation, Fitzgerald said funding was no longer an issue. 'It's not that we've discovered an oil well under the Civic Offices. Most of the public sector funding has come from other sources', he explained. 'As a result, we can now deal with all the black spots. The time for preparing glossy brochures and engaging in study tours of social black spots in Scandinavia is finished.' The six areas scheduled to benefit are Ballymun, Inchicore/Kilmainham, O'Connell Street, the North East Inner City, Liberties/Coombe, and the HARP area, from Henry Street to Collins Barracks. Paul Maloney, project manager for the North East Inner City IAP, who made his name for introducing wheel-clamping, said the area still had a very strong community spirit, despite high crime and unemployment levels, and very little evidence of any economic spin-off from being next door to the IFSC. Under the IAP, the area's 'bleak landscape' dominated by run-down blocks of Corporation flats is to be transformed by replacing the worst of them with new housing and renovating others. Michael Stubbs, who is overseeing implementation of the Liberties/Coombe IAP, said the long-delayed Cork Street-Coombe Bypass road scheme would now be used as a vehicle to secure the redevelopment of this blighted area. The most innovative project is Dublin's first 'foyer', a remarkably successful French concept which provides sheltered housing and training for young people at risk. Designed by London-based architects Brady+Mallalieu, this £4 million scheme, incorporating a multi-purpose community sports hall, is being built on the old Wills factory site, hard by the edge of Marrowbone Lane, and looks set to tackle some of the real problems on the ground with the active involvement of local people. Other major projects include a £12 million refurbishment by publican Martin Keane of the Iveagh Markets, including the addition of a seventy-bedroom hotel, a high-tech 'media village' centred on the Guinness Hop Store, to be developed in association with MIT, and a £30 million 'Guinness Experience'. The latter will make use of the brewery's 1904 Market Street Store House, one of Ireland's earliest and most impressive steel-framed buildings, with a glazed atrium in the shape of a pint of stout, topped by a revolving restaurant with spectacular views over the city. Equally remarkable, in its own way, is the restoration of St Catherine's in Thomas Street *as a church* by an evangelical wing of the Church of Ireland.

Some progress has also been made on implementing the O'Connell Street IAP, despite setbacks over the controversial *Monument of Light*. Its aim, says project manager Ciarán McNamara, is to recreate the atmosphere which Dublin's main street used to have before it became so 'tacky' and 'user-unfriendly' that people 'just don't want to be there'. The first element likely to be completed is a formal square, fringed by well-clipped trees, in front of the GPO. Costing an estimated £2.5 million, McNamara said its dark granite paving flecked with white 'spot stones' will create a 'tablecloth effect', through which pedestrians and four lanes of traffic will move. The Anna Livia fountain, commissioned by Michael Smurfit in 1988 to commemorate his father, will probably have to be taken out to facilitate construction of the 'Spike', assuming that it receives Noel Dempsey's imprimatur, though no decision had been taken at the time of writing on the Floozie's final resting place. With the street already overwhelmed by fast-food joints and cheap trinket shops, it was inevitable that the Corporation would have to take a stand against Ann Summers, the British chain of adult shops. When it took over a store near the North Earl Street corner, once occupied by Madam Nora's, ladies outfitters, an enforcement notice under the 1963 Planning Act was immediately served on the basis that selling kinky underwear, dildos and other 'sex aids' represented a material change of use. The store responded by referring this issue to An Bord Pleanála as well as seeking a High Court judicial review, and amid much hilarity in the media, Ciarán McNamara found himself in the unenviable position of having to defend the Corporation's action on the *Late Late Show*. He emphasised that it had nothing to do with being censorious, but rather a conviction that the unchallenged opening of a sex shop on O'Connell Street would 'send out the wrong message' and possibly even jeopardise the Integrated Area Plan, though loopholes in the planning laws forced the Corporation to withdraw its action in January 2000. What it was up against was the simple fact of 'dustbins or dildos, it's all retail', as planning consultant Fergal MacCabe put it. But the real value of the IAP approach had already been demonstrated when Joe Linders was refused planning permission to build a multi-storey car park on the corner of Talbot Street and Corporation Street, on the grounds that such a scheme would not be compatible with the North East Inner City IAP. As a result, he had to change his plans, commissioning Anthony Reddy Associates to design a more acceptable development of retail and enterprise units at street level, with offices and apartments overhead.

In opting for area-based management to achieve urban renewal objectives, the Corporation was emulating Temple Bar Properties, the State agency set up in 1991 to develop Dublin's designated 'cultural quarter'. KPMG et al, in their study, noted approvingly that TBP's adoption of an architectural framework plan

Eric Luke / *Irish Times*

Frank McDonald

Nightlife in Temple Bar. By 1997, the much-hyped cultural quarter was thronged by drinkers on a seemingly endless pub crawl, including large numbers of English stag-party types who had discovered Dublin as a fun destination. The area, in Michael Smith's phrase, was turning itself into the 'Temple of Bars'.

Square Wheel Cycleworks on Temple Lane in its psychedelic coat of many colours. Now trading behind a business-grey front, it was one of the many 'alternative' facilities, including art galleries, clothes shops, restaurants and rock band rehearsal studios that gave Temple Bar a unique bohemian atmosphere, thanks in large measure to the responsible approach adopted by CIÉ.

– the first to be drawn up for any urban area in the State – was 'in marked contrast to the largely ad hoc development observed in most other designated areas', and said it could usefully be adopted as a model for integrated planning. But the consultants were also critical of the role played by Temple Bar Renewal, TBP's sister company, which effectively had the say-so on what projects would receive tax incentives, noting that it had never invoked its power to refuse approvals on the ground that one use type – pubs, for example – might have been overdeveloped to the detriment of the area in general. And though Brendan Howlin rashly described Temple Bar in 1996 as a 'model of sustainability in an urban context', even the dogs in the streets knew that there were too many licensed premises in the area. In the previous five years, almost an acre of extra drinking space had been added to it, with TBP itself directly involved in the creation of four large pubs – Fitzsimons, the Porterhouse, the Front Lounge and Isolde's Tower – and in facilitating the expansion of three existing premises, including the emblematic Temple Bar pub, a multi-part boozerama with around ten times the floor area it had in 1991. In some cases, licences were acquired elsewhere and reversed into the area. In others, the provision of a new 'hotel' entitled the developer to install a large pub at ground-floor level with its own entrance from the street, usually in tandem with a noisy nightclub in the basement. Danger Doyle's, for example, was created in 1995 by demolishing all but the front façades of a pair of listed early 18th-century buildings on Eustace Street in defiance of their status, installing the requisite number of bedrooms above and excavating the basement for a 'hotel function room', first known as the Mission, then Club Za Zu and more recently as Switch. Two of the area's State-funded cultural facilities, the Temple Bar Music Centre and the Irish Film Centre, also generate a very high proportion of their revenue from selling alcohol. By 1997, the much-hyped cultural quarter was well on its way to becoming Dublin's version of Sachsenhausen, the 'night town' zone of Frankfurt, where nearly every building is either a bar, a restaurant, a nightclub or a tourist trinket shop. At weekends, Temple Bar was thronged by drinkers on a seemingly endless pub crawl, including large numbers of English stag-party types who had discovered Dublin as a fun destination. The area, in Michael Smith's phrase, was turning itself into the 'Temple of Bars'.

This was not what was meant to happen. Indeed, the word 'pubs' was barely mentioned in TBP's 1992 Development Programme, which aimed to create 'a bustling cultural, residential and small business precinct that will attract visitors in significant numbers'. That was in line with its mandate under the 1991 Temple Bar Renewal and Development Act, introduced with great fanfare by the then Taoiseach, Charlie Haughey, for whom it had become something of a *grand projet*. In 1987, when the area was still threatened with evisceration by CIÉ's plans for a bus station and transportation centre, topped by office blocks and shopping malls, he had described Temple Bar as 'one of the most important, traditional, historic, attractive and interesting parts of Dublin', and memorably declared that he 'wouldn't let CIÉ near it'. But it would be wrong to think that

Haughey alone 'saved' the area. Much of the running had been made by conservationists, urbanists and an indigenous arts community working in some of the buildings CIÉ intended to demolish. None of these buildings would have existed at all if the national transport company had emulated the scorched-earth policy pursued over the years by Dublin Corporation's road engineers. Instead, they were rented out on short leases to art galleries, alternative clothes shops, restaurants, and rock band rehearsal studios. Thus, Temple Bar developed a unique Bohemian atmosphere thanks in large measure to the responsible approach adopted by CIÉ, which unwittingly created a monster that devoured its ziggurat bus station plan.

Significantly, too, four years elapsed between Haughey's famous pledge and the establishment of appropriate structures to implement it. After the legislation was finally passed in 1991, Paddy Teahon, then assistant secretary and later Secretary General of the Taoiseach's Department, was appointed as TBP's first managing director, with accountant Pat Kenny, later revealed as one of those who did Haughey's books, put in as chairman. Though working on a part-time basis, Teahon revelled in his new role, forecasting at an early stage that Temple Bar would have no less than 5,000 residents by the time its renewal programme was completed. And while this prediction turned out to be wildly optimistic, the entrepreneurial Kerry-born civil servant threw himself into the task at hand. He was ably assisted by Owen Hickey, a sagacious chartered surveyor (and, latterly, a successful barrister) poached from CIÉ where he had been property manager, Laura Magahy, former administrator of the IFC, Patricia Quinn, who went on to become the first woman director of the Arts Council, and John Quillinan, who had been prominently involved in the campaign to defeat CIÉ's plan. Their mission was to develop Temple Bar as Dublin's Cultural Quarter, 'building on what has already taken place spontaneously in the area'. To that end, TBP commissioned an architectural framework plan, becoming the first public agency to do so, following a limited competition among twelve Dublin design practices. The winners were Group 91,* a consortium of eight firms which had come together to design an innovative and much-acclaimed housing project in the Liberties called *Making a Modern Street*, which no developer at the time had the bottle to build. That particular scheme for South Earl Street eventually materialised in another form, long after this influential group, who had something of a head-start on their rivals, secured a real platform on which to realise their rationalist architectural and urban design ideas.

Inevitably, there was intense rivalry over how the individual projects were divided up between them, and some are barely on speaking terms as a result of this ego-bruising experience. But the results were so startlingly new and different

---

*Shay Cleary Architects, Grafton Architects, Paul Keogh Architects, McCullough Mulvin Architects, McGarry Ní Éanaigh Architects, O'Donnell & Tuomey Architects, Shane O'Toole Architects, and Derek Tynan Architects

Tony Higgins / courtesy of Group 91

Jack McManus / Irish Times

that Temple Bar came to be featured in architectural and lifestyle magazines across the world, not just for its own significance but also because of what it seemed to be saying about Dublin as a modern, forward-looking European city. By then, Laura Magahy had succeeded Teahon as TBP's managing director and become part of the story. For the media, there was something quite stunning about this stylish, attractive young woman, the beguiling daughter of a Bank of Ireland manager, taking over at the helm of a State agency with millions of pounds to spend at the tender age of thirty-one. But Magahy wasn't just a pretty face. Apart from her experience as a persuasive arts administrator, she had an MBA from Trinity, and over the years proved herself well capable of doing the business. Altogether, TBP secured a total of £41 million in public money – half of it from Europe – to develop ten cultural centres and create new public spaces in the designated Temple Bar area, extending from Westmoreland Street to the Civic Offices at Wood Quay. Because the EU funding came from the Operational Programme for Tourism, TBP had to show that pedestrian movement in the area was increasing all the time – it trebled in the first six years – and that there was also a spin-off in terms of hotel bed-nights. In short, it had to put bums on seats. But there was some doubt about whether Temple Bar's patrons were coming for the cultural centres or for the drink and the *craic*. Magahy's initial reaction to a broadside by this writer in 1997* was to deny that anything had gone awry. She pointed to the fact that Dublin Corporation, as the planning authority for the area, had granted permission for all the new pubs and extensions to existing premises. Furthermore, they were all approved for extremely lucrative tax incentives by Temple Bar Renewal, the State company set up with a brief to ensure that there would be a balanced mix of uses in the redevelopment of the area. Yet although its board was widely representative – including Bord Fáilte, for example – it singularly failed to achieve this objective. Despite repeated complaints from representatives of local residents, Finian Matthews, the senior DoE official on TBR's board, maintained that it didn't have the power to control the extent of any use, including pubs. The fact that it was chaired by rotating Lord Mayors, distracted by so many other functions, meant that it also lacked a firm hand on the tiller. Thus, far from performing as an effective watchdog with its eye on long-term sustainability, TBR was reduced to a rubber stamp.

Making a Modern Street... and much else besides. The influential Group 91 consortium of architects, who devised the winning architectural framework plan for Temple Bar, with a model of their project for South Earl Street in the Liberties. *Front (left to right)*: Paul Keogh, Rachael Chidlow, Siobhán Ní Éanaigh, Yvonne Farrell, Valerie Mulvin and Shane O'Toole. *Rear (left to right)*: Michael McGarry, Derek Tynan, Sheila O'Donnell, Shelly McNamara, Niall McCullough, Shay Cleary and John Tuomey.

Laura Magahy, managing director of Temple Bar Properties, pictured in 1993 testing the stability of the Poddle or 'Wibbly Wobbly' Bridge in the scale model of Dublin's designated cultural quarter.

* *Irish Times*, 21st April 1997

Within weeks of the *Irish Times* opinion piece, it finally stirred itself to take action, adopting a new set of guidelines which amounted to a ban on giving further tax incentives to publicans for yet more licensed space in Temple Bar. Shortly afterwards, Laura Magahy announced a twenty-point action programme aimed at tackling the problems on a broad front. She also conceded publicly that there were 'definitely enough pubs and pub-hotels' in the area. TBP then proceeded to engage architects and planning consultants to examine every single planning application for Temple Bar, appealing to An Bord Pleanála against any decision by Dublin Corporation to sanction additional licensed space. One of the casualties was a proposed 'Irish Language Cultural Centre' for Cecilia House, once the Catholic University Medical School. Though Gael Linn was nominally involved, the Fitzers group was the driving force behind it, with the ultimate objective of creating a mega-pub, with a floor area of some 10,000 square feet, extending from Cecilia Street to Temple Bar Square. Another was a plan to redevelop Blazes Restaurant at Essex Gate into a fully licensed premises, with a public bar counter – a proposal that one senior Corporation planner, Michael Reynolds, found quite acceptable on the basis that there were already two large pubs in the immediate vicinity (the Turk's Head and Isolde's Tower). Even after the adoption of an amendment to the 1991 City Plan putting the lid on further mega-pubs in the area, it took a while for the message to get through. However, the record of An Bord Pleanála shows that it knew what needed to be done. All of its decisions, from mid-1997 onwards, cited 'the extent of public bars/restaurants in the vicinity' as the principal reason for refusing to approve more of the same. Against this background, it's no wonder that Magahy was 'shocked' when developer Paddy Shovlin, who created the Thunderbird and All Sports themed restaurants on Fleet Street, opened a brash chrome-and-steel bar called XS in mid-1998 on the ground floor and basement levels of a 23-bedroom extension to the Morgan Hotel. Joe Vanek, the award-winning stage designer, described it as 'a real Dante's inferno of blue neon, expanded metal, glass bricks and slash mirrors'. Not only did this depart from the plans approved by the Corporation, which provided for a greatly extended hotel foyer with a small 'cocktail bar' to the rear, it also breached a written undertaking given by Shovlin to Magahy that 'there will be no bar installed [in the premises] for the purposes of the sale of intoxicating liquor'. It was on foot of this undertaking that TBP had agreed to withdraw an appeal to An Bord Pleanála over the installation even of the small 'cocktail bar'. Nearly two years later, what the Corporation described as 'one of the most blatant pieces of unauthorised development' it had ever seen was still before the High Court.

In 1998, when neither Bord Fáilte nor the Department of Tourism showed any interest whatsoever in establishing the scale of 'stag-party tourism' in Dublin, TBP's managing director commissioned her own review by consultants Indecon, which found that its disproportionate impact turned off other, more high-spending visitors, resulting in an estimated loss of £57 million a year in tourism revenue across the city. Subsequently, she called in all of the publicans in Temple Bar and got them to agree not to serve stag or hen party groups. When TBR refused to approve tax incentives for a major extension to the Quays pub in Temple Bar Square, publican Louis Fitzgerald sued the company on the basis that it had exceeded its powers – and lost. Delivering his judgment in December 1998, the President of the High Court, Mr Justice Frederick Morris, said the provisions of the 1991 legislation 'were at all times operative, and these provided that, if the respondents [TBR] were of the opinion that the granting of an approval would be detrimental to a suitable mix of uses and activity in the area or any part thereof, it was mandatory upon them to refuse the approval.' In other words, TBR always had the statutory power to control the spread of pubs in Temple Bar. It had simply failed to exercise this power until after the proverbial horse had well and truly bolted. Sore about losing the tax incentives, Fitzgerald has not yet built anything on the site next door to his pub, and it has been left to fester, fronted by railings and a painted hoarding, as an unfortunate gash in the urban fabric of Temple Bar Square. It is also a pity that early plans to develop a major element of student housing on Fleet Street, in partnership with Trinity College, came to nothing. The intended site is largely occupied by a multi-storey car park.

Nonetheless, the development of Temple Bar was an extraordinary achievement. 'It is hard to think of a single person who has had as much impact on an Irish city as Laura Magahy has had on Dublin', the *Sunday Tribune* declared in 1995* as many of TBP's flagship projects were coming to fruition, but before the pub problem had become evident. Magahy did not do it unaided, of

The Crow Street entrance of the Green Building, designed by Murray O'Laoire in collaboration with Conservation Engineering. One of the doorways, designed by artist Remco de Fouw, features a Belfast sink with plumbing fittings rising out to form a tree.

John Searle / Gandon Archive

———
Sunday Tribune, 4th June 1995

Curved Street, one of the new public spaces in Temple Bar, could have been developed with Arthouse on one side *(above)* facing a less monolithic and more diverse scheme than the Music Centre *(left)*.

opposite

Meeting House Square, Temple Bar's architectural set-piece, comes into its own on Saturdays when it is the venue for a thriving food market, and on balmy summer nights movies are shown on a big screen.

The exquisitely detailed flight of steps leading down from Eustace Street into Meeting House Square.

John Searle / Gandon Archive

John Searle / Gandon Archive

course. The company's headquarters in a refurbished Georgian house on Eustace Street was always a hive of activity throughout the intensive planning and development phases, with young, creative people such as Maeve Jennings and Eve-Anne Cullinan, and pragmatic surveyors like Pat Walsh and Joe Melvin engaged in a seemingly endless round of meetings with architects and other consultants. The youthful Jennings had a natural empathy with Temple Bar's bohemian constituency, and a keen sense of the grain and texture of the area. Combining creativity with hard-nosed commerciality, she rose rapidly to the position of Development Manager, overseeing the design and construction of most of TBP's earlier mixed-use schemes and coming up with radical new ideas such as the Green Building on Crow Street / Temple Lane, which was designed by Murray O'Laoire in collaboration with Conservation Engineering, run by Tim Cooper of Trinity College. Cooper also devised a combined heat and power scheme for the 190 apartments planned for Temple Bar's 'west end', recycling excess heat from the nearby Civic Offices. For everyone involved in the project, many of them still in their twenties when it started, there was a sense of being at the cutting edge of urban development, even if the Corporation continued to exercise planning control. Inevitably, mistakes were made. Converting the Regency Gothic SS Michael & John's church into a Dublin Tourism-driven Viking Adventure at a cost of £5.6 million was by far the worst. In hindsight, the church would have made an ideal location for the Temple Bar Music Centre, retaining its entire volume as a venue and reusing the ancillary school buildings as offices and recording studios. But Paddy Dunning, who became the centre's manager, and others involved in the area's pre-existing rock band scene wanted it to remain in the vicinity of Temple Lane. Had it been relocated, the Curved Street could have been developed with Shay Cleary's Arthouse on one side facing a less monolithic and more diverse scheme than McCullough Mulvin's companion building on the other. It was also an error to retain the relatively nondescript, late-19th-century building at the corner of Essex Street and Sycamore Street. This severely compromised the landmark effect of O'Donnell & Tuomey's award-winning DIT School of Photography and National Photography Archive building at the entrance to Meeting House Square. But it was the hasty demolition in 1993 of five much-altered early 18th-century buildings on Essex Quay, which were about to be listed, that brought TBP into direct conflict with An Taisce and made bitter enemies of its Dublin City Association. For Magahy, who had a low tolerance of criticism and a high interest in PR, it was also a salutary lesson, though she took some comfort from the positive reaction to Gilroy McMahon's scheme for the Essex Quay site and from a roll-call of architectural awards for other developments in the area. She was also given an honorary fellowship by the RIAI. Magahy's antennae were so well tuned that when Owen Hickey became president of the Society of Chartered Surveyors in 1995, she could immediately see the downside of his participation in a debate, organised by the society, on the motion, 'The Destruction of Dublin – Let's Get On With It'. Hickey wanted to speak in favour

– half in jest, of course – but PR considerations meant that he had to speak against the motion. The PR hype reached its zenith in 1996, with the publication by TBP of a lavishly illustrated book on the entire project, entitled *The Power of an Idea*, under the editorial direction of Patricia Quinn, just prior to her departure for the Arts Council. Cynics suggested *The Idea of the Power* as an alternative title.

The Temple Bar project was not just about constructing new buildings of real quality, but also about the creation of new public spaces in the city, even if these were not always appreciated by rowdier elements of the public. Meeting House Square, the area's architectural set piece, has to be gated every night after Eden (a restaurant) closes because of fears that it might be trashed. Much of the time, the square is almost deserted because it is such a hidden place and none of the surrounding buildings actually opens into it. During the daytime, its silence is punctuated by whoops from aspiring actors in the Gaiety School of Acting, above Eden. The restaurant, too, hasn't helped by railing off its outdoor tables with shrubs in tubs, effectively privatising a portion of the public space. Apart from a thriving weekly food market, it comes into its own on balmy summer nights when the cultural division of TBP shows movies on a big screen, rolled down over the Box Brownie façade of O'Donnell & Tuomey's award-winning but wafer-thin Gallery of Photography from a projection box mounted on the archive building. Sitting there in this outdoor room in August 1996 watching Fritz Lang's *Metropolis* as a small orchestra playing the score from the stage of The Ark (on one of the rare occasions that the curtain has been lifted) was almost a surreal experience. It just didn't feel like Dublin, or look like Dublin, surrounded as we were by all of this sophisticated new architecture, built on the site of a surface car park from the era of dereliction and decay. The new square had just been inaugurated to mark Ireland's presidency of the European Union, and there could be no doubt that it was the right venue. Not only could the Eurocrats see that their money had been well spent, but the square itself was a potent symbol of the Europeanisation of Dublin. It wouldn't have happened at all if it wasn't for Michael Gough, then a senior planner with the Corporation. He stuck his neck out for The Ark, even though it meant demolishing all but the façade of a 1720s List 1 building and punching a pedestrian route through the hall-floor level of another listed early 18th-century building next door. A former president of the Irish Planning Institute and one of the most insightful planners in Ireland, he could see what the architects, Shane O'Toole and Michael Kelly, were trying to achieve. Inspired by Martin Drury, who went on to become its director, they were creating the first purpose-built children's cultural centre in Europe, and Gough suspected that it would also be the finest single project in the whole area, both socially and architecturally, combining a unique set of facilities for children from all backgrounds with six artists' studios, a cast-aluminium 'stage curtain' to the square by Santiago Calatrava, and an exquisitely detailed flight of steps leading down from Eustace Street. So he went for it.

John Searle / courtesy of Derek Tynan Architects

John Searle / courtesy of Derek Tynan Architects

The Printworks in Temple Bar, designed by Derek Tynan Architects. It came closest to expressing Group 91's agenda through its complex mix of new-build and renovation, with ten apartments laid out around a first-floor courtyard over shops and showrooms at street level.

courtesy O'Donnell & Tuomey Architects

On balmy summer nights, movies are shown on the big screen of O'Donnell & Tuomey's award-winning Gallery of Photography on Meeting House Square. Films are projected from a projection box mounted on the National Photography Archive building which was designed by the same architects.

Bill Hastings, ARC / courtesy O'Donnell & Tuomey Architects

Along with Dick Gleeson, Gough steered the first, most crucial phase of the Temple Bar development programme through the planning department of a body that regarded the developer, TBP, as some sort of alien being which had assumed authority over a significant chunk of the city centre. A year before it was set up, the Corporation had prepared its own area action plan for Temple Bar, and it saw no reason why this should be superseded by TBP's highfalutin' architectural framework plan. There was also a real clash in philosophy. The Corporation's blueprint, drawn up by executive planner Dermot Kelly, who was one of the few officials with any empathy for the area at this early stage, had a strong conservation bias and would have imposed a 'contextual' form on new buildings, as if it was possible to pick a period for such an eclectic area as Temple Bar. Illustrations in an appendix to the plan showed two possible treatments for Crampton Court beside the Olympia Theatre – one was neo-Georgian pastiche and the other Tudorbethan theme park stuff with half-timbered fronts and medieval overhangs, presumably to complement the re-cobbled streets and fake-Victorian lamps from the days of Jack the Ripper. The kind of thing Kelly had in mind was something like Bachelors Walk, the Hollywood set Georgiana which he later effectively designed for Zoe Developments. But TBP won the battle for contemporary architecture in Temple Bar, not just because the whole initiative was sponsored by the Taoiseach's Department, but also because of the stalwart support it received from Michael Gough and Dick Gleeson. And whereas Gleeson went on to become Deputy City Planning Officer in 1996, after being recommended for the post by a Local Appointments Commission interview board chaired by Laura Magahy, Gough found himself consigned to Dublin Corporation's equivalent of the Gulag before escaping to become Deputy Planning Officer of Dun Laoghaire-Rathdown in late 1999. Coincidentally, Magahy chaired that interview board, too. As for Gleeson, a brilliant planner with an infectious enthusiasm for the city, some of his colleagues still bristle over his elevation, and wait expectantly for him to fall flat on his face, which he shows no sign of doing.

Serious friction between the Corporation and Temple Bar Properties turned into open hostility after the DoE became TBP's parent department in late-1993, even though a senior Corporation planning official, Derek Brady, was a member of its board. Brady, a very efficient but somewhat autocratic administrator who took over as Dun Laoghaire-Rathdown County Manager in September 1998, was never part of Magahy's charmed circle and did nothing to assist when she ran into serious trouble over the ill-fated Poddle Bridge plan. Having worked his way up from the rank of clerk after leaving Synge Street CBS at the age of eighteen, just as Frank Feely had done, he was a 'Corpo man' through and through, and shared its pique at the notion that an upstart State agency would have the effrontery to throw a pedestrian bridge across the River Liffey between Ormond Quay and Wellington Quay. As a result, the 'Wibbly Wobbly Bridge', so dubbed because of its wavy form, became a casualty of the wider power struggle between TBP and the Corporation. Its design, by McGarry Ní Éanaigh, didn't help. The copper roof, in particular, seemed like an architectural conceit, and the tubular steel bracing required to support the structure turned out to be far too chunky. The Corporation's planners threw the book at it, issuing a request for the most detailed set of further information yet required from any developer, before refusing permission for the project. They described it as arbitrary, dense, warped, unsettling and unacceptable. Magahy was determined not to be defeated, and took the risk of appealing to An Bord Pleanála, but she got no joy there either. The board pulled no punches in upholding the Corporation's decision in June 1995, saying the proposed bridge would be a 'discordant and obtrusive feature' on the Liffey quays because of its height, mass, curved profile and lack of transparency. But even if the decision had been positive, the Corporation – through Ciarán de Burca, one of its senior engineers – had made it clear at the two-day oral hearing that TBP would not be given access to the quay walls to build it. Three years later, the planners drafted a tight brief for an international design competition for a new millennium footbridge, stressing the need for a more traditional form that would respect its context. Dublin-based architects Howley Harrington, in collaboration with London structural engineers Price & Meyers, won the contest, and their beautiful bridge, costing £1.5 million, was opened by the Lord Mayor, Cllr Mary Freehill, a few days before Christmas 1999, with the designers' names, plus Freehill's, the City Manager's, the Corporation's top engineers and the contractors memorialised in bronze plaques at both ends.

One of Temple Bar's real strengths has been the quality of TBP's residential developments, compared to some of the dross being built in other parts of the inner city. Queues formed before the 'launch' of the Green Building in September 1994, with prospective purchasers camping out overnight to make sure of getting the apartments they wanted. And though this was a unique scheme, designed by Murray O'Laoire in collaboration with Conservation Engineering, featuring wind turbines and solar panels on the roof, and eye-catching 'art doors' by Maud Cotter and Remco de Fouw, such was the interest in every subsequent development in Temple Bar that queuing became de rigeur. The Printworks by Derek Tynan Architects, came closest to expressing Group 91's agenda through its complex mix of new-build and renovation, with ten apartments laid out around a first-floor courtyard over shops and showrooms at street level. In many ways, it was the prototype on a small scale for TBP's largest and most challenging development – the construction of 189 apartments, twenty-two retail units, a crèche and a new street in the 'West End' of Temple Bar, in line with a revised master plan for this area laying down guidelines on height, scale, materials, and even energy conservation. And whereas private sector developers would have commissioned a single firm of architects to do the lot, TBP sought to promote variety and inventiveness, including the novel idea of heating the buildings by recycling excess energy from the Civic Offices. But so many obstacles were placed in its path that it became known internally as 'Nightmare at West End'. At one point,

Joe St Leger / *Irish Times*

Joe St Leger / *Irish Times*

Magahy almost threw in the towel until she realised that the two-acre site might then be sold off to Zoe Developments. The site had been used for twenty years as a place to park cars and mobile libraries, and although it was known to be archaeologically significant, the Corporation had done nothing to facilitate an excavation. That burden fell on TBP, which invested around £1.5 million in the largest 'dig' carried out in Dublin since Pat Wallace excavated much of the adjoining Wood Quay site, on top of paying the Corporation £1.2 million for the property. It also had to take on board a requirement that 30% of the apartments west of Parliament Street must be social housing, as well as contending with a contentious appeal by An Taisce's Dublin City Association against the entire scheme.

Five firms of architects* had been selected to design the various buildings, mainly drawn from runners-up in the 1991 competition, and their shared aspiration was to create a new quarter that would be an exemplary exercise in urban renewal, laid out along Essex Street West and a new north-south street aligned on the axis of SS Michael & John's. They were all drawing on a development brief inspired by IBA, the highly influential International Building Exhibition in Berlin during the 1980s, and by the master plan for the Olympic Village in Barcelona by Martorell Bohigas Mackay. One of its most controversial features was a timber-clad tower, designed by de Blacam & Meagher for a mid-block site on Exchange Street Upper. Indeed, it became something of a lightening conductor for the scheme, drawing attention away from other issues. If this tower had been located elsewhere, such as the corner of Fishamble Street, opposite Wood Quay's 'bunkers', it might have survived. But John Martin, Deputy City Planning Officer, who was otherwise very positive about the scheme, made it clear to TBP that the thirteen-storey tower presented a problem for the Corporation's planners, as did the width of the north-south street, which they felt would be too narrow at six metres. So the tower was reduced to just eight storeys and the street increased to nine metres, wide enough to accommodate market stalls but tragically throwing it off the axis of the former church. Michael Smith was still not satisfied, and appealed to An Bord Pleanála on height and other grounds, describing as a 'procrustean contrivance' any notion that the stepped-out tower, clad in iroko, recalled the medieval towers of Siena or San Gimigiano. Magahy responded by labelling the appeal as 'crazy'. Five months later, in July 1996, the board upheld the Corporation's decision, declaring with approval that the 'appropriate archi-

---

* Anthony Reddy Associates, Burke-Kennedy Doyle & Partners, de Blacam & Meagher, McGarry Ní Éanaigh and O'Dowd O'Herlihy Horan.

opposite

The Wooden Building, designed by de Blacam & Meagher, which became an architectural lightning conductor for Temple Bar's most ambitious scheme – 191 apartments over street-level retail units in the area's 'west end'. Had there not been a failure of nerve by TBP in the face of the planners, it would have been four storeys higher.

tectural treatment and integrated approach' being pursued by TBP 'would enhance the amenity of the area'. That cleared the way for perhaps the most important fine-grained urban renewal scheme carried out in Dublin since the 1901-1904 Iveagh Trust flats, but in a wholly modern idiom and built by Rohcon to a very high standard. Not surprisingly, it sold like hot cakes for steep prices, with the tower's thirteen apartments, including a duplex penthouse, fetching a staggering total of £4.65 million at auction in March 2000. Inevitably, most were bought by investors in what some saw as a betrayal of TBP's mission to create a real residential community in the area. The penthouse, which sold for £865,000, was no exception. It's just a shame that had there not been a failure of nerve, Shane de Blacam could have taken it much higher. The archaeological mentality also triumphed over common sense at the other end of the site, with Kennan's arch painstakingly retained and then rebuilt in situ, bizarrely askew of the new building line, and an unremarkable brick wall, believed to be a survivor of the Fishamble Street Musick Hall, preserved as a tumbledown relic in the Handel's *Messiah* memorial courtyard. Nearby, directly opposite the expensive private apartments, is Smock Alley Court, a 53-unit scheme laid out around a private courtyard, which TBP sold to the Corporation at cost. Completed in 1997, it is largely occupied by middle-aged tenants who agreed to surrender houses in the suburbs after their families had grown up. They are all delighted with themselves.

Whether the West End's retail element will work remains to be seen, but its success is critically important as TBP is retaining all of the shop units to provide an income stream to support loss-making cultural centres in the area. Even east of Parliament Street, retailing in the core of Temple Bar has had a tough time, with several flagship shops closing down because they were not generating enough profits to pay the rent. Two factors played a role here – firstly, most of the pedestrian movement in the area is at night-time when the shops are shut, and secondly, TBP's policy was to sign up tenants on high rent commercial leases and then sell on their units to private investors looking for tax shelters. Even its Urbana shopping mall ran into trouble, with the tenants accusing TBP of 'pulling the plug' on them in January 2000. The bohemian atmosphere which Temple Bar once had is gone. Even the Project Arts Centre, whose ramshackle building on Essex Street East was one of its totems, gave serious consideration to moving to Smithfield before finally agreeing to settle for a spanking new building by Shay Cleary Architects on its original site. But at least Crampton Buildings, that unique little enclave of old Temple Bar, was saved. When its owners, Sir Robert and Lady Goff, put this entire city block on the market in September 1998, the Corporation stepped in to purchase the fifty-four artisan-style flats for £2.1 million, with the *Irish Times* reporting that its greatly relieved residents celebrated

Excise Walk in Dublin's docklands, designed by Urban Projects – a consortium formed by Gerry Cahill, Derek Tynan and McGarry Ní Éanaigh – will provide a total of 190 apartments in six 8-storey towers and three lower blocks forming garden courtyards, along with some retail spaces.

with champagne supplied from the Civic Offices – something that would have been inconceivable just a few years earlier. The eleven retail or restaurant units at street level, including Johnny Ronan's favourite, the Elephant & Castle, were gobbled up by Treasury Holdings for £3.6 million. TBP also won an award for its TASCQ (Traders in the Area Supporting the Cultural Quarter) initiative in persuading publicans, hoteliers and other business interests to fund a £200,000 programme of street theatre, additional cleansing and marketing in the summer of 1999. A contemporaneous opinion survey commissioned by TBP also found that most people thought the area was settling down, with fewer complaints about rowdiness in the evenings. The fact that it will end up with around 2,000 residents should help to keep it that way. As the development phase neared its end, Laura Magahy gradually wound down her involvement to make more time for other interests, including film production and consultancy work as a project manager for such schemes as the relocation of Temple Street children's hospital to the grounds of the Mater Hospital in half-destroyed Eccles Street.

However, despite the idealistic inclusion of a crèche, few could argue that Temple Bar would be an ideal place to bring up a family. The great hope is that Docklands will break that mould, offering the type of housing and general environment that might induce young couples with children to take the plunge into urban life. The Dublin Docklands Development Authority's master plan envisages that the 1,300-acre area under its control will become an attractive residential location, 'a living, breathing, self-sustained community', including family living, to counteract suburban sprawl. This is to be achieved by creating a 'beautiful and sustainable urban environment', in the words of architect Seán O'Laoire, who headed the Riverrun group which advised the DDDA on the plan – though it did not go along with the consultants' gung-ho proposal that the Docklands area should 'set itself in complete contrast' to the dominant low-rise skyline of the city by going much higher. And given the Temple Bar experience, there was also a strong emphasis on achieving a balanced mix of development through a series of area action plans for the various zones requiring renewal. One of the first such plans to be unveiled was for the Grand Canal Docks area in August 1999. Within five years, the authority said, around 9,000 people were likely to be living here in a 'new, vibrant city quarter' with a range of shops, pubs and restaurants, after the 24-acre former gasworks site is decontaminated. The area action plan envisages making much greater use of the dock basins for water-based activities, as well as creating safe play areas for children and a new civic space for concerts and other events at the junction of Hanover Quay and Grand Canal Quay. With proposals for two lifting or turning pedestrian bridges over the Liffey giving access to Luas, a bus-only bridge across the mouth of the Grand

Aerial view of Docklands from the Dublin City Development Plan 1999. The great hope is that it will break the mould, offering the type of housing and general environment that might induce young couples with children to take the plunge into urban life.

Canal, and a new DART station at Barrow Street, 'nobody living in the area will be more than a five-minute walk from high-quality public transport', according to the DDDA's chief executive, Peter Coyne. He also made a commitment, in line with the firm view of the authority's broadly based council, that 20% of the new housing would be 'social or affordable'.

It had already demonstrated its bona fides by allocating thirty-seven of the 190 apartments planned for Excise Walk in the twelve-acre IFSC extension, for social housing. This innovative scheme, designed by Urban Projects, a consortium formed by Gerry Cahill, Derek Tynan and McGarry Ní Éanaigh, consists of six eight-storey towers, standing like soldiers in a line, and three lower blocks forming garden courtyards, along with a crèche and some ground-floor retail. Practically surrounded by Scott Tallon Walker's office campus and a new 200-bedroom hotel designed by the same firm, the Excise Walk housing is one of the major components of Terry Durney's area master plan because it will frame the access to a new urban square. It is also being developed by the DDDA in a joint venture with the Campshire Partnership, formed by the McCormack family's Alanis investment vehicle, house-builder Paddy Kelly, and major contractor Ged Pierse, who has acquired stakes in several of the tax-driven developments in the vicinity. The company takes its name from those narrow strips of land between roadway and water along the old Liffey and canal docks. Once partially covered by sheds, the campshires are being developed by the DDDA as attractive amenity walkways and cycle paths, enclosed by curved nautical-style railings. It shows what can be done, even by small interventions, to upgrade the whole public realm.

Along Mayor Street, Chesterbridge Developments Ltd has completed a superb scheme on the site of Sheriff Street flats, where cars used to be set ablaze by the wild youth of a deeply disaffected community. The property world thought estate agent Paul Newman, solicitor Paul Hanby, and builder Michael Whelan were mad when they bought the eight-acre site for £4 million in 1994, setting up Chesterbridge for the purpose. Newman, who had spent most of his life telling developers what to do, was putting his own money on the line, and now had a chance to show what he was capable of achieving. When de Blacam & Meagher were commissioned to design the scheme, the development trio's intention was to refurbish four of the existing eight blocks. However, this proved impossible because the ground level had to be raised by more than a metre in an area prone to flooding, and the developers were also dubious about the scheme's financial viability. Newman had worked with Anthony Reddy Associates (ARA) on the two-phase redevelopment of Patrick Street and hired his firm to redesign it, retaining the essentials of de Blacam & Meagher's master plan. The result is of European quality, as good as anything in Barcelona or Berlin: 580 apartments laid

Rus in urbe: If people are to live closer together in a higher-density urban environment, they will need green spaces such as the two public parks created in Paris during the 1990s – Parc André Citroën (above) and Parc du Bercy (below).

Frank McDonald

Frank McDonald

out in five- to six-storey blocks, topped by projecting zinc canopies, around generous landscaped courtyards with double-height entrance halls, underground
parking, and a large number of retail units on the main street frontage. To the
rear, a curved block looks out across a new urban park towards the toytown
three-storey houses built for the previous residents of Sheriff Street – urbanity
versus suburbanity – and contrary to the early suspicion of local community
activist Seánie Lamb, who rather surprisingly appeared in a promotional video
for the Spencer Dock project, it does not include a moat filled with alligators or
piranhas. This park may have been intended as a *cordon sanitaire*, but it is surely needed in an area which is not at all well served in terms of green spaces.

Despite the area's notorious reputation, the first phase of Custom House
Square – as Chesterbridge called its scheme – sold out in a single day, with the aid
of lucrative tax incentives. Like the West End of Temple Bar, it offered a wide
range of apartment sizes, with single-bedroom units accounting for only 10% of
the total, and the flexibility of combining workplace and living space in some of
the larger ones. Fifteen of the apartments are laid out in a five-storey circular
tower, clad in cedar, which forms a striking focal point for the first-phase courtyard. This, too, is one of the elements carried over from de Blacam & Meagher's
original scheme, its use of timber being one of their trademarks. Unlike nearly
every development completed by Zoe, which rely on cheap, but wasteful electric

Chesterbridge's Custom House Square is a development of European quality, with 580 apartments laid out in five- to six-storey blocks around generous landscaped courtyards with double-height entrance halls, underground parking, and retail units on the main street frontage.

courtesy of Anthony Reddy Associates

'Gold Shield' radiators, the apartments in Custom House Square are heated from a gas-fired CHP (combined heat and power) plant which recycles waste energy from nearby office buildings. This is another feather in the developers' cap, as it represented a significant additional cost to them. The animating effect of retail units at street level, introduced by ARA, also contrasts favourably with the stand-alone islands of apartments in the adjoining Custom House Docks site, designed by Burke-Kennedy Doyle for the Hardwicke-British Land consortium and completed in 1995. When all of the office blocks and apartment buildings on the twelve-acre site are occupied, there will be more than enough people in the area to sustain the new shopping facilities and provide a clientele for the pub being developed by the DDDA in a limestone-arched former excise store on Mayor Street. Getting rid of the high stone wall separating the original IFSC site from the extended area must surely be a priority, though residents on the Custom House Docks side are understandably fearful of the security implications.

With a good mix of apartments for single people, couples and even families, the Docklands area might become a series of living city neighbourhoods. It is possible to imagine children playing in the semi-private courtyards, though where they might go to school is another matter. The south docks area is accessible to what are called good schools, but there is a dearth of these middle-class icons on the northside, and this would be a huge issue for many families. Seán O'Laoire recalls putting forward the case for 'competitive schools for middle class kids' after the Riverrun consortium was commissioned to draft the Docklands master plan, though nothing much came of his suggestion that we need to find a new idea of an urban school – perhaps something on the lines of the Stockholm model. More leisure facilities are also required, whether in the form of multi-purpose sports centres or public parks. But if there are to be parks, they should take their cue from the new parks in Paris, at Bercy near the Palais des Sports and on the site of the former Citroën motor works in the south-western sector of the city. The park at Bercy, just across the River Seine from the four 'open-book' towers of François Mitterand's Bibliotheque Nationale, is a prime example of the French landscaping style, particularly in its division into quite different component parts, fringed to the north by well-designed apartment buildings. The Parc André Citroën also provides much-needed breathing space for residents of the densely built apartment and office blocks nearby. On any Sunday afternoon, it is full of people, young and old, lying on the grass, strolling around, or admiring the plants in a variety of formal garden settings. Given the high land values in the Docklands area, it would be difficult, if not impossible, to lay out new green spaces on anything like the scale of Bercy or Citroën. It will certainly not be done by developers, left to their own devices. Mayor Square, for example, is only coming into existence because it was a central element of the area master plan. But then, as Barcelona-based architect David Mackay, external assessor for the Temple Bar architectural framework plan competition, has repeatedly pointed out, the creation of new public space in the city is a public responsibility.

5. Muddling Through

D ublin does not stand alone. Like other European cities, it is involved in the cut-throat competition for highly mobile investment by global corporations – and they are taking a lot more into account nowadays, in deciding where to locate their outposts, than the mere availability of grants or low corporate tax rates. Increasingly, they want to know about culture and leisure facilities, about where senior executives might live, what schools are available for their children, and how the transport system works. A 1999 survey by the American Institute of Architects of elected representatives and officials at state, county and municipal levels found that 'livability' issues such as education, suburban sprawl, traffic congestion and housing provision were now among the most serious political issues facing people in the US, with more than two-thirds of the respondents saying they believed that such concerns are growing. 'In the 21st century, it is the skilled worker, as well as the global company, who will be footloose. Cities must work hard to attract and retain both', according to the British government's Urban Task Force. 'An attractive, well-designed environment can help create a framework for promoting economic identity and growth. It can fulfil a role at a strategic level by providing the city with the mix of cultural, commercial and infrastructure facilities which it will require to compete on the global economic map. But perhaps more importantly, it can ensure that the city does not stagnate, by continually recycling buildings and spaces to perform new economic functions compatible with its business needs.'

What worries IBEC, among other interest groups here, is that the stresses and strains brought about by our booming economy – notably the enormous increase in traffic – threatens to strangle Dublin's ability to grow and prosper in

Aerial view of the centre of Dublin, with the Liffey meandering through it. Increasingly, global corporations investing in cities want to know about culture and leisure facilities, about where senior executives might live, what schools are available, and how the transport system works.

a sustainable manner. Unless the current 'infrastructural logjam' is resolved, IBEC's Dublin Regional Executive warned in its *Competitive Capital City* policy document (July 1999), that Ireland's most important economic zone will lose out to other, better-organised northern European cities such as Amsterdam, Copenhagen, Helsinki and Stockholm. If Dublin is to stay competitive, it 'must address the needs of commerce as it is now', says architect Tony Reddy. 'The city centre, including Docklands, should be the first port of call for office functions that require large floor plates. Otherwise, we will continue to see the development of an edge city on the M50.' Yet Dublin Corporation, the region's principal local authority, frankly admitted in December 1999 that it was in the dark about how its economy actually functions. 'We do know that companies invest in cities for a wide range of reasons and that quality of life is an important consideration. [But] we are not well-informed on the nature of specialism in the modern economy of Dublin. We are hazy about aspects like clustering, job numbers, land demand, gross domestic product, etc. We cannot speak with conviction about linkages or support systems. How can we market Dublin without this basic information?'

The Corporation's candour was expressed in its brief to the Rotterdam-based Erasmus Institute for a study aimed at enhancing Dublin's ability to compete in the 'premier league' of European cities. Overseen by Philip Maguire, assistant city manager, the study was intended to enable the Corporation to become more 'proactive' in promoting or retaining a competitive edge in such areas as financial services, tourism, retail, information technology, education, manufacturing, and an increasingly diverse office market. Citing the 'galvanising' effect of such sensational projects as the Guggenheim Museum in Bilbao, the brief recognised that culture has become central to the agenda of every contemporary 'city-state', with architecture, great galleries or museums, and major cultural events all featuring on 'the battleground for international recognition'. And while Dublin has many fine buildings and memorable clusters like Trinity College and the southside Georgian core, its reputation for literature, music and theatre finds only a weak physical expression. The 'urban elements for the 21st century' include the spine formed by the River Liffey from Heuston Station to the East Link bridge, the 'grand civic thoroughfare' linking Christchurch with Parnell Square, and the creation of a new 'sense of place' in such long-neglected areas as Smithfield and Spencer Dock. For the first time in its history, the Corporation now has an Economic Development Unit – headed by Alan Taylor, formerly its chief valuer – with a proactive role to secure the development of derelict sites and all remaining under-utilised land in the city. Realistic plans and strategies aimed at tackling social exclusion, in co-operation with 'a myriad of statutory and voluntary organisations', as well as devising up-to-date transport solutions, again in co-operation with numerous other agencies, are also integral elements of the Corporation's agenda.

And therein lies the rub. For Dublin is bereft of anything approaching a metropolitan government. What struck Matt Moran, IBEC's Dublin regional director, most forcefully in researching its study was 'the sheer complexity and breadth of Dublin's institutions' and their frequently overlapping, even contradictory, responsibilities. He was not the first to spot this bureaucratic miasma. Altogether, three Government departments, four local authorities, the Dublin Transportation Office, the National Roads Authority and the Garda Siochána all have some responsibility for the supply, maintenance and management of the region's transport infrastructure, as CIÉ's chief executive, Michael McDonnell, told an Oireachtas committee in 1997. 'Each of these has separate budgets and separate vested interests. So despite goodwill on all sides and formalised consultation mechanisms, it is inevitable that progress must be based on the lowest common denominator.' The City Manager, John Fitzgerald, who was in charge of carving up the old county council to create three new local authorities, is equally frank: 'If I was told to invent a model of government for the Greater Dublin Area, I'm fairly certain it wouldn't be what is there now.' But though he maintains that present arrangement, however loose and imperfect, 'should be well able to do whatever needs to be done', this confidence is not widely shared. Despite a managerial revolution in recent years, the system has not delivered the goods.

Transportation is the most glaring example. 'Major infrastructural projects in the Dublin area, such as the Southern Cross Route, are often dogged by delays prior to the actual construction stage, thus exacerbating the problems they were designed to alleviate. Often the delays are predicated on legal challenges which can literally add years to the completion of a project', Fitzgerald said in a December 1999 report to the City Council. And he presented a catalogue of examples to illustrate this point. Though only eight kilometres long, the Southern Cross Route will have taken thirty years to complete compared to twelve years each for the second Severn bridge linking England with Wales and the huge Oresund bridge/tunnel stretching across the narrow neck of the Baltic between Copenhagen and Malmo. Even the Portuguese, hardly in the first rank of any international efficiency league, managed to complete the eighteen-kilometre Vasco da Gama bridge across Lisbon harbour in just seven years. In common with the Government, Fitzgerald favours the introduction of 'fast-track procedures' to procure major public projects more rapidly, while protecting, at least to some degree, 'the requirements of natural and constitutional justice'. Fast-tracking is seen to be the only way of implementing a raft of projects in the £40 billion National Development Plan. On roads alone, the plan proposes to increase annual spending to £671 million – equivalent, as NTR engineering director Ciarán Blair has pointed out, to building the Waterford bypass, the Limerick bypass, the Kilcock-Kinnegad stretch of the N4, the Dublin Port Tunnel and the South Eastern Motorway *every year* until 2006. 'Putting projects in the NDP doesn't mean they're going to happen', he told the SIMI annual conference in December 1999. Even though there had been record investment in roads year on year over the previous half-decade, what the National Roads Authority didn't spend, either through lack of competence or time, amounted to £1.94 billion, by Blair's calculations. Its actual investment averaged £228.5 million a year – nearly three times less than the annual figure now being so boldly planned.

Capacity and political will are real issues. Whatever about Bertie Ahern saying that we are now 'able to decide what we want and go out tomorrow and pay for it', major pieces of infrastructure cannot be magicked out of the air. 'We may have the money to pay for it, but we can't necessarily buy it', according to one seasoned observer. 'Even if we bought all the pieces and brought them in packing cases through Dublin Airport, would we be able to put them together? Based on the experience with Luas or the Port Tunnel, it would appear that major infrastructural projects that require more than four years to realise have no chance of success, given that any government will have a five-year term at best and will tend to regard them as potential election disasters unless they can be fully completed within that time frame and the electorate can see the benefits. As a result of the type of democracy we have at the moment, grand visions simply cannot be achieved.' In terms of capacity, the indigenous construction industry is working flat out to meet the demands of the 'Celtic Tiger' economy, with skills shortages reported right across the board, so we will have to look to our fellow Europeans to help build the plethora of infrastructural projects outlined in the NDP. The likelihood is that civil engineering contractors, such as those engaged in building Potsdamer Platz in Berlin, will be drawn to Ireland – bringing their own construction gangs with them – to work on joint ventures with their Irish counterparts or directly with public agencies under much-vaunted public-private partnerships (PPPs).

But whether fast-tracked or not, 'bad projects are still bad projects', as the ESRI's John FitzGerald and Edgar Morgenroth said in their commentary on the NDP. An awful lot of money is to be spent over the next six years. If not invested sensibly, it will do an awful lot of damage. Even the plan itself concedes, ever so tentatively, that the 'possibility of the emergence of some unsustainable patterns of development ... cannot be excluded [because of] the pace of the current economic development, unforeseen interactions between measures or unanticipated consequences of particular measures'. That's why Arthur Hickey, recently elected president of the RIAI, warned of the 'grave' consequences for Irish society if the plan is implemented 'in too much of a hurry'. As he said in March 2000, 'this unprecedented effort to solve the country's infrastructural problems could create a host of other difficulties, lasting long into the future, if we don't keep our eye on the issue of quality.' Much earlier, An Taisce called for a strategic envi-

---

The Government-sponsored boardwalk along Bachelors Walk and Ormond Quay Lr seemed to be an inspired idea, but An Taisce criticised the design as 'utilitarian' and 'gimmicky'.

According to An Taisce, Santiago Calatrava's road bridge between Blackhall Place and Usher's Island would cut off the first view of the quays, with the tower of St Paul's Church and the Four Courts dome providing a memorable visual composition for visitors arriving from the west.

ronmental assessment of the NDP to ensure that it complied with the principles of sustainable development, in line with the latest thinking in Brussels. 'By 2005, Ireland will have a standard of living equal to the EU average. There is no longer – if there ever was – any excuse for low environmental standards. Affordability is no longer the issue. What is required is imagination. If we do not now get a plan for sustainability, then when?' it asked. In this regard, the Government's admission that its own plan could actually produce unsustainable patterns of development 'does not inspire confidence either as to its thoroughness or its methodology', according to An Taisce. Yet it has become an EU requirement that compliance with its environmental and nature protection legislation 'must be incorporated into the definition and implementation of measures supported by Structural Funds and Cohesion Funds'. An Taisce would go further in proposing that the measurement of economic progress by increases in Gross Domestic Product needs to be broadened to include 'quality of life' indicators like crime, literacy, poverty and unemployment rates, as well as life expectancy, water quality, waste production, area of public open space, length of time spent commuting, and carbon dioxide emissions.

CO$_2$ is a serious matter. It is the principal greenhouse gas blamed by scientists for causing climate change, or 'global warming', already being witnessed in such extreme events as the ferocious storm that devastated France in December 1999, leading to Paris being declared a disaster area, or the spraying of New York against killer mosquitoes three months earlier. 1999 itself was also the hottest year since records began, perhaps even for a thousand years. Under the Kyoto Protocol, agreed in December 1997 to begin reducing human-induced changes to the Earth's climate system, Ireland – still technically an underdeveloped country by EU standards – is permitted to increase its greenhouse gas emissions by 13% on their 1990 levels by 2008. By 1999, because of economic growth, they were already 18% higher and, at the rate we are going, these emissions are likely to be at least 2.5 times the internationally agreed target. Since road transport is the fastest-growing contributor to greenhouse gas emissions, An Taisce argued that the proposed expansion of this sector, on the basis that more roads produce more traffic, was 'in direct conflict with Ireland's and the EU's greenhouse gas obligations', quite apart from making a serious impact on the environment and human health. Under the NDP, according to its calculations, 75% of transportation investment would go to roads countrywide and only 25% to public transport over the seven-year period. It called for 'a state-of-the-art study of the desirability of the proposed proportionate distribution of funds', noting that more developed countries such as France or Germany would no longer contemplate such an equation. 'Rail is far more energy-efficient than road transport. Without a substantial transfer of traffic to rail, there is no possibility of Ireland meeting its greenhouse gas emission targets', An Taisce warned.

However, given that the vast bulk of heavy-goods traffic in Ireland is now carried by road rather than rail, it is clear that inter-urban routes will have to be improved to facilitate more balanced regional development. It is obviously in the national interest that Greater Dublin does not continue growing disproportionately by absorbing two-thirds of the State's net population growth of 1,000 per week. That influx of people, mainly returning from overseas, has contributed to high house prices and rising levels of traffic congestion in the capital. A laissez-faire approach to the development of Greater Dublin will inevitably turn it into Brian Hughes's envisioned 'city-state of the 21st century', with more than half of the population living there by 2047, if not sooner. However, if anyone was expecting firm guidance on where alternative growth centres would be located, the NDP abjectly failed to provide it. All it offered was the promise of a National Spatial Strategy that would identify 'broad spatial development patterns' and the infrastructure required to underpin a better balance between regions, as well as setting out 'a scenario for the future role of Irish cities and towns' and nominating 'a small number of new strategic regional centres'. But since this is two years down the road, we still have no map of the Dublin and the Ireland we are destined to create, for good or ill, over the next decade. In postponing such crucial decisions, the Government has yet again flunked the issue of regional development, just as one of its predecessors did thirty years earlier when presented with the Buchanan report. For it was in 1969 that Prof Colin Buchanan first proposed an alternative growth centre strategy to take some of the pressure off Dublin. The problem then, as now, was that politicians could not bring themselves to take the hard decisions to designate, say, Sligo as a growth centre when such a move would implicitly put Longford and Castlebar at a disadvantage. Even within counties, how would Mullingar react if Athlone was to be chosen? Clientilism demanded that there had to be 'something for everyone in the audience', so the IDA bought fields and built advance factories outside almost every provincial town, in our own unique version of the cargo cult. And in the absence of any national physical plan, Dublin continued to grow like Topsy.

Perhaps Buchanan was unpalatable at a time when only 32% of the Republic's population was urbanised, but this proportion has since risen to 58%, suggesting that there is no longer any excuse for political cowardice on the designation of alternative growth centres. The fact that Dublin is bursting at the seams, making it a less pleasant place to live, has already encouraged a voluntary migration to other towns in Leinster. However, this is based on long-distance commuting to jobs in the capital, usually by road rather than rail, and the pressure on Dublin will only be eased if jobs, too, are relocated by directing growth elsewhere, in line with a coherent regional development strategy. In its critique of the NDP, An Taisce emphasised that the development of more far-flung towns such as Athlone, Sligo, Castlebar and Tralee as expanded regional settlements must be based on the principles of environmental sustainability. Otherwise, they would end up mirroring Dublin's problems on a smaller scale. But long before the emergence of any coherent strategy, several Ministers had taken the proverbial bull by the horns by announcing the transfer of elements of the State bureaucra-

Martyn Turner

Martyn Turner's logo for the Dublin Crisis Conference in 1986 depicting Dublin as an octopus strangling itself and the rest of the country

cy to their constituencies, even to their own home towns. 'They see power, not as an opportunity to shape the destiny of future generations, but as a short-term, smash-and-grab project', as Fintan O'Toole wrote in the *Irish Times*. 'The public good, yet again, is sacrificed to private ends and the pathetic culture of the raider-politician is given a new lease of life.' The relocation of a further 10,000 civil servants to provincial centres, on top of some 14,000 already 'decentralised', will also be proceeding in advance of the promised National Spatial Strategy, with the Department of Finance in the driving seat, as usual. Its latest programme of dispersal was used as an excuse not to proceed with a new headquarters for the Department of Arts, Heritage, the Gaeltacht and the Islands. This project had been the subject of an international architectural competition in autumn 1999, and the winning entry by a London firm, Avery Associates, was intended to be built on a former car pound beside the main gates of the Phoenix Park. But Finance balked at the bill of £40 million, with officials raising their eyebrows about the lavish proportions of the ministerial suite, in particular, and the result of the competition was never announced, never mind published or exhibited. It simply died the death. Instead of a prestige State-owned building on the edge of the Park, what we are likely to get is another batch of cheap and cheerful office blocks on the edges of provincial towns, procured through 'design-and-build' packages under which architecture competes with cost. The idea that the residue of civil servants left in the capital might benefit from working in better quality offices does not appear to have occurred to those who welshed on the competition. And despite the Government's ostensible commitment to devolution, the new regional bodies – one for the BMW (Border-Midlands-Western) 'region' and the other covering the Southern and Eastern 'region' – are likely to be little more than toothless talking shops. Given the determination of the Department of Finance to retain complete control, the two regional assemblies, one headquarted in Ballaghadereen, Co Roscommon, and the other in Waterford, will be lucky to end up administering 10% of total spending under the NDP. They will be as powerless as the French 'parliament' that met at the casino in Vichy during the Second World War.

One of the unforeseen consequences of the failure to create new growth centres in the past was that it undermined the viability of what survived of the national railway network, after it had been gutted and filleted by Todd Andrews. The Cork and Belfast lines are the only ones that make a profit, primarily because the cities they serve have populations large enough to sustain two-way traffic with Dublin at the other end. If Sligo was three times its current size, as Buchanan envisaged, the railway line that terminates there would be in a less parlous state. France is a much more populous country, and despite the pre-eminence of Paris, the SNCF manages to sustain itself because there are numerous other cities on its network, such as Bordeaux, Nantes, Lille, Lyon, Marseille, Montpelier and Toulouse, with substantial populations and high-speed TGV trains serving them all. Montpelier, indeed, has been developed as the country's scientific capital, drawing in major investment from knowledge-based industries. Here, however, Dublin's critical mass makes it more difficult to 'sell' alternative locations with poorer facilities to inward investors, who will continue to cluster in the capital as a result. And far from heralding a new era for the railways, most of the £500 million earmarked by the NDP for mainline investment is intended to make clapped-out lines safer to travel on, following a number of accidents in recent years. Amounting to marginally more than the NRA's budget to turn the N9 into a dual carriageway between Kilcullen and Waterford, this miserable sum is driven by dread of the compensation culture, reflecting a realisation by the Government that it cannot knowingly preside over unsafe railways. The huge sums of money spent or planned to be spent on the E01 route between Larne and Rosslare merely serve to underline the Cinderella status of the railways. Though the Dublin-Belfast Enterprise express is of European quality, attracting a large number of long-distance commuters, the 'service' between Dublin and Rosslare is among the worst in Ireland, and there is only a commitment to upgrade it as far as Arklow.

Despite all the guff about sustainable development and the importance of integrating environmental considerations into decision-making at every level, the European Commission is pursuing legal actions against Ireland over uncontrolled dumping, illegal asbestos dumping, inadequate waste management planning, water pollution, and drinking-water quality. It maintains that we are also in breach of EU law relating to protection of the architectural heritage, carbon dioxide emissions, peat extraction, afforestation, and the protection of birds and habitats. On foot of a complaint by Lancefort over the handling of planning permission for the Hilton (now Westin) hotel on the edge of College Green, the Government may soon find itself indicted before the European Court of Justice. Lancefort also intends to pursue a separate case with the Commission over the marked reluctance of the Supreme Court to refer environmental cases to the ECJ in Luxembourg because of 'the national obsession with expediting development', according to Michael Smith, who is himself well versed with litigation. Within the next two years, he forecasts that the Supreme Court would 'suffer a major constitutional shock' when it comes to realise that 'the law of the land is

Frank McDonald

The first phase of the Civic Offices at Wood Quay, disparagingly known as 'The Bunkers' *(above)*, and the second phase *(below and right)* by Scott Tallon Walker, which reinstated the line of the Liffey quays and seemed to herald a new era of openness and accountability. Its interior features a plant-filled atrium

Frank McDonald

European'. In the meantime, the Government high-level task force monitoring infrastructural development has been devising a range of measures aimed at short-circuiting the legal process, including the establishment of a special division of the High Court to deal expeditiously with judicial reviews. It should be noted, however, that the environmental sector was not among the cozy club of 'social partners' consulted about what went into the NDP, which was handed down like a tablet of stone from the top of the mountain on 18th November 1999.

But where do An Taisce and Lancefort stand when the process of public consultation leads to unsustainable development, by the will of the people, as happened in Ballymun and Fatima Mansions? Smith, who resigned as a director of Lancefort after becoming national chairman of An Taisce in September 1999, said: 'I believe planning is for people. Anyone who is against community-led planning is anti-democratic in the truest sense.' But what if the community involved is not well informed about the nuances of sustainability? According to Smith, this problem could be resolved by 'progressive professional advice and demonstration', using the round table concept as a planning tool to achieve consensus between planners, architects, developers, conservationists and local community representatives. If people were shown new models that worked, he maintains, it would change their attitudes and obviate the need for repeated rounds of 'public consultation'. The City Manager agrees that Dublin Corporation cannot simply ride roughshod over people and expect to make progress at the same time. 'If you take out undergrounding Luas and the Eastern Bypass, there is very little dispute about the rest of the transport infrastructure projects

Dave Meehan Photography / courtesy of Dublin Corporation

for the city', he said. Fitzgerald has been trying to promote a 'can-do' culture to overcome what he regards as one of Dublin's principal drawbacks – 'our inability to get on and implement plans' – and talks with pride about the fact that, long before Ardnacrusha, the Corporation built the Pigeon House power station in 1899 to provide electric lighting on Dublin's streets. 'To discharge our responsibility for city government, we need to generate a culture of civic leadership in a manner that is not in evidence at present', he bluntly told the City Council in November 1999. 'The question is: Who is in charge of the city? Who controls its direction and future?' Fitzgerald said he was assuming that the council's five new area committees and its strategic policy committees, which involve a cross-section of interests, would lead to a greater political focus on the city, and 'reposition Dublin Corporation at the centre of local government in Dublin'. If that didn't happen, he asked pointedly, 'Where do we go from here?'

Where, indeed? There was a time when some councillors were ahead of the officials in terms of progressive thinking. Now, it is the other way around. The second phase of the Civic Offices, designed by Scott Tallon Walker, has come to symbolise a new era of transparency and accountability, just as the 'bunkers' of Sam Stephenson's uncompleted original project were the metaphor for a civic bureaucracy dug in against the city. It is hard to credit, looking at the splendid result, that the STW scheme was sanctioned on a casting vote in December 1992. *Obedientia civium urbis felicitas* (the obedience of the citizens is the happiness of the city) may still be Dublin Corporation's official motto, but there can be no doubt that the organisation has changed. The atrium of the new Civic Offices, which would never have been built but for the single-minded determination of Derek Brady, is regularly used for public meetings at which senior Corporation officials explain its policies and take questions from the floor. At the same time, Fitzgerald's managerial style has turned elements of the bureaucracy from a purely administrative structure into something that resembles a thrusting, go-ahead firm with its own agenda and mission statement. He had done the same with the newly formed South Dublin County Council as its first county manager, and this had a ripple effect on the other artificially created 'counties' in what used to be Co Dublin. They have all provided themselves with fine civic offices, in Tallaght, designed by Gilroy McMahon, Dun Laoghaire (McCullough Mulvin) and Swords (Bucholtz & McEvoy with BDP), but it still seems improbable that any of the *soi-disant* counties over which they preside will develop a real sense of identity until they have their own GAA teams. In the meantime, whatever about the Strategic Planning Guidelines and the 'metropolitan interest', they can get on with the business of aggrandising their commercial rates revenue by granting planning permission for anything that moves. That's what gives them a discretionary income. Local government would also have more clout if local authorities had the power to levy rates on residential property, a prerogative they had until it was senselessly taken away from them in 1978 on foot of Fianna Fáil's giveaway manifesto in the previous year's general election. Just as there can be no taxation without representation, there can be no real representation without the power of taxation. Funding the local authorities from the proceeds of motor taxes makes them marginally better off, but it fails to establish the principle that a 'property-owning democracy', as Thatcher called it, should contribute directly to the administration of the city.

So who speaks for Dublin? Nobody, really. Certainly not, in any coherent way, the city and county's forty-seven Dáil deputies or its 130 councillors. And most of the sixteen TDs and seventy-eight councillors for Meath, Kildare and Wicklow do not even see themselves as representing the Greater Dublin Area, even though they're in it. The IFA only needs to whisper about a meeting to highlight another crisis in farming and it can be certain that every rural TD in the country will turn out to be counted. Dublin, as an entity, does not exercise the same pulling power. The city has its lobbies alright, notably the Chamber of Commerce and the City Centre Business Association, as well as numerous residents associations, community groups, professional bodies and what conservationists may be mustered by An Taisce. But although it has a better claim than most to speak for the public interest, all of these represent different sections of civic society, each with its own agenda. The titular head of of the city is the Lord Mayor, wearing King Billy's handsome chain of office, a bauble that's passed around from Mary to Jack on an annual basis. Though decisions are still taken in the name of 'The Right Honourable, the Lord Mayor, Aldermen and Burgesses of the County Borough of Dublin', executive power resides with the City Manager, so a great deal depends on that office-holder's leadership and vision. Of the fifty-two members of the City Council, 'about a dozen would have a very clear understanding of what needs to be done, another dozen will never have, and the rest respond to whatever they feel has to be responded to', according to one experienced observer. The fundamental issue they all have to confront, in John Fitzgerald's view, is to decide whether their role should continue to be representational, revolving around clientilist service delivery, or be redefined to 'deal with city government in the way the Wide Streets Commissioners did'. Local government reform aims to re-balance the relative powers of councillors and officials by, among other measures, having a directly elected Lord Mayor, with at least some executive functions, from 2004. The same will apply to the mayors of other cities and towns and the chairs of county councils. Coincidentally, Noel Dempsey made this move after Britain's New Labour government decided to give London a directly elected mayor, even though this ran the risk that maverick Ken Livingstone, who had railed against Thatcher for abolishing the GLC in 1984, would snatch the glittering prize. There has been concern here, too, in both official and political circles, about the outcome of a Dublin mayoral contest. Might it, for, example lead to the election of a populist candidate such as Senator David Norris, who they feared would more than likely make policy as he played to the gallery? (Norris himself says he has no interest in the post. He had quite enough to contend with following the outbreak of trench warfare over his controversial plan – perhaps foolishly adopted by the Corporation – to install a set of Regency gates from Santry Court near the bottom of North Great George's Street.) Another concern, mirroring the fears in Whitehall, was that a full-time mayor with an executive role would create an alternative power centre in the city, in opposition to the Government.

The shining example of what can be achieved by inspired political leadership must surely be Barcelona. Though the record of elected mayors throughout the world is highly variable – Washington's Marion Barry, for example, was jailed on drug charges – Pasqual Maragall proved that dizzying heights could be scaled. Repeatedly elected (by the city council) to serve as executive mayor of the Catalan capital between 1982 and 1997, he was able to realise his bold vision of turning Barcelona around to face the sea – an amazing idea, first outlined here by John de Courcy Ireland at the 1986 Dublin Crisis Conference. The young Catalan socialist, said our old man of the sea, was 'looking far ahead, not sitting there constrained by being brought up to think that things can't be changed except when large amounts of money are available, and then they might even be changed for the worst'. Steeped in the extraordinary cocktail of resurgent Catalan nationalism in the years after Franco's death in 1975, Barcelona imprinted itself on the map of European cultural consciousness as a capital of architecture, art and urban design, bringing the Olympic Games in 1992 and such well-deserved accolades as Britain's Royal Gold Medal for architecture in 1999 – the first time it had ever been awarded to a city. In his speech at the award ceremony, Maragall spoke of the view of Europe from a satellite as a 'constellation of specks of light' indicating its cities, great and small, where the future of their respective countries would increasingly be shaped. 'When a city has gone through years of non-doing and passivity, ideas about its future mature and can be transformed into a fruitful, forceful and purposeful attitude, when the necessary political conditions to take action come into play', he said. The former mayor might equally have been talking about Dublin, which is fortunate to be twinned with Barcelona because we can learn so much from its experience of urban renewal. 'Let us call architecture back to its date with history', Maragall declared. 'No one can survive merely by conservation. If there is no new construction, the city cannot stand; not even the old will endure. Each city must find its own formula for combining existing symbols with new ones. Without the latter, antiquity becomes mere repetition.'

The future of Dublin, too, does not hinge on the preservation of individual historic buildings. That battle has been largely won, *pace* the perennial bull-in-a-china-shop syndrome and the unfortunate fact, illustrated yet again by the belated campaign to save Riversdale in Rathfarnham, WB Yeats' last home in Dublin, that too many of them are still taken for granted. (Houses associated with James Joyce have also suffered. His home in Drumcondra, where he lived while attending Belvedere College, was demolished, while the house on Ushers Island where he set his most famous short story, *The Dead*, languishes in a ruinous state despite repeated promises that it would be fully restored.) There has

Frank McDonald

City vision: Barcelona from the terrace of the Miró Museum on Montjuic. Under the enlightened leadership of Pasqual Maragall, its mayor from 1982 to 1997, the Catalan capital was transformed with new public spaces, remarkable buildings, and *(right)* a whole new city quarter, the 1992 Olympic Village.

Frank McDonald

been a real *rapprochement* between the Corporation and An Taisce, most evident from the acceptance of its submission on the 1999 Dublin City Development Plan, which resulted in a 50% increase in the number of listed buildings. The Corporation is also working in partnership with Dublin Civic Trust, which has demonstrated through a number of excellent projects how historic buildings can be saved and given viable new uses. The law, too, is being tightened. One of the most important changes in the consolidated Planning Bill, introduced in August 1999 by Noel Dempsey, broadens the definition of a 'listed building' to include its interior and curtilage, in line with the Government's stated policy on the preservation of Ireland's architectural heritage. And for the first time ever, starting with just £4 million, there is a Budget allocation to provide grants towards the repair and restoration of listed buildings in private ownership. Simultaneously, a new Government policy on architecture commits it to promoting high standards of design and construction in the State and private sectors by encouraging innovation and fostering a demand for high-quality architecture in the community as a whole. If this translates itself into the classroom, it could in time do wonders for our visual awareness. As for recalcitrant developers who avail of bank holiday weekends to get rid of listed buildings, the Bill should have a deterrent effect because it increases the maximum fine for a conviction on indictment from £1 million to £10 million. It also inaugurates a new planning enforcement

courtesy of Dublin Civic Trust

One of several projects by Dublin Civic Trust demonstrating how historic buildings can be saved and given viable new uses. This late-17th-century building on Aungier Street., which had been scheduled for demolition, is now a guest house.

The restored fanlight of No.4 Castle Street, a late-Georgian shop premises occupied for many years by Barnewall's shoe repairers. Once scheduled for demolition, it is now the headquarters of Dublin Civic Trust.

courtesy of the *Irish Times*

regime to remedy what many conservationists see as the Achilles' heel of the present system, particularly in Dublin, by imposing an obligation on local authorities to follow up 'genuine complaints' about unauthorised development within a given time frame.

The most serious problem facing Dublin lies at a more strategic level, in the interaction between the city and its hinterland. With no metropolitan authority and a non-legally binding set of Strategic Planning Guidelines, too much is left for the seven local authorities to determine individually. John Fitzgerald sees the guidelines as a contract to resolve the inevitable conflicts in the 'metropolitan interest', and insists that the other six authorities recognise that the whole region's prosperity is critically dependent on the success of the city. Others are not so sure that they do, pointing to the raft of rates-earning Edge City office parks which have been approved in recent years, the continuing urge to zone more land on the periphery for residential development, and the complex division of responsibilities for traffic and transport. In any sensible arrangement, these areas would fall within the remit of a Greater Dublin Authority, with a second tier of councils – for Tallaght, Clontarf, Rathmines, etc – to deal with service delivery and other local issues. But the City Manager says there are already 'more than enough structures – we're tripping over ourselves with bureaucracy', and he would be 'appalled at the prospect of devoting the kind of energy that would be required to reinvent it all. What we've got to do is identify the bits that are deficient and plug them.' In the meantime, the DoE exercises a de facto role as planning and development authority for Greater Dublin, issuing circulars, directives and guidelines from its much-prized headquarters in the Custom House. 'They make the rules, communicate them to us and we endorse them. If only we could get them off the pitch...', one senior Corporation official mused. However, if it wasn't for the DoE's intervention, the Corporation might have proceeded with publicly funded plans for a suburban housing estate on the site of Fatima Mansions.

There is also a lack of confidence in CIÉ's ability to provide a modern public transport system for the region, despite its acknowledged success in transforming both Connolly and Heuston stations. In what other European capital do bus and rail services close down at 11.30 pm, apart from the odd night bus at weekends? Riddled by restrictive practices built up and assiduously maintained by trade unions over the years, CIÉ is seen as incapable of meeting the challenge after more than a decade on a subsistence diet. But if this famine relief policy was meant to loosen things up, it did not succeed. In 1994, an innovative Glaswegian, Bob Montgomery, was forced to resign as managing director of Dublin Bus by pressure from trade unions which had opposed almost every attempt he made to introduce a more customer-orientated focus. His successor, Alan Westwell, a more low-profile Liverpool-born engineer with a PhD in transport planning, put up a spirited fight against the dire threat of competition, introducing new bus routes to and from Dublin Airport in response to the launch of Aircoach in

October 1999. He also resisted the Corporation's demand that the privately owned company, which had suffered intimidation from some Dublin Bus drivers (and from the more thuggish taxi men based at the airport), should be able to use its bus stops. But although Westwell rowed in firmly to ensure the success of the Stillorgan bus corridor, the traffic authorities remained sceptical. Every year, they were clearing road space to give buses more priority, yet the operator was slow in putting forward proposals for more cross-city and orbital bus routes – for example, on the M50. Poor enough basic pay of £330 per week prompted the bus drivers, led by their union, the NBRU, to take strike action in March 2000, ratcheting up from one day per week to two, three and four days per week, to press home their claim for a 20% increase. Dublin Bus said 'sorry' to its customers in a series of quarter-page newspaper advertisements, which explained that the drivers' claim would cost £95 million per year and could not be funded without productivity gains.

Iarnród Éireann also comes in for criticism, again mainly because of trade union resistance to change, with train drivers striking over the relocation of a depot at Connolly Station, and delaying the inauguration of DART extensions to Bray and Malahide for months on end to get better deals. Everything new in the CIÉ group seems to become an 'IR problem'. That's one of the main reasons why Mary O'Rourke has come out strongly in favour of ending Iarnród Éireann's rail monopoly and extending competition in the bus sector – something which Dublin Corporation also favours. Her proposals for a radical shake-up of the public transport sector, outlined to the Cabinet sub-committee on infrastructure in April 2000, are not quite so baldly Thatcherite as some had feared. What she has opted for is not complete deregulation, but rather a new regulatory regime which offers considerable scope for private sector participation. One of its key objectives is to decouple the design and procurement of public transport services from their operation, with a dedicated body established to oversee the franchising of bus routes, laying down standards of service and levels of subsidy. In the higher echelons of the Civic Offices, there is an acute awareness that the Corporation itself 'can't put one bus on a road or one railcar on a track'. Some senior officials even believe that Dublin should follow other European cities by entrusting transport provision to the municipal administration. 'Depending on an outside agency puts us in an impossible position', said one of them. 'At the very least, we should be nominating a transport authority for Dublin, with responsibility for everything that moves. It's to do with city governance.' O'Rourke must have heard this plea because what she is now toying with is the establishment of a Greater Dublin Authority, with overall responsibility for both transportation and land use.

But even though the bureaucracy of Dublin Corporation is being revitalised, officials with vision and great ideas are still swamped by cumbersome decision-making processes and structures. 'There is huge untapped potential and energy which is taking longer to release than anyone would wish', according to one observer. 'The city may be paying a high price in lost opportunities for fruit-ful collaboration because of a fragmented approach to development and prob-lem-solving. People in Dublin Corporation are unaccustomed to "thinking outside their box" because their sole focus has been on delivering essential serv-ices on very low budgets in the decades since the abolition of rates. And that behaviour is mirrored outside the Corporation, leading to a serious lack of engagement with the broader challenge of building a capital city with style and panache. The first question will never be "What's in it for the city?" but rather "What's in it for us?" So while we have public expectations of delivering the type of grand projects which are seen in Sydney, Paris and London, it will be an uphill battle to achieve these results with the current structures and mindsets. In reality, it takes far too much time to get even the simple things done. But with better communications and more project teams and project champions, things could be improved beyond recognition. More than anything, the city has to engage people who live and work in it. Improving the visual environment and amenity is the biggest challenge, and this demands a co-ordinated approach.' The Corporation might also benefit if there were some women in senior management posts. It is surely not appropriate that a 21st-century public service organisation whose deci-sions impact on our lives and on our futures should be a male management monolith. Throughout the State, indeed, only one of the thirty-five top city or county management posts – Ann McGuinness in Westmeath – is held by a woman, and there are few females in the next tier either. At central government level, only the Department of Tourism, Sport and Recreation has a female Secretary General – Margaret Hayes. But even if there were more women at the top, they would find themselves in a club of predominantly male civil servants who invest a lot of time and energy fighting bureaucratic wars which can often only be resolved at the Cabinet table.

Dithering is another endemic feature of the system. Take the waste man-agement strategy for the Dublin area. It was originally unveiled in draft form in January 1998, proposing a range of measures to reduce dependence on landfill by vastly increasing the proportion of waste recycled and building a municipal 'ther-mal treatment plant' – an incinerator, in shorthand – to dispose of the remain-der. Prepared by MCCK, an Irish-Danish consortium led by consultant engineers MC O'Sullivan, the £300 million strategy is designed to deal with the increasing volumes of waste produced by a throwaway society, now averaging at half a tonne per person per year. Though a public-private partnership is clearly on the cards for the proposed incinerator, probably involving a Danish company financing, building and operating it, implementation of the strategy as a whole depends on councillors having the guts to introduce commercial and domestic waste charges, in line with the 'Polluter Pays' principle. Yet, more than two years down the road, only Dun Laoghaire-Rathdown has moved to impose an annual charge or a fee-per-bag to collect the 'waste' deposited on every city street and suburban road. Rows will break out over the location of new composting and landfill sites to replace the exemplary facility run by South Dublin County Council near Kill, Co Kildare, and the battle lines are already being drawn over the consultants' recommendation that the 'thermal treatment plant' should be located on the Poolbeg peninsula, not far from the ESB power station. Even though it lacks a rail link, this is probably the best place to put it, as the heat it generates could be used to fuel the adjoining Ringsend sewage treatment plant, currently being upgraded as a central element of the £200 million Dublin Bay Project. The Amager incinerator in Copenhagen, on an island quite close to the city centre, has been operating since the mid-1970s with no adverse public health impacts, while the more recent thermal waste plant in Vienna, designed by the eccentric artist Hundertwasser, has become something of a tourist attraction. Meanwhile, the MV Sir Joseph Bazalgette, which used to take the sewage sludge out from Ringsend every day to dump it in the sea off the Nose of Howth, has been decommissioned, as of June 1999. It was later offered for sale.

Whatever about the plaudits garnered by Judge Seán O'Leary in disposing of three Luas inquiries in record time – though he bent over backwards to facilitate objectors, even where they didn't deserve to be accommodated – the Government would be making a big mistake if it thought that other major projects only needed a clever inspector to see them through. Unless all the preparatory work has been done, including a proper EIS, they will be seen as flawed and open to challenge at every opportunity. 'If you're in public sector, spending public money, the right thing to do is to publish everything from the beginning, push it all out. Otherwise, it's going to be dragged out of you', said Donal Mangan, the Luas project director. Even the National Gallery fell into that trap in planning a major extension in Clare Street. Assuming that it could get rid of a surviving 18th-century building on the site, the gallery did not specify that it should be retained in its brief for an international architectural competition in 1996 for the project, then estimated at £13 million. Having awarded the commission to Benson & Forsyth, architects of the much-acclaimed Museum of Scotland in Edinburgh, the gallery ran into serious flak from An Taisce and the Irish Georgian Society, which were outraged that a premier national cultural institution would demolish a Georgian house with a rare Regency ballroom at the entrance to Merrion Square. They were as stunned as the gallery when An Bord Pleanála upheld their appeal in January 1998, overturning Dublin Corporation's decision on the avowedly conservationist grounds that the replacement of these worthy, unlisted structures with a modern building would materially contravene its policy of protecting the area's architectural and civic design character. Having recovered from their shock, the gallery and its architects submitted a revised scheme, retaining No.5 South Leinster Street in its entirety, and this sailed through the planning process without a single objection. But time was needlessly lost, pushing up the price of the project to £17 million. To avoid a similar debacle, the Office of Public Works managed to secure agreement in advance on its plans for a major extension to Leinster House, cleverly designed by Dolan &

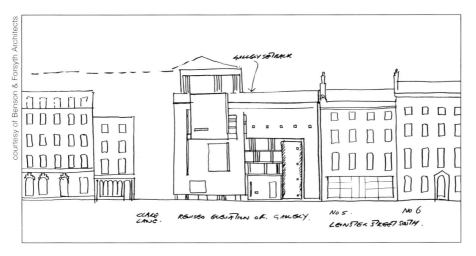

After An Bord Pleanála's rejection of its plans to demolish No.5 South Leinster Street, the National Gallery submitted a revised scheme, retaining the Georgian building in its entirety, and this sailed through the planning process without a single objection.

Donnelly, with Paul Arnold advising on the conservation aspects. The only delay here was caused by a construction workers strike, which simultaneously hit the National Gallery extension.

The format of public inquiries is also being changed. Under the 1999 Planning Bill, An Bord Pleanála will assume the functions of the Minister for the Environment in dealing with road and motorway projects, as well as continuing to perform its primary role of adjudicating on planning appeals and references. A new division, with extra staff, is required to administer this additional work-load, especially to meet deadlines specified in the legislation, with the informality characteristic of the board's oral hearings replacing the more hidebound style of public inquiries into road and motorway compulsory purchase orders. In future, the board will be blamed for avoidable delays in these areas, just as it already is for taking too much time to process planning appeals, particularly for larger, more contentious developments. Paddy O'Duffy, its figures-obsessed chairman since 1994, not unreasonably made the case that the delays in delivering Luas, the Port Tunnel and other major pieces of infrastructure have been much longer. At a press briefing in December 1999, he refuted criticisms from the Construction Industry Federation, among others, that third-party objectors were being over-indulged. In fact, more than 60% of the 4,000 planning appeals dealt with by the board in 1998 were made by developers. And while the number of 'frivolous or vexatious' appeals are very low, O'Duffy conceded that the appeal process is being abused by unscrupulous individuals for the purpose of extorting money from developers, a practice known to be rampant. This type of 'grubby stuff', as he termed it, could only be eliminated if the developers themselves were to prepared to report cases of attempted extortion to the Garda, which none of them were prepared to do. He also noted with satisfaction that, although the board had determined 15,881 planning appeals over the previous five years, of which 61 were the subjects of judicial review proceedings, only four of its orders were quashed on legal grounds. The quite reasonable legislative provision requiring third-party objectors to make their views known in writing to a local authority before any appeal to An Bord Pleanála will be deemed valid may help to deter would-be Dick Turpins.

But the truth is that planners in Dublin, as elsewhere in the Republic, spend most of their time dealing with planning applications in the essentially reactive process of exercising development control. After sanctioning the employment of additional planners to cope with the huge, Celtic-Tiger driven workload, Noel Dempsey said in February 1999 that the aim was to ensure that 'we don't create a whole new set of mistakes' due to development proposals being inadequately examined by local authorities or by An Bord Pleanála. Exactly a year later, planning consultant Bill Nowlan complained that the planning system was being 'stretched to breaking point', with far too few qualified planners trying to cope with a 66% increase in the number of planning applications since 1995. Writing in the *Irish Times*, Nowlan cited the 'not unusual' case of one local authority, where three of the nineteen planning posts were vacant while ten were held by planners with less than six months' experience. It was these inexperienced planners who had to bear the burden of grappling with the Celtic Tiger and the increasingly onerous duties imposed by new legislation and regulations. As a result, he argued, many planning applications were either being put on the long finger or, in some instances, 'unnecessarily refused'. It was also clear that the annual output of twenty to twenty-five planners per annum from the Republic's only planning school at UCD 'is not even going to scratch the surface of the problem'. Indeed, a joint report by the Irish Planning Institute and the RIAI suggested that the current complement of three hundred qualified planners would need to be more than doubled to deliver the kind of environment in which people would be happy to live, work and play. 'The key question', said Niall Cussen, former President of the IPI, 'is whether the city and county managers really want a quality planning service and are prepared to invest in the human, technical and other resources necessary to deliver it.' Creating a more visionary process will mean setting up inter-disciplinary teams of architects, planners, engineers and other professionals to articulate three-dimensional area action plans for, say, higher-density housing or the redevelopment of 'brownfield' sites. Britain's Urban Task Force also came down strongly in favour of such a design-led approach. 'We must re-establish the quality of urban design and architecture as part of our everyday urban culture, as it is in the Netherlands, Spain and the towns and cities of many of our other European neighbours', its report says. 'This is not a question of regulation. We must use the skills and talents of good designers, rather than depend heavily on manuals and controls which have often failed to deliver a quality product. We also have to regard good design as adding to the long-term sustainability of the city.' This is already happening to some extent through IAPs, but planners in Ireland – most of whom are not architects – are still way behind their counterparts in the Netherlands, who were trained primarily to design new towns from scratch. Irish architects are not much better off. Most of those over thirty received little or no training in urban design at college. What they know of it has been gleaned on-the-job or from reading books, taking part in seminars and visiting other European cities. The greatest of these cities have all had their conjurers – Haussmann in Paris, Cerda in Barcelona, Pombal in Lisbon. But Dublin, too, already had its Wide Streets Commissioners a century before Napoleon III made Haussmann the Prefect of Paris.

The Urban Task Force's visits to Barcelona, Germany and the Netherlands also 'confirmed the importance of urban design in turning cities round', according to its chairman, Richard (Lord) Rogers. What the successful urban projects analysed in its final report had in common is that they were all based on implementing a spatial master plan to drive the development process and secure a high-quality design product. Members of the task force, drawn from a wide range of interests, also found that there was a willingness to use architectural and urban design competitions to test innovative approaches, such as the idea of car-free areas. 'Well-designed urban districts and neighbourhoods succeed because they recognise the primary importance of the public realm – the network of spaces between buildings that determine the layout, form and connectivity of the city', their report said. 'New urban developments – whether infill or new-build sites – should do the same, with a clear hierarchy between the major through-routes and the more subtle structure of local streets and alley-ways.' As for what constitutes 'public space', the task force suggested that it 'should be conceived as an outdoor room within a neighbourhood, somewhere to relax and enjoy the urban experience, a venue for a range of different activities, from outdoor eating to street entertainment, from sport and play areas to a venue for civic or political functions. And most importantly of all, as a place for walking or sitting-out.' This vision, and many others put forward by the task force, seemed to mark a Continental drift in thinking about urban life, which probably explains why Rogers was greeted so sceptically by the rather narrow-minded, insular English, whose planning guidelines barely mention the importance of high-quality design – an oversight which was repeated here in the Government's 1999 Planning Bill.

Yet Ireland is in the midst of the biggest building boom in its history, with over 40,000 new homes being turned out annually – 'equivalent to a Cork city every year, which is pretty astonishing', as Niall Cussen put it – and this trend is likely to continue for a decade. 'The basic problem is that we have no vision of urban expansion, or of the form Dublin will take', according to Tony Reddy, who is a member of the London-based Urban Design Group. 'With a whole planning cadre that doesn't believe in framework planning, the danger is that we will simply end up with more of the same.' Dick Gleeson agrees that the system has institutionalised a lot of local authority officials, though he himself has long since broken out of that mode, travelling in from Naas every day to the planning and design laboratory that Dublin has become, and making various interventions with the aim of 'knitting and darning the urban tissue', as he puts it. 'The city centre had contracted to a really small core, so one of the things we're trying to do is to spread it out to the east and the west. But we only have a limited amount of time to achieve this during the present economic boom and we're also running out of land. That's why sites like Spencer Dock are incredibly important in estab-lishing the quality of inter-connection with the city centre, which the scheme put forward for it failed to do.' By contrast, the framework plan for Temple Bar had turned it into 'a model of European significance', largely because there was a commitment to urban design from the very outset, with TBP recognising that good architecture could best be achieved in the context of this wider agenda.

An Taisce wants more area action plans that would set down a full range of quality standards, with an in-built mechanism to review their effectiveness over time. This approach, Michael Smith maintains, could have averted the spread of 'mega-pubs' in Temple Bar, something the original framework plan never envisaged. And through the 'development forum' approach he has pro-posed, it should be possible for all sectors to reach an agreed agenda. However, we will first have to 'liberate our ways of thinking about urban living', according to Seán O'Laoire. 'Where are we now? Where is Dublin going? How are things going to fit? Or are we going to be left in a situation where change itself has basi-cally made us incapable of dealing with the constructs we've made? We've only started to think about these things.' As another leading architect, Derek Tynan, puts it: 'We are surprised by the success we've had in rebuilding the city, in look-ing at the public realm and how we deal with it. But unlike other northern European cities, we haven't tackled what "edge" or "brownfield" actually mean. So what is the new agenda?' Is Dublin becoming a multi-centred city, as Brian Brennan would wish, with a 'string of pearls' along the M50 competing with the diamond at its core? If so, what form should its urban extension take, both on the periphery and in brownfield areas such as Docklands? 'What we need is an urban diagram of the type of city we want, such as the famous 'finger diagram' of Copenhagen, so that everyone – including the politicians and administrators – could buy into it', Brennan said. The same issue was raised by Brian Hogan, urbane architect of the Setanta Centre and many other buildings, as long ago as 1986 at the Dublin Crisis Conference. Fundamentally, as he said then, it was a question of 'establishing, in the broadest possible way, how the people of Dublin perceive their city – as a monster village, as the largest country town in Ireland, or as a great city with all the magic and variety you would expect to find in the capital of a cultured and progressive nation'.

Though the Dublin Crisis Conference agenda has since become part of official policy to a quite remarkable degree, that central question is still waiting for a coherent answer. In its absence, we cannot realistically expect to achieve the most crucial task facing us – to put a sustainable form on the metropolitan area.

All we have is a loose set of Strategic Planning Guidelines and the growth patterns they envisage or endorse. But can it be said that there is a consensus on this settlement strategy? Do Dubliners agree, for example, that the area administered by Dublin Corporation would account for only 30% of the GDA's overall population in 2011? Colm McCarthy is surely not alone in suggesting that such an outcome would be unconscionable because of the heavy costs it would impose on infrastructure, air pollution, and 'stranded assets' in depopulated built-up areas. At the RIAI/IPI *Stopping the Sprawl* conference in November 1999, he called for the guidelines to be revised with the aim of returning the population of Dublin city to what it was in 1971, and thus set limits to suburban sprawl. In the intervening years, as planner Ciarán Treacy pointed out, the average occupancy of a house has fallen from 4.3 people to 3.2, with even lower levels of 1.8 in the inner city and 1.7 in the old borough of Dun Laoghaire. 'It's a time-bomb', according to Brian Brennan. 'We have a situation where the inner city's population is now increasing slowly but surely, because of all the apartments being built there, as well as a development edge that's exploding. In the areas in between the two, the population is falling so dramatically that, in ten to fifteen years time, there's not going to be enough people to buy tins of beans in the local shops.' This is recognised by all four Dublin local authorities. In April 1999, they called for incentives for elderly people with larger houses to 'downsize' to mixed schemes of sheltered housing. But would the Department of Finance see the point in, say, abolishing stamp duty on the sale of family homes which have turned into empty nests, to encourage a much higher level of household mobility?

Colm McCarthy's almost heretical idea of sacrificing under-used parkland for housing would find even less favour with An Taisce, which regards parks as 'sacrosanct'. Even with a scientific survey to establish levels of use, it would be very difficult to sell the proposition that half of St Anne's Park should be built on to help reverse population decline in Raheny and Clontarf. In John Fitzgerald's view, it would be an unwinnable battle and, therefore, pointless. But he would also accept that the adjoining 'counties' are growing because of a perception among developers that there is very little land left in the city to build on. Even leaving aside the thorny issue of building on parkland, it is clear that the planners need to take a long hard look at what land is usable and what acreages of open space are really required to meet a community's recreational needs. But whether or not parkland is sacrificed, Dublin remains Europe's lowest density capital city. Those responsible for running it must recognise that the suburbs, established or recently built, are part of the *urban* area. Even if there are serious implications in taking this thesis on board, they cannot ignore the fact that a policy of consolidation makes sense. In the light of statistics on changing household formation and declining family sizes, why are we still building three- or four-bedroom houses which will be occupied for most of their lifecycle by two people? At the very least, we should be allowing developers to sub-divide semi-detached houses into maisonettes, so that there will be enough people living in an area to sustain existing shops, schools and churches. The consultants who drew up the Residential Density Guidelines also favoured the conversion of larger houses to multiple occupancy, as well as the redevelopment of lands currently in institutional use – by religious orders, for example – providing that some of their open-space character is retained. Our reluctance to think in such terms about the built-up area is as pusillanimous as the Corporation management's opposition to Jim Mitchell's proposal in 1991 that the City Plan should have it as a goal to double the inner city's population in ten years. They were against setting down such a specific target because, at the end of the day, they didn't believe in the place.

Yet urban density is what makes cities interesting. In Barcelona, most people live in seven- to ten-storey apartment buildings with awnings over their balconies to keep the sun out. The way people live in other European cities, whatever their climate, is quite different to Dublin. That's the urban culture we have still not embraced because of our predilection for suburban houses with front and back gardens. 'As we become a more urbanised society, we will accept a higher ratio of apartments to semi-detached houses, and land values are a catalyst here', according to Brian Hughes. 'The housing market is much more diverse, so the idea of building six hundred identical semi-detached houses is yesterday's news.' Many planners agree that the *sine qua non* of new suburban housing estates is a mix of houses, duplex-over-garden-level units, and apartment buildings. They also talk about numbers of homes rather than houses in any new scheme. This does not mean 'placing artificial pressures on people to accept housing which does not meet their basic desires in terms of space and privacy', as the Rogers report put it. Rather, the task is to 'provide homes which reflect private needs and aspirations, but not at the expense of broader social, economic and environmental imperatives'. Those imperatives imply that we must be much more careful about how we use land. Issues about where housing should be located and what form it should take would have to be decided in advance of public consultation on the details about how individual needs might be met. Otherwise, it's Fatima Mansions all over again. 'There's no point in going to people with nothing on the table', one planner said.

Urban renewal has popularised the idea of apartment living, at least for unattached. Is it possible to imagine couples with young children living in multi-storey buildings around the Grand Canal Docks or in Smithfield, with Stoneybatter just up the street? Are the middle classes, in particular, prepared to live in apartments and even to consider the possibility of raising a family in such circumstances, just as many others do in cities all across the Continent? 'The most sought-after set in fashion shoots, movies and TV commercials is an apartment in the city with a glittering skyline in the background. That's the image of urbanism today', said John Graby, the RIAI's director. Younger people returning from abroad have no difficulty in adapting to the apartment lifestyle, and given the seemingly insatiable demand for living space in the inner city, either to purchase or rent, it is clear that the first hurdle has been crossed. A measure of social integration has also been achieved, with many new private apartment buildings located cheek by jowl with Corporation flats, albeit often separated by high walls and cowls of razor wire. Yet it is in areas like City Quay, Ringsend and parts of the north inner city that families have been raised for generations in tightly knit working-class communities. 'They're as poor in Pearse House as anywhere, having suffered all the problems of unemployment after the disappearance of the docks, but the stability of the community is incredible, compared to those who were uplifted and transported to Clondalkin or Tallaght', marvels John Fitzgerald. 'One of the things we have to do is to provide more social housing down there, so that their kids have some chance of staying in the area.' But this will require a redefinition of social housing on the European model, with much more involvement by housing associations, as well as the use of urban, rather than suburban, building forms. Finland, for example, has a very healthy mix of private and social housing. Even within a single apartment block, there might be a millionaire living in a luxury penthouse and a single mother on social welfare in a more modest flat on the first floor. As a result, there are no squalid ghettos in Helsinki. Such an approach was also firmly endorsed by the Rogers report. 'In future, we must develop on the basis of a mix of tenures and income groups. Indeed, our objective should be that a visitor to an urban neighbourhood is unable to tell the difference between social and market housing.' It concluded that, 'Without a commitment to social integration, our towns and cities will fail.'

There is also a pressing need for radical reform of the private rented sector, again on European lines, to strike a better balance between the rights of landlords and tenants. Under existing legislation here, as Threshold has repeatedly pointed out, tenants have no security of tenure. All of the rights are on the landlord's side, which is particularly curious in a country with a bitter experience of landlordism. From year to year, with property prices rising, tenants are often faced with the grim choice of paying much more in rent for their flats or finding lower-quality accommodation elsewhere if they can't afford the latest hike. Lest tenants establish any rights, leases are normally for a maximum of twelve months, and they may be terminated at a month's notice. 'In Holland', as RTÉ reporter David Nally noted in the *Sunday Tribune*,* 'you can only be evicted if you've misbehaved or if the landlord's need for the flat is greater than yours. In Germany, you can oppose your eviction on the grounds that it would bring hardship to your family. In Denmark, rent rises are restricted by a formula which ties them to [the rate of] inflation. But in Ireland, you're out on your ear at 28 days notice and your rent can rise by as much as the landlord likes.' Nally, whose two-part series for *Prime Time* was hailed as one of the finest pieces of investigative journalism on RTÉ television for years, also highlighted the fact that over 50% of flats inspected by Dublin Corporation since 1997 failed to meet minimum standards. And despite 1996 legislation requiring landlords to register their proper-

---

* *Sunday Tribune*, 16th April 2000

ties, four-fifths of them have still not done so – a tactical non-compliance open-ly advocated by the Irish Property Owners Association. Yet many of the same landlords have been beneficiaries of the Section 23 tax incentive scheme, which was ostensibly designed to encourage the provision of 'moderately priced' rented accommodation. In fact, they are doubly subsidised. As well as getting the very lucrative tax incentive for ten years, they are enabled to charge high rents to ten-ants on low incomes by the dint of a State-funded rent support scheme. In April 1999, it was estimated that the Eastern Health Board was paying out £40 million a year – nearly £770,000 per week – in subsidies to tenants in the private rental sector, and the Dublin local authorities expressed concern about the inflationary effect of this scheme on rents in the city. Not surprisingly, a significant propor-tion of these State-subsidised tenants are immigrants living on social welfare in a country that has refused them the right to work. They have also been made to queue in one of the most dispiriting places in Dublin, beside a bleak ramp lead-ing to the car park of a grim early 1980s office block on Lower Mount Street. But even without the unexpected arrival of up to 6,000 refugees per year, an influx that brought lurking racism to the surface, nobody could deny that more social housing was sorely needed.

In other northern European countries, housing is generally designed to much higher architectural and environmental standards, mainly because of cli-matic considerations, with much better insulation and more generous spaces, including higher ceilings. But in this part of the world, as Rogers noted, the plan-ning system actually encourages the lowest level of floor-to-ceiling heights by fix-ing a height for a new apartment block and then allowing the developer to cram in as many floors as he can get away with under the minimum standards laid down by the Building Regulations. 'We're so caught up with rules and regulations that we have lost the humanity of what we're supposed to be about', according to James Horan, head of the DIT School of Architecture. 'They have replaced the tyranny of the Catholic Church in the 1960s. Other countries which haven't been infected by this virus have a better quality of life. That's the bottom line and it has to be addressed.' He was commenting on the marked reluctance of the DoE to amend the Building Regulations and embrace the concept of 'lifetime-adapt-able housing' to suit the changing needs of people over time. With average life expectancy in Ireland likely to increase from 76 to 82 years of age by 2020, there are going to be a lot more people with disabilities which impact on their ability to use their homes and the surrounding environment. By building in such features as level entrances, wider doors and corridors, low-level switches, easy-to-open doors and windows, accessible bathrooms and a hall-floor toilet, a new home can cater not only for people with disabilities but also small children, pregnant women and the elderly. But though Noel Dempsey has described lifetime-adapt-able housing as basic to the promotion of environmentally sustainable buildings, the DoE has been slow to 'go the whole hog' because it is perceived as being too expensive, as architect Fionnuala Rogerson complained at a conference on the issue in December 1999. She cited the example of a small housing scheme where the DoE had ordered the omission of ground-floor toilets from six houses on cost grounds, at a net saving of £1,650. Later, when it transpired that one of the tenants had a disabled child, a single ground-floor toilet was retrofitted in one of the houses at a cost of £3,700 – more than twice as much as the original 'saving'.

In order to be sustainable, new housing must be designed to respond to the interlinked concepts of 'long-life', 'loose-fit' and 'low-energy', according to Britain's Urban Task Force. 'Together, these ensure that buildings are built to last, by considering each structure as a long-term investment.' It pointed out that tried-and-tested technologies are available to design new buildings that require a minimum energy input, by using both passive and active solar systems, hydrogen fuel cells, and CHP for district heating. 'In the Millennium Communities' design brief for Allerton Bywater, near Leeds, targets included 50% reduction in energy consumption, 50% household waste reduction, 30% reduction in construction costs, 25% reduction in construction time, and 0% defects at handover', the task force said. Its report also favoured optimising off-sites construction of the basic housing shell, using the types of prefabrication commonly employed in Germany and the Netherlands to speed up the construction process and make housing more affordable. However, given the salutary experience of Ballymun and other 'low-cost housing' schemes, the DoE and even the Construction Industry Federation remain sceptical about the value of prefabrication. As with the issue of lifetime-adaptable housing, this could be re-examined if significantly more money was invested in housing research. Indeed, since the demise of An Foras Forbartha following the drastic budget cuts of 1987, this whole area has been shamefully neglected, especially by comparison with the record of the Northern Ireland Housing Executive. And, depressingly, there is no sign of real support from the building industry either for more energy-efficient or lifetime-adaptable homes. One school of thought even sees the best as the enemy of the good. 'Quality is important, but Zoe residential is better than no residential', according to John Mulcahy, of Jones Lang LaSalle. 'But I have this curious optimism: I don't think the built environment is forever, unless they start preserving it. If some extraordinary excrescence appears, it can be cleared away within your working life and replaced by something better. Look at what's been happening in Lower Mount Street, for example.'

But quality is one of the main planks of sustainability, and Dublin's planners know that they will have to 'lift our game in lots of ways within the next ten years', as Dick Gleeson put it. Or, to quote the Rogers report: 'We need a vision that will drive the urban renaissance. We believe that cities should be well-designed, be more compact and connected, and support a range of diverse uses, allowing people to live, work and enjoy themselves at close quarters, within a sustainable urban environment which is well-integrated with public transport and adaptable to change. Urban neighbourhoods must become places where people of all ages and circumstances want to live.' In Dublin, numerous studies are in various stages of completion, as the various authorities attempt to grapple with the enormity of this task of pointing the city in a more sustainable direction. 'All over the world, cities are attracting investment because of their culture and quality of life', as Gleeson observed. 'The real trick is really to stitch the economic product and cultural product into the context of a spatial, physical city.' But how can that be done when power, or responsibility, is so fractured and dispersed, with each agency pursuing its own agenda to a greater or lesser extent? What Dublin Corporation has been doing is tending to the city centre, particularly its public realm, as the 'living room' of the metropolitan area. The number of individual projects it has initiated in recent years is impressive, ranging from the revamping of Henry Street and Mary Street, to the millennium footbridge, two major bridges by Santiago Calatrava, the spectacular restoration of City Hall, the remaking of Smithfield with its sensational gas brazier-topped lighting masts, as surrealistic as the liner scene in Fellini's *Amarcord*, and the plan to rejuvenate O'Connell Street, with Ian Ritchie's 'Spike' as its centrepiece. As for those who argued that the Corporation should be building houses for the homeless rather than 'meaningless' monuments for the millennium, the City Manager's response was that 'any decent society should be able to do the two things – to build civic monuments for everyone to enjoy and to deal with the problems of the homeless. If we can't handle that, we shouldn't be here.' In April 1999, he also made this important pledge: 'I guarantee that you won't recognise the north inner city in five years time. Have a good hard look at it now, take photographs of it, and come back and hit me over the head if I'm not right.'

A number of projects planned by the Corporation have been strongly criticised – and not just the *Monument of Light*. Doubts have arisen about some of the dramatic interventions planned for the Liffey, notably the boardwalk along the river side of Bachelors Walk and Ormond Quay Lower. This seemed to be an inspired idea when it was first mooted by Jim Barrett because it offered the prospect of providing a promenade for leisurely strolls, removed from the heavy traffic on the quays. As designed by McGarry Ní Éanaigh and shown by a full-scale mock-up near O'Connell Bridge, the boardwalk was to be at exactly the same level as the footpath, rendering the quay wall rather meaningless and allowing its 1.1-metre rail to protrude above it. An Taisce described it as 'utilitarian' and 'gimmicky', saying that it could very soon start to look 'shabby and tawdry', especially with the addition of kiosks and stalls. Despite this criticism, the Government's Millennium Committee adopted the project, stumping up £2 million in funding, though the architects did revisit the height issue by lowering the timber deck. An Taisce also rowed in against Santiago Calatrava's parabolic-arched road bridge proposed to link Blackhall Place and Usher's Island, saying its 'highly assertive design' would create a 'serious visual barrier' in the line of the Liffey, cutting off one of its most important vistas – the first view of the quays, with the tower of St Paul's Church and the Four Courts dome providing a memorable visual composition for visitors arriving from the west. 'The huge curved arch with its suspended cables is an aggressive conceit which has no structural logic, as demonstrated by the manner in which it meets the piers at each end. This is a case where Calatrava is supplying one of his hallmark highly profiled bridge designs in a location and context for which it is inappropriate', it declared. Noel Dempsey accepted that the conservationists had a point, and ordered that the height of the arches should be reduced to minimise the bridge's visual impact. By contrast, there was no controversy over other Corporation projects, such as a pair of glazed bookstall pavilions for Grattan Bridge, designed by Gilroy McMahon, or a variety of schemes by younger architects for a series of SLOAP (Space Left Over After Planning) sites throughout the city, such as the junction between Castle Street and Christchurch Place. Splendid work has also been carried out by the parks department, reaching a pinnacle in Pearse Square, even if its superintendent, Gerry Barry, had serious doubts about the competition-winning scheme (by Peter Cody, a young Dublin architect) for a radical transformation of Wolfe Tone Park in front of the retained Victorian façade of Jervis Street Hospital.

Many other projects could be undertaken to enhance the city. Replacing the hideous Loop Line bridge with a more slimline structure, so that the Custom House could be seen clearly from O'Connell Bridge, is surely one of them. Although an ideas competition was jointly sponsored by the OPW, CIÉ and the

Replacing the hideous Loop Line bridge with a more slimline structure so that the Custom House could be seen clearly from O'Connell Bridge is surely one of the projects that would benefit the city. Just such a proposal *(below)*, designed by consultant engineers Kavanagh Mansfield, emerged from an ideas competition held in 1995.

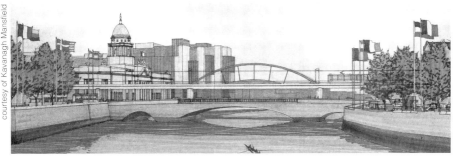

Institution of Engineers of Ireland in 1995, there was no commitment to build the very fine winning entry by Kavanagh Mansfield. The estimated £300,000 a year CIÉ earns from the awful advertising hoardings hanging from the iron and steel lattice work – which once proclaimed Dublin as 'The Home of the World's Biggest Pint' – shouldn't enter into it. Then, the Government's Millennium Committee balked at the idea of funding the replacement scheme, even though it could have been built for around £5 million – equivalent to the additional cost of incorporating a pivot in Calatrava's dramatic suspension bridge further downriver. (The late Tom Roche, founder of Roadstone and National Toll Roads plc, would have gone much further. Three weeks before he died in July 1999, he presented a proposal to get rid of the Loop Line altogether by putting it underground.) Serious consideration should also be given to building a barrage on the river, east of Matt Talbot Bridge. A sketch design by James Horan and Peter McGovern in 1997 showed an elegant structure, topped by a pedestrian walkway, lit at night, to link City Quay with the Custom House Docks, and incorporating lock gates on its southern side to provide for water traffic, an artificial island adjoining the lock, and a salmon run to allow fish to pass upstream. Its effect would be to transform the city stretch of the Liffey into a sheet of water, with low-slung Amsterdam-style water buses plying to and fro between the IFSC and Heuston Station. Gone forever would be the whiff at low tide and the sight of all the old tyres, prams, bicycles and supermarket trolleys stuck in the slimy mud. That vision of transforming the city's most memorable feature was put forward by Cornelius Sheehan as long ago as 1975, and never received a fair hearing. The

One of Dublin's most shameful wrongs: the triple-tiered steeple of St George's Church on Hardwicke Place which has been festooned with scaffolding for at least ten years. Money must be found to restore it and bring its bells back from Taney Church in Dundrum.

opposite

A weir, or barrage, for the Liffey designed in 1997 by James Horan and Peter McGovern. Topped by a pedestrian walkway, lit at night, it would link City Quay with the Custom House Docks, and incorporate lock gates on its southern side to provide for water traffic, an artificial island adjoining the lock, and a salmon run to allow fish to pass upstream.

least that the Corporation, in collaboration with the DDDA, could do is to commission a thorough study to examine the practicalities, and establish whether there is any ground for fears that a barrage might pose problems of flooding at basement level in the city centre or prevent the discharge of storm drains upstream. Perhaps there are also some people who would miss the action of a river, in its ebbs and flows, but ask anybody in Belfast about it. There are very few among them who do not believe that the Lagan Weir, especially lit up at night, is a marvellous addition to the city. Here again, however, the Millennium Committee wouldn't even dream of funding such a thing. Neither was it prepared to consider putting right one of Dublin's most shameful wrongs – the fact that St George's Church, one of the most important in the city, has had its distinctive neo-classical steeple festooned by scaffolding for at least ten years. Money has to be found somewhere to restore it and bring its bells back from Taney Church in Dundrum, where their installation was a local millennium project. South William Street, with its old Georgian houses and new street furniture, also has marvellous potential, if only the rag trade would relocate elsewhere, and so does the Markets area, if the wholesale trade and its associated juggernauts moved out to a site on the M50. Plans by the OPW to build a high-level pedestrian bridge over Conyngham Road to link the Phoenix Park with Edwin Lutyens' War Memorial Park at Islandbridge, vetoed in 1990 by Charlie Haughey because of his own knee-jerk nationalism, should also be dusted down and implemented. There might even be, as Jim Barrett has suggested, an upmarket restaurant on top of O'Connell Bridge House, with superb views over the capital's main street and the Liffey quays.

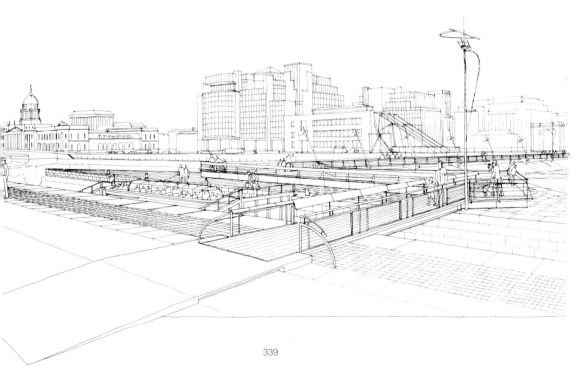

But even if all of these things and more were done, the Edge City will continue to expand, fed by blobs of housing, office parks, industrial estates and shopping/leisure centres. This is happening so rapidly that it's doubtful anyone can keep track of the output. Politicians are generally complacent about it all. Most of them still equate development, in a generic sense, with 'progress', in the way that word was used with great gusto in the 1960s. At the *Stopping the Sprawl* conference, Minister of State Dan Wallace took comfort from the fact that Ireland is not the only country experiencing the phenomenon of suburban sprawl, and the scale of our problems is smaller, or so he thought. What he did not seem to realise is that the scale of the challenge facing us is proportionately much larger, because we must meet the demand for housing and change the culture at the same time. The prospects are grim, according to Fergal MacCabe, principal author of the Residential Density Guidelines. 'We will go through a very bad period over the next couple of years as aspirations hit the wall of low design skills.' He also believes that rural Ireland 'is being wrecked on an unprecedented scale. It is absolutely out of control.' Yet the same county managers who see nothing wrong with bungalows in the countryside now face the task of 'densifying' the outer Leinster towns to cope with Dublin's elastic commuter belt. Even in Dun Laoghaire-Rathdown, over half of the land area is still 'rural', of which nearly 80% consists of upland or mountain terrain, and its county plan aims to protect the Dublin Mountains from 'visual and physical erosion by urban-generated development'. The unspoiled parts of Howth and the Liffey valley are protected by very rare Special Amenity Area Orders. But what is to be done to protect Bray Head, following An Bord Pleanála's controversial decision in March 1999 to approve a housing scheme on its lower slopes? And while Fingal is advising Meath on a vision for Navan (first freeman: Pierce Brosnan), developers are 'building acres and acres of rubbish around the town', as one planner complained.

Does anyone take the density guidelines seriously? Perhaps if they were presented with copious 'how to do it' illustrations, as in the Northern Ireland Housing Executive's excellent *Housing Layout and Design* manual, they might have more impact on the designers of new housing. As published in September 1999, the guidelines contain no images at all, apparently on the basis that good architects don't need such a steer, and professional hacks will continue producing rubbish, however pretty the pictures. The 1999 Planning Bill also gave no comfort to planners on the issue of design, with no provision of powers to refuse permission for new development purely on the basis of poor design. Yet quality design is regarded as essential to the achievement of higher-density housing. Without it, the resulting residential environment will fail, casting the whole idea in bad odour. This would be very good news indeed for councillors with an itch to rezone land at the behest of its owners. They are not remotely interested in more intensive development because it implies that they wouldn't actually need to zone so many fields. But even they must be aware that there is a requirement to review the various local authority development plans to ensure compliance with the GDA Strategic Planning Guidelines, which endorse higher densities, especially in urban centres and along public transport routes. That had not happened at the time of writing, and there was no indication that it would, especially with just one full-time official and a part-time assistant given responsibility to co-ordinate implementation of the SPGs. The only way Noel Dempsey can make the strategic planning and residential density guidelines stick is by giving them statutory force in the form of ministerial policy directives – subject, of course, to the SPGs being amended with the twin aims of consolidating the city and completing the 'new towns'. The bottom line, as the Rogers report noted, is that developing brownfield sites within the built-up area must become more attractive than building on greenfield sites around its edge. But do our councillors have the gumption to rescind land-rezoning decisions where these are blatantly in conflict with planning policy objectives?

And meanwhile, the housing crisis deepens, with more and more people – including those priced out of the private market – signing their names on the waiting lists. In April 1999, the four Dublin local authorities announced a common action programme aimed at relieving this crisis by providing sites for an additional 66,000 new homes. A strategic review of housing, agreed by the capital's chief administrative officers, bluntly conceded that affordable housing 'is simply not available' to many citizens. Though the number of households had risen by 50,000 over the previous ten years, they acknowledged that waiting lists for public housing were 'unacceptable', and the settlement programme for Travellers had proved to be 'painfully slow' because it was being 'resisted at every turn', particularly in middle-class areas. A multi-disciplinary and inter-authority Strategic Response Team was set up to monitor the 'fast-track' implementation of a massive water, sewerage and transport programme, as well as almost forty other initiatives. These included plans to augment the Ballymore Eustace water supply scheme to produce up to 573 million litres per day. The four authorities called on the Government to amend the planning laws to remove 'any possible legal doubt about the requirement to include a proportion of social housing in all new private housing developments' – something which was done, very controversially, under Part 5 of the 1999 Planning Bill. And though several major road schemes were also given priority, they warned that Dublin's future economic prosperity was 'wholly dependent' on proper transport, 'in particular, a revamped and radically improved public transport system'. This message was underlined exactly a year later, in April 2000, in a 'review and update' of the Strategic Planning Guidelines, now to be undertaken annually to ensure that they remain relevant. Compiled again by Brady Shipman Martin on behalf of the GDA's seven local authorities, this review does not depart from the broad thrust of the original set of guidelines in terms of the allocation of population growth, apart from revising it upwards. According to the consultants, the target population of 1.65 million in 2011 could be reached much earlier, in 2006, because the

GDA is growing more rapidly than envisaged just twelve months previously. Based on the assumption that the economy will continue to perform strongly, the review concludes that over 20,000 new housing units would be required every year to meet demand by 2006. 'The high level of population, household and employment growth now envisaged further strengthens the need to implement the strategy of consolidation, with its associated emphasis on public transport. This is the only way forward. The alternative would be unsustainable and unacceptable sprawl, accompanied by intolerable traffic congestion', the review bluntly declares. 'It is now especially important that a commitment be made to the location and character of the fixed elements of a public transport system, as these will determine the detailed location of future land uses and will reduce the pressure for sprawl.' The authors also stressed the need for local authorities in the area to review their own development plans, not only to take the SPGs on board but also to ensure that they would fall into line with a future 'mesh' of public transport services.

I t always came back to transport, like a stylus stuck in a groove. If the core of the 1999 Planning Bill was to promote sustainable development instead of just paying lip-service to the concept, the GDA would have to be shaped around a real, functioning and accessible public transport *system*. To help achieve this objective, the 1999 City Plan explicitly seeks to 're-balance' transportation in Dublin in favour of public transport by facilitating the development of Luas and the various quality bus corridors, 'giving the car its rightful place without allowing it to dominate the city'. This reflects what can only be described as a seismic shift in thinking about traffic, brought about by the Dublin Transportation Initiative. And though the DTI got all of its forecasts wrong, the process itself left an enduring legacy of enlightenment. Through it, the city's planners came to realise two essential truths – firstly, that the traffic problem could not be solved simply by throwing more roads at it, and secondly, that far too much of the public realm had been ceded to private cars, and the time had come to start reclaiming it. The motorised city, that crazy dream nursed by generations of road engineers, had turned into a nightmare which their successors have tried to shake off. In theory, of course, everyone could be conveyed into the city centre by car, but only at the cost of massive urban blight and the wholesale demolition of historic buildings. Thanks to the DTI process, not even the most self-serving lobbyist for private transport would make that case anymore. Indeed, it is ironic that the widening of almost every arterial road in the past to cater for cars is now being used as an opportunity to provide additional space for public transport.

'There's no doubt that the DTI brought about a huge sea change in thinking', says Tim Brick, Deputy City Engineer in charge of roads. 'We've made a conscious decision that we want the European model of a livable urban environment, rather than the American model of car dependency.' Having worked abroad for seventeen years, mainly in Africa and the Middle East, Cork-born Brick knows the score – 'a traffic jam in Lagos can last for up to eight hours', he recalls – and personally subscribes to the new agenda of restraint. Though their predecessors were seen as bogeymen, the city's current cadre of transport planners are probably ahead of the populace in their acceptance of the need for harsh measures. Many Dublin drivers, caught up as they are in the adolescent phase of car ownership, have not thought things through quite as thoroughly, and may, therefore, still subscribe to the old agenda of 'predict and provide'. Unlike their counterparts in other European countries, most of them have not yet made a distinction between car ownership and use. They seem to believe that they have an automatic right to use their cars for any journey, however short, even when alternatives are available. As part of an EU-wide opinion survey in 1999, Forfás, the State's industrial policy agency, asked people what they considered to be the most useful invention of the 20th century. Top of the list here was not television, hi-fi stereos, CDs, microwave ovens, washing machines, passenger jets, or even mobile phones, but the car. We still believe its promise. This was confirmed by another survey in January 2000 which found that Irish Internet surfers 'prefer cars to sex', as a *Sunday Tribune* headline put it. So how can the car, that ultimate symbol of the Me Generation, be tamed to make transport in Dublin and other urban areas more manageable? How can we, wild and untameable people that we are, learn to accept a bit of regimentation, in the public interest? The answer to both is with difficulty and pain, particularly over the next five years. For unless a large number of Dubliners change their current habits, the 'multi-centred city' will quite literally be strangled by its traffic.

   Not even the most avid motorist could argue that the present situation works or, with any credibility, that the chaos on the streets can be sorted out by building more and more roads, like Ben Elton's demented transport minister. Yet there are solutions that work which have been implemented elsewhere. What we need to do is to learn from them. With travel demand in Ireland increasing at 7% per annum, and car ownership levels rising relentlessly, we simply cannot go on the way we're going. 'We should be moving into the adult phase now', John Henry says, adding that every 1% of commuters leaving their cars at home would save an estimated £25 million a year in congestion costs. Astonishingly, official figures show that one quarter of all journeys during the morning peak are less than a mile, many of them school-runs. Even more telling is the fact that nearly half of all journeys within three miles are undertaken by car. That's a measure of how devoted we are to the cult of personal mobility, whatever about the congestion it creates. What the figures suggest is that many Dubliners are within walking or cycling distance of their destinations. But even though they could easily do so, most commuters living in such inner suburbs as Glasnevin or Rathmines wouldn't stop using their cars. The only bikes some of them are likely to come in contact with are the stationary ones in a gym. In time, some of them may abandon their cars for mopeds, as many commuters are already doing, to get about town.

Is the writing on the wall for cars in the city? Almost two-thirds of motorists in Strasbourg said they believed that cars in towns are 'a thing of the past' in response to a 1998 survey. Its mayor, Roland Ries, agreed: 'The city does not belong to the car. Cyclists and pedestrians have more right to use the city.' Calling for political courage to deal with traffic, he said it was up to politicians to spell out what's at stake if unlimited car use continues and to propose alternative solutions. Otherwise, he warned, 'our cities will deteriorate into formless heaps' with ever-expanding sprawl. The Rogers report also concluded that urban planners need to reclaim the potential of the street to meet many different community needs rather than 'simply providing a conduit for motor vehicles', like Ranelagh, Stoneybatter, or the main streets of any number of other 'urban villages' in Dublin. It called for more public investment in walking, cycling and public transport, as well as reductions in the amount of land we give over to the car and in the distances we travel 'by consolidating development within a compact urban form, close to existing and new travel interchanges'. The task force also recommended that urban transport plans should include 'explicit targets for reducing car journeys and increasing year on year the proportion of trips made on foot, bicycle and by public transport'. Pierre Laconte, adviser to the International Union of Public Transport (UITP), strongly agrees that urban areas must be planned primarily for people, 'allocating to the motor car only the space which is compatible with a good quality of life' while taking decisive steps to upgrade public transport. A UITP opinion poll in 1998, involving a thousand citizens in each EU member state, found that 83% on average agreed that public transport should receive preferential treatment over private cars, while 73% would favour a similar priority for cyclists. Instructively, almost half of the Irish respondents said traffic management here was 'too favourable to cars', with 15% saying the opposite, while four out of five agreed that access to town centres should be 'severely restricted'. Commenting on the results, the EU Commission's cycling handbook said that politicians were 'more timorous' on these issues than anyone else, 'perhaps because they confuse their own mobility requirements with those of the average citizen'.

The Government's decision in May 1998 to force Luas underground between St Stephen's Green and Broadstone was perhaps the classic example of political timorousness. It was also made by ministers who are accustomed to being conveyed around the place in sleek black Mercs, on occasion travelling in convoy to the provinces to give the pretence that this had something to do with devolution. There was also something ludicrous about the notion of politicians gathered around a table redesigning Luas just hours before their shameful decision was announced. In opting to 'go under', they sabotaged the most important artery of the light rail project in terms of its civilising impact on the public realm through Dawson Street, Nassau Street, Lower Grafton Street, College Green, Westmoreland Street and O'Connell Bridge. Fears about the disruptive effects of constructing this crucial stretch were, and still are, irrational. Other cities have endured the pain with no regrets. Why is Dublin so different? It should also be borne in mind that the Calatrava bridges for Macken Street and Blackhall Place are designed to provide a relief route for city-centre traffic, and that the Corporation intends to go ahead with 'very painful' plans to ban the left turn from Dawson Street into Nassau Street, other than for buses and taxis, to reduce the volume of cars in O'Connell Street. This measure would also directly facilitate on-street light rail by removing much of the traffic along its originally planned route. With such a congenial operating environment in prospect, the proposal to put an essentially surface transit system underground is deeply flawed. The huge additional cost, with no return in passenger capacity, would be so utterly excessive and disproportionate as to make it barking mad.

Given that the Government has already allocated £300 million to dig a horizontal hole in the ground, it is imperative that the money is spent on the right hole – and the only one that seems to make sense is for an underground line between Spencer Dock and Heuston Station, connecting up with the Phoenix Park tunnel and the largely disused line looping around the north inner city. Not only does this proposal offer a high-capacity metro in the city centre, but it would also link up with every arterial public transport route, both existing and planned. This would give Dublin a public transport *system*, making it possible for most people to get around the place without having to use their cars. As in other European cities, bus routes would have to be reorganised to interface effectively with rail stations, producing what Dr Roy Johnston has called 'an easily read mesh-like map', on which the nodes would coincide with the city's principal urban villages. 'Until such a system exists, of a quality such as to enable appointments to be kept anywhere in the city, remote commuters will feel they have to bring their vehicles in, and we will have more stress and gridlock', he believes. Just as most people know London by a diagrammatic representation – the brilliantly designed Underground map – the updated version of an *Irish Times* diagram [see page 135] shows how Dublin's public transport system could be developed, with a Circle Line as the lynchpin of a regional railway network. It also presents a vision of the type of city that is now within our grasp, if only we had the political will to achieve it.

For the Circle Line works not just in transportation terms, but also in terms of urban development. Along with the planned Luas line linking Heuston and Connolly stations, it would consolidate the core of Dublin, drawing the whole western sector of the inner city into an 'elongated' central area by mitigating the south-easterly drift which has been under way since the halcyon days of the Pembroke Estate. Everything of importance now lurking in backwaters, such as the National Museum at Collins Barracks and the Museum of Modern Art at the Royal Hospital in Kilmainham, would suddenly become accessible by high-quality public transport. Future communities could also be built around nodes in the city centre, and, more particularly, along the routes of new rail links to Dublin Airport and Navan. Once developers realise where everything is going, they will move in that direction. That's why it is of the utmost importance for the Government to commit itself to a city-centre metro line, and spell out clearly, before the end of 2000, what route it and the other new lines will follow, thereby enabling sensible land-use planning to proceed. Such a statement would show that the politicians recognise that transportation links are the spines around which cities have grown historically and will grow in the future. As long ago as the 1890s, Berlin's first step in developing Charlottenburg was to install a U-bahn line, and there are photographs showing stations already open while this fashionable district was being developed for *belle époque* apartment blocks. In other countries, rural villages of 3,000 souls have grown into towns with a population of 20,000-plus within five years because of the provision of a rail link. Navan, for example, could end up with a population of up to 100,000 if Meath County Manager Joe Horan has his way, and the new line could also be routed to serve other expanding areas such as Blanchardstown, Mulhuddart and Clonee – site of the huge IBM plant – as well as Ashbourne and Dunshaughlin. The key to it all is that it should be public sector-led, rather than developer-led, probably through a PPP arrangement. According to the City Manager, the most efficient way of procuring the Circle Line and airport rail link would be through a joint venture involving CIÉ, Dublin Corporation and private sector interests, such as the Japanese company, Mitsui. Whatever about the politicians, at least he recognises that improved accessibility to the city centre by *public transport* is essential to maintaining its economic vitality in the face of competition from burgeoning Edge City development along the M50. 'If we don't deal with the traffic, we're in deep trouble', Fitzgerald said in September 1999.

Some transport planners may be under the illusion that they have all the solutions and computer models they need to deal with it. However, as Gerd-Axel Ahrens, senator in charge of planning in Bremen, told a conference in Dublin on sustainable urban travel in December 1999, 'the only problem is that people do not act, think and function like our models.' Chantal Duchene, director of infrastructure and transportation for Île de France, put it another way. The challenge presented by the urban mobility plan not only involved 'managing a complex system by pulling different levers', she said. People's behaviour also needed to be changed. 'To do so, we must provide convincing explanations in order to resolve conflicts between individual and public interest. We live in a democracy and the best solutions cannot be imposed, they must be accepted.' She was heartened, however, by changes in public opinion, which indicated that people in the Paris region 'are increasingly aware that there is a problem and it is therefore necessary to act'. In Dublin's case, as Tim Brick sees it, 'we have to make up our minds the kind of city we want – not the planners, the transport engineers or the architects, but the people themselves. Do they want the sustainable European model or the unsustainable American model of urban development? Because if they say they want the American model, they'll get it whether we like it or not.' And with the pattern of development so dispersed that parts of the metropolitan area are very difficult to serve by public transport, Dublin may already be unwittingly on the way to a hybrid of the standard US-style doughnut.

We have not yet reached the point of no return. The city can still be consolidated, if the Government is prepared to bite the bullet and double the level of investment proposed in the NDP to put in the calibre of public transport needed by a modern European capital. Otherwise, haphazard sprawl will continue, condemning thousands of people to a life of long-distance commuting by car. Sooner or later, however, it will dawn on them that the incoherent development of the metropolitan area and its hinterland is literally out of control. 'The scenario we're facing is genuinely frightening', in the words of one senior official. 'Huge cracks were already appearing in the Strategic Planning Guidelines within months of their publication, as exemplified by the incredible density of new office blocks in out-of-town locations such as Sandyford Industrial Estate. And then, there's all the new housing estates springing up everywhere. If things go on as they are, what we'll end up with is a Los Angeles-style conurbation stretching from Drogheda to Wicklow, but without the Los Angeles-style roads to serve it. We will have no way of getting around unless there is a huge quantum leap in the quality and range of public transport.'

The scale of that quantum leap was outlined by the DTO's director, John Henry, and its chairman, Conor McCarthy, to the Cabinet sub-committee on infrastructure in April 2000. They were reporting to the Taoiseach and other ministers on the outcome of the DTO's review of the original (1994) DTI strategy, which concluded that an immense amount of new 'hardware' would be required to provide Dublin with a proper public transport system. Taking a longer view to 2016, and based on optimistic assumptions that the economy would remain buoyant, the DTO put forward the most ambitious plan ever for transport in the capital, carrying a price tag of £8 billion. The plan goes beyond anything previously envisaged, with the aim of creating a 'mesh' of public transport services that would make it possible for anyone in the built-up area to gain access to any other part of the city without having to rely on using a private car. It endorses proposals in the CIÉ-commissioned Greater Dublin Strategic Rail Review for an east-west underground line in the city centre from Spencer Dock to Heuston Station, via St Stephen's Green, as well as metro lines serving Sandyford, Kimmage and Dublin Airport, a surface light rail line running in via Clanbrassil Street to Broadstone, Drumcondra and Ballymun, and a second orbital Luas line, outside the M50 C-ring, to serve Tallaght, Lucan-Clondalkin, Blanchardstown and Swords. Suburban rail services to Kildare and Maynooth would also be electrified under the DTO plan to form a loop in the inner city, running underground between Spencer Dock and Heuston, with intermediate stops at East Wall Junction and Westland Row (both connecting with the DART), St Stephen's

Green (connecting with the Sandyford-Airport line), and somewhere in the vicinity of St Patrick's Cathedral. All of these projects could be installed incrementally over the plan period, and in the meantime the emphasis would be on completing the remaining QBCs, reorganising the Dublin Bus network to provide more orbital services, and proceeding with the Luas project, subject to one caveat. In the longer term, the DTO wants the Sandyford line upgraded to a metro, running underground from Ranelagh to Broadstone and then onwards to Dublin Airport, using the old Midland railway line to Liffey Junction. A second metro is proposed to serve Tallaght, via Greenhills, Kimmage and Harold's Cross, joining with the Sandyford line beneath St Stephen's Green and then running north to Broadstone with intermediate stations at Nassau Street, Tara Street and Bolton Street.

Critics of the latest strategy say it is the equivalent in public transport terms of the 'predict and provide' philosophy which has driven the roads programme in Ireland and elsewhere. It is also based on the assumption that funding will present little or no problem. 'This plan is engineer-driven', one source said, adding that there was a danger in producing 'an aspirational list of metro lines going everywhere' and a fear that such an 'all or nothing' approach might fail in the event of an economic downturn. It was also too long-term, he believed. 'Saying that things will be sorted out in 2016 is all very well, but what about now? In the short-term, it's all about buses. But we also need to be thinking about road-pricing and imposing charges on workplace car parking.' The DTO plan could also be criticised for its failure to adopt the Circle Line idea, apparently because the computer modelling carried out by its in-house authors suggested that there would not be sufficient demand to warrant bringing the Phoenix Park tunnel back into use for frequent rail services. At the time of writing, it was unclear whether the Government would run with a PPP involving the Mitsui-Unified Proposal group, now formalised as a joint venture with its sights firmly focused on the potentially lucrative Sandyford-Dublin Airport line.

The idea of investing as much as £8 billion on public transport in Dublin would have been unimaginable in 1994 when the DTI unveiled what might, in retrospect, be regarded as a modest package for a relatively poor country. It was circumscribed by what one senior official termed the 'piggybank approach'. There was a limited pot of money available, so those involved in the DTI process asked what they could get for it, instead of identifying what the city needed, pricing the various elements, and then finding the funds to pay for it all. In that context, Fitzgerald is bemused by economists who have taken to blaming the planners for Dublin's huge transport infrastructure deficit. 'Even five years ago, there wasn't an economist who came remotely near forecasting the growth and prosperity we're now experiencing. And if we had planned for that, we would have been locked up for wasting public money.' At the end of the 1980s, it must be remembered, the State was nearly bankrupt. Public sector borrowing, much of it for current spending, accounted for up to 13% of GNP and Ireland was in danger of losing its international credit rating. The Fianna Fáil minority Government led by Charlie Haughey adopted a slash-and-burn strategy to curtail public spending, with every department's estimate pored over in minute detail to identify cuts. But things could not be more different today, with unexpected tax revenue windfalls of £800 million in 1998 and £1 billion in 1999 – plus massive receipts from the sale of such State assets as Cablelink (£535 million) and Telecom Éireann (£4.8 billion). Such an embarrassment of riches might even persuade us to abandon the debilitating notion that nothing will happen or, worse still, that nothing *can* happen, because of systemic inertia.

But the £1.58 billion allocated for public transport in Dublin under the National Development Plan falls well short of what the Government can now afford – with or without the use of PPPs to deliver projects on time and within budget. Fortified by the huge resources at our disposal, we are now in a position 'to decide what we want and go out tomorrow and pay for it', as Bertie Ahern himself has said, and that should include a public transport system so that most people in the metropolitan area would be able to access some element of it within 500 metres of where they live, or by driving to the nearest park-and-ride site. 'Public transport is the biggest item on the agenda and needs to be relentlessly pursued', according to City Planning Officer Pat McDonnell. 'Because once we have a proper system in place, it will attract more and more users.' Indeed, increasing levels of traffic congestion might in itself help to convince the electorate, and its political representatives, that serious money must be spent on transportation in Dublin. Cracking down on ad lib car-parking is another squeeze that works. A recent study in Bristol found that while currently available measures could reduce car trips to the centre by 21% at most, comprehensive parking controls could achieve a reduction of 77%. That's one reason why the Corporation is now insisting on traffic impact studies for all major developments, egged on by the DTO, whose views are increasingly being taken into account in adjudicating on major planning applications and appeals. 'The way forward is a mix of everything', says Tim Brick. 'The Eastern Bypass is one of a dozen things that need to be done. We need a quantum leap in the range and quality of public transport, with links across the C-ring to reduce long-distance car commuting, and we should also be thinking about "demand management", the euphemism for road pricing. Unfortunately, it's easier to put roads in place simply because we're practised at it and know how to do it. But everyone has to raise their sights and their ambitions, because otherwise Dublin is going to become an extremely unpleasant place. It will take a leap of courage and faith to take that extra step. But we have already changed the culture and philosophy and, with that, should come the will and the finance to implement it. We're no longer poor little Ireland. If we show a bit of courage, we will get the city we want.'

Judging by their track record, however, it may take some time to get this message through to the ostrich-like Department of Finance and its stubbornly individualistic political head, Charlie McCreevy, master of the solo run. Both the

Department and the Minister have flunked it on the issue of green taxation, even where only a marginal change would produce environmentally beneficial results. Apart from the BIK concession to employees in receipt of free public transport passes, and a slight tweaking of motor taxation to discriminate in favour of smaller, more fuel-efficient cars, they have done nothing. What is their frame of reference for refusing to vary excise duty or VAT on different fuels to encourage a changeover from dirty diesel oil to cleaner LPG? Have they made any link at all between such an alteration and Ireland's commitments under the 1997 Kyoto Protocol or the increasingly onerous requirements of EU directives on air pollution? Are they even aware of the progressive taxation measures introduced elsewhere, even in the UK? In Oslo, for example, drivers of electric cars pay no road tax, VAT or excise duty, as well as being exempt from tolls and entitled to receive subsidised electricity to recharge their batteries. Is there a snowball's chance in hell of persuading the mandarins of Merrion Street to do anything like this? And yet, the issue is confronting them. Ford, Fiat and Nissan are among the world's major motor manufacturers already producing electric cars and marketing them as 'easy to park, very nippy over short stretches and virtually noiseless'.

In twenty years time, or even less, many cars are likely to be running on batteries, flywheels or hydrogen fuel cells, rather than petrol or diesel engines. They will also be much less polluting, with fuel cells, for example, emitting only water vapour and carbon dioxide. At present, however, the overwhelming prevalence in Dublin of vehicles burning fossil fuels threatens to breach the EU guide level for benzene, a known carcinogenic, while nitrogen dioxide pollution in the city centre is also hovering close to the limits. Emissions from the transport sector are expected to account for over half of the increase in Ireland's greenhouse gas emissions by 2010, with car numbers estimated to increase by 25% to 1.5 million, and trucks by about 44% to more than 250,000. If they were all powered by batteries, solar panels or fuel cells, damaging emissions could be reduced close to zero. California's decision that 10% of new car sales in 2003 – about 100,000 cars

caricature by Martyn Turner / Irish Times

Charlie McCreevy, stubbornly individualistic political head of the Department of Finance and master of the solo run. Both he and his department have flunked it on the issue of green taxation, even where only a marginal change would produce environmentally beneficial results.

Frank McDonald

Self-sufficiency. Torbjorn Ryden, manager of the Bromma sewage-treatment plant in Stockholm, fills his petrol tank with bio-gas from the sewage works. Bio-gas, mainly methane recovered from the treatment process, now fuels nearly one-quarter of Stockholm's municipal fleet of 1,500 vehicles.

– must be 'zero emission vehicles' is expected to speed up technological progress in this area, thus making such cars more competitive. Biogas from sewage treatment plants already fuels more than 22% of Stockholm's municipal fleet of 1,500 vehicles, while Copenhagen reserves special parking spaces for electric vehicles, with free battery-charging facilities. Would it ever occur to Charlie McCreevy to provide such tax incentives for ZEVs, as they are called in the trade, or to support even more radical concepts such as car-sharing? This seemingly outlandish idea has been taken up in 250 European cities and towns through car-sharing clubs, all of which give their members the benefit of being able to use a car whenever they need to without having to bear the burdens of owning one in terms of insurance, depreciation, road tax, loan repayments and the problem of finding a parking space. Munich's StadtAuto club, for example, has 1,700 members and a fleet of 64 vehicles, distributed around 32 reserved parking locations in the city, Every member has a personal key or smart card and a booklet showing the cars available, and getting access to them is 'as easy as booking a tennis court', according to European Car Sharing, a Hamburg-based umbrella group promoting the initiative. Essentially a co-operative car-rental scheme, it is aimed at people living in inner city areas, where parking is at a premium, who might want a car for heavy shopping, excursions to the countryside, or whatever. Europe-wide, ECS forecasts 350,000 car-sharers by 2003, on current trends. But not in Dublin.

A pilot scheme, started by Co Clare-based transport consultant Graham Light-foot in 1997 had to be scrapped after the first year because no Irish company would insure it. Lessons from abroad also show that car-sharing schemes need to be very well run, and are more likely to succeed where environmental conscious-ness is high.

Although the development of alternatives to fossil fuels will reduce the pollution caused by traffic, it will do nothing to relieve the problem of conges-tion. Whatever happens, this can only get worse, because with increasing pros-perity there will be a lot more cars, and people will 'continue to get orgasmic about them', as one traffic expert put it. The hurdle we must cross is to learn to make the distinction between car ownership and car use, just like many of our fellow Europeans. 'We are now in situation where we have to look at travel man-agement', according to John Henry. 'Motorists in Dublin have grown to accept a level of congestion greater than what prevails in most other European cities. Even with improved public transport, we would be doing well to hold congestion at the present level, rather than let it get worse and worse.' Thus, in addition to throw-ing vast sums of money at public transport, the authorities will need to develop much more sophisticated 'travel management' measures, including electronic congestion tolls, to get people out of their cars. Prof Phil Goodwin, the British government's transport policy adviser, believes that there is an urgent need to cre-ate safe, attractive streets for children to walk or cycle to school, to reinvent the old custom of home delivery of shopping, and to rediscover the role of land-use planning to reduce journey distances. Developing new residential areas at much higher densities with a more varied range of housing types in close proximity to public transport nodes is another imperative. Dublin Corporation's action plan for Pelletstown, off the Navan Road, shows the way in proposing to develop an urban neighbourhood on the city's last piece of farmland. 'We also need a new model for living accommodation linked to working space', in James Horan's view. 'Working from home is no longer unusual, but a lot of people don't like the concept of working and living in the same place. They need to put on their coat and go somewhere, so some new model is needed to cater for them.'

Such 'teleworking' has been made possible by the revolutionary develop-ments in computer and communications technology during the last decade of the 20th century, notably personal computers, modems, e-mail and the Internet. Nobody can say with any certainty at this stage what the long-term impact of the Internet is going to be, except that it will probably be enormous. In late-1999, it was estimated that on-line shopping would account for $200 billion worth of retail sales in the US alone within five years. This anticipated exponential growth in e-commerce sent shivers down the spines of shopping centre developers and owners – the 'bricks and mortar brigade', as they are known in cyberspace – because it raised the spectre that the value of their investments may be under-mined. Some of them take comfort from the belief that, whatever about clothes or furniture, people will want to *feel* an apple, onion or red pepper, while others foresee a future for shopping centres as 'resorts', with hotels catering for those who want to shop till they drop. But it is surely a straw in the wind that Wal-Mart, America's biggest retailer, has responded to the threat by decreeing that the design of its huge outlets should be flexible enough to allow them to be converted into delivery depots to cater for on-line shopping in twenty years time. Who can say where e-commerce is going to be then? Not much more than twenty years ago, in January 1979, while covering the Betelgeuse disaster in Bantry Bay, I recall dictating my story for the *Irish Times* to a copy-taker in Dublin from a magneto 'wind-up' telephone in a public call box on the town's main street. They didn't even have subscriber trunk dialling in west Cork in those days. Mobile phones, voice mail, e-mail, 'sat-packs', and the other gadgetry we now take for granted were all in the future.

There is also the very real danger that we are losing the run of ourselves. In January 2000, even as the GAA was redeveloping Croke Park as a modern 80,000-seater stadium and the Football Association of Ireland was proceeding with plans for its own stadium at City West, off the Naas Road, Bertie Ahern unveiled his grandiose vision of a national stadium and 'sports campus' at Abbotstown, off the M50. 'The thought that Dublin, which plays host to no major professional football teams of any kind, is to have three spanking new stadiums represents an extravaganza of wasted resources almost as criminal as the culture of neglect which for the longest time made the capital a dowdy backwater of the sporting world', wrote Tom Humphries in the *Irish Times*. Bernard O'Byrne, the FAI's chief executive, who had been a member of the steering committee for the Taoiseach's 'Abbotstown Albatross' project, otherwise known as the 'Bertie Bowl', made it clear that it would be going ahead with its own 45,000-seater Eircom Park scheme to provide Irish soccer with an 'emotional home' – at a cost of £65 million – and might make use of the £168 million national stadium every seven years or so. (The name was a pay-off for Eircom, which pledged £11 million to the project.) 'Bernard and Bertie will both be building stadiums just to spite each other. Bertie has deeper pockets and more powerful friends, however', Humphries commented, forecasting that Eircom Park, which would need a two-kilometre Luas extension to serve it, 'could be just one recession away from the white elephant's graveyard'. Even the choice of Davy Hickey Properties' CityWest business park was curious, as there was still an extant planning permission for another stadium at nearby Neilstown – a phantom of Owen O'Callaghan's interest in nailing down the Liffey Valley shopping centre at Quarryvale – and Dunloe Ewart plc had offered to present the FAI with an alternative thirty-acre site at Clonburris, right beside the Dublin-Cork railway line, provided this did not clash with the Government's plans, which, of course, it did. The Air Corps was also concerned that the huge structure of Eircom Park would compromise air navigation safety at Baldonnel, doubly so if it was to be developed as a commercial airport.

The GAA, bolstered by Ahern's earlier gifts totalling £25 million, had a head-start over the other two proposed stadiums because its £140 million rede-

concept design courtesy of Scott Tallon Walker

The 'Bertie Bowl' at Abbotstown, off the M50. It was almost as if the 'Celtic Tiger' was roaring so loud that it had to be pacified by an enormously extravagant gesture, with a price tag in excess of £300 million.

To its enormous credit, the GAA transcended its dismal record of breeze block and corrugated iron to commission Gilroy McMahon to design a marvellous amphitheatre for national games.

John Searle / courtesy of Gandon Archive

velopment of Croke Park was well under way. Back in 1992, the association had decided to stay in Jones's Road not only because it was hallowed ground, but also because it was persuaded that an in-town location was preferable to moving out to a site along the M50. To its enormous credit, the GAA transcended its dismal record of breeze block and corrugated iron to commission Des McMahon, of Gilroy McMahon Architects, to design a marvellous amphitheatre for the national games. One of McMahon's many selling points was that he had played minor football for Tyrone. Though it was fought all the way by local residents who felt ill-used by the Croke Park authorities over the years, the emerging result has more than vindicated their decision, even though it entails, by order of An Bord Pleanála in May 1999, losing the traditional open terraces of Hill 16 in the interests of public safety. The new stadium, built in four or five phases, was also a metaphor for changes in the GAA itself, as it started shedding the shackles of its *Faith of Our Fathers* heritage.

But instead of doing the sensible thing by requesting the GAA to host rugby and soccer internationals at Croke Park, the Taoiseach ran with Abbotstown plan, giving another personal endorsement to the Edge City. This followed a consultancy study, led by Price Waterhouse Coopers, which identified a site of 230 acres in State ownership (through the Department of Agriculture) as the most suitable location for Sports Campus Ireland, as the £281 million project is called. Apart from Stadium Ireland, which would be flexible enough to cater for rugby, soccer and Gaelic games as well as athletics, it is to include an indoor sports arena seating 15,000, a number of multi-purpose halls, nice new offices for various sporting bodies, a 50-metre swimming pool, parking space for 8,500 cars – most of them across the M50 on the former Dunsink dump – and a new railway station on the Sligo line. In concept, it was not unlike the ill-fated Sonas Centre for the Phoenix Park racecourse site, without its hotel and casino elements. Henry J Lyons & Partners had won the commission to provide architectural advice for the feasibility study, but they stepped down at the FAI's insistence because they were already designing Eircom Park, so the baton was passed to Scott Tallon Walker. Just over 150 acres of the Abbotstown site, could be sold off for development, raising around £50 million, and another £50 million was pledged by JP McManus, the rich, publicity-shy, Cork-born gambler, businessman and tax exile. But taxpayers would still have to pick up a tab of at least £181 million to realise Ahern's vision of providing a debt-free stadium from day one in 2005, even with the IRFU as its only major anchor. (The rugby authorities had also been toying with the idea of building a new stadium near Newlands Cross, where writer Katherine Tynan's home, White Hall, once stood in the fields, but dropped this ball in favour of running with the Government's plan.)

It was almost as if the 'Celtic Tiger' was roaring so loud that it had to be pacified by an enormously extravagant gesture. So this was what the Taoiseach meant when he said that we could now 'decide what we want and go out tomorrow and pay for it'. How Charlie McCreevy went along with it was anybody's guess. Some weeks later, it transpired that the entire agricultural establishment at Abbotstown, including the mad cow disease laboratory, was to be transferred to a State-owned farm in McCreevy's Kildare constituency, and its facilities replicated there at an estimated cost of £60 million. Everything on the site, even a noted mid-1980s building by John Tuomey and another £5 million project then under construction, is likely to be demolished to make way for Bertie Ahern's *grand projet*. All that was available on the day of the launch was a site plan and a computer-generated bird's-eye view of what the stadium might look like. Project architects had yet to be appointed, and the trust set up to oversee its implementation, with Paddy Teahon at the helm, still faced the daunting task of taking the scheme through the planning process. That night, the Minister for Sport, Jim McDaid, delivered an apt malapropism on RTÉ's *Prime Time*: 'Every other banana republic in the world has their (sic) own national stadium', the hapless Donegal doctor declared. The proposed behemoth would be 'a statement about the Irish people in the 21st century', though he frankly admitted that nobody could say what sport would be like in ten, fifteen or twenty years time. But even McDaid must have known that the US, which pioneered greenfield site stadiums in the 1970s, has reverted to downtown developments with proven spin-offs for urban regeneration in cities such as Baltimore, Cleveland and San Francisco. What will Ireland-Scotland rugby internationals be like in future if the IRFU sells off its valuable piece of real estate on Lansdowne Road and moves out to Abbotstown? In years to come, will anyone remember the times when every pub from Baggot Street to Merrion Strand was full of Scots in their kilts on match days? Yet the same Government that wants to splash out such largesse on a national stadium has earmarked prisons as likely candidates for PPPs, and sought to ensure that the National Conference Centre, another item on McDaid's agenda, was provided at no cost to the Exchequer. The idea that Dublin could end up with a surplus of stadiums also suggests that everyone involved has lost any sense of proportion. They seem to have forgotten that the combined popula-

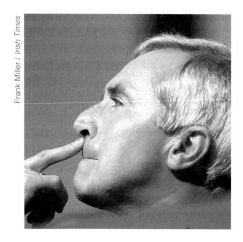

Frank Miller / *Irish Times*

Tourism and Sports Minister Jim McDaid. On the day Abbotstown was announced, he delivered an apt malapropism on RTÉ's *Prime Time*: 'Every other banana republic in the world has their (sic) own national stadium.'

tion of the Republic and Northern Ireland is just over five million whereas Manchester, home of Ahern's favourite team, has more than double that number of people in its catchment area and can therefore support a wide range of sports and leisure facilities. Even in terms of traffic, the implications of Sports Campus Ireland are potentially horrendous, especially with an £80 million privately owned leisure complex – including another Olympic-size swimming pool – planned for Coolock Lane, also feeding off the M50. Indeed, it was because of such traffic impacts that the DTI in its final report (1994) stressed the need to control commercial, retail and leisure developments along the motorway corridor. All things considered, as Tom Humphries wrote, Abbotstown brought a planning deficit to the point of absurdity.

As if this saga was not sufficient to fill us with foreboding about how the Government will spend £40,000 million between now and 2006, the millennium fiasco showed that we had even lost our ability to organise a good party. Having an alcohol-free concert in Merrion Street (with Government Buildings as a liggers' enclosure for the privileged few) and fireworks from the Great South Wall in Dublin Bay, rather than at Christchurch Cathedral, represented a twin triumph for the nanny State and the suburban mentality. It was pathetic. A proposal from Míle Átha Cliath, Dublin Corporation's millennium partnership, for fireworks on the Liffey was vetoed on cost grounds by the Government's Millennium Committee and on security grounds by the Garda Siochána. Risk-averse, as usual, the authorities just didn't want a quarter of a million people congregating in the city centre. In their view, the spectacular fireworks display at the Custom House to celebrate St Patrick's Day in 1999 was a crowd control 'disaster', even though everyone else thought it was absolutely wonderful. Tourists lured to Dublin by its 'party capital of Europe' reputation wandered around on New Year's Eve like lost souls in search of some solace, past shuttered shops, pubs and restaurants, all closed down by an explosion of naked greed. Shameless Seamus Brennan, the Millennium Committee's chairman, defended the lacklustre festivities here as a 'dignified' celebration, even as other cities throughout the civilised world revelled until dawn. He had spent £1 million on pound-shop candles, given £700,000 towards the cost of staging a bastardised version of Handel's *Messiah*, and otherwise sought to ensure, in classic clientilist style, that there would be something for everyone in the audience. The fact that the committee held its first meeting in November 1998, five years after Britain set up its Millennium Commission and just thirteen months before the due date, didn't help us to get our act together. If we hadn't managed to refashion the annual St Patrick's Day parade as a truly civic spectacle, one might have been reduced to black despair.

Much as some may regret it, the success of Ireland now depends critically on the success of Dublin, yet we have no vision other than to keep things going more or less as they are, making it up and muddling through, like Brennan's committee. 'Dublin is as it is because Ireland is now an urban society', as John Graby pointed out. 'Politicians wedded to the rural ethos of the past may not accept it, but people don't want to look up the backside of a cow anymore. They have come to the city. Yet the Department of Agriculture has over 4,000 civil servants, many of them involved in the pointless exercise of administering grants under the CAP. If there was even a tenth of their number involved in forward planning in the DoE and the local authorities, we might have more understanding of the forces that shape the city.' Unbelievably, the DoE employs just seven professional planners, while the local authorities are forced by the sheer volume of planning applications to allocate most of their planners to development control at the expense of forward planning. The paucity of personnel in this crucial area means that we are even less likely to chart a rational course, whatever the 1999 Planning Bill may say about the importance of 'proper planning and sustainable development'. And though architects and planners are beginning to examine and critically question Government strategy, they realise that they are merely enablers of the system, rather than component parts of it. Their role, in effect, is to deal with the problems it creates. 'We won't solve the problems within the next five to seven years. Indeed, there will probably be awful chaos', according to Graby. 'We should be talking about Dublin and Ireland in the year 2020. Where are we going? What vision do we have? And how are we going to realise it? These are the questions which the politicians must answer.' However, in common with most of his colleagues in Leinster House, where the patchwork stone façade is itself a symbol of systemic decay, Bertie Ahern's horizon is the next general election. As long as he can point to progress on the construction of two Luas lines, the Port Tunnel, the final phases of the M50 and the two Calatrava bridges, as well as indications that the Government is 'delivering' on the housing front, Fianna Fáil might hold or even increase its representation in Dublin, where elections are won or lost.

Dublin still has extraordinary assets – a beautiful bay, the proximity of the mountains, the Grand Canal, the cared-for parts of the Royal Canal, the Phoenix Park and numerous other public parks throughout the city and county. But even the bay cannot be taken for granted, given Dublin Port's controversial plan to reclaim a further fifty-two acres east of Alexandra Basin. What makes Dublin special, as architect Paul Keogh has written, is the human scale of the city's streets and squares, combined with its rich architectural inheritance from the 18th and 19th centuries. 'We owe it to ourselves and to future generations to ensure that these qualities are conserved and enhanced in the future development and expansion of the city.' In his appeal on behalf of Dermot Desmond against the Spencer Dock project, he argued that the successful regeneration of the inner city during the 1990s, combined with the strength of the economy, required that the primary criterion for assessing all future development proposals should be quality in terms of architecture, planning and urban design rather than 'expedient economic or financial issues'. And while it was generally agreed that there might be scope for some tall buildings to add interest to Dublin's skyline, Keogh insisted that the six- or seven-storey European street, as opposed to American-style 'mega-structures sitting in vacant open space', was 'still a perfectly valid model for urban development, even in the 21st century'. An Taisce has gone further in calling for a 'moratorium' on high-rise schemes, at least until the DEGW skyline study has been completed and properly debated. Rational decisions on tall buildings or, indeed, any large developments should be assisted by a DIT School of Architecture project to create a digital version of Dublin, which will enable planners to assess the impact of new buildings from every angle long before they are built. A model of the city, such as that which Cork Corporation has produced, might also help to avoid further failures in axial planning, such as the blank brick wall of the UCG multiplex terminating the vista northwards on Jervis Street, or the botched alignment of Cow's Lane in relation to SS Michael & John's Church.

Dublin is now a modern European capital city. Its future deserves to be properly planned, not simply allowed to happen in the error-filled ways of the past forty years. And we do not have to reinvent the wheel. Any number of other European cities have confronted the same problems and solved them, to a greater or lesser extent. Dublin can also look to its own proud tradition of urban planning, dating back to the Wide Streets Commissioners who laid out the city's finest streets and squares during the Georgian era. Even in the 1920s, the fledgling Irish Free State achieved extraordinary things, despite having very modest financial resources. In Dublin, the then government restored the Custom House, the Four

While it is generally agreed that there might be scope for some tall buildings to add interest to Dublin's skyline, the six- or seven-storey European street remains a perfectly valid model for urban development, even in the 21st century. Pictured below is the Stranden scheme in Oslo.

Courts and the GPO, while the City Architect, Horace Tennyson O'Rourke, had O'Connell Street rebuilt in grand neoclassical style to his own design, as well as overseeing plans for the development of Marino and Griffith Avenue. Ardna-crusha, the largest hydro-electric scheme in Europe at the time, was also achieved during that heroic period, and came to represent the image of a progressive little country, as depicted by Seán Keating's powerful murals for Michael Scott's brilliantly inventive Irish Pavilion at the 1939 New York World Fair. By then, Fianna Fáil had added to its predecessors' impressive record by creating the Sugar Company, Irish Shipping, Bord na Mona and CIÉ. 'All of this was done by the most idealistic, patriotic people who had the interests of the country at heart. Where and when did we lose the plot?' one senior official asked sadly. The lesson is that it's not just a question of money. It's about vision and political will too. The inertia that made Dublin 'a centre of paralysis', in the words of James Joyce, has been replaced by a new momentum, which is reflected in the exponential increase in construction output and the changed style of management in the Civic Offices. John Fitzgerald, said one architect, 'took something that didn't work and made it work'. Some critics suggest that the City Manager has a touch of the 'Pompidou syndrome' because of his determination to pursue signature projects such as the Calatrava bridge for Docklands, and his flexibility in dealing with the challenge of development, although few doubt his commitment to cre-

Miichael Scott's brilliantly inventive Irish Pavilion at the New York World Fair in 1939, with its shamrock footprint and powerful murals by Seán Keating, came to represent the image of a progressive little country.

Albert Rothschild / Gandon Archive

ating a better Dublin. But even he must ask himself sometimes what is the point of investing £1.5 million in the stylish remaking of Henry Street and Mary Street when nearly every one of its expensive stone paviors was spattered by chewing gum residue within days of being revealed. The fretted aluminium deck of the millennium footbridge also seems destined to become a gunge repository. Somebody threw up on it within twenty-four hours of the official opening in December 1999, and two months later a pair of stainless steel bollards had to be retrofitted at both ends because of well-grounded fears that motorists might be tempted to use it as a short-cut after hours. Meanwhile, streets which have been repaved are neither maintained nor repaired. Ordinary things that make a difference are not being done in Dublin, like removing half-dismantled wrecks from the shiny new bicycle stands or getting rid of the 'juice' that leaks out of litter bins.

Whose city is it anyway? Does Dublin belong to its people or is it turning a giant chessboard, with the pieces being moved around by unseen forces driven by profit? Perhaps it has already become 'Dublin City Incorporated – a place to be sold as a space for entrepreneurial activity', in Andrew MacLaran's phrase. Addressing a symposium on 'The Citizen and the City', hosted by the Architectural Association of Ireland and the UCD School of Architecture in January 2000, MacLaran – who is director of the Centre for Urban and Regional Studies at Trinity College – highlighted the profound implications of allowing unrestricted

The millennium footbridge, designed by architects Howley Harrington in collaboration with structural engineers Price & Meyers, which was unveiled in December 1999, may represent the new culture of civic improvement.

Frank McDonald

office development to mushroom on the outskirts of the city without reference to the availability of public transport. Until the mid-1990s, as he pointed out, most office development in Dublin was concentrated in the city centre. In 1999, however, a staggering 60% of the record volume of new office space completed during the year was in non-traditional areas on the urban fringe – all Edge City developments that would be wholly reliant on cars, and, therefore, 'totally unsustainable'. Saskia Sassen, Professor of Sociology at the University of Chicago and an influential theorist on globalisation, told the same symposium that cities have 'more bargaining power than they think' in dealing with global capital. It is not simply a question of tailoring their environment to suit niche markets by concentrating exclusively on the development of a 'glamour zone'. What every city needs to do, in her view, is to assert its own identity. And though global capital gravitates towards cities with a state-of-the-art infrastructure and world-class culture, Sassen warned that its very 'hyper-mobility' meant that it could also 'dematerialise' at the blink of a computer screen. Still, for those attending the symposium, it was hard to imagine that such a solid edifice as the huge Compaq office block that now dominates the UCD campus could vanish so easily. Approved by Dun Laoghaire-Rathdown County Council, this massive groundscraper, with 300,000 square feet of office space and two levels of commuter parking underneath, is just one of the physical symbols of the competition among Dublin's local authorities for their own slices of the luscious inward investment cake. With all of these competing forces, there is obviously a need for a major debate on the balance to be struck between the economic (the demands and needs of the city), the cultural (what Dublin is and should be) and the social (the rights and needs of the citizens). For unless there is a clear vision of what the city is and where it is going, Dublin cannot develop a negotiating stance in dealing with the demands of global capital.

There are many positive things happening. Good, thoughtful architecture is being created in response to the aspirations of increasingly discerning clients and the wishes of a more design-conscious public. Even in the most deprived areas, ordinary people have been empowered to some degree by a plethora of 'social economy' quangos, so that wherever victims exist they are represented by victim-organisers, usually on the public payroll. It is through them that a new, and often difficult, dialogue has emerged between what Jim Walsh, policy analyst with Combat Poverty, termed 'the social and physical realms'. Throughout the city and its suburbs, people at every level of the social scale have become much more vocal in demanding a real role in the planning process, even putting forward their own proposals for new parks, swimming pools and childcare facilities. In the city centre, whole streets have come back to life, none more spectacularly than Parliament Street, now crowned at one end by the sparkling City Hall, reinstated internally as the Royal Exchange, and by Tony Hanahoe's magnificently restored Sunlight Chambers at the other. A great deal of work remains to be done, however. Dublin Airport, the State's most important gateway, remains a visual disaster zone, unconsciously projecting an all-too-accurate first impression of Ireland as a country where what we do best is make it up as we go along. Apart from the most recent additions by Henry J Lyons & Partners (Pier C and the main terminal extension), there is no coherent vision, still less a three-dimensional master plan – a fact that's particularly evident from the jumble it presents when viewed from the M50's Northern Cross route. Indeed, no amount of theme park trickery by Aer Rianta, such as the ultra-kitsch parody of the Ha'penny Bridge leading to Pier B, can conceal the fact that Dublin Airport is a dog's dinner accretion of buildings over time. Yet there is no reason why we cannot have an architecturally attractive and harmonious approach to the development of the airport and, indeed, the city as a whole. With the alarmingly large resources now at our disposal, we can certainly afford it. The poor mouth excuse for bad taste no longer applies.

Without a real commitment to sustainable development, however, Dublin – and Ireland, too – is surely on the road to ruin. Even the outgoing chairman of An Bord Pleanála, Paddy O'Duffy, declared in December 1999 that it was 'time to stop giving lip-service' to this all-embracing concept, which has been at the core of international thinking on environment and development since the Earth Summit in Rio de Janeiro in 1992. We must also recognise that Dublin's current prosperity is critically dependent on a number of assumptions that may not turn

In the city centre, whole streets have come back to life, none more spectacularly than Parliament Street, now crowned at one end by the sparkling City Hall (reinstated internally as the Royal Exchange), and by the magnificently restored Sunlight Chambers at the other.

Joe St Leger / *Irish Times*

out to be valid. Quite apart from the risks associated with placing our faith, and our future, in hyper-mobile capital, serious dangers entirely outside our control include the British nuclear industry and, in the longer term, climate change. Just imagine what a major accident at fault-prone Sellafield would do for property values in Dublin or anywhere else on the east coast. Depending on which way the wind was blowing, the whole place might have to be evacuated, like the exclusion zone imposed around Chernobyl after it blew up in 1986. We can no longer be complacent about climate change either. Extreme weather events are now occurring with monotonous regularity, even in the world's major capitals, notably Paris and New York. If changes in the ocean 'conveyor belt', induced by melting polar ice caps, diverted the Gulf Stream away from Ireland, Dublin would end up with a climate not dissimilar to Spitzbergen in the Arctic Circle. That would do wonders for property values, too.

'All things are connected', said that great environmental hero, Chief Seattle, as long ago as 1854. 'Whatever befalls the Earth befalls the sons of the Earth ... Continue to contaminate your bed, and you will one night suffocate in your own waste.' Instinctively, people recognise this essential truth and respond to it by making token gestures, such as driving to the nearest bottle bank in their BMWs. But beneath all of the trappings of prosperity, there is a deep, underlying anxiety among Dubliners about where the city is going, and a growing sense of their own powerlessness in the face of unprecedented social and environmental change. The traffic and transport crisis is its most obvious manifestation, and yet nearly everyone is implicated in creating it. We all need to stand back and examine what we ourselves, individually, are doing to contribute to the problem – to have an 'out-of-body experience', as it were. We must ask ourselves the question 'is this journey really necessary?' and, if so, can it be done some other way – on foot, by bike or by public transport? One small vignette might serve to illustrate the point. Late on the last Saturday before Christmas 1998, I recall walking with my bicycle down Andrew Street, past ENFO, the environmental information service. The street was jammed by a line of cars inching forward very slowly towards one or other of the multi-storey car parks, with a view to some frenzied last-minute shopping. An architect I know beeped the horn of his big Volvo and wished me the compliments of the season. Suddenly, his plight dawned on me, and I said: 'You're trapped in that thing, aren't you?' He smiled weakly because he knew that the only thing he could do was to go with the flow, such as it was, whereas I was almost as free as a bird. I could lock my bike to the next pole and go anywhere I wanted, into a shop, a pub, a coffee bar or a restaurant. And though Dublin's traffic moves at a snail-like pace in peak periods, we should also seriously consider reducing the general speed limit within the built-up area from 30mph to 20mph to make the streets safer for everyone, particularly children.

What is certain in the meantime is that Dublin will extend itself by half as much again as all of the households that currently exist in the city. 'Household Growth: Where shall we live?' was the title of a 1996 British government green paper on precisely the same issue, produced by the estimable John Gummer in response to forecasts that our neighbouring island needs to provide at least three million new homes over the next ten years or so. It dealt with all the issues revolving around greenfield versus brownfield development, housing densities and transport implications. Whatever about the Strategic Planning Guidelines for the Greater Dublin Area and the other *aides-mémoires* on residential density and retail developments, our own Government has not answered the fundamental question about where we should live because it has no frame of reference in the absence of a national spatial plan. But if we do have to provide 200,000-plus new homes in the GDA in the years to 2011, Dublin's die will be cast, perhaps forever – or for as long as we can conceive of it. John Beresford, Luke Gardiner and the Wide Streets Commissioners who did their bidding may have been skilled in the art of sharp practice, but at least they left us with a hugely impressive legacy. Might their successors – the politicians, planners, architects and property developers of our era – devote themselves to the even more important task of recreating Dublin in a new dispensation? We are now at that point again where we have not just a once-in-a-lifetime, but a once-in-two-hundred-years opportunity to change the city. The millennium footbridge and O'Connell Street 'Spike', the Smithfield beacons and Calatrava bridges as well as imaginative plans for leftover spaces throughout the city may well be microcosms of what the new culture of civic improvement can produce. But they are merely emblems for what might be achieved *writ large* on a much broader canvas, if only we had a clue about where we are going. For make no mistake about it – what we do now, in the next ten years, will have a lasting impact for at least two centuries. Dublin, our 'wilful, wicked old city', as Denis Johnston called it, demands that we give it our best shot.

Index